The Regulations and Establishment of the Houshold of Henry Algernon Percy

by Unknown

Address:
HardPress
8345 NW 66TH ST #2561
MIAMI FL 33166-2626
USA
Email: info@hardpress.net

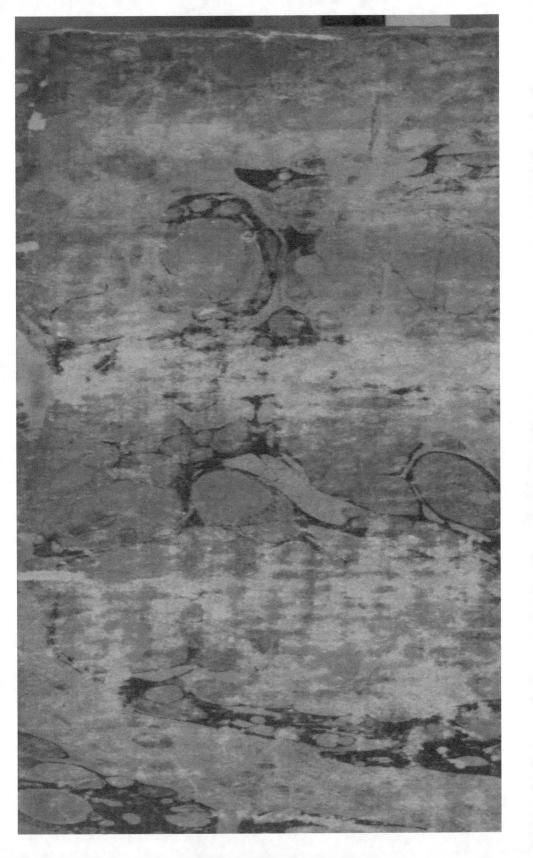

The EARL of

NORTHUMBERLAND'S

HOUSHOLD - BOOK.

THE
REGULATIONS AND ESTABLISHMENT
OF THE
HOUSHOLD
OF
HENRY ALGERNON PERCY,
THE FIFTH EARL OF
NORTHUMBERLAND,
AT HIS CASTLES OF
WRESILL AND LEKINFIELD
IN YORKSHIRE.

BEGUN ANNO DOMINI
M.D.XII.

LONDON PRINTED
M.DCC.LXX.

T H E

P R E F A C E.

THE following pages are copied from an ancient Manuscript in poſſeſſion of the Duke and Ducheſs of Northumberland, who conceiving that ſo ſingular a curioſity might afford the ſame amuſement and pleaſure to others, which it hath given to themſelves, have cauſed a ſmall impreſſion to be taken off merely to beſtow in preſents to their friends.

The original Manuſcript, which fills a very large folio volume, and is finely ingroſſed upon a ſtrong thick paper, had by ſome accident or other been loſt to the Northumberland family, but was happily preſerved in that of the Lords DACRE; till the preſent nobleman reſtored it to the Duke and Ducheſs with a politeneſs that deſerved their particular thanks. Nor ought the very obliging offices of Lord CAMDEN to

paſs

pass unacknowledged ; by whose kind interpofition it was prefented to the family.

It was prefumed, fo curious a monument of ancient times deferved to be refcued from oblivion, and to be perpetuated at leaft in a fmall impreffion, upon feveral accounts.

In the FIRST place, as it exhibits a curious PICTURE OF ANCIENT MANNERS. Here we fee the great magnificence of our old nobility, who feated in their caftles, lived in a ftate and fplendour very much refembling and fcarce inferiour to that of the Royal Court. Their Houfhold was eftablifhed upon the fame plan, their Officers bore the fame titles, and their Warrants ran in the fame form and ftile [a]. This remarkable refemblance to the Royal Eftablifhments will ftrike the Reader the moment he opens this Book. As the King had his Privy Council and great Council of Parliament, to affift him in enacting ftatutes and regulations for the public weal ; fo the Earl of Northumberland had his Council, compofed of his principal officers, by whofe advice and affiftance he eftablifhed this Code of Oeconomic Laws [b]. As the King had his Lords and Grooms of the bed-chamber, who waited in their refpective turns ; fo the Earl of Northumberland was attended by the Conftables and Bailiffs of his feveral caftles, &c [c]. who entered into waiting in regular fucceffion. The two firft offices about his perfon, were occafionally to be filled by his own younger fons [d]. Nor can we doubt but all the head officers of his houf-

[a] See p. 109, &c. &c.   [b] See p. 1. & paffim.   [c] See fect. vii. p. 53.   [d] See pag. 362.

houſhold were Gentlemen both by birth and office [e]; ſuch as the Comptroller, Clarke of the kitchen, Chamberlain, Treaſurer, &c. &c. This appears from the ſervants and horſes kept for their uſe [f], and from the table where they ſat being called the KNIGHT'S-BOARD [g]. Among other inſtances of magnificence, we cannot but remark the number of PRIESTS that were kept in houſhold, not fewer than ELEVEN, at the head of whom preſided a Doctor or Batchelor of divinity, as dean of the chapel [h]. This redundance of clergymen muſt not be altogether attributed to the ſuperſtition of that prieſt-ridden age, but to the ſuperior intelligence of the men of that order, who ſeem to have been almoſt the only perſons capable of exerciſing any office of ſkill or ſcience; ſo that the Surveyor of my lord's lands, his Secretary [i], and the Clarke of his foreign expences [k], were all Prieſts; notwithſtanding which, the laſt officer was weekly to make up his accounts on Sunday [l].

It appears however from many curious inſtances in this book, how deeply the devotion of that age was tinctured with ſuperſtition, and how much the nobles were influenced by the Clergy [m]. Indeed nothing more ſtrongly ſhows the great devotion of our anceſtors in the middle ages, than the number of CHAPELS in ſome of the Northern Caſtles. In buildings

---

[e] See pag. 310, 315, 318.   [f] See pag. 37, 43, &c. pag. 87, &c. pag. 330. See alſo ſect. xlv. However many of the head officers found their own horſes, or to uſe the language of the book, " were at their own horſing."   [g] Pag. 301. See alſo pag. 310, 315, 318.   [h] Pag. 323.   [i] Ibid. [k] Pag. 364.   [l] Pag. 398.   [m] Pag. 337, &c. &c.

ings of this fort, where multitudes of men were often long confined within very narrow limits, every inch of fpace one would think muft be valuable, and yet in caftles of very moderate fize one often finds more than one Chapel.   Thus in WARKWORTH and PRUDHOW caftles in Northumberland (both of them belonging to the PERCY family) are ftill to be feen the remains of two Chapels, one in the bafe court among the outer buildings, the other within the keep or body of the caftle.   And yet both thefe fortreffes are by their fitu-ation much ftraitned for room, which is remarkably the cafe of Prudhow caftle : and as for that of Wark-worth, befides its two Chapels, in the court are alfo to be feen vaults defigned for a confiderable building. This, in the old Surveys[n], is faid to have been in-tended for a COLLEGE ; by which, I fuppofe, we are to underftand fome monaftic foundation [o].

SECONDLY, this book contains a compleat SYSTEM OF ANCIENT OECONOMICS.   Here may be feen all the Provifions, Conveniencies, and Accommodations, which our nobility had procured in that half-civilized age ; and even moft of their Diverfions and Amufe-ments may be collected from it[p]. Here are the Bills of fare, the domeftic Regulations of every kind, and the methods

[n] See the Survey taken in 1567, by Geo. Clarkfon, Auditor to Tho. VIIth. Earl of Northumberland.   [o] Foundations of this fort were not unufual in Caftles.   In 1362, a perpetual Chantery was founded in Alnwick Caftle for three Priefts, who were daily to celebrate mafs in the Chapel of the caftle for the fouls of the de-ceafed Lord Percy and others of his family.   See Clarkfon's MS. Survey in 1567 : and Dugdale's Mon. Ang. vol. 3. p. 164.   [p] See pag. 339, &c

methods of providing for each contingency. The minute attention paid to every the moft inconfiderable article of domeftic expence, and the formal ftated orders eftablifhed with regard to many particulars which appear to us extremely trivial, are very remote from our modern ideas and prefent manners: but this minutenefs is not peculiar to our Houfhold Book. The eftablifhing a fyftem of Domeftic Oeconomy appears to have engaged the attention of our Anceftors nearly in the fame degree, as the enacting public Laws and fettling the Conftitution of the Kingdom. In the celebrated FLETA, amidft the moft important heads of Government and Law, the Author introduces a plan of Houfhold Management, and gives the minuteft Directions for regulating the moft petty domeftic concerns [q]. Our nobility in the more early times, lived in their caftles with a grofs and barbarous magnificence, furrounded with rude and warlike followers, without control and without fyftem. As they gradually emerged from this barbarity, they found it neceffary to eftablifh very minute domeftic regulations, in order to keep their turbulent followers in peace and order: and from living in a ftate of diforderly grandeur, void of all fyftem, would naturally enough run into the oppofite extreme of reducing

[q] Vid. Lib. 2. where he defcribes very minutely every thing that pertains to the Office of almoft every kind of Houfhold Servant: viz. not only of the Senefchal, Bailiff, Marfhall, &c. but of the Cook, Oxdriver, Shepherd, Swineherd, Baker, Mower, Carter or Waggoner, (*De Carrectario* from *Carrecta*, Fr. *Chariot*, a Waggon) Cowkeeper, Dairy-man, &c. — The FLETA is fuppofed to have been written in the Reign of Edward II.

B

ducing every thing, even the moſt trifling diſburſements, to ſtated formal rules. It may be conſidered further, that a nobleman in the dark ages, when retired to his caſtle, had neither books, nor news-papers, nor literary cor-reſpondence, nor viſits, nor cards, to fill up his leiſure : his only amuſements were field-ſports, and as theſe, however eagerly purſued, could not fill up all his va-cant hours, the Government of his Houſhold would therefore be likely enough to engage his attention, if he happened to be a prudent man ; and having little elſe to do or think of, from a meer deſire of employ-ment, he would be led to deſcend to the moſt ſtudied minuteneſs in his regulations and eſtabliſhments.

To a perſon unacquainted with the ancient value of Money, the Allowance in this book may perhaps appear ſcanty, and hardly conſiſtent with the ideas entertained of the old bountiful houſekeeping ; as the weekly ſum divided to each perſon taken one with another, amounts to little more than 2 s. per week. But this is not ſuffi-ciently eſtimating the value of Money at the time this book was compiled. A Thouſand Pounds was the ſum annually aſſigned for the keeping of my Lord's houſe [r] : the number of Perſons in houſhold was one hundred and ſixty-ſix [s]. That ſum divided equally amongſt them (omitting the fractions) amounted an-nually to 6 l. 0 s. 5 d. $\frac{3}{4}$ each perſon ; and weekly to 2 s. 3 d. $\frac{1}{4}$. At a time when Wheat was ſold at 5 s. 8 d. per Quarter [t], 6 l. 0 s. 5 d. $\frac{3}{4}$ would purchaſe juſt twenty-two quarters, three buſhels and a half of

Wheat;

[r] See pag. 224. [s] See pag. 45. [t] See pag. 4.

Wheat; which at 5 s. a bufhel now, would coft 44 l. 17 s. 6 d. Confequently, at this eftimate, the annual proportion to each perfon then was nearly equivalent to 45 l. per annum of our prefent money, a very great allowance to be diftributed through fo large a family as that of the Earl's houfhold.

But even this is ftating the account as much as pof-fible in conformity to modern ideas, for it appears pretty evidently that Wheat was not the moft general bread-corn ufed in that age, (as indeed it is hardly yet in the northern counties) but that Rye, Barley, or Oats, were the common food of the lower or middle ranks of people, who at prefent (in the fouthern parts of England at leaft) difdain any but the fineft wheaten bread; the great difference therefore in the value of money is further to be increafed by the difproportion of value between Wheat and other inferior grains.

It may further be obferved, in the words of a very eminent writer [*], that " the value of Money has ano-
" ther variation, which we are ftill lefs able to afcer-
" tain. The rules of cuftom, or the different needs
" of artificial life, make that revenue little at one time,
" which is great at another. Men are rich and poor
" not only in proportion to what they have, but to
" what they want. In fome ages not only neceffaries
B 2   " are

[*] See the life of Ro. Afcham, prefixed to Bennet's edition of his Works in Englifh. 4to.

" are cheaper, but fewer things are neceffary. In the
" reign of Hen. VIII. moft of the elegances and ex-
" pences of our prefent fafhions were unknown: com-
" merce had not yet diftributed fuperfluity through
" the lower claffes of people," and therefore the fame
Revenue (though the different value of money were out
of the cafe) would have gone in thofe times a great
way further than it will at prefent.

But indeed to fhow, what might be done in that age
with a much fmaller fum, than is here allowed to the
Earl's loweft fervants; we need only refer to that noted
paffage in Latimer's fermons ᵗ, which has been fo often
quoted : " My father was a yoman, and had no landes
" of hys owne, onely he had a farme of iij or iiij pound
" by yeare at the uttermoft, and hereupon he tilled
" fo muche as kept halfe a doffen men. He had
" walke for an hundred fheepe, and my mother milked
" xxx kyne. He was able, and did finde the king a
" harneffe, with himfelfe and his horfe, while [i. e.
" until] he came to the place that he fhould receiyve
" the kinges wages. I can remember that I buckled
" his harneffe, when he went unto BLACKHEATH fielde.
" He kept me to fchole...He maryed my fifters wyth
" five pound or xx nobles a piece....He kept hofpi-
" tality for his poore neighboures. And fome almes
" he gave to the poore, and all thys did he of the
" fayde farme. Where he that now hath it, payeth
" xvi

See his firft Sermon before King Edw. VI. 1549.

" xvi pound by yeare or more, and is not able to do
" any thyng for hys prince, for himfelfe, or for hys
" children, or geve a cup of drinke to the poore."

If any thing further is neceffary on this fubject ; it
will fufficiently fhow the plenty and liberality of the
Earl's houfekeeping, if we do but confront it with that
which then prevailed among the other orders of men.
At the time when fo plentiful an allowance of good
Bread and Beef was delivered out fo many times a day
to every the meaneft fervant in this Earl's family ; the
Commons of England in general lived at a meaner rate
and fared more hardily than we can at prefent well conceive. To inftance only in one article of their food,
viz. that of their Bread, even fo late as the reign of
Elizabeth (when great advances had been made in
luxury and refinement) the lower fort of people fed on
what would not now be offered to dogs. This appears
from the defcription of England * prefixed to Hollinf-
hed's Chronicle, edit. 1586, where we are told " " the
" Bread through the land is made of fuch graine as
" the foile yeeldeth, nevertheleffe the gentilitie com-
" monlie provide themfelves fufficientlie of Wheat for
" their own tables, whilft their houfbold and poore
" neighbours in fome fhires are inforced to content
" themfelves with Rie or Barleie, yea and in time of
" dearth manie with bread made either of Beans, Pea-
" fon, or Otes, or of altogither and fome Acorns among.
" I will

* By Will. Harrifon, 1 edit. 1577. See Tanner's Bibl. " P. 168.

" ---I will not faie that this extremitie is oft fo well
" to be feene in time of plentie as of dearth, but IF I
" SHOULD, I COULD EASILY BRING MY TRIALL."
He afterwards fpeaks of the artificer and poor labour-
ing man as feldom able to tafte any other than the bad
bread above-mentioned ; and proceeds to defcribe more
particularly the feveral forts of Bread ufually made in
England, viz. MANCHET, CHEAT, or Wheaten
bread, another inferior fort of wheaten bread called
RAVELLED, and laftly BROWN-BREAD, " of which,"
fays this writer, " we have Two forts, One baked up as
" it cometh from the mill, fo that neither the bran nor
" the floure are anie whit diminifhed.---The Other hath
" little or no floure left therein at all,---and it is not
" onlie the worft and weakeft of all the other forts,
" but alfo appointed in OLD TIME for fervants, flaves,
" and the inferior kind of people to feed upon. Here-
" unto likewife becaufe it is drie and brickle in the
" working---fome adde a portion of Rie meale IN OUR
" TIME, whereby the rough drineffe---therof is fome-
" what qualified, and then it is named Mefcelin, that
" is, bread made of mingled corne. Albeit that di-
" verfe do fow or mingle Wheat and Rie---and fell the
" fame at the markets under the aforefaid name." He
adds, " " In champeigne countries much Rie and Bar-
" leie Bread is eaten." By the author's addition of
the " Rie meale in OUR TIME," it may fairly be concluded that the OLD TIME when the Bran-bread was
                                        baked

" Pag. 169.

baked for fervants, was not further diftant back than the date of this Houfhold Book, and it prefents a very ftriking contraft to the liberal appointments provided for in it.

Before I quit this head of " Things provided," I cannot but obferve that fome of the articles appear to us now extremely unaccountable, as the hire of ROUGH PEWTER VESSEL[x], at the fame time that a fmaller quantity was ordered to be bought[y]. As the Earl and his family ordinarily ufed Wooden Trenchers[z], Pewter muft have been a very ornamental addition on great holidays,[a] and efpecially the garnifh or fervices of COUNTERFEIT VESSEL;[b] which, I prefume, was fome metal gilt or wafhed over.

It is remarkable that they fhould be obliged to carry all the Beds, Hangings, and Furniture along with them whenever they removed. Indeed the ufual manner of hanging the rooms in the old caftles, was only to cover the naked ftone walls with Tapeftry or Arras hung upon tenter hooks, from which they were eafily taken down upon every removal.[c] On fuch an occafion the number

ber

[x] Pag. 17. [y] P. 19. [z] P. 73, 75, 78. [a] P. 17. [b] P. 19.
[c] One department of the king's wardrobe is the REMOVING WARDROBE, which confifted chiefly of the Arras, that was thus to be hung up againft the naked walls of the king's bedchamber, and perhaps another room or two of reception.—The Polifh nobles now, travel in this manner, they drive the Jews out of their houfes, whilft in their progrefs; and their attendants fix the tapeftry hangings, which they carry with them, fo as to make the lodgings tolerably comfortable. B.

ber of Carts [d] employed in a family of this fize, muſt have formed a caravan nearly as large as thoſe which traverſe the deſerts of the Eaſt.

I cannot conclude this part of my ſubject without remarking, that from the total ſilence throughout the book with regard to GLASS, I am led to believe that this very beautiful and uſeful material, though it had been perhaps long applied to the decorating Churches, [e] was not as yet very commonly uſed in Dwelling-houſes or Caſtles. The author of the Deſcription of England, (before quoted) writing about ſixty years after, ſays [f] that " of OLD TIME," (probably meaning times not much older than that of this Houſhold Book) " our " countrie houſes inſteede of Glaſſe did uſe much Lat- " tiſe and that made either of wicker or fine rifts of " oke in checkerwiſe. I read alſo that ſome of the " better ſort in and before the times of the Saxons, " (who notwithſtanding uſed ſome Glaſſe alſo ſince the " time of Benedict Biſcop the Monk that brought the " feat of Glaſſing firſt into this land) did make panels " of Horne inſteed of Glaſſe, and fix them in woode " calmes. But as Horne in windows is now [A. D. " 1577.] quite laid downe in every place, ſo our Lat- " tiſes are alſo growne into leſſe uſe [i. e. not quite " laid aſide] becauſe Glaſſe is come to be ſo plentifull, " and within very little ſo good cheape, if not better " then the other." The writer afterwards adds this

re-

---

[d] See p. 386.   [e] See Drake's Hiſt. of York, p. 527.   [f] P. 187.

remarkable paſſage. " Heretofore alſo the houſes of
" our princes and noblemen were often glaſed with
" Berill (an example whereof is YET to be ſeen in Sud-
" leie caſtle) and in diverſe other places with fine
" Chriſtall, but this eſpecially in the times of the Ro-
" mans, whereof alſo ſome fragments have been taken
" up in old ruines." But with regard to Glaſs (now
ſo cheap and common a conveniency) even after it began to be uſed in windows, it was ſtill preſerved with
great care, as a precious rarity ; as appears from the ſur-
vey of Alnwick caſtle made in 1567, in which is this
very remarkable paſſage : " And becauſe throwe ex-
" treme winds the Glaſſe of the windowes of this and
" other my Lord's caſtles and houſes here in the coun-
" trie dooth decay and waſte, Yt were good the whole
" Leights of everie windowe at the departure of his
" Lordſhippe from lyinge at any of his ſaid caſtels and
" houſes, and dowring [i. e. during] the tyme of his
" Lordſhip's abſence, or others lying in them, were
" taken doune and lade upe in ſafety : And at ſooche
" tyme as ather his Lordſhipe or anie other ſholde lye
" at anie of the ſaid places, the ſame might then be ſet
" uppe of newe with ſmale charges to his Lp. wher
" [i. e. whereas] now the decaye thereof ſhall be verie
" coſtlie and chargeable to be repayred."

    L a s t l y, This Book may be conſidered as a
very valuable SUPPLEMENT TO THE CHRONICON
PRETIOSUM ; and the more ſo, as Biſhop FLEET-
C

WOOD's

wood's excellent Essay on that subject is remarkably defective with regard to the period of time comprehended in this Book. Of this the learned author himself complains, declaring that all his diligence could not procure him sufficient information to render this part of his work compleat. The curious investigator therefore of subjects of this sort, will be glad to find the peculiar defects of the Bishop's Book so happily supplied in the present work : Wherein the Prices of all kinds of provisions and marketable commodities are clearly laid down ; wages and stipends fixed and stated ; current expences settled and adjusted, and even arbitrary gifts and rewards reduced to a regular invariable rule [g]. From the following pages also the just proportion of food to labour, and of money to both, may be easily deduced. All these and many other particulars of the same curious nature, are here exhibited ; and the whole disposed in so regular and clear a manner, that no Supplemental Tables were necessary to new-arrange or distribute them.

It is necessary only to give the Reader one caution in the use and application of the Rates and Prices : viz. that some allowance ought to be made for their being fixed and adjusted at such a distance from the capital. In that age there was little or no communication between one part of England and another : no regular conveyance from the provinces to the metropolis ; and there-

[g] See sect. xliv.

therefore the product of the inland countries was for the most part obliged to be consumed at home. This would naturally occasion things to be at a much lower price in a remote northern county like Yorkshire, than they would in the south, or in the neighbourhood of London. And yet the Prices of WHEAT and OATS, as given in the CHRONICON PRETIOSUM, remarkably agree with those laid down at the Beginning of this Work. [h] e. g.

	Chronicon Pretiosum	Houshold Book, 1512.
" In 1504. Antiq. Canterb.		
" Appendix, p. 27. WHEAT		
" the Quarter. - - - - -	0 l. 5 s. 8 d.	0 l. 5 s. 8 d.
[Chron. Pret. p. 114.]		
" In 1512. OATS the Quarter.	0 l. 2 s. 0 d.	0 l. 2 s. 0 d.
[Ibid. p. 116.]		

I say " at the Beginning of this Work," because the Prices of the very same articles are found to vary in the succeeding pages : [i] but this is easily accounted for, as we know the book was compiled at different times, and the Warrants bear so many different dates, [k] viz. from 1512 to 1525. This difference of Date the Reader will advert to in his Computations.

[h] See p. 4. p. 22. [i] P. 177. 186. &c. p. 216. &c. [k] See p. 1. p. 109. p. 131. p. 223. p. 230. p. 239. p. 242. p. 259. p. 275. p. 287. p. 291. p. 294. p. 297.

AS the Reader will expect some account of the great Earl and his Family, whose Œconomic Rules he is going to peruse, it is proper to inform him here, that

HENRY ALGERNON PERCY, fifth Earl of Northumberland, was born on the thirteenth of January, 1477-8. His father was slain, while he was a minor, in a popular insurrection in Yorkshire, April 28, 1489. In 1497, young as he was, he was one of the chieftains that commanded at the battle of BLACKHEATH, against the lord Audley and his adherents; and was early engaged in other public services. But what principally distinguished him, was the very magnificent and splendid manner in which he conducted the princess Margaret to the borders of Scotland, on her marriage with James IV. in 1503, on which occasion his dress, furniture, equipage and attendance was more like that of a prince than a subject, as is particularly observed by HALL in his Chronicle; where may be seen at large a full description of this very gallant show; as also in the late curious Additions to the COLLECTANEA of LELAND. [1] For the other particulars of this Earl's history, we must refer the reader to Dugdale or Collins; and shall only observe here, that having been early installed a Knight of the Garter, he died about the middle of the year 1527.

He

[1] See Vol. IV.—An Extract from the same MS Account is given by Drake in his Hist. of York. Appendix, p. xviij.

He appears to have been a nobleman of great magnificence and taste : as is inferred not only from the instance above-mentioned, and the splendid Establishments in the following Book ; but from the very noble monuments which he erected in Beverley minster to the memory of his father and mother (the fourth Earl of Northumberland ᵐ and his Countess). These are executed in the finest style of Gothic architecture, and remain to this day lasting proofs of his love and taste for the arts, as well as of his generosity and filial piety. He appears also to have had a great passion for literature, and was a liberal patron of such genius as that age produced. This was the more to his honour, as perhaps at no period of time his brother peers in general were more illiterate. ⁿ He encouraged SKELTON, the only professed poet of that reign, who wrote an Elegy on the death of his father. But still stronger proofs of his literary turn may be collected from a very curious and splendid MS. which had formerly belonged to this nobleman, and is at present preserved in the British Museum. ᵒ It contains a large collection of Poems, finely engrossed upon vellum, and richly illuminated, which had been transcribed for his use. The Poems are chiefly those of Lydgate ; after which follow the above Elegy of Skelton and some smaller compositions,

---

ᵐ In Peck's Desiderata Curiosa, vol. 2. p. 10. are the particulars of this Earl's Interment, &c.　　ⁿ See Reliques of Anc. Eng. Poetry, 2d Ed. vol. 2. p. 273. Mr. Walpole's Noble Authors, 2d Edit. vol. 1. p. 59. Biog. Brit. vol. 2. p. 1236.　　ᵒ Reg. Bib. No. 18. D. II.

tions, which evidently prove his love of letters and passion for poetry. Among these are a History in Verse of the PERCY family, presented to him by a Chaplain of his own; and what is still more remarkable, a large series of POETICAL INSCRIPTIONS, which he had caused to be written on the Walls and Ceilings of the Principal Apartments at Leckenfield and Wressel.[p] Though these are rather to be commended for their grave moral cast, than for their poetical merit, they are at least as good as any other compositions of the same period. To these proofs of this Earl's literary character, may perhaps be further added the remarkable provision in the following book, that his Almonar should be "a Maker of Interludes;"[q] and even the bare mention in it of my Lord's and my Lady's LIBRARIES[r] deserves notice, at a time when many of the first nobility could hardly read or write their names.

He

[p] See a particular account of these two Castles, at the end.

[q] See pag. 44. By the Statutes of Trinity college, Cambridge, (granted by Q. Elizabeth) the Head-Lecturer is to compose one Latin Play, and the four Sub-Lecturers, one between two of them, to be acted by the Scholars of the house during the Christmas holidays.

CAP. xxiv. *Novem domestici Lectores, quo Juventus majore cum fructu tempus natalis Christi terat, bini ac bini singulas* COMOEDIAS, TRAGOEDIASVE *exhibeant; excepto primario Lectore, quem per se solum unam* COMOEDIAM *aut* TRAGOEDIAM *exhibere volumus: Atque hasce omnes Comœdias seu Tragœdias in Aulâ privatim vel publice, prædictis duodecim*

[r] Pag. 378.

He married CATHARINE, daughter and coheir of Sir Robert Spenser, Knt. and of Eleanor his wife, daughter and coheir of Edmund Beaufort, duke of Somerset. By this lady, who was second cousin to king Henry VII. he had the following Children ', viz.

HENRY Lord PERCY, his eldest son, who succeeding him in his titles and estate, became sixth Earl of Northumberland, and is recorded by our historians for his unsuccessful passion for queen ANN BULLEN:

Sir THOMAS PERCY, Knt. his second son, who suffered death, for being concerned in the Yorkshire insurrection in 1538; but whose two sons, THOMAS and HENRY, were afterwards restored, and became successively Earls of Northumberland:

Sir INGELRAM PERCY, Knt. third son, of whom nothing particular is recorded:

Lady MARGARET PERCY, who became wife of Henry lord Clifford, first Earl of Cumberland of that family.

Lady

cim diebus, vel paulo post, pro arbitrio Magistri et octo Seniorum, agendas curent.

So the Statute stands at present; but in the more ancient Statutes given by K. Edward VI. the passage runs thus:

COMOEDIA *aut* TRAGOEDIA, *una Græca, altera Latina, post Epiphaniam, ante initium Termini, quotannis Collegii sumptibus agatur: Eas diligentius curent Magister Aulæ et Reliqui Quæsitores.* [The answer to the Head-Lecturer and Sub-Lecturers.]

These Statutes were compiled by Thomas [Goodrich] Bishop of Ely, Sir John Cheke, Dr. May Dean of St. Paul's, and Thomas Wenday the King's Physician.   L.

ᵃ Called ' Childre,' ' Childer,' and ' Chillder,' in the Book.

All thefe are mentioned in the Houfhold Book : but befides the above, he had another younger daughter, viz. Lady MAUD PERCY, who was married to William lord Coniers, and who, from the filence of the Houfhold Book with regard to her, it is evident was not born till after the articles were compiled which relate to the Nurfery (contractedly called ' Nurcy' in the book) : whence it may be inferred, that moft of the other Children were extremely young; for the exact dates of their Births are not preferved.

As mention is made of the Earl's Brethren, (defectively written ' Breder' or ' Brether' in the book) it may be proper to enumerate them. Thefe were

Sir WILLIAM PERCY, Knt. who bore a principal command, and fignalized his valour at the battle of Flodden.

ALLAN PERCY, Clerk, who was Warden of Trinity college at Arundel in Suffex, and

JOSCELINE PERCY, who married the heirefs of Walter Froft, Efq; of Featherfton and Beverley in Yorkfhire, and became anceftor of the PERCIES of Beverley, fince extinct.

He had alfo three Sifters, ELEANOR, wife of Edward Stafford, duke of Buckingham ; ANNE, married to William Fitz-Allan, earl of Arundel ; and ELIZABETH, who died an infant.

No-

NOTHING now remains but to assure the Reader; that the following Copy hath been printed from the Original with all possible exactness, and it is hoped will be found to contain fewer Errata than could have been expected in so difficult a work. All the peculiarities of Style and Orthography, and even the very Errors of the MS. have been retained with as scrupulous a fidelity as the most rigid Antiquary could desire. No Points or Stops occurred in the original, and therefore none have been inserted in the printed copy; but the want of them is occasionally supplied by the proper disposal of the Capital Letters. Only one innovation hath been admitted, and that for the sake of clearness and distinctness, viz. the subjoining to some of the articles the Algebraic Mark of Equation $=$, which had not been invented when this book was written.

It was once intended that a Glossary should have been given of the more unusual Words, but upon minute inquiry there were found to be few obscure in themselves; and as for such as were meerly rendered so by the uncouth, obsolete, or defective Orthography, it was judged that a small degree of attention in the Reader would easily enable him to decypher these. With regard to the obscurities in the Style or Expression, whether they proceed from the provincial dialect, the antiquated idiom, or the ungrammatical phrase of the writer, they will be generally removed or explained by the context. The greatest difficulties will be found to arise from the sub-

D

ject

ject matter itſelf; from the frequent alluſion to ancient
manners, cuſtoms or things; and it was thought beſt to
give the illuſtration of theſe in the form of NOTES at
the End of the Book. Few and inconſiderable as theſe
will be thought, the collecting them coſt much time
and labour: for the ſubjects were ſo much out of the
common track of reading, that it was difficult to know
where to look for information; and if many paſſages
equally obſcure are paſſed over without notice, it was
becauſe the Editor could not meet with any explana-
tions that were ſatisfactory to himſelf, and he rather
choſe to leave them to the Reader's own ſagacity and
reſearch, than to trouble him with vague and uncer-
tain conjectures.

T. P.

A D V E R-

ADVERTISEMENT.

☞ IT will be neceſſary to premiſe here, that the ancient modes of Computation are retained in this book : According to which it is only in Money that the Hundred conſiſts of Five Score : in all other articles the Enumerations are made by the old Teutonic Hundred of Six Score, or 120.

All Numbers are expreſſed (not by Figures, but) by the old numerical Letters as in the MS. and that in a manner ſomewhat particular, thus,

V^{xx}. is Five ſcore. Pag. 139.
V^{c}XLVIII. is Five hundred and forty-eight. P. 384.
V^{M}CCLX. denotes Five thouſand, two hundred and ſixty. P. 3.
CCCCiiij^{xx} xvj. reads Four hundred, four-ſcore and ſixteen. Pag. 138.

After all, frequent Miſtakes occur in the Arithmetical Computations : nor does the Sum Total always agree with the Enumeration of the Particulars : but theſe are generally left as they ſtand in the MS.

With regard to the Contractions, the following are the moſt common, viz.

Di. or Dim. is Dimidium, or Half.
Ob. or Obol. is Obolus, or Half-penny.
Qu. or Quad. is Quadrans, or Farthing.
Lb. is the Pound weight, as L. is the numerical Pound
  in money.

D 2   M^{c}.

ADVERTISEMENT.

Mᶜ. is Mark, or 13s. 4d.

Bz. is Bushel.

Pᶜ. is Peck.

j—at the end of an article, only denotes One Article or Paragraph, as in pag. 78.

One or two peculiarities of Phrase may just be noted here, thus,

'The pece' or 'piece,' is now expressed by 'a piece,' (Which is also sometimes used, pag. 190.) E. g. p. 2. 'Mutons, after xvijd the pece,' would now be—'after 'xvijd a-piece,' or xvijd each.

'Lefs or more at all,' would now be writ 'lefs or more 'in all.' Thus pag. 139. 'fave xd. more at all:' i. e. 'except 10d. more in all;' or 10d. over and above the fum total.

Laftly, It may be proper to inform the Reader, that where it was neceffary to infert or alter any Word in the Text, it is carefully inferted between inverted Commas, 'thus.'

THE

THE BOOKE OF

ALL THE

DIRECTIONS AND ORDERS

FOR KEPYNGE OF

MY LORDES HOUS

YERELY.

THE KALENDAR.

HERE BEGYNNYTHE THE KALLENDER OF THIS BOOKE of all Manner of Direccyones and Orders for Keapinge of my Lordes Hous As the Names of the faid Orders And what Ordurs they be Ande in what place And where ye fhall fynde every of the faid Orders one after an outher HEREAFTER FOLLOWITH in this Booke.

XXII.

XLIII.

XLIIII.

XLV.

XLVI.

XLVII.

XLVIII.

XLIX.

L.

* By ' Houfes ' here are meant the different Stories of a Manfion ; which was reckoned to be of fo many Houfes-height as it contained Stories.

THE

THE

DIRECTIONS and ORDERS

FOR

Kepynge of my Lorde's Houſe yerely.

✠✕✕✕

I.

THIS IS THE ASSIGENEMENTE made by me and my Counſaill at Wreſill to Richard Gowge Countroller of my houſe and Thomas Percy Clark of the Kechynge of my ſaid houſe ſtondynge charged with my ſaid houſe Which ys for the hole expenſys and kepynge of my ſaid houſe for one hole Yere begynnynge on Monday the xxxᵗʰ day of September which was Michaelmas day laſt paſt in the thyrd Yere of my Soveraigne Lorde Kynge Henry the viijᵗʰ and endynge at Michaelmas next cumynge which ſhal be by the grace of God in the iiijᵗʰ yere of my ſaid Soveraigne Lorde as the names of the Parcells that they ſhall have payd by th'hands of my Cofferers for the tyme beynge With the names of the Sommes that they ſhall pay hereafter folowyth in the Booke.

B   REMANETH.

REMANETH.

FURST there ys payd to the said Richard Gowge and Thomas Percy as in the price of divers Vitalls and Stuff remanynge in my house of the Remaneth takyn at Michaelmas last past in the third yere of the reigne of my Sovereigne Lorde Kynge Henry the viij^th and delyverd to the aforesaid Richard Gowge Countroller of my house and Thomas Percy Clark of the Kechynge of my said house charged with my said Countroller as parcell of th'assignement of the hole Somme for kepynge of my said house for oone hole Yere begynnynge at the said Michaelmas last past and endynge at Michaelmas next cummynge which shal be with the grace of God in the iiij^th yere of Kynge Henry the viij^th As the parcells with the prycys of the said Remanyth hereafter folowyth delyvertt to theme.   That is to say

Of Whete iij quarters dimid: after vj s. viij d. the quarter = xxiij s. iiij d.

Of Wyne a ton a hogishede & xj sestrons after iiij l. xij s. iiij d. the ton = vj l. xvj s. x d.

Of Ale vij gallons after ij d. the gallon = xiiij d.

Of Breid cccv score ij loofys after vj loofys j d. = vj s. vj d.

Of Beire xiiij hogisheds dimid: contenynge diiij score xvj gallons after obol. quadr. the gallon = xliij s. vj d.

Of two Stotts and iij Whies after x s. the pece oone with another = l s.

Of Mutons ccij after xvij d. the pece = xvij l. ij s. x d.

Of Beiff in the larder iiij carcas after viij s. the carcas = xxxij s.

Of Mutons theire viij casys after xiij d. the pece = ix s. iiij d.

Of Salt Fish ij after vj d. the pece = xij d.

Of Hoppys cclvj lb. after xij s. iiij d. the c. = xxxij s. iiij d.

Of White Salt j quarter dimid: after iiij s. the quarter = vj s.

Of Parisch Candle viij dosson x lb. after xij d. the dosson = viij s. x d.

Of Weik xij lb. after j d. obol. the lb. = xviij d.

Of Wax and Rosell myxt v lb. after iij d. the lb. = xv d.

Of

Of Wax wroght in Torches xxxvj lb. after iiij *d.* the lb.
= xij *s.*

Of Wax wroght in Quarions j lb. dimid: after viij *d.* the
lb. = xij *d.*

Of Wax wroght in Tapers j lb. = viij *d.*

Of Piper iij quarterons after xvj *d.* the lb. = xij *d.*

Of Mace and Clovves j quarteron after viij *s.* the lb. = ij *s.*

Of Gynger two unces after iiij *s.* the lb. = vj *d.*

Of Prones iiij lb. after j *d.* obol. the lb. = vj *d.*

Of Tornefole j lb. dimid. after ij *s.* the lb. = iij *s.*

Of Sugar x lb. dimid. after iiij *d.* obol. the lb. = iij *s.* x *d.* quadr.

Of Powder of Licoras j lb. = vj *d.*

Of Saunders j lb. iij quarterons after iij *s.* iiij *d.* the lb. = v *s.* x *d.*

Of Safferon j unce after xiij *s.* iiij *d.* the lb. = x *d.*

Of Datys dimid lb. after v *d.* the lb. = ij *d.* obul.

Of Blaynfch Powder iij quarterons after xij *d.* the lb. = ix *d.*

Of Granes iij quarterons after xij *d.* the lb. = ix *d.*

Of Racyns of Corens j lb. = ij *d.*

Of Fagotts at Wrefill Mcccclx after ij *s.* viij *d.* the c. =
xxxviij *s.* viij *d.*

Of Fagotts at Lekyngfeld ^Mvcclx after xvj *d.* the c. = lxx *s.*

Of Fagotts in the Wefthaill at Lekyngfeld M after xv *d.* the c.
= xij *s.* vj *d.*

Of Shids at Lekyngfeld in the Wodyarde xxx lode after viij *d.*
the lode = xx *s.*

Of Hey at Lekyngfeld clxxij lode after xv *d.* the lode = xij *l.*

Of Hey at Wrefill xlvj lode after xiij *d.* quadr. every lode
= l *s.* ix *d.* obol.

' The hole ys ' = lviij *l.* xxij *d.*

And as it aperith more playnly by a bill of the faid Remaneth figned .with my hand which ys delyvert into the
kepynge of the faid Richard Gowge Countroller and Thomas
Percy Clark of the Kitchynge.

WHEET.

W H E E T.

I T E M to be payd to the faid Richard Gowge and Thomas Percy for to make provifion for cv fcore xvj quarters dimid. of Whete for th'expenfys of my houfe for an hole Yere after v *s*. viij *d*. the quarter by eftimacion Somme = lxxviij *l*. xvj *s*. viij *d*. Whereof xxxix *l*. viij *s*. iv *d*. to be payd for the fyrft paymentt unto the faid Richard Gowge and Thomas Percy at Saynt Andro day afore Criftynmas for the provifion of v fcore xviij quarters ij bufhells of Whete to ferve my houfe bitwixt Candlemas laft paft and our Lady day in Lentt next foloynge And xxxix *l*. viij *s*. iiij *d*. to be payd to the faid Richard Gowge and Thomas Percy for the ij^th paymentt at our Lady day in Lentt for the provifion of v fcore xviij quarters ij bufhells of Whete to ferve 'my' houfe frome our faid Lady day to Michaelmas next after and fo the hole Somme for full contentacion of the faid Whete for an hole Yere ys = lxxviij *l*. xvj *s*. viij *d*.

M A L T E.

ITEM to be payd to the faid Richard Gowge and Thomas Percy for to make provifion for ccix quarters j bufhell of Maltt after iiij *s*. the quarter by eftimacion for th'expenfys of my houfe for an hole Yere Somme = xlix *l*. xvj *s*. vj *d*. Whereof xxiiij *l*. xviij *s*. ij *d*. to be payd for the furft paymentt unto the faid Richard Gowge and Thomas Percy at Sayntt Andrew day afore Criftynmas next cummynge for the provifion of ciiij quarters dimid. and dimid: bufhell of Maltt for to ferve my houfe frome Michaelmas laft paft unto our faid Lady day in Lentt next foloynge And xxiiij *l*. xviij *s*. ij *d*. to be payd to theym for the fecund paymentt at our Lady day in Lentt for the provifion of ciiij quarters dimid. and dimid: bufhell of Maltt for to ferve my faid houfe frome our faid Lady day in Lentt unto Michaelmas next after And fo the hole Somme for full contentacion of the faid Maltt for oone hole Yere ys = xlix *l*. xvj *s*. vj *d*.

B E E F I S.

BEEFIS.

ITEM to be payd to the said Richard Gowge and Thomas Percy for to make provision for cxxiiij Beiffs for th'expensys of my house for an hole Yere Whereof v score ix Fatt Beiffs after xiij *s*. iiij *d*. a pece by estimacion to be bought at All Hallowtide for to serve my house from that tyme to Midsomer next after And xxiiij Leyn Beiffs after viij *s*. the pece by estimacion to be boght at Sayntt Elyn day and put into the Pastures assigned to my house to feyd for to serve my said house frome Midsomer aforesaid to Michaelmas next after The hole Somme of the said Beiffs ys iiij score vj *l*. v *s*. iiij *d*. Whereof lxxij *l*. xiij *s*. iiij *d*. to be payd for the fyrst payment to the said Richard Gowge and Thomas Percy at the foresaid All Hallowtide for the paymentt of the noumbre of the Fatt Beiffs afore named and xiij *l*. xij *s*. to be payd for the secund paymentt at Saynt Elyn day for the paymentt of the noumbre of the said leyn Beiffs to be bought to fede in my said Pastures assigned to my said house And so the hole Somme for the full contentacion of the said Beiffs for an hole Yere ys = iiij score vj *l*. v *s*. iiij *d*.

MUTTUNS.

ITEM to be payd to the said Richard Gowge and Thomas Percy for to make provision for Dclxvij Mutons for th'expensys of my house for an hole Yere after xx *d*. the pece by estimacion oone with another the ffatt and the leyn Somme = lxviij *l*. xij *s*. ij *d*. Whereof lx *l*. vij *s*. ij *d*. to be payd for the fyrst paymentt to the said Richard Gowge and Thomas Percy at All Hallowtide for the provision of Dlxviij Mutons to serve my house frome Michaelmas last past unto Lammes next cummynge And viij *l*. v *s*. to be payd to theme for the secund payment at Sayntt Elyn day for the provision of v score xix Mutons to serve my house frome Lammes aforesaid to Michaelmas next after And so the hole Somme for the full contentacion of the said Mutons for an hole Yere ys = lxviij *l*. xij *s*. ij *d*.

GASCOIN WYNE.

ITEM to be payd to the said Richard Gowge and Thomas Percy to make provision for x ton ij hogisheds of Gascoigne Wyne for th'expensys of my house for an hole Yere Viz. iij ton of Rede Wyne — v ton of Clarett Wyne — and ij ton and ij hogisheds of White Wyne — after iiij *l.* xiij *s.* iiij *d.* the ton by estimacion Somme xlix *l.* Whereof xxiiij *l.* x *s.* to be payd to the said Richard Gowge and Thomas Percy for the fyrst paymentt at Saynt Andro day afore Cristynmas for the provision of v ton and j hogishede of Gascoigne Wyne to be bought at the said Saynt Andro day to serve my house frome that tyme unto our Lady day in Lentt next foloynge And xxiiij *l.* x *s.* to be payd to theme for the secund paymentt at our Lady day in Lentt for the provision of v ton and j hogishede of Gascoigne Wyne to serve my house frome our Lady day unto Michaelmas next after And so the hole Somme for full contentacion of the said Wyne for an hole Yere ys = xlix *l.*

POORKS.

ITEM to be payd to the said Richard Gowge and Thomas Percy for to make provision for xxv Poorks for th'expensys of my house for an hole Yere after ij *s.* the pece by estimacion Somme L *s.* Whereof xx *s.* to be payd to the said Richard Gowge and Thomas Percy for the fyrst paymentt at Saynt Andrew day next cummynge for the provision of x Poorks to serve my house frome the said Saynt Andro day to Candlemas next after And xxx *s.* to be payd to theme for the secund paymentt at the said Candlemas for the provision of xv Poorks to serve my house frome the said Candlemas to Shroftide next after bicause of the more occupiynge of theme the said tyme in Meitts and otherwise And so the hole Somme for full contentacion of the said Poorks for an hole Yere ys = L *s.*

V·EELIS.

V E E L I S.

ITEM to be payd to the said Richard Gowge and Thomas Percy for to make provision for xxviij Veills for th'expensys of my House for an hole Yere after xx *d.* the pece by estimacion Somme xlvj *s.* viij *d.* Whereof xxiij *s.* iiij *d.* to be payd to the said Richard Gowge and Thomas Percy for the fyrst payment at Sayntt Andrew day next cummynge for the provision of xiiij Veills to serve my house frome Michaelmas last past unto Saynt Elyn day next cummynge And xxiij *s.* iiij *d.* to be payd to theme for the secund paymentt at Saynt Elyn day for the provision of xiiij Veills to serve my house frome the said Saynt Elyn day unto Michaelmas next after And so the hole Somme for full contentacion of the said Veills for an hole Yere ys = xlvj *s.* viij *d.*

L A M B E S.

ITEM to be payd to the said Richard Gowge and Thomas Percy for to make provision for lx Lambes for th'expensys of my house for oone hole Yere Whereof x at xij *d.* the pece by estimacion to serve my house frome Cristynmas to Shroftide And L at x *d.* the pece by estimacion to serve my house frome Ester to Midsomer next after Somme lj *s.* viij *d.* Whereof x *s.* to be payd to the said Richard Gowge and Thomas Percy for the fyrst payment at Candlemas next cummynge And xlj *s.* viij *d.* to be payd to theme for the secund paymentt at Sayntt Elyn day next cummynge And so the hole Somme for full contentacion of the said Lambes for oone hole Yere ys = lj *s.* viij *d.*

S T O K F I S H.

ITEM to be payd to the said Richard Gowge and Thomas Percy for to make provision for cxl Stokfisch for th'expensys of my house for an hole Yere after ij *d.* obol. the pece by estimacion All the said Fisch to be bought at Candlemas next cummynge to serve my house frome Shroftide to Ester next
after

after and to be occupied frome the said Shroftide to Ester Viz. all the Lentt season Somme xxxiij *s.* iij *d.* Which ys to be payd all to geder to the said Richard Gowge and Thomas Percy at the said Candlemas bicause of the occupyinge of theym in the said Lent foloynge And so the hole Somme for full contentacion of the said Stokfische for oone hole Yere ys = xxxiij *s.* iij *d.*

S A L T   F I S H E.

ITEM to be payd to the said Richard Gowge and Thomas Percy for to make provision for pccccxlij Salt fisch for th'expensys of my house for an hole Yere after iiij *d.* the pecé by estimacion Somme xviij *l.* xiiij *s.* Whereof xiiij *l.* xiiij *s.* to be payd to the said Richard Gowge and Thomas Percy for the fyrst paymentt at All Hallowtide for the provision of pccxlij Salt fisch to serve my house frome Michaelmas last past unto Sayntt Elyn day next cummynge And iiij *l.* to be payd unto theme for the secund paymentt at Sayntt Elyn day for the provision of cc Saltfisch to serve my house frome the said Sayntt Elyn day to Michaelmas next after And so the hole Somme for full contentacion of the said Saltfisch for an hole Yere ys = xviij *l.* xiiij *s.*

W H Y T   H E R I N G.

ITEM to be payd to the said Richard Gowge and Thomas Percy for to make provision for ix barells of White Herynge after x *s.* the barell by estimacion for th'expensys of my house betwixt Shroftide and Ester next after Which ys to serve all the Lentt Season Somme iiij *l.* x *s.* which ys apoynted to be payd to the said Richard Gowge and Thomas Percy all to geder at Candlemas next cummynge bicause it must be purveyed all at oons And so the hole Somme for full contentacion of the said White Herynge for an hole Yere ys = iiij *l.* x *s.*

R E D E

REDE HERYNGE.

ÏTEM to be páyd to the faid Richard Gowge and Thomas Percy for to make provifion for x cades of Rede Herynge for th'expenfys of my Houfe from Shroftide to Efter next after Which ys to ferve all the Lent Seafon after vj *s*. iiij *d*. the Cade by eftimacion Somme lxiij *s* iiij *d*. Which ys apoynted to be payd to the faid Richard Gowge and Thomas Percy all to geder at Candlemas next cummynge bicaufe it muft be purveyd all at oons And fo the hole Somme for full contentacion of the faid Rede Herynge for oone hole Yere ys ═ lxiij *s*. iiij *d*.

SPROOTIS.

ITEM to be payd to the faid Richard Gowge and Thomas Percy for to make provifion for v cades of Sproytts for th'expenfys of my Houfe betwixt Shroftide and Efter next after Which ys to ferve all the Lentt Seafon after ij *s*. the cade by eftimacion Somme x *s*. Which ys apoynted to be payd to the faid Richard Gowge and Thomas Percy all to geder at Candlemas next cummynge bicaufe it muft be purveyd all at oons and fo the hole Somme for full contentacion of the faid Sproytts for oone hole Yere ys ═ x *s*.

SALMON.

ITEM to be payd to the faid Richard Gowge and Thomas Percy for to make provifion for ciiij fcore Saltt Salmon for th'expenfys of my Houfe frome Shroftid to Whitfontid next after Which ys to ferve all the Lentt Seafon and to Whitfontide next foloynge after vj *d*. the pece by eftimacion Somme c *s*. Which ys apoynted to be payd to the faid Richard Gowge and Thomas Percy all to geder at Saynt Andro day next cummynge bicaufe it muft be purveyd all at oons And fo the hole Somme for full contentacion of the faid Saltt Salmon for oone hole Yere ys ═ c *s*.

C   SALTT

SALTT STURGION.

ITEM to be payd to the said Richard Gowge and Thomas Percy for to make provision for iij ferekyngs of Saltt Sturgion for th'expensys of my House frome Shroftide to Ester next after Which ys to serve all the Lentt season after x s. the ferekynge by estimacion Somme xxx s. Which ys apoynted to be payd to the said Richard Gowge and Thomas Percy all to geder at Candlemas bicause it must be purveyd all at oons and so the hole Somme for the full contentacion of the said Saltt Sturgion for oone hole Yere ys = xxx s.

SALTT ELIS.

ITEM to be payd to the said Richard Gowge and Thomas Percy for to make provision for v caggs of Saltt Elys for th'expensys of my House frome Shroftide to Ester next after Which ys to serve all the Lentt season after iiij s. the cagg by estimacion Somme xx s. Which ys apoynted to be paid to the said Richard Gowge and Thomas Percy all to geder at Candlemas next cummynge bicause it must be purveyd all at oons And so the hole Somme for full contentacion of the said Saltt Elys for oone hole Yere ys = xx s.

FIEGGS.

ITEM to be payd to the said Richard Gowge and Thomas Percy for to make provision for iiij coppetts of Fieggs for th'expensys of my House frome Shroftid to Ester next after Which ys to serve all the Lentt Season after xx d. the coppett by estimacion Somme vj s. viij d. Which ys apoynted to be payd to the said Richard Gowge and Thomas Percy all to geder at Candlemas next cummynge bicause it must be purveyd all at oons And so the hole Somme for the full contentacion of the said Fieggs for oone hole Yere ys = vj s. viij d.

GREAT

GREAT RASINS.

ITEM to be payd to the faid Richard Gowge and Thomas Percy for to make provifion for iiij coppetts of Great Rayfyngs for th'expenfys of my Houfe frome Shroftid to Efter next after Which ys to ferve all the Lentt Seafon after xx *d.* the coppett by eftimacion Somme vj *s.* viij *d.* Which ys apoynted to be payd to the faid Richard Gowge and Thomas Percy all togeder at Candlemas next cummynge bicaufe it muft be purveyd all at oons And fo the hole Somme for full contentacion of the faid Great Rafyngs for oone hole Yere ys ═ vj *s.* viij *d.*

HOPPS FOR BREWYNGE.

ITEM to be payd to the faid Richard Gowge and Thomas Percy for to make provifion for plvj lb. of Hopps for Brewynge of Bere for th'expenfys of my Houfe for oone hole Yere after xiij *s* iiij *d.* the c by eftimacion Somme lxxiij *s.* iiij *d.* Whereof xl *s.* to be payd to the faid Richard Gowge and Thomas Percy for the fyrft payment at our Lady day in Lentt for the provifion of ccc lb. Hopps to ferve my Houfe from Michaelmas laft paft unto Midfomer next after And xxxiij *s.* iiij *d.* to be payd to theme for the fecund payment att Midfomer for the provifion of cclvj lb. Hopps to ferve my faid Houfe frome Midfomer aforefaid unto Michaelmas next after And fo the hole Somme for full contentacion of the faid Hopps for an hole Yere ys ═ lxxiij *s.* iiij *d.*

HONY.

ITEM to be payd to the faid Richard Gowge and Thomas Percy for to make provifion for a barell dimid. of Hony for th'expenfys of my Houfe for oone hole Yere after xxij *s.* the Barell by eftimacion Somme xxxiij *s.* Whereof xj *s.* to be paid to the faid Richard Gowge and Thomas Percy for the furft payment at Criftynmas next cummynge for the provifion of half a barell of Hony for to ferve for th'expenfys of my faid Houfe frome Michaelmas laft paft unto Criftynmas aforefaid And

And xxij *s.* to be payd unto theme for the fecund payment at our Lady day in Lentt next foloynge for the provifion of oone hole barell of Hony to ferve my Houfe frome Criftynmas next cummynge unto Michaelmas next after And fo the hole Somme for full contentacion of the faid Hony for oone hole Yere ys = xxxiij *s.*

O I L E.

ITEM to be payd to the faid Richard Gowge and Thomas Percy for to make provifion for a barell dimid. of Oyll for th'expenfys of my houfe for oone hole Yere The barell contenynge xxiiij gallons after xj *d.* ob. the gallon and ij *d.* les at all And after xxij *s.* x *d.* the barell by eftimacion Somme xxxiiij *s.* iij *d.* Whereof xj *s.* v *d.* to be payd to the faid Richard Gowge and Thomas Percy for the fyrft paymentt at Criftynmas next cummynge for the provifion of dimid. barell of Oyll for to ferve for th'expenfys of my Houfe frome the faid Criftynmas unto Shroftide And frome the faid Shroftide unto Efter next after And xxij *s.* x *d.* to be payd unto theme for the fecund paymentt at Shroftide aforefaid for the provifion of oone hole barell of Oyll to ferve for th'expenfys of my faid Houfe unto Michaelmas than next foloynge And fo the hole Somme for full contentacion of the faid Oyll for friynge of Fifh for oone hole Yere ys = xxxiiij *s.* iij *d.*

W A X E.

ITEM to be payd to the faid Richard Gowge and Thomas Percy for to make provifion for cc iiij fcore vij lb. dimid. of Wax for th'expenfys of my Houfe for oone hole Yere Viz. Syfez Pryketts Quarions and Torches after ix *d.* the lb. by eftimacion Somme xij *l.* v *s.* vij *d.* obol. Whereof iiij *l.* to be payd to the faid Richard Gowge and Thomas Percy for the furft paymentt at Criftynmas next cummynge for the provifion of v fcore vij lb. Wax which did ferve my houfe frome Michaelmas laft paft unto Criftynmas next after And iiij *l.* v *s.* vij *d.* obol.

obol. to be payd to theme for the fecund payment at Candlemas
next cummynge for the provifion of v fcore xiiij lb. Wax to
ferve my faid houfe frome criftynmas unto Efter next after And
iiij l. to be payd unto theme for the thyrd paymentt and laft at
Midfomer for the provifion of v fcore vj lb. dimid. of Wax
to ferve my faid houfe from Efter aforefaid unto Michaelmas
next after And fo the hole Somme for the full contentacion
of the faid Wax for oone hole Yere ys = xij l. v s. vij d. obl.

ROSIN.

ITEM to be payd to the faid Richard Gowge and Thomas
Percy for to make provifion for xxix lb. of Rofyn for
Torches for th'expenfys of my Houfe for oone hole Yere after
j d. obl. the lb. by eftimacion Somme iiij s. x d. obl. Which
ys apoynted to be payd to the faid Richard Gowge and
Thomas Percy all to geder at Criftynmas next cummynge
bicaufe it muft be purveyd all at oons And fo the hole Somme
for full contentacon of the faid Rofyn for oone hole Yere
ys = iiij s. x d. obol.

WEIK FOR LIGHTYS.

ITEM to be payd to the faid Richard Gowge and Thomas
Percy for to make provifion for lj lb. Weik for to ferve for
all manner of lyghts of Wax for th'expenfys of my Houfe for
oone hole Yere after ij d. the lb. by eftimacion Somme viij s. vj d.
Which ys apoynted to be payd to the faid Richard Gowge and
Thomas Percy at Sayntt Andro day next cummynge bicaufe
it muft be purveyd all at oons And fo the hole Somme for the
full contentacion of the faid Weik for oone hole Yere
ys = viij s. vj d.

BAY SALTTE.

ITEM to be payd to the faid Richard Gowge and Thomas
Percy for to make provifion for x quarters of Bay Saltt for
th'expenfys of my Houfe for oone hole Yere after iiij s. the
quarter

quarter by eftimacion Somme xl*s*. Whereof xx*s*. to be payd theme for the fyrft payment att Sayntt Andro day next cummynge for the provifion of v quarters of Bay Saltt to ferve my faid Houfe frome Michaelmas laft paft unto Shroftide And x*s*. to be payd to theme for the fecund paymentt att Efter next after for the provifion of ij quarters dimid. of Bay Saltt to ferve my Houfe frome Shroftide aforefaid unto Midfomer next cummynge And x*s*. to be payd unto theme for the thyrd and laft paymentt att Midfomer for the provifion of ij quarters dimid. of Bay Saltt for to ferve my faid houfe frome Midfomer aforefaid unto Michaelmas next after And fo the hole Somme for the full contentacion of the faid Bay Saltt for oone hole Yere ys = xl*s*.

WHITE SALTTE.

ITEM to be payd to the faid Richard Gowge and Thomas Percy for to make provifion for vj quarters dimid. of White Saltt for th'expenfys of my houfe for oone hole Yere after iiij *s*. the quarter by eftimacion Somme xxvj*s*. Whereof xij*s*. ys apoynted to be 'paid' to the faid Richard Gowge and Thomas Percy for the fyrft paymentt at Sayntt Andro day for the provifion of iij quarters of White Saltt to ferve my Houfe frome Michaelmas laft paft unto our Lady day in Lentt next after And xiiij*s*. to be payd unto theme for the fecund paymentt and laft at our Lady day in Lentt for the provifion of iij quarters dimid. Saltt to ferve my houfe frome our Lady day in Lentt unto Michaelmas next after And fo the hole Somme for the full contentacion of the faid White Saltt for oone hole Yere ys = xxvj*s*.

PARISHE CANDELL.

ITEM to be payd to the faid Richard Gowge and Thomas Percy for to make provifion for iiij fcore xj doffon ij lb. of Parifch Candle for th'expenfys of my Houfe for oone hole Yere after xij*d*. the doffon by eftimacion Somme iiij *l*.xj*s*. ij*d*. Which ys apoynted to be payd to the faid Richard Gowge and Thomas Percy

Percy at Michaelmas next in th'end of the said Yere bicause
the Talow ys myne owne And nott be rekynned for unto
the said Michaelmas in th'end of the said Yere And so the
hole Somme for full contentacion of the said Parishe Candle
for oone hole Yere ys = iiij *l.* xj *s.* ij *d.*

V I N A C R E.

ITEM to be payd to the said Richard Gowge and Thomas
Percy for to make provision for xl gallons of Vinacre for
th'expensys of my house for oone hole Yere after iiij *d.* the
gallon by estimacion Somme xiij *s.* iiij *d.* Whereof vj *s.* viij *d.*
ys apoynted to be payd to the said Richard Gowge and
Thomas Percy for the fyrst paymentt at Sayntt Andro day
for the provision of xx gallons of the said Vinacre to
serve my House frome Michaelmas last past unto our Lady
day in Lentt And vj *s.* viij *d.* to be payd unto theme for
the secund paymentt and last at our Lady day in Lentt
aforesaid for the provision of other xx gallons of Vinacre to
serve my house frome our Lady day in Lentt aforesaid
unto Michaelmas next foloynge And so the hole Somme
for full contentacion of the said Vinacre for oone hole Yere
yff the said Vinacre cannott be made of myne owne Lagge
of my Cellar ys = xiij *s.* iv *d.*

V E R G E O U S.

ITEM to be payd to the said Richard Gowge and
Thomas Percy for to make provision for iiij score x gallons
of Vergeous for th'expensys of my house for oone hole
Yere after iij *d.* the gallon by estimacion Somme xxij *s.* vj *d.*
Whereof vij *s.* vj *d.* ys apoynted to be payd to the said Richard
Gowge and Thomas Percy for the fyrst paymentt at Candlemas
for the provision of xxx gallons of Vergeous to serve my
house frome Michaelmas last past unto our Lady day in
Lentt And xv *s.* to be payd unto theme for the secund and
last paymentt at Ester for the provision of lx gallons of
Vergeous

Vergeous to ferve my houfe frome our faid Lady day in Lentt unto Michaelmas next foloynge And fo the hole Somme for the full contentacion of the faid Vergeous for oone hole Yere ys $=$ xxijs. vjd.

LYNNON CLOTHE.

ITEM to be payd to the faid Richard Gowge and Thomas Percy, for to make provifion for lxx elnys of Lynon Cloth yerde brode Which muft ferve for all manner of Lynon that muft be occupied for th'expenfys of myne houfe for oone hole Yere after viijd. the elne by eftimacion Furft for viij Boordeclothes yerde brode for the Hall Viz. For oone Boorde Cloth in lenght v elns iij quarters — And for vij other Boordeclothes every of theym of iiij elnys longe — oone to the Knyghts boord in the great Chambre of v elnys iij quarters longe — oone Ewery Cloth ij elnys longe — two Wefchynge Towells for my Lorde to wefch with for the Ewery ij elnys long a pece and a quarter brode — iiij Towells for Carvers and Sewers of ij elnys long a pece and a quarter dimid. brode — xviij Napkyns vij elnys and a quarter after a yerde longe and half a yerde brode every pece — for a Cupbard Cloth of ij breids for the Sellar iiij elnys Viz. ij elnys longe and ij yerds brode a pece. — A fingle Cupbard Cloth for the faid Seller ij elnys longe and a yerde brode — for two Berynge Towells for the Pantre two elnys dimid. after ij elnys longe and a quarter dimid. brode a pece — viij Pantre Towells for Lyverys ij yerds after a quarter brode and a yerde longe a pece — A Portpayne for the faid Pantre an elne longe and a yerd brode — two Dreffor Clothes for the Kechynge ix 'elnys' after iiij Elnys dimid. longe and a Yerd brode a pece. — Somme of all the faid Cloth ys xlvjs. viijd. Which ys apoynted to be payd to the faid Richard Gowge and Thomas Percy, at Sayntt Andro day next cummynge all to geder bicaufe it muft be purveyd all at oons And fo the hole Somme for
full

full contentacion of the faid Lynon Cloth for oone hole Yere ys $=$ xlvj*s*. viij*d*.

RUGHE VESSELL.

ITEM to be payd to the faid Richard Gowge and Thomas Percy for to make provifion for the hyre of c doffon of Rugh Veffell to ferve my houfe for oone hole Yere after iiij*d.* the hyre of every doffon by eftimacion Somme xl*s*. Wherof xiij*s*. iiij*d*. ys apoynted to be payd to the faid Richard Gowge and Thomas Percy for the fyrft paymentt at Criftynmas for the hyre of xl doffon of the faid Rugh Veffell to ferve my houfe in the tyme of Criftynmas next cummynge And xiij*s*. iiij*d*. to be payd to theme for the fecund paymentt at Efter next after for the hyre of xl doffon of the faid Rughe Veffell to ferve my houfe the faid tyme of Efter And xiij*s*. iiij*d*. to be payd unto theme for the thyrd and laft paymentt at Whitfonday next cummynge for the hyre of other xl doffon of Rugh Veffell to ferve my houfe at the fame tyme of Whitfonday And fo the hole Somme for the full contentacion for the hyre of the faid Rugh Pewder Veffell for oone hole Yere ys $=$ xl*s*.

BRASS POTTIS.

ITEM to be payd to the faid Richard Gowge and Thomas Percy for to make provifion for ij Bras Potts for to ferve my faid houfe for oone hole Yere after xiij*s*. ij*d*. the pece by eftimacion Somme xxvj*s*. iiij*d*. Which ys apoynted to be payd unto the faid Richard Gowge and Thomas Percy at Sayntt Andro day next cummynge all to geder bicaufe they muft be purveyd all at oons for to ferve my faid houfe at Criftynmas foloynge And fo the hole Somme for full contentacion of the byinge of the faid ij Bras Potts ys $=$ xxvj*s*. iiij*d*.

D   MUSTARDE.

MUSTARDE.

ITEM to be payd to the faid Richard Gowge and Thomas Percy for to make provifion for clx gallons of Muftard to be redy made in the Squyllery for th'expenfys of my houfe for oone hole Yere after ij*d*. quad: the gallon and iij*d*. more at all by eftimacion Somme xxxiiij*s*. iiij*d*. Whereof xvij*s*. ij*d*. ys apoynted to be paid to the faid Richard Gowge and Thomas Percy for the fyrft paymentt at our Lady day in Lentt to make provifion for iiij fcore x gallons of the faid Muftard to ferve my houfe frome Michaelmas laft paft unto our Lady day in Lentt aforefaid And xvij*s*. ij*d*. to be payd unto theme for the fecund and laft paymentt at Midfomer for the provifion of other iiij fcore x gallons of the faid Muftard to ferve my houfe frome our faid Lady day in Lentt unto Michaelmas next foloynge And fo the hole Somme for the full contentacion of the faid Muftard for oone hole Yere ys = xxxiiij*s*. iiij*d*.

STONE CRUSIS.

ITEM to be payd to the faid Richard Gowge and Thomas Percy for to make provifion for xx doffon of ftoone Crofez for to ferve my houfe for oone hole Yere after vj*d*. the doffon by eftimacion Somme x*s*. Whereof v*s*. ys apoynted to be payd unto the faid Richard Gowge and Thomas Percy for the fyrft paymentt at Sayntt Andro day next cummynge for the provifion of x doffon Crofez to ferve my houfe frome Michaelmas laft paft unto Efter next after And v*s*. to be payd unto theme for the fecund paymentt and laft at Efter for the provifion of other x doffon of Stoone Crofez to ferve my houfe frome the faid Efter unto Michaelmas next foloynge And fo the hole Somme for the full contentacion of the faid Stoone Crofez for oone hole Yere ys = x*s*.

COUNTERFOOT

COUNTERFOOT VESSELL.

ITEM to be payd to the faid Richard Gowge and Thomas Percy for the byinge of two Garnyfch of Counterfeitt Veffell for fervynge of my houfe an hole Yere after xxxv*s.* the Garnyfch by eftimacion Somme lxx*s.* Which ys apoynted to be payd to the faid Richard Gowge and Thomas Percy all to geder at Sayntt Andro day next cummynge bicaufe they muft be purveyd all to geder And fo the hole Somme for full confentacion of the faid Counterfeitt Veffell ys = lxx*s.*

RUGHE PEWTER VESSEL.

ITEM to be payd to the faid Richard Gowge and Thomas Percy for the byinge of vj doffon Rugh Pewter Veffell for fervynge of my houfe for oone hole Yere after vj*s.* viij*d.* the doffon by eftimacion Somme xl*s.* Which ys apoynted to be payd to the faid Richard Gowge and Thomas Percy all to geder at Sayntt Andro day afore Criftynmas next cummynge bicaufe they muft be purveyd all att oons And fo the hole Somme for full contentacion for the byinge of the faid Rugh Pewter Veffell ys = xl*s.*

ALL MANNER OF SPICES.

ITEM to be payd to the faid Richard Gowge and Thomas Percy for to make provifion for all manner of Spices for th'expenfys of my houfe for oone hole Yere ; Viz. of Piper L lb. j quarteron dimid. — Rafyns of Corens ciiij fcore lb. — Prones cxxxj lb. dimid. — Gynger xxj lb. dimid. — Mace vj lb. — Clovvez iij lb. dimid. — Sugour ciiij fcore lb. j quarteron — Cinamom xvij lb. iij quarterons dimid. — Allmonds cxxxij lb. — Daytts xxx lb. — Nuttmuggs j lb. j quarteron — Granes vij lb. — Tornefolle x lb. dimid. — Saunders x lb. — Powder of Annes iij lb. j quarteron — Rice xix lb. — Coumfetts xix lb. dimid. — Galyngga j quarteron — Longe Piper dimid. lb. — Blaynfhe Powder ij lb. — And Safferon iij lb. — Somme of all the faid Spices by eftimacion
ys

ys xxv *l.* xix *s.* vij *d.* quad. Whereof xiij *l.* ys apoynted to be payd to the faid Richard Gowge and Thomas Percy for the fyrft paymentt at Sayntt Andro day next cummynge for the provifion of all manner of Spices for to ferve my houfe frome Michaelmas laft paft unto our Lady day in Lentt next foloynge And vj *l.* to be payd unto theme for the fecund paymentt at our Lady day in Lentt for the provifion of all manner of Spices to ferve my houfe frome our faid Lady day in Lentt unto Midfomer next f oynge And vj *l.* xix *s.* vij *d.* quad. to be payd to theme for the thyrd and laft paymentt at Midfomer next cummynge for the provifion of all manner of Spices to ferve my houfe frome the faid Midfomer un-to Michaelmas next foloynge And fo the hole Somme for full contentacion of the faid Spices for oone hole Yere ys = xxv *l.* xix *s.* vij *d.*

SEE CHOLYS.

ITEM to be payd to the faid Richard Gowge and Thomas Percy for to make provifion for iiij fcore Chawder of Seecolys for th'expenfys of my houfe for oone hole Yere Whereof xx Chawder after iiij *s.* ij *d.* the Chawder And lx Chawder after v *s.* the Chawder by eftimacion Somme xix *l.* iij *s.* iiij *d.* Whereof xv *l.* ys apoynted to be payd to the faid Richard Gowge and Thomas Percy for the fyrft paymentt at Sayntt Andro day next cummynge for the provifion of lx Chawder of Seecolys to ferve my houfe frome Michaelmas laft paft unto our Lady day in Lentt next after And iiij *l.* iij *s.* iiij *d.* to be payd to theme for the fecund and laft paymentt at our Lady day in Lentt for the provifion of xx Chawder of Seecolys to ferve my houfe frome our Lady day afore unto Michaelmas next after And fo the hole Somme for full contentacion of the faid Seecolys for oone hole Yere ys = xix *l.* iij *s.* iiij *d.*

CHAR

CHAR CHOLIS.

ITEM to be payd to the faid Richard Gowge and Thomas Percy for to make provifion for xx quarters of Charcolys for th'expenfys of my houfe for oone hole Yere after xij*d*. the quarter with the cariage Somme xx*s*. Which ys apoynted to be payd to the faid Richard Gowge and Percy all to geder at Sayntt Andro day next cummynge bicaufe they muft be purveyd all at oons for to ferve in the tyme of Criftynmas next after Which ys bicaufe the Smook of the ßeecolys wold hurtt myne Arras when it ys hunge And fo the hole Somme of full contentacion for the faid Charcolys for oone hole Yere ys = xx*s*.

FAGOOTS.

ITEM to be payd to the faid Richard Gowge and Thomas Percy for to make provifion for ᴍᴍᴍᴄᴄᴄᴄlx Fagotts which ys for Bakynge and Brewynge for th'expenfys of my houfe for oone hole Yere after ij*s*. viij*d*. the c by eftimacion Somme iiij *l*. xij*s*. ij*d*. Which ys apoynted to be payd to theme all to geder at Candlemas next cummynge bicaufe they muft be purveyd all at oons And fo the hole Somme for full contentacion of the faid Fagotts for oone hole Yere ys = iiij *l*. xij*s*. ij*d*.

GREET WOODE.

ITEM to be payd to the faid Richard Gowge and Thomas Percy for to make provifion for lxiiij loodd of Greatt Wodd for th'expenfys of my houfe for oone hole Yere after xij*d*. the loode with the cariage oone with another by eftimacion Somme lxiiij*s*. Which ys apoynted to be payd to the faid Richard Gowge and Thomas Percy at Candlemas all togeder Which ys bicaufe Colys will not byrne withowte Wodd And fo the hole Somme for full contentacion of the faid Greatt Wodd for oone hole Yere ys = lxiiij*s*.

OOTTYS.

OOTTYS.

ITEM to be payd to the faid Richard Gowge and Thomas Percy for to make provifion for v fcore quarters of Oytes for th'expenfys of my Horfes in Houfehold for oone hole Yere after ij*s*. the quarter by eftimacion Somme x *l*. Whereof c*s*. ys apoynted to be payd to the faid Richard Gowge and Thomas Percy for the fyrft paymentt att Criftynmas next cummynge for the provifion of L quarters Oytts to ferve for th'expenfys of my faid Hors in Houfehold frome Michaelmas laft paft unto our Lady day in Lentt next after And c*s*. to be payd to theme for the fecund and laft paymentt att Efter for the provifion of other L quarters of Ottes for th'expenfys of my faid Hors in Houfehold frome our Lady day aforefaid unto Michaelmas next after And fo the hole Somme for full contentacion of the faid Ottes for an hole Yere ys = x *l*.

BORD WAGIS.

ITEM to be payd to the faid Richard Gowge and Thomas Percy for to pay for the Boord Waigies of divers of my Servantts who be putt to Boord Waigies att certain tymes of the Yere for divers caufes by eftimacion x *l*. Which ys apoynted to be payd to the faid Richard Gowge and Thomas Percy att Michaelmas next foloynge in th'end of the faid Yere for full contentacion of the faid Boord Waigies = x *l*.

REWARDS TO PLAYARS.

ITEM to be payd to the faid Richard Gowge and Thomas Percy for Rewards to Players for Playes playd in Chriftynmas by Stranegers in my houfe after xx*d*. every play by eftimacion Somme xxxiij*s*. iiij*d*. Which ys apoynted to be payd to the faid Richard Gowge and Thomas Percy at the faid Chriftynmas in full contentacion of the faid Rewardys = xxxiij*s*. iiij*d*.

LAUNDERERS

LAUNDERERS OF HOUSEHOLD.

ITEM to be payd to the said Richard Gowge and Thomas Percy for to pay to the Launderes of Household for the Weschynge of all the Lynonn Stuff belongynge 'to' my house Viz. the Chapell the Ewery the Sellar the Pantre the Kechynge and the Warderobe for the space of oone hole Yere by estimacion = xlvj*s.* viij*d.* Whereof xj*s.* viij*d.* ys apoynted to be payd to the said Richard Gowge and Thomas Percy for the fyrst paymentt at Cristynmas for to pay for the Weschynge of the said Lynonn Stuff of Household frome Michaelmas last past unto Cristynmas aforesaid And xj*s.* viij*d.* to be payd to theme for the secund paymentt at our Lady day in Lentt to pay for the Weschynge of all the said Lynonn Stuff of Household frome Cristynmas aforesaid unto our said Lady day And xj*s.* viij*d.* to be payd unto theme for the thyrd paymentt at Midsomer for to pay for the Weschynge of all the said Lynonn Stuff of Household frome our Lady day aforesaid unto the said Midsomer And xj*s.* viij*d.* to be payd unto theme for the iiij*th* and last paymentt at Michaelmas for to pay for the Weschynge of all the said Lynonn Stuff of Household frome Midsomer aforesaid unto Michaelmas next after And so the hole Somme for full contentacion of the said Weschynge of all the said Lynonn Stuff of Household for oone hole Yere ys = xlvj*s.* viij*d.*

COSTS NECESSARY.

ITEM to be payd to the said Richard Gowge and Thomas Percy for to pay theire Costs for rydynge owte for all manner of necessary provisions that shal belonge to my house for oone hole Yere by estimacion = xx*l.* Whereof c*s.* ys apoynted to be payd to the said Richard Gowge and Thomas Percy for the fyrst paymentt at Christynmas next cummynge for to pay all manner of necessary Costs that shal belonge for the provision of my house frome Michaelmas last past unto the aforesaid Christynmas And c*s.* to be payd unto theme

theme for the fecund paymentt at our Lady day in Lentt
for to pay for all manner of neceffary Cofts for the provifion
of my houfe frome Chriftynmas aforefaid unto our faid Lady
day in Lentt And c*s*. to be payd unto theme for the thyrd
paymentt at Midfomer next cummynge for to pay for all
manner of neceffary Cofts for the makynge of provifion for
my houfe frome our faid Lady day in Lentt unto Midfomer
aforefaid And c*s*. to be payd unto theme for the iiijth
paymentt and laft at Michaelmas for to pay for all manner
of neceffary Cofts for the makynge of provifion for th'expenfys of my houfe frome Midfomer aforefaid unto the faid
Michaelmas And fo the hole Somme for full contentacion
to be payd for all manner of neceffary Cofts for the
makynge of provifion for th'expenfys of my houfe for oone
hole Yere ys = xx *l.*

HORSSYS SHOING.

ITEM to be payd to the faid Richard Gowge and Thomas
Percy for to pay for the Shoynge of all fuch Horfys of
myne as ys apoynted to ftond in my Stable at the charge
of the houfe which ys = xxvij. Viz. Gentill Horfys vj
Pallfrays iiij Naggs and Hobbies iiij Clothfek Horfe ij Chariott
Horfe vij Malehorfe j and v Horfys for theme that ar at
my Lords Horffynge after ij*s*. viiij*d.* every Hors Shoynge
for the hole Yere by eftimacion Viz. a Hors to be fhodd
oons in iij moneths withowt they jornay Which ys at my
charge Somme lxxij*s.* Which ys apoynted to be payd to
the faid Richard Gowge and Thomas Percy at Michaelmas
next cummynge at th'end of the Yere for full contentacion to be payd for Shoynge of all the faid Horfys for
oone hole Yere = lxxij*s.*

MAWING MAKYNGE AND CARYAGE OF HEY.

ITEM to be payd to the faid Richard Gowge and Thomas
Percy for to pay for the Mawynge Makynge and Cariage
of

bf all my Hey growynge of ciiij fcore v acres of Medowe ground which ys affigned as parcell of th'affignementt for my houfe Viz. xxxiiij acres at Wrefill after x d. for Mawynge and makynge of every acre in Hey And for the Cariage of lv lood of Hey growynge of the faid xxxiiij acres there after iiij d. every lood Cariage to the Caftell of Wrefill And for Mawynge makynge of clj Acres of Medow ground at Lekyngfeld after x d. every Acre makynge and mawynge in Hey And for the cariage of cxxxix loods of Hey that grew upon the faid Acres Viz. xlvij lood after ij d. the lood which ys ftakked in the Demayns lx lood after ij d. the loode cariage which ys ftakked in the Demayns in likcafe And lij lood after iiij d. the lode cariage which ys caried frome the faid Demayns to the barne at the Mannor And les at all than the prices of the parcells aforefaid iiij s. ix d. Somme for Mawynge Makynge and Cariage of all the faid Medowys in Hey as well at Wrefill as at Lekyngfeld for th'expenfys of my faid houfe xj l. Which ys apoynted to be payd to the faid Richard Gowge and Thomas Percy at Lammes next cummynge in full contentacion of the faid hole Somme for oone hole Yere = xj l.

FARMYS OF MEDOWS AND PASTURS.

I T E M to be allowed to the faid Richard Gowge and Thomas Percy for to pay for the Farmes of all fuch Medowys and Paftures which ys affigned as parcell of th'affignementt of my houfe Viz. at Newifham the Halle Ryddynge and Nefchdaills lvj s. A Medow ground called the Hollefike xiij s. iiij d. And oone other Medow called Langdaills vj s. viij d. And for the Farme of divers Medowys and Paftures at Lekyngfeld Viz. Hadcroft lx s. Cudbert Leys cvj s. viij d. Heynnyngs xxx s. and Hugheholme xxxiij s. iiij d. Somme of all the faid Medowys and Paftures ys = xvj l. vj s. Which ys apoynted to be allowed to the faid Richard Gowge and Thomas Percy and ys delyvert as fyrft parcell of th'affignementt

E

at Michaelmas in the begynnynge of the Yere and allowed theme at Michaelmas in th'end of the Yere for all manner of Medowys and Paſtures occupied for th'expenſys of my houſe and allowed as laſt parcell of the Somme of th'aſſignementt in full contentacion of the hole Somme aſſigned for kepynge of my ſaid houſe for the hole Yere$=$xvj *l.* vj *s.*

CATOR PARCELLS.

ITEM to be payd to the ſaid Richard Gowge and Thomas Percy for to make proviſion for all manner of Cator Parcells as ſhal belong for th'expenſys of my houſe for oone hole Yere by eſtimacion the Somme of cv *l.* xv *s.* iiij *d.* Whereof c *s.* ys apoynted to be payd to the ſaid Richard Gowge and Thomas Percy for to pay for the Cator Parcells in the moneth of Octobre And c *s.* vj *d.* to be payd unto theme for the ſaid Cator Parcells in the moneth of Novembre And xvij *l.* ix *s.* to be payd unto theme for the ſaid Cator Parcells in the moneth of Decembre wherein ys Criſtynmas to New Yere Day And xxiij *l.* xxij *d.* unto be payd unto theme for the ſaid Cator Parcells in the moneth of January wherein ys Twelfth Day And cvij *s.* vj *d.* to be payd unto theme for the ſaid Cator Parcells in the moneth of February And vij *l.* iij *s.* ix *d.* to be payd unto theme for the ſaid Cator Parcells in the moneth of March And ix *l.* xix *s.* v *d.* to be payd unto theme for the ſaid Cator Parcells in the moneth of Aprill wherein ys Eſter and Sayntt George Day And vj *l.* x *s.* x *d.* to be payd unto theme for the ſaid Cator Parcells in the moneth of Maye And ix *l.* xj *s.* viij *d.* to be payd unto theme for the ſaid Cator Parcells in the moneth of June wherein ys Whitſonday And c *s.* ij *d.* to be payd unto theme for the ſaid Cator Parcells in the moneth of July And cx *s.* iij *d.* to be payd unto theme for the ſaid Cator Parcells in the moneth of Auguſt And vj *l.* v *d.* to be payd unto theme for the ſaid Cator Parcells in the moneth of Septembre And ſo the hole Somme for full

conten-

contentacion to be payd to the ſaid Richard Gowge and Thomas Percy Monethly for all the ſaid Cator Parcells for oone hole Yere ys ═ cv *l.* xv *s.* iiij *d.*

CHAPELL WAGIS.

ITEM to be payd to th'hands of Sir John Norton my Chamberlayn and Mr. Gefferay Proctor my Treaſurer for the contentacion of my Chapell Waigies for oone hole Yere as aperyth more playnly by the Chequirerolle and the Stile of the ſame what they ſhall have the Somme of xxxv *l.* xv *s.* to be payd quarterly Viz. To be payd for the fyrſt quarter at Criſtynmas next after the ſaid Michaelmas begynnynge the ſaid Yere viij *l.* xviij *s.* ix *d.* of the Money of my Lands of Cumberland cummynge to the Coffers at the ſaid Michaelmas upon the Auditt And to be payd for the ſecund quarter at our Lady day in Lentt viij *l.* xviij *s.* ix *d.* to be payd of the Revenuys of my Lands of Northumberland of this Yere dew at Martynmas after the ſaid Michaelmas aforenamed and payable at Candlemas and to be payd to theme at the ſaid Lady day And to be payd for thyrd quarter at Midſomer foloynge viij *l.* xviij *s.* ix *d.* to be payd of the Revenuys of my Lands in Yorkſchyre dew and payable at Whitſonday afore ſaid Midſomer and payd at the ſaid Midſomer to theme And to be payd for the iiijth quarter at Michaelmas foloynge endynge the ſaid Yere in full contentacion viij *l.* xviij *s.* ix *d.* to be payd of the Revenuys of my Lands of Yorkſchyre of the ſaid terme of Whitſonday by-paſt afore the ſaid Michaelmas and payable at Michaelmas and payd to theme at the ſaid Michaelmas in full contentacion of the ſaid hole Yere And ſo the hole Somme for full contentacion of the ſaid Chapell Waigies for oone hole Yere ys ═ xxxv *l.* xv *s.*

HOUSEHOLD

HOUSEHOLD WAGIS.

ITEM to be payd to th'hands of my said Chamberlayne and my said Treasurer the Somme of cliij *l.* vj *s.* viij *d.* for the contentacion and paymentt of the Household Waigies of my Servantts for oone hole Yere besids the Chapell Waigies as aperyth more playnly by the Chequirerolle and the Stile of the same what Waigies every man shall have by Yere to be payd at two Terms Viz. To be payd for the Fyrst Half Yere at our Lady day in Lentt lxxvj *l.* xiij *s.* iiij *d.* of the Revenuys of my Lands in Northumberland cummynge to my Coffers of this Yere dewe at Martynmas and payable at Candlemas next foloynge and to be payd to theme at the said Lady day And to be payd for the Secund Half Yere at Michaelmas foloynge endynge the said Yere in full contentacion lxxvj *l.* xiij *s.* iiij *d.* to be payd of the Revenuys of my Lands in Yorkschyre cummynge to my said Coffers of the Terme of Whitsonday by-past afore the said Michaelmas and payable at Lammes next after the said Whitsonday and payd to theme at the said Michaelmas for the contentacion of the said hole Yere = cliij *l.* vj *s.* viij *d.*

WYNTER HORSEMET.

ITEM to be payd to th'hands of my Chamberlayn and my Treasurer for the contentacion and paymentt of all my Servantts for theire Wynter Horsemeitt after x *s.* every Man as aperyth more playnely in the Chequirerolle of the said Wynter Horsemeitt What they be And how many And what rowme they serve in apoynted to be of my Rydynge Household Viz. Frome Michaelmas which day the said Wynter Horsemeitt begynnyth upon And Sayntt Elyn day next foloynge which day the said Wynter Horsemeitt goyeth owt on Somme xxiiij *l.* Which ys apoynted to be payd at the said Sayntt Elyn day all at oone paymentt of the Revenuys

ꝟenuys of my Lands in Northumberland of the Martynmaſ
Farme of this preſentt Yere dew to be payd at our Lady
day in Lentt next after the ſaid Martynmas and to be payd
to theme at the ſaid Sayntt Elyn day for full contentacion
of the ſaid Wynter Horſemeitt = xxiiij *l.*

SOMER HORSSEMET.

ITEM to be payd to th'hands of my Chamberlayn and my
Treaſurer for the contentacion and paymentt of all my
Servantts apoynted to be of my Rydynge Houſehold for
theire Sommer Horſemeitt after iij *s.* iiij *d.* every Man as
aperyth more playnly in the Chequirerolle of the ſaid Sommer
Horſemeitt What they be And how many And what rowme
they ſerve in Viz. Frome Sayntt Elyn day which day the
ſaid Sommer Horſemeitt begynnyth on And Michaelmas next
foloynge which day the ſaid Sommer Horſemeitt goyeth
owte on Somme viij *l.* Which ys apoynted to be payd to
theme at the ſaid Michaelmas all at oone paymentt of the
Revenuys of my Lands in Yorkſchyre cummynge to the
Coffers of the Term of Whitſonday of this preſentt Yere dew
to be payd to theme Lammes next after the ſaid Whitſonday
And to be payd to theme at the ſaid Michaelmas for full
contentacion of the ſaid Horſemeitt = viij *l.*

SOMME TOTALL for the hole Aſſignementt
apoynted for the Hole Expenſys for Kepynge
of my houſe for oone hole Yere with the
Houſehold Waigies and Wynter and Sommer
Horſemeitt and all other charges thereto
belongynge as more playnly aperyth by the
Book of th'Aſſignementt with the Ordors and
Directions for kepynge of my ſaid Houſe
ᴅᴄᴄᴄxxxiij *l.* vj *s.* viij *d.*
Whereof

II. The

II.

THE FYRST PAYMENTT of the Affignemente to my Countroller and Thomas Percy Clark of my Kechynge of my faide houfe frome Michaelmas to Criftynmas.

Somme of the paymentts bitwixt Michaelmas and Criftynmas next foloynge in the fyrft quarter ys ccciiij fcore vj *l.* iij *s.*

Whereof at

MICHAELMAS as in the price of certayn Vitaills unfpentt remanynge of the laft Yere and parcell of th'affignementt for this Yere Which ya the fyrft parcell payd to theme for th'affignementt of my faid Houfe = lviij *l.* xxij *d.*

ALL HALOWTIDE of the Money of my Lands of Yorkfchire dew to my Coffers upon th'auditt at Michaelmas Which ys fecund paymentt payd to theme for th'affignementt of my faid Houfe Viz. for Beiffs Mutons and Saltfifch to be bought = iiij fcore xvj *l.*

SAYNTT ANDRO DAY of the Money of my Lands in Cumberland dew to my Coffers upon th'auditt at Michaelmas Which ys the thyrd paymentt payd to theme for th'affignementt of my faid Houfe Viz. for White-Saltt Wyne Poorks Veills Saltt-Salmon Grea-Saltt White-Saltt Vinacre Lynon-Cloth Spice Stoone-Crofez Cunterfeitt-Veffell Rughe-Veffell Bras-Potts Seecole Charcolys and the Cator Parcells = c *l.*

CRISTYNMAS of the Money of my Landys in Northumberland dew to my Coffers upon th'auditt at Michaelmas Which ys the iiij[th] paymentt payd to theme for the Affignementt of my faid Houfe Viz. for Hony Oyll Wax Rofell Otes Rewards to Players Hyre of Pewder-Veffell Expenfys neceffary The Chapell Quarter-Waigies and The Launderer Quarter-Waigies = cxxxij *l.* xiiij *d.*

THE

THE SECUND PAYMENTT of th'affignement to my Countroller and Thomas Percy Clark of my Kechynge of my faid Houfe frome Criftynmas to oure Lady day in Lentt

Somme of the paymentts bitwixt Criftynmas and our Lady day in Lentt next foloynge in the fecund quarters ys cclviij *l.* xix *s.* j *d.*

Whereof at

CANDLEMAS of the Money of my Lands in Yorkfchire dew to my Coffers of the Martynmas Farme payable at the faid Candlemas Which ys the fyfth paymentt payd to theme for th'affignementt of my faid Houfe Viz. for Poorks Lambes Stokfifch White-Herynge Rede-Herynge Sprotes Sturgion Salt-Elys Rafyngs Wax Fieggs Vergeous Fagotts and Hard wodd = c *l.*

OURE LADY DAY IN LENTT of the Money of my Lands in Yorkfchire dew to my Coffers of the Martynmas Farme payable at Candlemas aforefaid Which ys the vjth paymentt payd to theme for th'affignementt of my faid Houfe Viz. for Whete Maltt Wyne Hoppys Hony Oyle White-Salt Vinacre Muftard Spice Seecole Expenfys neceffary The Chapell Quarter Waigies The Launderer Quarter Waigies and The Houfehold Waigies for the fyrft half Yere Viz. frome Michaelmas to our faid Lady day in Lentt = clviij *l.* xix *s.* j *d.*

THE

THE THYRD PAYMENT of the Affignementt to my Countroller and Thomas Percy Clark of my Kechynge of my faid Houfe frome our faid Lady day in Lentt to Midfomer

Somme of the paymentts bitwixt our Lady day in
Lentt and Midfomer next foloynge
in the thyrd quarter ys
clxvij *l.* iij *s.* x *d.*

Whereof at

ESTER of the Money of my Lands in Northumbreland dew to my Coffers of the Martynmas Farme payable at Candlemas Which ys the vij[th] paymentt payd to theme for th'affignementt of my faid Houfe Viz. for Bay-Saltt Vergeous Stoone-Crofez Hyre of Pewder-Veffell and Otes to be boght = vij *l.* iij *s.* iiij *d.*

SAYNTT ELYN DAY the Money of my Lands in the faid Northumbreland dew to my Coffers of the Martynmas Farme payable at Candlemas Which ys the viij[th] paymentt payd to theme of the affignementt of my faid Houfe Viz. for Beiffs Mutons Veills Lambes Salttfifch Spice and My Servantts Wynter Horfe Meitt = cx *l.* xix *d.*

MIDSOMER of the Money of my Lands in the faid Northumbreland dew to my Coffers of the Whitfonday Farme payable at the faid Midfomer Which ys the ix[th] paymentt payd to theme for the affignementt of my faid Houfe Viz. for Hoppys Wax Bay-Saltt Muftard Expenfys neceffary The Launderer Quarter Waigies The Chapell Quarter Waigies and The Cator Parcells = xlix *l.* xviij *s.* xj *d.*

THE

THE FOURST PAYMENTT and Laft of the hole Affignementt in full contentacion for the kepynge of my Houfe for oone hole Yere endynge at the faid Michaelmas to my faid Countroller and Thomas Percy Clark of my Kechynge in full paymentt of the hole Somme apoynted for the fame.

Somme of the paymentt bitwixt Midfomer and Michaelmas next foloynge in the iiijth Quarter which ys
in full contentacion of the hole Affignementt
for kepynge of my faid Houfe for oone hole
Yere endynge at the faid Michaelmas
cxxj *l.* ix*d.*

Whereof at

LAMMES of the Money of my Lands in Northumbreland dew to my Coffers of the Whitfonday Farme payable att Lammes Which ys the xth paymentt payd to theme for th'affignementt of my faid Houfe Viz. for Wynnynge of my Hey and The Cator Parcells = xx *l.* viij*s.* viij*d.*

MICHAELMAS of the Money of my Lands in Yorkfchyre dew to my Coffers of the Whitfonday Farme payable at Lammes Which ys the xjth paymentt and laft in full con-tentacion of the hole affignementt for kepynge of my faid Houfe for the forefaid Yere Viz. for Boord Waigies of my Servantts Shoynge of all my Horfys with Farmes of Medowys and Paftures Expenfys Neceffary concernynge the Houfe The Chapell Waigies for the laft quarter of the Yere With the Waigies for the laft half Yere of all the Houfehold Servantts in full contentacion of the Yere The laft quarter Waigies in full contentacion of the Launderer of Houfehold and The Somer Horfemeitt = c *l.* xij*s.* j*d.*

F   III. THIS

III.

THIS IS THE ORDORE of the CHÈQUIREROULLÉ of the Noumbre of the Perſons aſſignyde by my Lorde and his Counſaill to be of my Lordes Rydynge Houſehold Yerely And to have WYNTER HORSEMEYTT allowyde theym The ſaid Wynter Horſmeytt begynaynge every Yere at Michaelmas and endynge at Sayntt Elyn day next after And all the ſeid Perſons to be paide for theire ſaid Wynter Horſmeytte at the ſeid Saynt Elyn day which day the ſeid Wynter Horſmeit goith owt on Allways providytt that the Bill of Wynter Horſemeitt yerely be apoynted and made redy for my ſeid Lorde to ſigne at the ſeid Michaelmas And every Man to be allowed for their Wynter Horſmeit ═ x ſ.

MY LORDIS BRODER.

FURST that my Lordys Broder if he be here His Clerk His Servaunt and His Horſekepar have their Wynter Horſmeitt allowide after x ſ. for every of theym ═ iiij.

MY LORDIS HEDE OFFICERS AND COUNSAILL IN HOUSHOLD.

ITEM that my Lordis hede Officers have theire Wynter Horſmeytt Viz. His Chambreleynn his Clerk his two Servanttſ and the Childe of his Chambre The Treaſurer his Clerk and his Horſekepar And other ij of my Lordes Counſaill if they be dayly in Houſhold And ather of 'them' j Servantte — Every of theym to have after x ſ. the pece ═ xij.

SECRETARY AND CLERK OF THE SIGNETT.

ITEM that the Secretary if he be in Houſholde to be allowede a Servante And ells the Clerk of the Signett without Servante And every of theym to be allowed x ſ. for theyr Wynter Horſmeitt ═ ij

GENTILLMEN-

GENTILLMEN-USHERS YOMEN-USHERS,

ITEM that a Gentyllman Ufher and iij Yomen Ufhers have x s. every of theym in the Yere for theyr Wynter Horfmeytt = iiij

CHAPLEYNS.

ITEM that j Chapleyn be allowed x s. by Yere for his Wynter Horfmeit = j.

GENTILLMEN OF HOUSHOLDE.

ITEM that Gentillmen of Houfholde Viz, a Keryer j Sewar j Cupberer two Gentillmen Waiters for the Boord-end And every of theym to have x s. for their Wynter Horfmeytte = v.

OFFICERS OF ARMYS.

ITEM that the Officers of Armys Viz. if he be Harrolde to have a Servaunte allowed hym And if he by Purfyvaunte to have noo Servaunte And every of theym to have x s. for theyr Wynter Horfmeit = iij.

YOMEN OF THE CHAMBRE.

ITEM the Yomen of the Chambre = iiij. And every of theym to have x s. allowede for theire Wynter Horf-meit = iiij.

YOMEN OFFICERS OF HOUSEHOLDE AND YOMEN WAITERS,

ITEM the Yomen Officers and Yomen Waiters vij Viz. of Yomen Officers v Whereof in the Buttre and Pantry j Yoman Cook j Yoman Herbigeor j Yoman Catorer j Yoman Porter j And Yomen Waiters ij Every of theym to have x s. allowed for theyr Wynter Horfmeite = vij.

GROMES

GROMES O'TH' CHAMBRE AND GROME OFFICERS OF HOUSEHOLDE.

ITEM the Gromys o'th' Chambre and Grome Officers of Householde v Whereof Gromes of the Chambre iij And Grome Officers ij Viz. j for the Sellar and Ewry And th'other Grome Cook for the mouth And every of theym to have x s. allowed for theyr Wynter Horfmeite = v.

CLERKYS OF THE RYDYNGE HOUSHOLDE.

ITEM the Clerks of Housholde iij Viz. Clerk of the Kychynge to ride about the makynge of provifion at the heede Officers Comaundmentt j A Coffurer for my Lorde j Clerk of the foren expenfis j and Every of theym to have x s. allowed for theyr Wynter Horfmeite = iij.

THE NOUMBRE of the PERSONS that ar at my Lordys Horfynge and hath no Wynter Horfmeit allowed theym becaufe the Horfe ftondith in my Lords Stabili at my Lords charge.

ITEM vij Perfons to be at my Lordes Horfynge and to have noo Wynter Horfmeitt allowed theym becaufe their Horfe ftondithe in my Lords owne Stable And to be in the hoole Noumbre of the Perfons apoynted to be of the Ridynge Household Viz. The Yoman of the Horfe A Yonge Gentillman at my Lordys fyndynge A Grome of the Chambre A Grome of the Wairdrobe for the Mayll The Grome of the Sterop A Grome of the Stable And a Grome Sumpterman = vij.

THE HOOLE NOUMBRE of all the PERSONS apoynted to be of my Lordys Ridynge Houfholde Yerely ys = Lvij.

IIII. THIS

IIII.

THIS IS THE ORDORE of the CHEQUIRE-ROULL of the Noumbre of the Perſons aſſignyd by my Lorde and his Counſaill to be of my Lordes Ridynge Houſehold Yerely and to have Somer Horſmeitt allowed theym The ſaid Somer Horſmeitt begynnynge every Yere at Saynte Elyn day and endynge at Michaelmas nextt after And all the ſaid Perſons to be payd for their ſeid Somer Horſmeit at the ſeid Michaelmas which day the ſeid Somer Horſmeitt goith owte on Allways provyded that the Bill of Somer Horſemeitt be apoynted and made redy Yerely for my ſeid Lorde to ſigne at the ſeid Saynte Elyn day And every Man to be allowed for theire Somer Horſmeitt = iij ſ. iiij d.

MY LORDIS BRODER.

FURSTE that my Lordes Broder if he be here His Clerk His Servauntt and His Horſekepar have their Somer Horſmeitt allowed after iij ſ. iiij d. for every of theym = iiij.

MY LORDIS HEDE OFFICERS AND COUNSAILL IN HOUSHOLD.

ITEM that my Lordys Heed Officers have theire Somer Horſmeitt Viz. His Chambrelayn his Clerk his two Servantts and the Childe of his Chambre The Treaſurer his Clerk and his Horſekepar and Other ij of my Lordes Counſaill if they be daily in Houſhold And ather of theym a Servantte Every of theym to have after iij ſ. iiij d. the pece = xij.

SECRETARY AND CLERK OF THE SIGNETT.

ITEM that the Secretary if he be in Houſehold to be allowed a Servantt And ells the Clerk of the Signett withoute Servante And every of theym to be allowed iij ſ. iiij d. for theire Somer Horſmeitte = iij

GENTYLLMEN

GENTYLLMEN USHERS AND YOMEN USHERS.

ITEM that a Gentillman Usher and iij Yomen Ushers have iij s. iiij d. every of theym in the Yere for their Somer Horsmeitt = iiij.

CHAPLAYNS.

ITEM that a Chaplayne be allowed iij s. iiij d. for his Somer Horsmeitt = j.

GENTYLLMEN OF HOUSHOLDE.

ITEM that Gentillmen of Household Viz. A Kerver A Sewer A Cupberer Two Gentillmen Waiters for the Boorde-end Every of theym to have iij s. iiij d. for their Somer Horsmeitte = v.

OFFICERS OF ARMYS.

ITEM that the Officers of Armes Viz. if he be Harrold to have a Servantte allowed hym And if he be Pursyvaunte to have noo Servante And every of theym to have iij s. iiij d. for theire Somer Horsmeit = iij.

YOMEN O'TH' CHAMBRE.

ITEM Yomen of the Chambre iiij And every of theym to have iij s. iiij d. allowed for theire Somer Horsmeitt = iiij.

YOMEN OFFICERS OF HOUSHOLD AND YOMEN WAITERS.

ITEM Yomen Officers and Yomen Waiters vij Viz. of Yomen Officers v Whereof in the Buttery and Pantry j Yoman Cooke j Yoman Herbigeor j Yoman Catorer j Yoman Porter j And Yomen Waiters ij Every of theym to have iij s. iiij d. allowed for their Somer Horsmeitte = vij.

GROMYS

GROMYS O'TH' CHAMBRE AND GROME OFFICERS OF HOUSHOLD.

ITEM the Gromes of the Chambre and Grome Officers of Houfhold v Whereof Gromes of the Chambre iij And Grome Officers ij Viz. Oone for the Cellar and Ewry And th'other Grome Cook for the Mouth And every of theym to have iij s. iiij d. allowed fore their Somer Horfmeitte = v.

CLERKIS OF THE RIDYNGE HOUSHOLDE.

ITEM the Clerks of Householde iij Viz. Clerk of the Kechynge to ride aboutte the makynge of provifion at the hede Officers comaundment j A Coffurer for my Lorde j Clerk of the foren expenfis j And every of theym to have iij s. iiij d. for their Somer Horfmeitt = iij.

THE NOUMBRE of the PERSONS that ar at my Lordis Horfynge and hath no Somer Horfmeit allowid theym bicaufe their Horfys ar at my Lordis fyndynge.

ITEM vij Perfons to be at my Lordys Horfynge and have no Somer Horfmeitt allowed theym bicaufe their Horfys ar at my Lordys fyndynge And to be in the hoole Noumbre of the Perfons apoyntyd to be of the Ridynge Houfehold Viz. the Yoman of the Hors A Yonge Gentillman at my Lords fyndynge A Grome of the Chambre A Grome of the Wairdrobe for the Male The Grome of the Sterope The Grome of the Stable and The Grome Sumpterman = vij.

THE HOOLE NOUMBRE of all the PERSONS apoynted to be of my Lordys Ridyng Houfeholde Yerely ys = Lvij.

GENTYLLMEN

GENTYLLMEN OF HOUSHOLD VIZ. KERVERS, SEWARS CUPBERERS AND GENTILLMEN WAITERS.

ITEM Gentillmen in Housholde ix Viz. ij Carvers for my Loords Boorde and a Servant bitwixt theym both except thai be at their frendis fyndyng and than ather of theym to have a Servant — Two Sewars for my Lordis Boorde and a Servant bitwixt theym except they be at their Friendis fyndynge and than ather of theym to have a Servant — ij Cupberers for my Lorde and my Lady and a Servant allowed bitwixt theym except they be at their Frendis fyndynge And than ather of theym to have a Servant allowid — And two Gentillmen Waiters and a Servant bitwixt theym bothe = xiiij.

MY LORDIS HANSMEN at the fyndynge of my Lorde and YONGE GENTYLLMEN at there Frendys fyndynge.

ITEM my Lordis Hansman iij Yonge Gentyllmen in Houshold at their Frendis fyndynge ij = v.

MY LORDIS OFFICERS OF ARMYS.

ITEM Officers of Armys Viz. if he be an Harrolde to have a Servaunt allowed hym And if he be Pursyvaunt to have noo Servaunt = iij.

GENTYLLMEN and CHILDERYN of the CHAPELL.

ITEM Gentyllmen and Childryn of the Chapell xiiij Viz. Gentillmen of the Chapell viij Viz. ij Bassys — ij Tenors — and iiij Countertenours — Yoman or Grome of the

---

* What follows seems to be part of a new division, the beginning of which is wanting in the Manuscript.

the Veftry j — Childeryn of the Chapell v Viz. ij Tribills
and iij Meanys = xiiij.

MARSHALLS AND USHERS OF THE HALLE.

ITEM Marfhallis and Ufhers of the Halle in Houfhold iiij
Viz. ij Marfhalles and a Servaunt allowid bitwixt theym
both — A Yoman Ufher and a Grome Or ellis a Marfhall
and two Yomen Ufhers = v.

YOMEN OF THE CHAMBRE IN HOUSHOLDE.

ITEM Yomen of the Chambre in Houfholde = vj.

YOMEN OFFICERS OF HOUSHOLDE.

ITEM Yomen Officers of Houfhold xij — Yoman of
the Robes — Yoman of the Hors — Yoman of the Sellar —
Yoman o'th' Pahtry — Yoman of the Buttry — Yoman o'th'
Ewry — Yoman Cook for the Mouth — Yoman Porter —
Yoman Baker — Yoman Brewer — Yoman Catorer — And
Yoman Bocher or Grome = xij.

YOMEN WAITERS.

ITEM Yomen Waiters in Houfholde = v.

GROMES O'TH' CHAMBRE AND GROME
OFFICERS OF HOUSHOLDE.

ITEM Gromys of the Chambre and Grome Officers of
Houfhold Viz. Gromys of the Chambre v — iiij for my Lorde
and one for my Lady — And Grome Officers of Houfhold xxiij.
Whereof of the Waredrobe v Whereof oon for the Robys
Oon for the Beddes One for the Wairdrobe and Oon for
my Ladys Wairdrobe And j Arrifmendar to amend Arres
ather Grome or Yoman Oon of the Cellar One of the
Pantre One of the Buttry Oone of the Ewery Two of the
Kychynge Viz. Grome for the Mouth and Grome of the
Larder Grome - Bocher Grome - Armorer Gromes of the

G   Stabill

Stabill — iiij Viz. A Grome of the Sterop A Grome of
the Stabill A Grome o'th' Palfrays for my Lady A Grome
Sumpterman A Grome-Hunt A Grome-Almonar A Grome
of the Chariote Two Gromes – Fawconars and a Grome-
Porter = xxviij.

CHILDERYN FOR OFFICES IN HOUSHOLDE.

ITEM Childeryn — v. Viz. Oon for the Wairdrob One
for the Stabyll Oone for the Skullery One for the Bakhous
and One for the Chariote = v.

MYNSTRALLS IN HOUSHOLD.

ITEM Mynſtralls in Houſhold iij Viz. A Taberett A Luyte
and A Rebecc = iij.

FOOTMEN IN HOUSHOLD.

ITEM Footman in Houſholde = j.

WARKMEN IN HOUSHOLD.

ITEM Warkmen in Houſhold iiij Viz. A Paynter A
Joyner and the Gardyner of the place where my Lorde
lyeth if their be oone And a Milnar = iiij.

CLERKIS IN HOUSHOLDE.

ITEM Clerkis in Houſhold ix Viz. The Coffærer The
Clerk of the Kechyng Two Clerks of the foren expences
The Clerk of the Warks The Clerk of the Brevements
Clerk-Avenar Clerk of the Dormont Booke and Clerk of
the Weryng Booke = ix.

V. THE

V.

THE KALENDAR BEGYNNYNGE at Michaelmas in the iij[th] Yere of the reigne of oure Sovereigne Lord Kynge Henry the viij[th] of the noumbre of all my Lords Servaunts in his Chequirroull daily abidynge in his Houfehold As the names of theym hereafter follouth.

Furfte My Lorde j My Lady j My Yonge Lorde and his Brether iij And theire Servaunts ij as to fay A Yoman and a Grome.

The Nurcy iij Viz. two Rokkers and a Childe to Attend in the Nurcy.

Gentillwomen for my Lady — iij.

Chamberers for my Lady — ij.

My Lordes Brether every of theym with theire Servaunts iiij as to fay if thei be Preifts his Chapleyn his Childe and his Horfkepar And if he be other ways his Clerk his Childe of his Chambre and his Harfkepar.

My Lordys hede Officers of Houfehold — iiij.

FURSTE the Chambrelayn and his Servaunts vij Viz. his Chapleyn his Clerk two Yomen a Childe of his Chambre and his Horfkepar.

The Stewarde and his Servaunts iiij charged as to fay his Clerk his Childe and his Horfkepar And uncharged — iij Viz. His Clerk Childe and his Horfkepar.

The Treafurer and his Servauntts iij as to fay his Clerk and his Horfkepar.

The Countroller and his Servaunts iij charged Viz. his Clerk and his Harfkepar And uncharged boot his Horfkepar.

The Dean of the Chapell and his Servaunt ij.

The Survifor and his Servaunt ij.

Two of My Lordys Counfaill and athir of theym a Servaunte iiij.

The Secretary and his Servaunt ij.

My

My Lordes Chapleyns in Houſeholde vj Viz. The Almonar and if he be a maker of Interludys than he to have a Servaunt to the intent for Writynge of the Parts And ells to have non The Maiſter of Gramer j a Chapleyn to ride with my Lorde j The Subdean j The Goſpellar j The Lady-Maſſe Preiſte j.

Two Gentillmen Uſhers and a Servaunt bitwixte thaym — iij.

Two Kervers for my Lorde and a Servaunte bitwixt theym iij — except they be at theire frendys fyndynge and than aither of theym to have a Servaunte.

Two Sewars for my Lorde and a Servaunte bitwixt theym iij — except they be at their Frends fyndynge and than athir of theym to have a Servaunte.

Two Cupberers for my Lorde and a Servaunt bitwixt theym iij — except they be at their Frends fyndynge and than athir of theym to have a Servaunt.

Two Gentillmen Waiters for the Boord end And a Servaunte bitwixt theym — iij.

Hanſman and Yonge Gentillmen at their Frendys fyndynge v as to ſay Hanſmen iij and Yonge Gentillmen ij.

Officer of Armys — j.

Yomen Uſhers of the Chambre ij.

Gentillmen of the Chapell — ix Viz. The Maiſter of the Childre j — Tenors ij — Countertenors iiij — The Piſtoler j — and oone for the Orgayns.

Childer of the Chapell — vj.

Two Marſhalls of the Halle and j Servaunte bitwixt theym — iij.

Yomen of the Chambre vj — Yoman Uſher of the Hall j — Yomen Waiters v.

Yomen Officers of Houſhold xj — as to ſay Yoman of the Robys j — Yoman of the Hors j — Yoman of the Veſtry

Veſtry j — Yoman of the Ewry j — Yoman of the Pantrye j — Yoman of the Seller j — Yoman of the Buttery j — Yoman Cook for the mouth j — Yoman of the Bakhouſe j — Yoman of the Brewhouſe j — And Yoman Porter j.

Gromes and Grome Officers of Houſhold xx — Viz. Gromes of the Chambre v As to ſay iij to ride with my Lorde and Oone to bide at home and Oone for my Lady — Gromys o'th' Wairdrobe iij Viz. Grome of the Roobes j Grome of the Bedds j Grome of the Wairdrobe for my Lady j — Grome of the Ewry j Grome of the Pantre j Grome of the Sellar j Grome o'th' Buttery j — Gromys of the Kechyng ij Viz. A Grome for the mouth And a Grome for the Larder Grome of the Hall j Grome Porter j Grome o'th' Sterope j —Grome o'th' Pallfreys j Grome Sumpterman j And Grome of the Charioote j.

Childer for Offices in Houſhold vj Viz. The Wairdrobe j. The Kechyng j The Squillery j The Stable j The Charioote j The Bakhous j The Ariſmendar j The Bocherry j The Catory j and the Armory j.

Mynſtralls iij Viz. A Taberett a Luyte and a Rebecc.

Footman j Fawconars ij Paynter j Joynar j Huntt j.

Gardynar in Hous j Viz. The Gardynar of the place where my Lorde lyeth for the tyme to have Meitt and Drynke within.

Under Almonor of the Hall j — and to ſerve the Gromes of the Chambre with Wood.

My Lords Clerks in Houſhold x Viz. A Clerk of the Kechynge j — Clerk of the Signett j — Clerks of the foren expenſys ij — Clerk of the Brevementts j — Clerk Avenar j — Clerk of the Warks j — Clerk of the Werynge Booke j — Clerks to wryte under the Clerks of the foren expenſys ij.

Milnar j.

The hoole noumbre of all the ſeid perſons in Houſhold is clxvj.

WHICH

WHICH is Ordenyd be my Lorde and his Counfaill and
fhall nott be exceded boot kepte ALLWAYS PROVYDED
how they fhall enter to theire Wagies at thaire quarter
days As to fay Michaelmas Criftynmas oure Lady day in
Lentt and Midfomer after the ufe and manner as is accuftomed That is to fay Who fo ever cumys to my Lords
Service in Houfholde within a moneth affore any of the
faid iiij quarter Days or within a Moneth after Than
they to enter Wagies at the faid quarter day And if they
cum nott within a Moneth affore or after any of the faid
iiij quarter days than they to tarry and not to enter Wagies
to the next quarter day that fhall cumm after Without it fhall
pleafe my Lorde to rewarde theyme any thynge for it at
his pleafure ALSO when foever the feid Noumbre is not
full than my Lorde to be informed by his Heed Officers
that his Lordfhipe may tak in fuch as his Lordfhip fhall
thynk beft for the fulfillynge of the feid Noumbre if the
caas fo require

ALLWAYS PROVIDITT the Wagies accuftommyde
of my Lordes Hous that every Perfon belongynge to every
rowme accuftomed in the forefaid roull fhall have by Yere
after this forme foll,owynge if they be payde by th'affignemente of the Hous

FURST every rokker in the Nurcy — xx s.

Every Gentillwoman attendynge upon my Lady and nott
at my Ladys fyndynge — v marc.

Every Chamberer to my Lady not at my Ladys fyndynge — xl s.

The hede Officers of Houfhold Viz. Furfte the Chambrelayn to have x l. fee in Houfhold if he have it nott
by Pattentt.

The Steward charged in Houfhold — xx l. And uncharged
x l. And commynge and goynge x mark.

The

The Trefaurer of the Hous abidynge in Houfhold ftandynge charged xx *l*. And charged with his Fellay x *l*. And uncharged comynge and goynge x mark.

The Countroller of Houfe abidynge in Houfhold ftandynge charged xx *l*. And charged with his Fellowe or a Clerk of the Kechynge x *l*. And uncharged x mark.

The Survifur in Houfhold x mark if he be nott promoted by Patentt.

The Dean of the Chapell iiij *l*. if he have it in houfholde and not by Patentt.

Every oone of my Lordes Counfaill to have c *s*. fee if he have it in Houfhold and nott by Patentt.

The Secretary in Houfhold if he be nott promoted c *s*.

The Clerk of the Signett liij *s*. iiij *d*.

Every Scolemaifter techynge Gramer c *s*.

Every Chaplayn graduate v marc.

Every Chaplayn not graduate xl *s*.

Preifts of the Chapll iij Viz. Oone at c *s*. The fecunde v marc And the thrid at iiij marc — Allways provyded that the mofte difcreit Perfon of the feid iij Preifts of the Chapell be apoynted to be Subdean and to have no more Wagies than he had.

Every Gentillman Ufher v marc.

Every Kerver Sawar and Cupberer for my Lorde and my Lady v marc.

Every Gentillman Waiter for the Boord end iiij marc.

Every Yoman Ufher of the Chambre iiij marc.

The Hanfmen to be at the fyndynge of my Lord.

Every Officer of Armys if he be Harrold x marc And if be Purfyvaunte v marc if he be paid in Houfhold and nott by Patentt.

Gentillmen of the Chapell x As to fay Two at x marc a pece — Three at iiij *l*. a pece — Two at v marc a pece — Oone

at

at xl*s*. .— And oone at xx*s*. Viz. ij Baſſys ij Tenors And vj Countertenors Childeryn of the Chapell vj after xxv*s*. the pece.

Yoman of the Veſtry xl*s*. And if he be charged with ane othir Office than to have boot xx*s*.

Every Marſhall of the Hall v marc.

Every Mynſtrall if he be Taberet iiij *l*. Every Luyte and Rebecc xxxiij*s*. iiij*d*. and to be payd in Houſholde if they have it nott by Patentt or Warraunt.

Every Yoman of the Chambre xl*s*.

Every Yoman Officer xxxiij*s*. iiij*d*.

Every Yoman Waiter xxxiij*s*. iiij*d*.

Every Grome of the Chambre xx*s*.

Every Armorer to have iiij marc for kepynge of my Lordes ſtuff as well his Armory in his Hous as other where He fyndynge al manar of ſtuf for Clenſynge of the ſaid ſtuf.

Every Arriſmendar if he be Yoman xxxiij*s*. iiij*d*. for his Wagies and xx*s*. for fyndyng of al manar of ſtuf belonging to his facultie except Silk and Golde And if he be Grome xx*s*. for his Wagies and xx*s*. for fyndynge of his ſtuf in like caſe.

Every Fawconer if he be Yoman xl*s*. And if he be Grome xx*s*.

Every Huntte xx*s*.

Every Grome Officer of Houſhold xx*s*.

Every Childe in every Office xiij*s*. iiij*d*.

Every Warkman in Houſholde xl*s*. — and comynge and goynge xx*s*.

Every Footman xl*s*. bicauſe of the moch Werynge of his ſtuf with labor.

Every Bocher if he be Yoman to have xxxiij*s*. iiij*d*. And if he be Grome to have xx*s*. And to be owte of Meit and Drynk and all other charges of the Hous.

Every

Every Under Almonar of the Hall xx s. bicaufe he fhall hew Wood for the Gromes of the Chambre and brynge it to them.

Every Clerk of the Kechynge v marc.

Every Clerk of the Brevementts xl s.

Every Clerk of the Warks lxvj s. viij d.

Every Clerk of the Foren Expenfys iiij marc.

Every Clerk Avenar xx s.

Every Clerk of the Werynge xl s.

Every Clerk that writes under the Clerks of the Foren Expenfys xxvj s. viij d. without thei be other wife agreed with.

THE KALENDAR endynge at Michaelmias next for to com after the date hereof Which be Wagis accuftomed for the Houfholde Servaunts that be not promoted Allways Provided that what Perfons foever they be that hath promocion except the forefaid Hede Officers fhall have no Wagies in Houfholde after thei be fo promoted Without the confideracion of his Lordefhipe pleafure be forther fhewid theym in the faid Chequyrroull Allwais Provided that what Perfon foever he be that commyth to my Lordes Service that incontynent after he be intred in the Chequyrroull that he be Sworn in the Countyng-Hous by a Gentillman Ufher or a Yoman Ufher in the prefence, of the Hede Officers And on theire abfence before the Clerk of the Kechynge aether by fuch a Ooth as is in the Booke of Othes yff any fuch be Or ells by fuch a Oth as thei fhall feyme befte by their difcrecion.

H

VI. THE

VI.

THE COPPÉ HOWE THE STILES of the QUARTER CHEQUIRROILL ſhal be made quarterly thorowoute the Yere as here after followeth

THE KALENDAIRE begynnyng at Michaelmas in the vjth Yere of the Reign of oure Sovereign Lord Kyng Henry the viijth of all my Lords Noumbre in his Chequirroill daſly abiding in his Houſeholde as the names of theym hereafter followeth ande how they ſhall entre to their Wagies in houſholde at their Quarter Daies as to ſay Michaelmas Criſtynmas Eſture ande Midſomer ALWAIES Provyded by my Lorde and his Counſaill aftir the Uſe and manar afore accuſtomed That is to ſaye Whoſoever comes to my Lordes ſervice in Houſehold within a Moneth afore or aftir any of the ſaid iiij quarter Dayes aforeſaid than to entre to Wagies at the ſaide quarter Dayes Ande if they come not within a Moneth afore any of the ſaide iiij Quarter Dayes or within a Moneth aftir thanne they to tarry and not entre too Wagies to the next Quarter Daye that ſhall comm aftir Without it ſhall Pleaſe my ſaid Lorde to reward theym any thyng for it at his Lordeſhips pleaſure.

THE NOUMBRE of theym that ſhal be kept daly in Houſehold quarterly is the noumbre of WHICHE noumbre is appointed by my Lorde and his Counſaill whiche ſhall not be exceded but kept ALWAIES PROVIDED that whenſomever the ſaid noumbre is not full my Lorde to be informed to tacke in ſuche as his Lordeſhip ſhall thinke beſt for fulfilling of the ſaide noumbre if the caaſe ſo require ALWAIES PROVIDED that the Wagies accuſtomed of my Lords Servaunts that every Parſon belongyng

longyng to every rowme accuftomed in this forefaid Roill
fhall have by Yere aftir this form followyng.

FYRSTE the Heed Officers of Houfhold as to fay

The Steward ftandyng charged with the Houfehold xx *l.*
Ande uncharged x *l.* And coming and going x marks.

The Trefaurer of the Hous abidyng in Houfhold ftanding
charged xx *l.* Ande with his fellow x *l.* And uncharged
comying and goyng x marks.

The Comptroller o'th' Hous abidyng in Houfehold ftandyng charged xx *l.* Ande charged with his Fellow or a Clerk
of Kechynge x *l.* Ande uncharged x markes if he be not
promoted.

The Survifor in Houfehold x markes if he be not promoted by Patent.

The Secretary in Houfehold if he be not promoted c *s.*

The Clarke of the Signet iiij marks.

The Dean of the Chapell iiij *l.* if he have it in Houfehold ande not by Patent.

Every Scolemaifter techyng Grammer in the Hous c *s.*

Every Chaplayn graduate lxvj *s.* viij *d.*

Every Chaplayn not graduate xl *s.*

Every Gentleman Ufher v 'marks'.

Every Carver Cupberer and Sewer v marks.

Every Gentlemen Waiter and Yoman Ufher of the
Chambre iiij marks.

Every Yoman of the Chambre xl *s.*

Every Yoman Waiter xxxiij *s.* iiij *d.*

Every Yoman Officer of Houfehold xxxiij *s.* iiij *d.*

Every Grome of the Chambre Groim Officer of Houfeholde and Gromes of the Stabill xx *s.*

Every Heede Clark of the Keching v marks.

Every Under Clark xl *s.*

THE

¶ THE KALENDARRE begynnyng at the faide Michael-mas ande endyng at Criftynmas next following in the vjth Yere of the Reign of Kyng Henry the viijth aforefaide whiche be the wagies appointed for the Houfehold Servaunts whiche be not officed — ALWAIES Provided that what Parfonne foever they be except the forefaide Heed Officers aftir the forme aforfaid have no Wagies in Houfehold whiche haith any promocion by my Lorde without the confideracion of his Lordefhip Pleafure be further fhewid in this faid Chequirroill.

VII. THIS

VII.

THIS IS THE ORDRE of the CHEQUIRROULLE of the Noumbre of my Lordis Officers and Servaunts which ar apoynted to be Waiters in every Quarter of the Yere and to have no Houfhold Wagies bicaufe thei be officed And what they be that fhall awaite As the names of the Officers hereafter followith How thei be apoynted to attend.

GENTYLLMEN and YOMEN apoynted to be Quarter Waiters yerely from Michaelmas to Criftynmas.

FURSTE theym that fhall awaite Yerely bitwixt Michaelmas and Criftynmas Viz. The Steward of my Lordis Laundes at Lekyngfeld if he be not Knyght to ferve for a Kervour — The Feodary of Yorkfhire and to ferve for Gentilman Ufher of my Lordes Chambre — The Maifter of the Gam at Topclif and Kervour for my Lorde when he waitts — The Baillif of Helaigh Yoman Ufher of the Chambre — The Baillif of Lekyngfeld The Baillif of Topclif and the Baillif of Hundmenby Yomen of the Chambre — and the Baillif of Lethlay and the Baillif of Kildaile Yomen Waiters = ix.

GENTILMEN and YOMEN apoynted to be Quarter Waiters yerely from Criftynmas to our Lady day in Lentt.

ITEM theym that fhall waite Yerely bitwixt Criftynmas and our Lady day in Lentt Viz. The Maifter of the Gam at Wrefill and Newifham if he be no Knyght to ferve for Sewar for my Lorde — The Maifter of the Gam at Wafhdaile-hede too ferve for Kervour when he waits —
The

The Baillif of Spofforde Yoman Ufher of the Chambre ——
And The Kepar of Catton Oone of the Kepars of the great
Parke at Topclif The Ballif of Poklyngton The Ballif of
Egremond Yomen of the Chambre — Oone of the Kepars
of Langftroth The Keper of Ruglay Wood and The Ballif
of Newifham in Cravyn Yomen Waiters = x.

GENTILMEN and YOMEN apoynted to be Quarter
Waiters yerely from our Lady day in Lent to
Midfomer.

ITEM theym that fhall waite Yerely bitwixt our Lady
day in Lent and Midfomer Viz. The Maifter Fofter of
the Weftwarde Cupberer for my Lorde — The Conftable
of Warkworth Gentyllman Ufher — The Conftable of
Prudowe to ferve for Carver for my Lorde — The Baillif
of Helaigh Yoman Ufher of the Chambre — The Baillif
of Alnewike The Kepar of Spofforde Parke Oone of the
Kepars of the Weftwarde Yomen of the Chambre — The
Kepar of Helaigh Parke Oone of the Kepars of Callege
Parke and Oone of the Kepars of Rothberry Forefte Yomen
Waiters = x.

GENTILMEN and YOMEN apoynted to be Quarter
Waiters yerely from Midfomer to Michaelmas.

ITEM theym that fhall waite Yerely bitwixt Midfomer
and Michaelmas Viz. The Steward of Prefton in Cravyn if
he be no Knyghf to ferve as a Carver — The Conftable
of Alnewike to ferve for Cupberer — The Lieftennant of
Cokermouth to ferve for Sewar for my Lord — The
Conftable of Langlay Sewar for the Boord-end — The
Baillif of Spofford Yoman Ufher of the Chambre — Oone
of the Kepars of Langftroth The Baillif of Chatton The
Ballif of my Lordis Laundis in Yorke Yomen of the
Chambre = xj.

VIII. THIS

VIII.

THIS IS THE ORDRE of the CHEQUIRROULL of the noumbre of all the Horſys of my Lordis and my Ladis that ar apoynted to be in the charge of the Hous Yerely as to ſay Gentill-Hors Palfreys Hobyes Naggis Clothſek-Horſe and Male-Horſe which ſhal be at hardmeit in my Lordis Stable and every Hors ſhal be allowid on the day A Pek of Otes or ells j*d*. in Breid.

GENTYL HORS of my Lords ſtondynge dayly at the charge of the Hous.

FURST Gentylhors to ſtonde in my Lordis Stable Yerely = vj.

PALFREYS for my Lady and hir Women at the charge o'th' hous.

ITEM Pallfrays of my Ladis to ſtond in my Lordis Stable Yerely Viz. Oone for my Lady and Two for her Gentyllwomen and Oone for her Chamberer = iiij.

HOBBYES and NAGGS for my Lorde at the charge of the Hous.

ITEM Hobbyes and Naggs to ſtond in my Lordis Stable Yerely for my Lordis own Saddill Viz. Oone for my Lorde to Ride upon Oone to lede for my Lord and Oone to ſpare at home for my Lorde = iij.

SUMPTER HORS and MAILE HORS at the charge of the Hous.

ITEM Clothſek-hors and Maile-Hors to ſtond in my Lords Stabill Yerely Viz. A Clothſek-Hors for the Bedd a Clothſek-Hors for the Coffuris And a Maile Hors = iij.

HORSYS

HORSYS of my Lords at the charge of the Houſe ſtoundynge in my Lords Stable for theym that ar at my Lords Horſynge.

ITEM Horſys to ſtond in my Lordis Stable Yerely for theym that ar at my Lordis Horſyng Viz. William Wormes Hors — The Yoman o'th' Stable Hors — Grome of the Chambre Hors — Grome o'th' Sterope Hors — and ij Horſys for the ij Sumptermen who ledis the Sumpter Hors = vj.

HORSES for the **CHARIOTT** to ſtond in my Lordys Stable at the charge of the Houſe.

ITEM Chariott Horſe to ſtond in my Lords Stable Yerely viij Viz. vij Great Trottynge Hors to draw in the Chariott and a Nagg for the Chariott Men to ride upon = viij.

HORSES for the **MILNE** to ſtond in my Lords Stable at the charge of the Houſe.

ITEM Milne Horſe to ſtond in my Lords Stable Yerely iij Viz. ij to draw in the Milne and Oone to cary Stuff to the Milne and fro: Which Horſes ys allowed nothynge bott Hay except ſuch as cumys of the Milne and Granes of the Brewhouſe = iij.

IX. THEIS

IX.

THEIS BE THE DEFAWTTIS which ar founde in the making of Provifion for my . Lordis Hous of the Yere endit at Michaelmas laft paft in the iijth Yere of the reigne of our Sovereigne Lord Kyng Henry the viijth As the names of the Percells wherein the faid Defawttis was hereafter followith for the Provifion thereof to be Amendit yerely frome hens furth.

FURST that theire be noo Brede bought to be occupied in my Lordis hous bot onely to be Baked in my Lordis Houfe.

ITEM that their be no Bere bought to be occupied in my Lords Hous bot oonly to be Brewid in my Lordis Hous.

ITEM that theire be noo Stokfifh bought bicaus of the better cheipe of theym when the Saltfifh be dere.

ITEM that theire be no Rede Heryng White Heryng and Sproittes bought for fervynge of my Lordis hous in Lent for Breikfafts and Scamlyngs and as well for other tymes of the Yere when thei be in Seafon for to ferve for Braikfafts bicaus of occupying of les See Fifh and Frefh Watter Fifh.

ITEM that theire be no White Salt occupied in my Lordis Hous withowt it be for the Pantre or for caftyng upon meit or for feafonynge of meate.

ITEM that Vinacre be made of the brokyn Wynes in my Lordis hous And that the Laggs be provide by the Clerks of the Hous and markid after thei be paft drawyng

I

that

that thei can be set no more of broche And see it put in
a vessell for Vinacre.

ITEM whereas Erthyn Potts be bought that Ledder
Potts be bought for theym for serving for Lyveries and
Meallis in my Lordis hous.

ITEM that theire be no Pewder Vessell hired to serve
in my Lords hous frome hens furth bot as theis days followyng that ys to say at Cristynmas Esture Saynt George
day and Whitsontide.

ITEM that thei have Counter Vessell boght which shall
serve at no tyme of the Yere bot at Cristynmas Estur Saynt
George-day Whitsonday and All-Hallowday And bitwixt
the tymes to be kept in the Conntyng hous and to be
delyveret from the Countyng-hous at the seid Festis.

ITEM that theire shal be no Horsbrede bought for my
Lordis Horsis bot to be Bakid in my Lordis Hous and
for that caus to agre with my Lordis Baker in hous for
a reward for the Bakynge of it for the hoole Yere.

ITEM that the Trenchor Brede be maid of the Meale
as it cummyth frome the Milne.

ITEM that their be no Horsys of my Lordis owne which
be assigned to be in the charge of the hous be put to Gres
bot oonly in the Pastures that ar assigned to the house.

ITEM that their be no Lambes bought when thay ar
at the darrest without it be bot for my Lords Boorde the
Chamberlayns meas and to the Stewards meas And that
their be no comon service of theym thrugh the hous when
they be dere.

X. THEIS

X.

THEIS BE THE DIRECTIONS takyn at Wrefill by my Lorde and his Counfaill at Michaelmas in the thrid Yere of the reigne of our Sovereigne Lorde Kyng Henry the viij^th how the Clerkis of the Brevementts fhall Ordore theym Yerely afwell concernynge the Brevementts in the Countynghous as to have an Ee and on fight dayly to every Officer in theire Offices to be kept dayly thrugout the Yere hereafter folowith.

DAILY.

FURST that the faid Clerkis be dayly at the Brevynge every day by vij of the Cloke in the Mornynge And theire to Breve every Officer accordynge as the cuftome is unto half howre after viij^th of the Cloke And that theire be no Braikfafts delyveret unto the tyme that all the Officers have Breved.

DAILY.

ITEM that the faid Clerkis of the Brevementts allow no other Brede Aile Bere Wyne Flefh Fifh nor non-other thyngs that ar Breved except they fee a good caus why And if they thynk th'expens be to moch then they to reafon with th'officers why it is fo And if they fee not a good confideracion why it fhuld be fo then they not to allow it upon theym bot as a deficient.

DAILY.

ITEM that the faid Clerkis of the Brevements allow no Wyne for Drynkyngs to the Yoman or Grome of the Sellar except it be by recorde of an Ufher Nor Wyne to be allowid that is ferved for Mealls in the Great Chambre or in the Hall except it be by record of an Ufher of the Chambre or of the Hall and they to be at the Brevements.

DAILY.

DAILY.

ITEM that the faid Clerkis of the Brevements allow no Braikfafts that ar ferved by any Officer bot fuch as ar apoynted in the bill of Braikfafts except it be by the comaundment of an Hede Officer an Ufher of the Chambre or of the Halle.

DAILY.

ITEM that the faid Clerkis of the Brevements allow noo Lyverys that ar ferved by any Officer except it be apoynted in the bill of Lyverys or ells be comaundit by an Hede Officer an Ufher of the Chambre or of the Halle.

DAILY.

ITEM that the faid Clerkis of the Brevements Breve every Officer after other in Ordore As to fay Furft the Grome of the Halle The Pantre The Sellar The Buttery The Kechyng The Ewery and the Grome or the Kepar of the Wodyarde.

WEEKLY.

ITEM that if any of the Officers of the faid Offices be not at the Countynghous by vij of the Cloke in the mornynge for to Breve Then the faid Clerkis of the Brevements to fhew it to the Hede Officers for reforma-.cion thereof.

WEEKELY.

ITEM that the faid Clerkis of the Brevements entre all the Taillis of the Furmunturs in the Jornall Booke in the Countynghous every day furthwith after the Brede be delyveret to the Pantre and then the Stoke of the Taill to be delyveret to the Baker and the Swache to the Pantler.

WEEKELY,

WEEKELY.

ITEM that the said Clerkis of the Brevements entre all the Taills of the Brasyantors in the Jornall Booke in the Countynghous at every tyme furthwith after the Bere be delyveret into the Buttry and then the Stoke of the Taill to be delyveret to the Brewar and the Swatche to the Butler.

WEEKELIE.

ITEM that the Clerkis of the Brevementts entre all the Necantours at every wekis end in the Jornall Booke in the Countynhous and when they ar enterid that the Yoman or Grome of the Larder and the Slaghterman be bothe present by when they so enter.

DAILY.

ITEM the said Clerkis of the Brevements see all manar off Grosse Empcions that ar boght to be entred furthwith in the Jornall Booke when thei ar bought.

MOUNETHLY.

ITEM that the said Clerkis of the Brevements see the Reconynge made every Moneth before theym in the Countynghous bitwix the Tannar and the Slaghterman of all the Hides of the Beiffs that ar slayn for th'expensis of my Lordis hous.

MOUNETHLY.

ITEM that the said Clerkis of the Brevements see the Reconynge made every Moneth afore theym in the Countynghous bitwixt the Glover and the Slaghterman of the Fellys or Skyns of the Mutons that ar Slayn for th'expensis of my Lordis Hous.

MOUNETHLY.

MOUNETHLY.

ITEM that the faid Clerkis of the Brevementts fee the Reconynge made every Moneth bifore theym in the Countynghous bitwixt the Tallow Chaundeler and the Slaghterman of all the Tallow that commyth of the Beiffs and Mutons that ar flayn for th'expenfis of my Lordis hous.

MOUNETHLY.

ITEM that the faid Clerks of the Brevements fee the Reconynge made every mouneth bifore theym in the Countynghous bitwixt the Yoman or Grome of the Paiftry and the Baker of all fuch Flowre as is delyveret out of the Bakhous to the Kechynge.

DAILY.

ITEM the feid Clerkis of the Brevements fee furely that every Groffe Empcion that is bought for th'expenfis of my Lordis hous be brought in and to fee whether it be abil Stuf or not after the price that is fet upon it or not or it be entered or occupyed.

MOUNETHLY.

ITEM the faid Clerkis of the Brevements enter in the Countynghous monythly all the Pretereas in the Title of Coftis Neceffary where they wer wount to be entered before tyme after the Catorer's Parcells of every Mouneth.

DAILY.

ITEM that the faid Clerks of the Brevements fee the Catorer enter his Parcells every Morenynge at the Brevyng tyme of the Officers and if he fo do not than they to fhew it to the Hede Officers for to be reformed or ells to be entered over Nyght every day.

DAILY.

DAILY.

ITEM that oone of the Clerkis of the Countynghous luke dayly upon the Catorer's Stuf that he bryngyth in and that it be broght up into the Countynghous and if it be not able Stuf nor worth the price that he fittythe upon it to delyver it hym again and not to be receyvyd ne occupied for my Lordis ufe.

WEEKLY.

ITEM that the faid Clerkis of the Brevements by th'advice of the Countroller and the Hede Clerk of the Kechynge caufe the Catorer to goo abrode in the Contry weikly for byinge of Stuf in fuche Places as is thoght it fhal be beft cheip and to by it feldomeft about where my Lorde lyith except it may be had as good chepe there as other where.

DAILY.

ITEM that if the faid Clerkis of the Brevements fee the Catorer raife his prices of his Stuf otherwife than he was wont to doo then thay to reafon with hym upon it And if thay fee good caus why it fhuld be rayfed fo to allowe it and if not to abait his price accordyng as it is worth.

DAILY.

ITEM that the faid Clerkis of the Brevements have a overfight to every Office And if they fee the Officers of the fame have any refort of Perfons into theire faid Offices than they too fhew it to the Hede Officers for reformacion of it.

WEEKELY.

ITEM that whereas Muftard hath beyn boght of the Sawce-maker affore tyme that now it be made within in my Lordis Hous And that one be providit to be Grome of the Skullery that can make it.

WEEKLY.

WEEKLY.

ITEM that the Potts of the Sellar and the Cahnys of the Buttery be mefured And if th'Officers afk more allowaunfe than they be of than it to be fett as a Deficient upon there hodes.

DAILY.

ITEM that every day at the Brevynge a Ufher of the Chambre to be there to Breve for the Chambre what Comaundmentis is theire.

DAILY.

ITEM that the Ufhers of the Chambre and of the Hall fe whether the Potts be fyllid as they oght to be when th'Officers brynges theym or not And if they be not than they to fhew it to the faid Clerkis at the Brevynge And they to reforme it.

DAILY.

ITEM that the faid Clerkis, of the Brevements inquyre every day of the Ufhers at the Brevynge what Defawtts they fynde with th'Officers and the faid Clerkis to reform the fame.

QUARTERLY.

ITEM that the faid Clerkis of the Brevements make a Copy of the Chequyrroull a Senet affore every Quarter Day that it may be fhewid to my Lorde to be corrected and made up and figned affore the next Quarter begyn and all the namys of the Perfons that fhal be in my Lords Houfe the faid quarter.

DAILY.

ITEM that all th'Officers of Houfhold brynge up theire Keys of theire Offices every nyght when my Lorde is ferved for all nyght into the Countyng-hous and that thai have theym

not

not downe unto the tyme that they have Brevyd in the Mornynge without an Usher a Yoman of the Chambre or an Hede Officer's Servaunt com for theym And also that the said Officers bryng up their said Keys in to the Countynghous every day when the latter Dynar is doyn and to fetch theym again at iij of the Cloke to serve for Drynkyngs.

MOUNETHLY.

ITEM that the Cator Parcells be cast up every moneth to knowe whoether thay doo lak of the Somme that is assign'd for theym or ells they excede above the said Somme.

MOUNETHLY.

ITEM that the said Clerkis of the Brevements mak up the Pyes * of th'Expendunturs at every moneth end.

MOUNETHLY.

ITEM that the said Clerkis of the Brevements take the Remaneth at every Moneth end and a Bill to be made of the Percells what remaneth And to be broght to my Lorde to see.

QUARTERLY.

ITEM that the said Clerkis of the Kechynge or of the Brevementts when so ever my Lord breks up hous they shall make my Lord a Chequirerolle of the names of the Persons that shall giff theire attendance where my Lord doth abide and shal be at Meills at mete at Drynk within where his Lordshipp ys With the names of theme And in what rowmes they shall serve And at every such tyme as my Lord so doys breke up hous a Bill to be made and to be signed with my Lords hand.

QUARTERLIE.

ITEM that the said Clarks of the Kechynge or of the Brevementts make my Lorde a Bill of the names of the Persons

K

fons

* So the original MS.

fons that fhall remayn ftyll at Boordwaiges where my Lord did kepe hous unto the tyme that his Lordfhipp fett up houfe agayn And that every Perfon fo goyng to Boordwaiges fhall have allowed xij *d.* a weik for the tyme of his Boordwaiges And the faid Bill to be figned with my Lords hand.

QUARTERLIE.

ITEM that the faid Clarks of the Kechynge or of the Brevements make my Lord a Bill of the names of all fuch Perfons that defireth to have licence and hath leffe of my faid Lord or of his Counfaill to go home abowte theire owne bufynes when my Lord doth brek up hous at any tyme unto the tyme that his Lordfhipp fett up hous agayn Which Per-fons ar not ordened to have Boordwaiges allowed theyme the faid tyme bicaufe they go abowte theire owne bufynes and giffes none attendance on my Lord and doyth not continew theire where other theire feloys doth abyde And at every tyme that my Lord dothe breke up hous to make a Bill of the names of fuch Perfons and what rowme they longed to that hath licence fo to depart And to be figned with my Lords hand Bicaufe they fhall have none allowance of Boordwaiges for the faid caufes.

QUARTERLY.

ITEM that the faid Clarkis of the Kechynge or of the Brevementts make my Lorde a Bill of the names of the Gen-tilmen of the Chapell at every quarter bicaufe they ar accufto-med to be payd theire Houfehold waiges quarterly With the names of the Perfons and the Sommes that they take by Yere with the Sommes that every of theme fhal be payd the faid quarter for theire houfehold waiges And the faid Bill to be figned with my Lords hand.

QUARTERLY.

QUARTERLY.

ITEM that the said Clarks of the Kechynge or of the Brevements make my Lorde a Bill at every quarter of the names of the Gentilmen of the Chapell that ar departed fro my Lords Service withowte licence And alfo the abfence how longe every of theme abfented themefelf in the faid quarter withowte leve And how much they fhal be abayted of theire quarter waiges or half Yere after the rate that they take by the quarter for the tyme of theire abfence And to declare unto theme in the faid Bill why they be fo abaited of theire waiges And at every quarter or tyme that they fhal be payd, the faid Bill to be maid and figned with my Lords hand.

HALF YERE.

ITEM that the faid Clarks of the Kechynge or of the Brevements make my Lord a Bill at every Half Yere Viz. At our Lady day in Lentt and Michaelmas next foloynge of the Names of my Lords houfehold Servants that ar accuftomed to be payd theire houfehold waiges at the faid Half Yere with the Titles of the rowmes that every man ferves in with the Sommes that they take by Yere with the Sommes that every of theme fhal be payd the faid Half Yere for theire waiges And the faid Bill to be figned with my Lords hand.

HALF YERE.

ITEM that the faid Clarks of the Kechynge or of the Brevementts fhall make my Lord a Bill at every Half Yere when Half Yere waiges fhal be payd Viz. At our Lady day in Lentt and Michaelmas next foloynge of the Names of my Lords Servaunts that abfented themefelf fro my Lords Service withowte licence in the faid Half Yere and what fpace they wer abfentt and for what caufes with the Sommes that they take by Yere with the Sommes that they fhal be abayted of theire Half Yere waiges after the rate of the tyme of theire abfence And the faid Bill to be figned with my Lords hand.

YERELY.

YERELY.

[ITEM that the said Clarkis of the Kechynge or of the Brevementts make my Lord a Bill yerely at Michaelmas of the Names of my Lords Houſehold Servaunts that war put to Boordwaiges and abſented themeſelf withowte licence frome the places where they wer apoynted to be at Boordwaiges and to giff theire attendance theire and what ſpace they wer abſentt and for what cauſes with the Sommes of the Money that they ſhal be abaited of theire Boordwaiges after the rate of the tyme of theire abſence And the said Bill to be ſigned with my Lords hand bicauſe that they wer not redy theire to attend or ride where my Lord wold comand them.

YERELY.

ITEM that the said Clarks of the Kechynge or the Brevements make my Lorde Yerely at Saynt Elyn day when the Perſons ſhal be payd that ar apoynted in the Chequirerolle of Wynter Horſemete a Bill of the Names of his Servaunts that ſhal be payd for theire said Wynter Horſmete at the said Sayntt Elyn day with the Titles in what rowme every Man ſerves with the Sommes that every of theme ſhal be payd for theire said Winter Horſmete at the said tyme And the said Bill to be ſigned with my Lords hand.

YERELY.

ITEM that the said Clarks of the Kechynge or of the Brevementts make my Lord Yerely at Saynt Elyn day when the Perſons ſhal be payd that ar apoynted in the Bill of Wynter Horſmete a Bill of the Names of my Lords Servaunts that wer abſent and gaffe not Attendance upon my Lord the said Wynter and were apoynted in the said Bill As well thoys that abſented themeſelf frome attendance upon my Lorde that was apoynted in the said Wynter Horſmete withowte licence as thoys that were in my Lords buſynes and had allowance by the

day

day that thoys at were at my Lords lyvery if his Lordschipp continewed at a place They to be abayted for theire abfence of the Somme allowed for theire said Wynter Horfmete after the rate of the weiks and moneths acordynge to the rate of the valor allowed for theire said Wynter Horfmete And the said Bill to be signed with my Lords hande.

YERELY.

ITEM that the said Clarkis of the Kechynge or of the Brevementts make my Lord Yerely at Michaelmas when the Perfons shal be payd that ar apoynted in the Bill of Sommer Horfmete a Bill of the Names of his Lordschips Servaunts that shal be payd for theire said Sommer Horfmete at the said Michaelmas with the Sommes that every of theme shal be payd for theire said Sommer Horfmete at the said tyme with the Titles of the rowmes that every man ferves in And the said Bill to be Signed with my Lords hand.

YERELY.

ITEM that the said Clarks of the Kechynge or of the Brevementts make my Lord Yerely at Michaelmas when the Perfons shal be payd that ar apoynted in the Chequirerolle of Sommer Horfmete A Bill of the Names of my Lords Servaunts that were abfentt and gaffe nott theire attendance upon my Lord the said Somer and wer apoynted in the said Bill of Somer Horfmeite As well thoys that abfented themefelf frome attendance upon my Lord withowte licence as thoys that were in my Lords bufynes and had allowance by the day as thoys that were at my Lords Lyveray if his Lordschip continewed at a place They to be abaited for theire abfence of the Somme allowed for theire said Somer Horfmete after the Rate or Weiks or Moneths acordynge to the rate of the valor allowed for theire said Somer Horfmeite And the said Bill to be signed with my Lords hand.

QUARTARLIE.

QUARTARLIE.

ITEM that the Clarkis of the Kechynge or of the Breve-mentts make my Lord at every quarter and half Yere a Bill of the Names of the Perſons in the Chequirerolle that departed owte of my Lords ſervice With the Titles of the rowmes that they ſerved in And what Waiges they toke To th'entent that my Lord and his Counſaill may provide for Perſons agayn for the ſaid rowmes And the ſaid Bill to be ſigned with my Lords hand.

QUARTERLIE.

ITEM that the ſaid Clarkis of the Kechynge or of the Brevementts make my Lorde at every quarter and half Yere a Bill of the rowmes in the Chequirerolle that laks Perſons in theme accordynge to the Ordor of the Chequirerolle in this Book of Ordors And to brynge the ſaid Bill to my Lord when the Chequirerolle of houſehold for the ſaid quarter ſhal be ſigned to th'ententt that my Lord may ſhew his pleaſure whether his Lordſchip will have Perſons in the ſaid rowmes that ar vacantt accordynge to the Book of Ordors or nott.

MOUNETHLY.

ITEM that the ſaid Clarks of the Kechynge or of the Brevementts make my Lord at every mouneth end a Bill of the Names of the Perſons that ar daily in Houſe and ar nott in the Chequirerolle and for what cauſes they ſo continew in the houſe that my Lord and his Counſaill may take direccion other to put theme into rowmes or ells to cauſe theme to de-parte owte of the houſe And the ſaid Bill to be ſigned with my Lords hand.

QUARTERLY.

ITEM that the ſaid Clarkis of the Kechynge or of the Brevements call of my Lords Cofferer or Clark of the Treſaury
every

every quarter and half Yere when Houſehold Waiges ſhal be payd for the Bill of all ſuch Priſts * of Waiges that he hays payd by my Lords comandmentt to any of my Lords Houſeholde Servaunts in partie of payment of theire Waiges that yt may be abayted in theire ſaid Waiges when they ſhal be payd at every quarter or half Yere And the ſaid Bill to be ſigned with my Lords hand.

DAILYE.

ITEM it is orderyde by my Lorde and his Counſaill that whoſomever ſtands charged with th'expences ande Kepinge of my Lords Hous for the Yere as the Steward Treſſorer or Comptroller or his Clark of the Kechyn or any other within my Lordis Hous ſhall at all ſuch tymes as my Lords doith excede in the fayre of his Lordſhips hous otherwyſe than the ordynary ſervice accuſtomed appoynted in his book of Orders as well at principal ffeaſts double feaſt or feriall dayes as in tymes that Strangers comys to his Lordſhip when his Lordſhip than doyth caus his fayer to excede above the ordynary fayre of the Service of the hous accuſtomede The ſaide Officer or Officers or any other charged with th'expences of my Lords hous for the Yere with a Clarke of the Kechyn ſhall brynge my Lord a Bill of the names of ſuch freſh Acaytts in fleſh or fiſh which is expendide above the ordinary faire accuſtomed for that day Ande in what ſervice it is expendyt in With names of the Parcells with Parts † of the ſame That his Lordſhip may daily ſe at all ſuch tymes as Strangers be with him wherein he doith excede above the fair ordynary of his hous Orderede in the booke of Orders wherby he may ſe howe it excedith in every thynge.

DAILLY.

---

* i. e. Preſts or Impreſts.
† This Word is contracted in the MS. and may poſſibly be, Prices.

DAILLY.

ITEM it is Ordeigned by my Lord and his Counſaill that all manner of Yardwod which commes into the Wodyerd at the charge of the houſe the Clerke of the Wodyerde the Huyſhers and Gromes of the Hall which be charged with the Wodyerd ſhall alwaies ſe as ſonne as the ſaid wod is broughte in to the ſaid Wodyerd that they ſe it reven and every hunderith of Hardwod which comes into the ſaid Wodyerd to be revenne and maid in ccc Shedes the ſhedes to be maid of the ſaid Hardwode to be in leinth a Yerde and in thikenes a Spanne and that they from tyme to tyme ſe all their Hardwod which comes dailly into the Wodyerde for the houſehold revenne and ordorid for the keaping of the breve- mentes and bycauſe they ſhall knowe how farre every hun- derith ſhall goe and to nycke with an ax uppon the Shides the merkis from on to ij and ſo unto three and no Shide to paſſe the nombre of iij nyckes bicauſe the Officers may breve what ſhede gois to every Levery.

XI. THIS

XI.

THIS IS THE ORDRE of all fuche BRAIKFASTIS as fhal be allowid daily in my Lordis hous EVERY LENT begynnynge at Shroftide and endyng at Eftur And what they fhall have at theire Braikfafts as to fay SONDAY TEWISDAY THURSDAY and SETTERDAY Except my Lordis Childeryn which fhall have Braikfafts every day in the weik in Lent: As the Names of the Perfons and What they be And What they fhall have the faid days allowid theym hereafter follouyth in this Book.

BRAIKFASTE for my Lorde and my Lady.

FURST a Loif of Brede in Trenchors ij Manchetts a Quart of Bere a Quart of Wyne ij Pecys of Saltfifch vj Baconn'd Herryng iiij White Herryng or a Dyfche of Sproits — j.

BRAIKFASTE for my Lorde Percy and Maifter Thomas Percy.

ITEM half a Loif of houfhold Brede a Manchet a Potell of Bere a Dyfch of Butter a Pece of Saltfifh a Dyfch of Sproits or iij White Herrynge — j.

BRAIKFAST for the Nurcy for my Lady Margaret and Maifter Ingeram Percy.

ITEM a Manchet a Quarte of Bere a Dyfch of Butter a Pece of Saltfifch a Dyfch of Sproitts or iij White Herryng — j.

BRAIKFAST for my Ladis Gentyllwomen.

ITEM a Loof of Brede a Pottell of Bere a Pece of Saltfifche or iij White Herrynge — j.

BRAIKFASTS for my Lords Breder and Hede Officers of Houſhold.

ITEM ij Loofs of Brede a Manchet a Gallon of Bere ij Peces of Saltfiſch and iiij White Herrynge — ij.

BRAIKFAST for Gentilmen Uſhers and Marſhalls of the Halle.

ITEM a Loof of Brede a Pottell of Bere and a Pece of Saltfiſch — j.

BRAIKFASTS for Gentilmen of Houſhold Viz. Kervers Cupbearers Sewars and Gentilmen Waiters for the Boord-end.

ITEM a Loof of Brede a Pottell of Bere and a Pece of Saltfiſch — j.

BRAIKFAST for ij Meas of Gentilmen o'th' Chapel and a Meas of Childeryn.

ITEM iij Loofs of Brede a Gallon dimid of Bere and iij Peces of Saltfiſch or ells iiij White Herryng to a Meas — iij.

BRAIKFAST for my Lordis Clerks Viz. Clerk o'th' Kechyn Clerks of houſhold Clerks of the Foren expenſes and Clerks o'th' Signett.

ITEM a Loof of Brede a Pottell of Bere and two Peces of Saltfiſche — j.

BRAIKFASTS for Yomen Officers of Houſhold Yomen o'th' Chambre and Yomen Waiters.

ITEM ij Loofs of Brede a Gallon of Bere and two Peces of Saltfiſch — ij.

DRYNKYNGS for the Porter Lodge.

ITEM a Quarter of a Loof of Brede and a Quart of Bere — j.

DRYNKYNGS for the Stable.

ITEM a Quarter of a Loof of Brede and a Quarte of Bere — j.

XII. THIS

XII.

THIS IS THE ORDRE of all fuche BRAIK-
FASTS that fhal be lowable dayly in my Lordis hous
THOROWTE THE YERE from Michaelmas unto Michaelmas and What they fhall have to their Braikfafts as well on
FLESCHE DAYS as FYSCH DAYS in Lent and out of Lent
As the Namys of the Perfons and What they be and What they
fhall have allowid theym to their Breikfaftis hereafter follouyth
in this Book Begynnynge on Sonday the fecond day of February
which was Candlemas day laft paft In the fecund Yere of the
reign of our Sovereigne Lorde Kyng Henry the viij[th] That be
daily in the hous

BRAIKFASTIS OF FLESCH DAYS DAYLY
thorowte the Yere.

BRAIKFASTIS for my Lorde and my Lady.
FURST a Loof of Brede in Trenchors ij Manchetts j Quart
of Bere a Quart of Wyne Half a Chyne of Muton or ells a
Chyne of Beif boilid — j.

BRAIKFASTIS for my Lorde Percy and Mr.
Thomas Percy.
ITEM Half a Loif of houfhold Breide A Manchet j Potell
of Bere a Chekynge or ells iij Muton Bonys boyled — j.

BRAIKFASTS for the Nurcy for my Lady Margaret
and Mr. Yngram Percy.
ITEM a Manchet j Quarte of Bere and iij Muton Bonys
boiled — j.

BRAIKFASTS for my Ladys Gentylwomen.
ITEM a Loif of Houfhold Breid a Pottell of Beire and iij
Muton Bonys boyled or ells a Pece of Beif boilid — j.

BRAIKFASTS

BRAIKFASTS for my Lords Breder his Hede Officers of Houshold and Counsaill.

ITEM ij Loifs of Houshold Breid a Manchet a Gallon of Beire ij Muton Bonys and ij Peces of Beif boilid — j.

BRAIKFASTS for Gentylmen Ushers and Marschalls of the Halle.

ITEM a Loif of Houshold Breid a Pottell of Bere and a Pece of Beif boilide — j.

BRAIKFASTS for Gentilmen of houshold as to say Kervers Sewars Cupberers Gentilmen Waiters for the Boord-end.

ITEM a Loif of Houshold Brede a Pottell of Bere and a Pece of Beif boilid — j.

BRAIKFASTS for ij Meas of Gentylmen o'th' Chapel and a Meas of Childer.

ITEM iij Loif of Houshold Breid a Gallon dimid of Bere and iij Peces of Beif boyled — j.

BRAIKFASTS for my Lords Clerks as to say Clerk of the Kechynge Clerks of Houshold and Foren Expenses and Clerks of the Signett.

ITEM a Loif of houshold Brede a Pottell of Bere and a pece of Beif boylid — j.

BRAIKFASTS for Yomen of the Chambre Yomen Officers of Houshold and Yomen Waiters.

ITEM ij Loif of Houshold Breid a Gallon of Bere and ij Pecys of Beif boylid—j.

DRYNKYNGS

DRYNKYNGS for the Porter Lodge.

ITEM a Quarter of a Loif of Houfhold Breid and a Quarte of Bere — j.

DRYNKYNGE for the Stable.

ITEM a Quarter of a Loif of Houfhold Breid and a Quarte of Bere — j.

XIII. THIS

XIII.

THIS IS THE ORDURE of all fuch **BRAIKFASTIS OF FYSCHE** as fhal be allowid within my Lordis hous on SETTERDAYS thorowte the Yere OUTE OF LENT And what they fhall have at theire Braikfaftis and the NAMES of the Perfons and What they be and What they fhall have allowid theym here after followith in this book Begynnynge on Sonday the fecond day of February which was Candlemas day laft paft in the fecond Yere of the reigne of our Sovereigne Lorde King Henry the viij^{th}.

BRAIKFASTE for my Lorde and my Lady.

FURST a Loif of Breid in Trenchors ij Manchetts a Quarte of Bere a Quarte of Wyne a Dyfch of Butter a Pece of Saltfifch or a Dyfch of Butter'd Eggs — j.

BRAIKFAST for my Lorde Percy and Maifter Thomas Percy.

ITEM a Loif of Houfhold Brede a Manchett a Pottell of Bere a Dyfch of Butter a Pece of Saltfifch or a Dyfch of Butter'd Eggs — j.

BRAIKFASTE for the Nurcy for my Lady Margaret and Maifter Ingeram Percy.

ITEM a Manchet a Quarte of Bere a Dyfch of Butter a Pece of Saltfifch or a Dyfch of Butter'd Eggs — j.

BRAIKFAST for my Ladys Gentyllwomen.

ITEM a Loif of houfhold Brede a Pottell of Bere a Pece of Saltfifch or a Dyfch of butter'd Eggs — j.

BRAIKFASTIS for my Lords Breder and Hede Officers of Houfhold.

ITEM ij Loifs of houfhold Brede a Manchett ij Pecis of Saltfifch a Dyfch of Butter or a Dyfch of Butter'd Eggs — j.

BRAIKFAST

BRAIKFAST for Gentylmen Uſhers and Marſchalls of the Halle.

ITEM a Loif of Houſhold Brede a Pottell of Bere and a Pece of Saltfiſch — j.

BRAIKFAST for Gentlemen Viz. Carvers Sewars and Cupberers and Gentilmen Waiters for the Boord-end.

ITEM a Loif of Houſhold Breid a Pottell of Bere and a pece of Saltfiſch — j.

BRAIKFASTS for ij Meas of Gentilmen o'th' Chapel and a Meas of Childer.

ITEM iij Loifs of Houſhold Breid a Gallon dimid of Bere and a Pece of Saltfiſche — j.

BRAIKFASTE for my Lordis Clerks as to ſay Clerk of the Kechyng Clerks of Houſhold Clerks of the Foren Expences and Clerk o'th' Signett.

ITEM a Loif of Breid a Pottell of Bere and a Pece of Saltfiſche — j.

BRAIKFAST for Yomen Officers of Houſhold Yomen o'th' Chambre and Yomen Waiters.

ITEM a Loif of Breid a Pottell of Bere and a Pece of Saltfiſche — j.

DRYNKYNGS for the Porter Lodge.

ITEM a Quarter of a Loif of Houſhold Breid and a Quarte of Bere — j.

Drynkyngs for the Stable.

ITEM a Quarter of a Loif of Houſhold Breid and a Quarte of Bere — j.

XIIII. THIS

XIIII.

THIS IS THE ORDRE of the Service of Meat and Drynk to be servyd upon the SCAMLYNGE DAYS in LENT Yerely as to say Mondays and Setterdays thrughe out Lent and what they shall have att the said Scamlyngs as the Namys of the Persons and what Persons they be and what they shall have allowid theym at the Scamlynge hereafter follouth WHICH ORDRE was takyn upon Ashwednesday in the secund Yere of the reign of our Sovereigne Lorde Kynge Henry the viijth And so to be kept accordynge to the said Ordre and Direccion Yerely in my Lordis hous as hereafter follouyth.

MY LORDE and MY LADY and the Namys of the PERSONS apoyntyd to waite upon theme and to have their Revercion.

SERVICE for my Lorde and my Lady at Suppers upon Scamlynge Days in Lent Viz. Mondays and Setterdais with the Namys of the Persons that shall gif attendaunce upon theym and have their Revercion FURST the Pantler The Yoman or Grome of the Cellar The Kerver The Sewar ij Cupberers A Yoman of the Chambre A Grome of the Chambre A Gentyllman-Usher Or a Yoman-Usher Which Persons shall have nothynge allowid bot the said Revercion except Breid and Drynk = iij Mease.

Service for my Lord and my Lady and theme that shal be at their Revercion.

FURST v Manchetts a Potell of Bere a Pottell of Wyne xl Sprotts ij Peces of Saltfisch a Quarter of Salt Salmon ij Sclifis of Turbot A Dysch of Flunders Turbot Bakyn or a Disch of **Fryed**

fryed Smeltts And iij Loofs of Breid And iij Pottells of Bere
for theym that ar at the Revercion Viz. a Loif of Brede and
a Pottell of Bere for every of the faid iij Meafes = vj Dyfchis.

MY LORDE PERCY and his BRETHER and the PERSONS that ar apoynted to wait upon theym and to have theire Revercion.

SERVICE for my Lord Percy and his Breder at Suppers
upon Scamlyng Days in Lent as to fay Mondays and
Setterdays with the Names of the Perfons that fhall gif attendaunce upon theym and have their Revercion. FURST He that
hath the reuyll of theym iij Yonge Gentilmen Viz. a Kerver
a Sewar and a Cupberer A Yoman and a Grome to waite
upon theym Which Perfons fhal have nothyng allowid bot
their Revercion except Breid and Drynk = j Meas.

SERVICE for my Lorde Percy and his Breder and theym that fhal be at theire Revercion.

ITEM a Manchet a Quarte of Bere iiij White Herrynge
broiled a Dyfch of Frefch Lyng a Slyce of Turbot and a
Dyfch of Buttre and ij Loofs of Brede and ij Quartes of Bere
for theym that ar at their Revercion = iiij Dyfchis.

MY LADYS DOGHTERS and GENTYLWOMEN and the PERSONS that ar apoynted to wait upon theme and to have theire Revercion.

SERVICE for the Nurcy as to fay my Ladys Doghters and
my Ladys iij Gentylwomen at Suppers upon Scamlyng
Days in Lent Viz. Mondays and Satterdais with the Namys
of the Perfons that fhall gif attendaunce upon theym and
have theire Revercion. FURST my Ladys Chamberer ij
Rokkers in the Nurcy and the Childe of the Nurcy Which

Perfons

Perſons ſhall have nothynge allowed bot theire Revercion excepte Brede and Drynk = j Meas.

SERVICE for my Ladys Doghters and Gentilwomen
and theme that ſhal be at theire Revercion.

ITEM a Manchet a Loof of Breid a Pottell of Bere iiij White Herrynge broiled a Pece of Saltt Fyſch fryed a Dyſch of Freſch Lynge or a Slyſe of Turbott And a Loof of Brede and a Pottell of Bere for theym that ar at the Revercion = iij Dyſchis.

My Lordis HEDE OFFICERS and COUNSAILL
IN HOUSHOLD and there SERVAUNTS apoynted
to waite upon theme and to have theire Revercion.

SERVICE for my Lordis Hede Officers and Counſaill in Houſhold at Suppers upon Scamlynge days in Lent Viz. Mondays and Setterdays. FIRST my Lords Chambrelayn and his Servaunt The Treſaurer and his Servaunt The Countroller and his Servaunt The Surviour and his Servaunt And ij of my Lords Counſaill in Houſhold Which Servaunts ſhall have nothyng allowid bott their Maiſters Revercion except Breid and Drynk = j Meaſſe.

SERVICE for my Lords Hede Officers and Counſaill
in Houſhold and theire Servaunts that ſhal be at
theire Revercion.

ITEM ij Loofs of Brede a Pottell of Bere iiij White Herrynge broiled a Dyſh of Stokfiſch and a Dyſche of Codd or a Dyſch of Lynge And a Loof of Breid and a Pottell of Bere for their Servaunts that ar at their Revercion = iij Dyſchis.

GENTILMEN

GENTILMEN and YOMEN USHERS of the Chambre.

SERVICE for a Meaffe of Gentilmen Ufhers and Yoman Ufhers o'th' Chambre at Suppers upon Scamlynge Days in Lent Viz. Mondais and Setterdays. FIRST ij Gentilmen Ufhers and ij Yomen Ufhers = j Meaffe.

SERVICE for Gentilmen and Yomen Ufhers of the Chambre.

ITEM a Loif of Brede a Pottell of Bere iiij White Herrynge and a Dyfh of Stokfifch = ij Dyfchis.

GENTILMEN OF HOUSHOLD as to fay Kervers Sewars and Cupberers for my Lord and GENTIL-MEN-WAITERS for the Boord-end.

SERVICE for ij Meafe of Gentilmen of Houfhold at Suppers on Scamlynge Days in Lent when my Lord fupps not Viz. Mondays and Setterdays And when my Lorde fuppes bot for one Meafe as to fay Kervers Sewars and Cupberers for my Lorde and Gentilmen Waiters for the Boord end = ij Meas.

SERVICE for Gentylmen of Houfhold Viz. Kervers Sewars and Cupberers and Gentyllmen Waiters for the Boord-end.

ITEM to ather Meas a Loof of Brede a Pottell of Bere iiij White Herrynge and a Dyfch of Stok-fyfche = iiij Dyfchis.

GENTYLLMEN and CHILDRYN of the Chappell.

SERVICE for iiij Meas of Gentilmen and Childeryn o'th' Chapel at Suppers upon Scamlynge Days in Lent Viz. Mondays and Setterdays. FURST x Gentilmen and vj Childre of the Chapell = iiij Meaffe.

SERVICE

SERVICE for Gentyllmen and Childeryn o'th' Chapell.

ITEM to every Meas a Loof of Breide a Potell of Bere iiij White Herrynge and a Dyfch of Stokfifch = viij Dyfchis.

MARSHALLS OF THE HALL and OFFICERS OF ARMYS.

SERVICE a Meafe of Marfhalles of the Halle and Officers of Armys at Suppers upon Scamlynge Days in Lent as to fay Mondays and Setterdays. FURSTE two Marfhallis of the Halle and a Officer of Armys = j Meas.

SERVICE for Marfhalls of the Halle and Officers of Armys.

ITEM a Loof of Breide a Pottell of Bere iiij White Herrynge and a Dyfch of Stokfifch = ij Difchis.

YOMEN O'TH' CHAMBRE and YOMEN WAITERS.

SERVICE for iij Meas of Yomen of the Chambre and Yomen Waiters at Suppars upon Scamlynge Days in Lent as to fay Mondais and Setterdays. FURST the Yoman of the Hors the Yoman of the Wairdrobe iiij Yomen of the Chambre and vj Yomen Waiters = iij Meas.

SERVICE for Yomen o'th' Chambre, and Yomen Waiters.

ITEM to every Meafe a Loof of Brede a Pottell of Bere iiij White Herrynge and a Dyfche of Stokfifche = vj Dyfchis.

YOMEN

YOMEN OFFICERS OF HOUSHOLD.

SERVICE for ij Meas of Yomen Officers of Housholde at Suppers upon Scamlynge Days in Lent as to say Mondays and Setterdays. FURST Yoman Porter Yoman o'th' Buttery Yoman of the Ewery Yoman Usher of the Halle Yoman Cooke for the Mouth Yoman Coke Yoman of the Larder Yoman of the Baikhous and the Grome Usher of the Halle = ij Measse.

SERVICE for Yomen Officers of Housholde.

ITEM a Loof of Brede a Pottell of Bere iiij White Herrynge and a Dysch of Stokfische = iiij Dyschis.

GROMYS OF THE CHAMBRE for my LORD and my LADY.

SERVICE for a Meas of Gromys of the Chambre at Suppers on Scamlynge Days in Lent as to say Mondays and Setterdays. FURST iij Gromes o'th' Chambre for my Lorde and Oon for my Lady = j Measse.

SERVICE for Gromes o'th' Chambre for my Lord and my Lady.

ITEM a Loof of Breide j Pottell of Bere iiij White Herrynge and a Dysch of Stokfisch = ij Dyschis.

MYNSTRALLS and FOOTMEN in Houshold.

SERVICE for a Mease of Mynstrallis and Footmen at Suppers upon Scamblynge Days in Lent Viz. Mondays and Setterdays. FURST a Taberet a Loit a Rebecc and a Footman = j Measse.

SERVICE

SERVICE for Mynſtralis and Footmen in Houſhold.

ITEM a Loof of Brede a Pottell of Bere iiij White Her-rynge and a Dyſche of Stokfyſche = ij Dyſchis.

GROME OFFICERS OF HOUSHOLD.

SERVICE for iiij Meas of Gromes in Houſhold at Suppers on Scamlynge Days in Lent Viz. Mondays and Setterdays. FURST Grome of the Pantry Grome of the Buttery Grome o'th' Ewery Grome o'th' Steropp Grome o'th' Roobis Grome o'th' Bedds Grome o'th' Wairdrobe Grome Porter Grome o'th' Brew-hous Grome o'th' Stable ij Gromys Sumptermen Grome Hunt Grome Falconer Grome o'th' Chariote and Under Almoner o'th' Halle = iiij Meas.

SERVICE for Grome Officers of Houſhold.

ITEM to every Meaſſe a Loof of Brede a Pottell of Bere iiij White Herrynge and a Dyſch of Stokfiſche = viij Dyſchis.

CHILDRE OF HOUSHOLD IN OFFICES.

SERVICE for a Meaſe of Childre of Houſhold in Offices at Suppar upon Scamlynge Days in Lent as to ſay Mon-days and Setterdays. FURST a Childe of the Wairdrobe a Childe of the Bakhous a Childe of the Squyllery and a Child of the Chariote = j Meaſſe.

SERVICE for Childre of Houſhold in Officers.

ITEM a Loof of Brede a Pottell of Bere iiij White Her-rynge or a Dyſch of Stokfyſch = j Dyſche.

CLERKS

CLERKS IN HOUSHOLD.

SERVICE for two Meaſſe of Clerkis in Houſhold at Suppers on Scamlynge Days in Lent Viz. Mondays and Setterdays. FURST Clerk o'th' Signet The Coffurer the Clerk o'th' Kechynge ij Clerks of the Foren Expenſis Clerk of the Warks Clerk of the Brevements Clerk Avenar Clerk o'th' Dormount Book and Clerk o'th' Werynge Book = ij Meas.

SERVICE for Clerks in Houſhold.

ITEM to ather Meas a Loof of Brede a Potell of Bere iiij White Herrynge and a Dyſch of Stokfyſch = iiij Dyſchis.

GENTILMEN SERVAUNTS IN HOUSHOLD.

SERVICE for v Meaſſe of Gentillmen Servaunts at Suppars upon Scamlynge days in Lent as to ſay Mondays and Setterdays. FURST iiij Servaunts of my Lordis Brothers a Servaunt of my Lordis Kynſwomans iiij Servaunts of the Chamberlayns a Servaunt of the Treſaurers a Servaunt of the Deanys a Servaunt of the Secretarys a Servaunt of the Almanars two Servaunts of two of my Lordis Counſaill a Servaunt too two Gentyllmen Uſhers a Servaunt to ij Kervours a Servaunt to ij Sewars ij Servaunts to ij Cupberers a Servaunt to two Gentyllmen Waiters for the Boord-end and a Servaunt to two Marſhallys of the Halle = v Meaſſe.

SERVICE for Gentilmen Servaunts in Houſhold.

ITEM to every Meaſe a Loof of Brede a Pottell of Bere iiij White Herrynge or a Dyſch of Stokfiſche = x Diſchis.

XV. THIS

XV.

THIS IS THE ORDRE of the Service of MEAT and DRYNK to be ferved upon Tewifday at Nyght in the ROGACYON DAYS Yerely And what they fhall have at the faid Service With the Namys of the Perfons and What they be and What they fhall have allowid theym to theire fervice the faid Nyght hereafter follouyth WHICH ORDRE was takyn upon Tewifday the xxvij[th] day of May in the third Yere of the reigne of our Sovereigne Lorde Kynge Henry the viij[th] And fo to be kept accordynge to the faid Ordre and direccion Yerely in my Lordis hous as hereafter follouyth.

MY LORDE and MY LADY and the Namys of the PERSONS that ar apoynted to wait upon theym and to have their Revercion.

SERVICE for my Lorde and my Lady at Suppar on Tewifday in the Rogacion Days with the Namys of the Perfons that fhall gif attendaunce upon theym and have theire Revercion. FURST the Pantler The Yoman or Grome of the Sellar The Kerver The Sewar Two Cupberers A Yoman of the Chambre A Grome of the Chambre A Gentyllman Ufher or A Yoman Ufher Which Perfons fhall have nothynge allowid bot the faid Revercion except Breide and Drynk = iij Meas.

SERVICE for My Lorde and My Lady and them that fhal be at their Revercion.

FURST v Manchettis a Gallon of Bere a Potell of Wyre a Cake of Butter ij Peces of Saltfifche a Quarter of frefch Codd a Quarter of frefche Lynge ij Slyces of Turbot a Quarter of Byrt fowfed and a Dyfch of Flounders or a Dyfch of Roches and iij Loofs of Brede and iij Pottells of Bere for theym that ar at
their

their Revercion Viz. a Loof of Brede and a Pottell of Bere for every of the said iij Meas — vj Dyschis.

MY LORDE PERCY and his BREDER with the PER-SONS that shall attend upon theme and have their Revercion.

SERVICE for my Lorde Percy and his Brether at Supper upon Tewisday in the Rogacion days with the Namys of the Persons that shall gif attendance upon theym and have theire Revercion Furst that shall have the rawill of theym iij Yonge Gentyllmen as to say a Kerver a Sewar a Cupberer a Yoman or a Grome to waite upon theym Which Persons shall have nothynge allowid bot theire revercion except Brede and Drynk — j Measse.

SERVICE for my Lorde Percy and hys Breder with the Persons that shall attend upon theme and have their Revercion.

ITEM a Manchett a Quarte of Bere a Dysch of Butter a Dysch of Fresch Lynge a Slyce of Turbot or a Dysch of Floun-ders And ij Loofs of Brede and a Pottell of Bere for theym that ar at theire Revercion — iij Dyschis.

MY LADYS DOGHTERS and GENTILLWOMEN and the PERSONS that ar apoynted to waite upon theme and have their Revercion.

SERVICE for the Nurcy as to say My Ladys Doughters and my Ladys iij Gentillwomen att Suppar upon Tewisday in the Rogacion days with the Namys of theym that shall attend upon theym and have their Revercion Furst my Ladys Chamberer two Rokkers in the Nurcy and the Childe of the

N   Nurcy

Nurcy Which Perſons ſhall have nothyng allowid bot their Revercion except Brede and Drynk — j Meaſſe.

SERVICE for my Ladys Doghters and Gentilwomen and theme that ſhall attend upon theme and have their Revercion.

ITEM a Manchett a Loof of Brede a Pottell of Bere a Dyſch of Butter a Pece of Salt-fiſche a Dyſch of freſch Lynge and a Slyce of Turbott And a Loof of Brede and a Pottell of Bere for theym that ar at theire Revercion — iiij Dyſchis.

MY LORDYS HEDE OFFICERS and COUNSAILL in HOUSHOLD and theire SERVAUNTS that ar aſſigned to have their Revercion.

SERVICE for my Lordis Hede Officers and Counſaill in Houſhold at Suppar upon Tewiſday in the Rogacion days Furſt my Lordis Chambrelayn and his Servaunt Treaſaurer and his Servaunt The Countroller and his Servaunt Surviour and his Servaunt and two of my Lordys Counſaill in houſholde Which Servaunts ſhall have nothynge allowid bot their Maiſters Revercion except Brede and Drynk — j Meas. .

SERVICE for my Lordis Hede Officers and Counſaill in Houſhold and theire Servaunts that ſhal be at their Revercion.

ITEM ij Loofs of Brede a Pottell of Bere a Dyſche of Buttre a Pece of Saltfiſche a Dyſch of freſch Codde and Dyſch of Lynge And a Loof of Brede a Pottell of Bere for theym that ar at their Revercion — iiij Dyſchis.

GENTILMEN

GENTILMEN and YOMEN USHERS o'th' CHAMBRE.

SERVICE for Gentillmen Ushers and Yomen Ushers of the Chambre at Suppar upon Tewisday in the Rogacion days Furst two Gentilmen Ushers and two Yomen Ushers — j Meas.

SERVICE for Gentylmen and Yomen Ushers of the Chambre.

ITEM a Loof of Brede a Pottell of Bere Half a Disch of Butter and a Pece of Saltfisch — ij Dyschis.

GENTILMEN of HOUSHOLD Viz. Kervers Sewars and Cupberers for my Lord and Gentyllmen Waiters for the Boord end.

SERVICE for two Mease of Gentyllmen of housholde at Suppar upon Tewisday in the Rogacion days when my Lorde suppes nott And when my Lorde suppes bot for oone Meas As to say Kervers Sewars and Cupberers for my Lorde and Gentyllmen Waiters for the Boord end — ij Meas.

SERVICE for Gentylmen of Houshold Viz. Kervers Sewars and Cupberers for my Lord And Gentyllmen Waiters for the Boord end.

ITEM to athir Mease a Loof of Breide a Pottell of Bere half a Dysch of Buttre and a Pece of Saltfisch — iiij Dyschis.

GENTYLLMEN

GENTYLLMEN and CHYLDRE of the CHAPELL.

SERVICE for iiij Meafe of Gentyllmen and Childre of the Chapell at Suppar upon Tewifday in the Rogacion days Furft x Gentylmen and vj Childre of the Chapell — iiij Meas.

SERVICE for Gentylmen and Childer o'th' Chapell.

ITEM to every Meas a Loof of Bred a Pottell of Bere Half a Dyfch of Buttre and a Pece of Saltt-fyfche — viij Dyfchis.

MARSHALLS of the HALLE and OFFICERS of ARMYS.

SERVICE for a Meas of Marfhalls of the Hall and Officers of Armes at Suppar upon Tewifday in the Rogacion days Furft two Marfhalls of the Halle and a Officer of Armes — j Meas.

SERVICE for Marfhalls of the Hall and Officers of Armis.

ITEM a Loof of Brede a Pottel of Bere Half a Dyfch of Buttre and a Pece of Salt-fifch — ij Dyfchis.

YOMEN o'th' CHAMBRE and YOMEN WAITERS.

SERVICE for iij Meas of Yomen of the Chambre and Yomen Waiters at Supper upon Tewifday in the Rogacion days Furft the Yomen of the Hors the Yoman of the Wairdrobe iiij Yomen of the Chambre and vj Yomen Waiters — iij Meas.

SERVICE

SERVICE for Yomen of the Chambre and Yomen Waiters.

ITEM to every Meas a Loof of Brede a Pottell of Bere Half a Dyfch of Buttre and a Pece of Salt-fyfche — vj Dyfchis.

YOMEN OFFICERS of HOUSHOLDE.

SERVICE for ij Meas of Yomen Officers of houfhold at Supper upon Tewifday in the Rogacion days Furft Yoman Porter Yoman of the Buttery Yoman of the Ewery Yoman Ufher of the Halle Yoman Cooke for the Mouth Yoman Cooke Yoman of the Larder Yoman o'th' Bakhous and the Grome Ufher of the Halle — ij Meas.

SERVICE for Yomen OFFICERS of HOUSHOLDE.

ITEM to ather Meas a Loof of Brede a Pottell of Bere Half a Dyfch of Buttre and a Pece of Salt-fyfche — iiij Dyfchis.

GROMYS o'th' CHAMBRE for my Lord and my Lady.

SERVICE for a Meas of Gromys o'th' Chambre at Supper upon Tewifday in the Rogacion days Furft iij Gromys of the Chambre for my Lord and Oone for my Lady — j Meas.

SERVICE for GROMES of the CHAMBRE for my Lorde and my Lady.

ITEM a Loof of Brede a Pottell of Bere Half a Dyfch of Buttre and a Pece of Saltfifche — ij Dyfchis.

MYNSTRALLS and FOOTMEN in HOUSHOLDE.

SERVICE for a Meas of Mynftralls and Footmen at Supper upon Tewifday in the Rogacion days Furft iij Mynftralls a Taberet a Luyte a Rebecc and a Footman — j Meas.

SERVICE

SERVICE for Mynſtralls and Footmen in Houſhold.

ITEM a Loof of Brede a Pottell of Bere Half a Dyſche of Buttre and a Peice of Saltfiſche — ij Diſchis.

GROME OFFICERS of HOUSHOLD.

SERVICE for iiij Meas of Gromys of houſhold at Supper upon Tewiſday in the Rogacion days Furſt Grome of the Pantry Grome of the Buttery Grome of the Ewery Grome of the Sterop Grome of the Robys Grome of the Bedds Grome of the Wairdrobe Grome Porter Grome of the Brewhous Grome of the Stabill ij Gromes Sumptermen Grome Hunt Grome Falconar the Grome of the Chariot and Under Almonar of the Halle — iiij Meas.

SERVICE for Grome Officers of Houſhold.

ITEM to every Meas a Loof of Brede a Pottell of Bere Half a Dyſche of Buttre and a Pece of Saltfiſche — viij Dyſchis.

CHILDRE of HOUSHOLD in OFFICES.

SERVICE for a Meas of Childeryn off houſhold in Offices at Suppar upon Tewiſday in the Rogacion days Furſt Childe of the Wairdrobe a Childe of the Bakhous a Childe of the Squyllery and a Childe o'th' Chariote — j Meas.

SERVICE for Childre of Houſhold in Offices.

ITEM a Loof of Brede a Pottell of Bere and a Pece of Salt-fiſche — j Dyſche.

CLERKIS

CLERKIS in HOUSHOLD.

SERVICE for ij Meas of Clerkis in houfhold at Suppar upon Tewifday in the Rogation days Furft the Clerk of the Signett the Clerk of the Kechyng the Coffurer ij Clerks of the Foren Expences the Clerk o'th' Warks the Clerk of the Brevements Clerk Avenar Clerk of the Dormount book and the Clerk of the Werynge book — ij Meas.

SERVICE for Clerks in Houfhold.

ITEM to ather Meas a Loof of Breide a Pottell of Bere Half a Dyfch of Buttre and a Pece of Saltfifche — iiij Dyfchis.

GENTYLLMEN SERVAUNTS in HOUSHOLDE.

SERVICE for v Meas of Gentyllmens Servaunts at Suppar upon Tewifday in the Rogacion days Furft iij Servaunts of my Lords Brothers a Servaunt of my Lordis Kynfwomans iiij Servaunts of the Chamberlayns a Servaunt of the Trefaurers a Servaunt of the Deanys a Servaunt of the Secretarys a Servaunt of the Almonars and ij Servaunts of ij of my Lordis Counfaill a Servaunt to two Gentyllmen Ufhers a Servaunt to two Kervers a Servaunt to two Sewars ij Servaunts to two Cupberers a Servaunt to ij Gentilmen Waiters for the Boordend and a Servaunt to two Marfhallis of the Halle — v Meas.

SERVICE for Gentilmen Servaunts in Houfhold.

ITEM to every Meas a Loof of Breid a Pottell of Bere Half a Dyfch of Buttre and a Pece of Saltfyfche — x Dyfchis.

XVI. THIS

XVI.

THIS IS THE ORDER of all fuch LYVERAYS of BREID BERE WYNE WHITE-LIGHTS and WAX as fhall be allowid Dayly in my Lordis Hous fro Michaelmas to Michaelmas thorowt the Yere As to fay from Alhallowtide to our Lady day in Lent for Hole Lyverays and from our faid Lady day unto Alhallowtide Half Lyverays And what they fhall have at their faid Lyverays dayly as the Namys of the Perfons and what Perfons they be and what they fhall have allowid theym hereafter followith.

The NAMYS of LYVERAYS of BREDE BERE WYNE and LIGHTTS.

The LYVERAYS for my Lord and my Lady.
FIRST two Manchetts a Loof of Houfhold Breid a Gallon of Bere a Quarte of Wyne a Pound of White Lightts conteynyng xij Candles and vj Syfez Viz. iij to my Lordis Footfheit and iij to my Ladys Chambre.

LYVERAYS for my Lord Percy and Maifter Thomas Percy.

ITEM a Manchett Half a Loof of Brede a Potell of Bere iij White Lightts and a Syfe.

LYVERAYS for the Nurcy for my Lady Margaret and Maifter Ingeram Percy.

ITEM a Manchett Half a Loof of Brede a Potell of Bere and iij White Lyghtts.

LYVERAYS for my Ladys Gentyllwomen.

ITEM a Manchett a Pottell of Bere a Quarte of Wyne and iij White Lyghtts.

LYVERAYS

LYVERAYS for my Lordys Brether.

ITEM a Manchet a Pottell of Bere a Quarte of Wyne and iij White Lyghts.

LYVERAYS for every of my Lords Hede Officers and Counsaill Viz. the Chamberlayn The Steward The Tresaurer The Countroller And the Counsaill.

ITEM a Manchett Half a Loof of Houshold Brede a Pottell of Bere a Quarte of Wyne and iij White Lyghts.

LYVERAYS for the Dean of the Chapell.

ITEM a Manchett a Potell of Bere a Quarte of Wyne and iij White Lyghtts.

LYVERAYS for the Sub-dean of the Chapell and Preists if thay be two and if they be mo to have larger Lyveray.

ITEM a Quarter of a Houshold Loof of Brede a Quarte of Bere and a White Light.

LYVERAY for Gentyllmen Ushers.

ITEM a Quarter of a Houshold Loof of Breid a Quarte of Bere and a White Lyght.

LYVERAYS for Gentyllmen of Housholde.

ITEM Half a Loof of Houshold Breide a Pottell of Bere and two White Lyghts.

LYVERAYS for the Maister of Gramer in Houshold.

ITEM a Quarter of a Loof of Houshold Brede a Quarte of Bere and a White Lyght.

O   LYVERAYS

LYVERAYS for Gentyllmen of the Chapell and Childer.

ITEM a Loof of Houſhold Breid a Gallon of Bere and iij White Lyghtts.

LYVERAYS to the Chambre of Yomen Officers Yomen Waiters and Grome Officers in Houſhold lying all togeder.

ITEM a Loof of Houſhold Brede a Pottell of Bere and a White Light.

LYVERAY for the Clark of the Signett and the Clark o'th' Foryn Expenſis.

ITEM a Quarter of an Houſhold Loof of Brede a Quarte of Bere and ij White Lyghtts.

LYVERAY for my Lordis Almonar.

ITEM a Quarter of a Loof of Houſhold Breid a Quarte of Bere and a White Lyght.

LYVERAY for the Countynghous and Clarks of Houſhold.

ITEM a Quarter of a Loof of Houſhold Brede a Quarte of Bere and ij White Lyghtts.

LYVERAY for the Porter Lodge.

ITEM a Quarter of a Loof of Houſhold Brede a Quarte of Bere and iij White Lyghtts.

LYVERAY for the Stable.

ITEM a Quarter of a Loof of Houſhold Brede a Pottell of Bere and ij White Lyghtts.

XVII. THYS

XVII.

THYS YS THE ORDER of all fuch HOOLE LYVEREYS of WOD and COOLES as ar allowed within my Lordis hous in Wynter As to fay from Alhallowtyde unto our Lady day in Lent And what they fhall have for theyre fayde Lyverey dayly As the Namys of the Perfons and what they be and what they fhall have allowed theme that ar dayly in the hous hereafter followith.

The NAMYS of LYVEREYS of Fewell as to fay WOODE and COOLES.

NAMYS	SHIDES	COOLES
My Lordes great Chambre where he dyeneth − −	Furfte — j	— j bz. ij peks
My Ladys Chambre where fhe lyeth − − − − − −	Item — ij	— j bz. iiij peks
My Lordes Chambre where he maketh hym redy − − −	Item — ij	— j bz. iiij peks
My Lordes Lybrary − − −	Item — j	— j bz. ij peks
The Knyghtts Chambre − −	Item — j	— j bz. iiij peks
My Lorde Percy Chambre −	Item — ij	— ij pᶜ.
The Nurcy if my Lordes Chil-der be byneth − − − −	Item − −	ij pᶜ.
My Lordes Brether − − −	Item — j	— j pᶜ.
Maifter Chambreleyn − − −	Item — j	— ij pᶜ.
The Steward − − − − −	Item − −	j pᶜ.
The Trefaurer − − − − −	Item − −	j pᶜ.
The Countroller − − − −	Item − −	j pᶜ.
The Surviour − − − − −	Item − −	j pᶜ.

Namys	Shides	Cooles
Gentyllmen Strangeors as to say Knyghttes Eſquyers and Gentilmen to theire Chambre	Item — j	— j pᶜ.
The Dean o'th' Chapell – –	Item –	– j pᵉ.
Kervers Sewers Cupberers and Gentylmen Waiters – –	Item –	– j pᶜ.
My Lordes Waredrobe – –	Item –	– j pᶜ.
The Allmonar – – – – –	Item –	– j pᶜ.
The Maiſter of Grammer as to fay j pᵉ. for his Lyvery and j pᵉ. for the Scolehous – –	Item –	– ij pⁿ.
Gentyllmen Uſhers – – –	Item –	– j pᵉ.
The Countyng Hous – – –	Item –	– j pᵉ.
The Porter Lodge – – –	Item –	– j pᵉ.
The Clarkys o'th' Sygnett and Foren Expenſis – – – –	Item –	– j pᶜ.
The Maiſter and Childer of the Chapell – – – – –	Item –	– j pᵉ.
The Reveſtry oones in the Weike – – – – – –	Item –	– j pᵉ.
The Halle – – – – – –	Item — j	— iiij bz.
The Kechynge – – – –	Item — ij	— vj bz.
The Kechynge when they bake in the grett Ovyn – – –	Item Fagottes vj	
The Kechynge when they bake in the litle Ovyn – – –	Item Fagottes iij	
The Brewhouſe at every Brew-ynge – – – – – – –	Item Fagottes iiij ſcore xvj	
The Backehouſe at every Bak-ynge – – – – – – –	Item Fagottes xvj	

XVIII. THYS

XVIII.

THYS YS THE ORDRE of all ſuch HALF LYVEREYS of WOOD and COLES as ar allowed wythin my Lordes hous this Yere As to ſay Half Lyvereys to be ſerved in Somar as to ſay from our Lady day in Lent th'Anunciacion unto Michaelmas next enſuynge As the Namys of the Chambres which ſhal be allowed theyre ſaid Half Lyverey hereafter followith in this Booke.

NAMES	SHIDES	COOLES
My Lades Chambre where ſhe lyeth - - - - - - - }	Furſt — j —	j bz.
My Lordes Chambre where he makith him redy - - - }	Item — j —	j pᵉ.
My Lords Lybrary - - - -	Item — j —	j pᵉ.
My Lorde Percys Chambre -	Item — j —	j pᵉ.
The Nurcy if my Lordes Childre ly byneth - - - - }	Item - -	j pᵉ.

XIX. THEYS

XIX.

THEYS BE THE DIRECCIONS taken by my Lorde and his Confeill at Wrefill upon Sonday the xxviij[th] day of Septembre which was Michaelmas Day in the iij[th] Yere of the reigne of our Sovereigne Lorde Kynge Henry the viij[th] concernynge the PROVISION of the CATOR PARCELLS as well of FLESCH as of FYSCH which fhall be provyded for thrugheout the Yere And at what tymys of the Yere And what Cator Parcells fhal be provided and ordenyd to be ferved in my feyd Lordes hous at the Meells for the Clerkys of the Kechynge to be executed hereafter followyth in this Booke.

WEEKLY.

FYRST it is devyfed that from hensforth no CAPONS to be bought bot onely for my Lordes owne Mees and that the faid Capons fhal be bought for ij d. a pece leyn and fed in the Pultry and that Maifter Chambreleyn and the Stewardes be ferved with Capons if theyre be Straungers fyttynge with theym.

MOUNTHLY.

Item yt is thought good that PYGGES be bought fo they be good and at iij d. or iiij d. a pece for of a Pygge theire may be mayde to ferve iiij Mees.

MOUNETHLY.

Item it is thought good to by GEYSSE fo that they be good and for iij d. or iiij d. at the mofte feynge that iij or iiij Mees may be ferved thereof.

WEEKELY.

WEEKELY.

Item it is thought goode that CHEKYNS be bought for my Lordes Mees onely and Maifter Chambreleyn and the Stewards Mees fo that they be at ane ob. a pece.

WEEKELY.

Item it is thought goode that HENNYS be bought from Cryftynmas to Shroftyde fo they be good and at ij *d.* a pece and my Lord Maifter Chambreleyn and the Stewardes Mees to be ferved with theym and noo other.

WEEKELY.

Item it is thought good to by PEGIONS for my Lordes owne Mees Maifter Chambreleyn and the Stewardes Mees fo they be bought after iij for j *d.*

WEEKLEY.

Item it is thought good that CUNYS be bought for my Lorde and Maifter Chambreleyn and the Stewardes Mees if theire be Straungers fyttynge with theym fo they be bought after ij *d.* a pece and be goode.

YERELY.

Item it is thought goode that my Lordes SWANNYS be taken and fedde to ferve my Lordes hous and to be paid fore as thay may be bought in the Countre feynge that my Lorde bathe Swannys inew of hys owne.

MOUNETHLY.

Item it is thought good that no PLUVERS be bought at noo Seafon bot oonely in Chryftynmas and princypall Feeftes and my Lorde to be fervyde therewith and his Boordend and non other and to be boght for j *d.* a pece or j *d.* ob. at mofte.

AT

AT PRINCIPALL FEESTS.

Item it is thought that CRANYS mufte be hadde at Cryftynmas and other principall Feeftes for my Lordes owne
Mees fo they be boght at xvj*d.* a pece.

AT PRINCIPALL FEESTES.

Item it is thought in like wyfe that HEARONSEWYS be
bought for my Lordes owne Mees fo they be at xij *d.* a pece.

MOUNETHLY.

Item it is thought goode that MALLARDES be bought
onely for my Lordes own Mees fo they be good and boght
for ij*d.* a pece.

MOUNETHLY.

Item it is thought good that noo TEYLLES be bought
bot if fo be that other Wyldefowll cannot be gottyn and to
be at j*d.* a pece.

MOUNETHLY.

Item it is thought good that WOODCOKES be hade for
my Lordes owne Mees and non other and to be at j*d.* a pece
or j*d.* ob. at the mofte.

MOUNETHLY.

Item it is thought goode that WYPES be hade for my
Lordes own Mees onely and to be at j*d.* a pece.

MOUNETHLY.

Item it is thought good that SEEGULLES be hade for my
Lordes owne Mees and non other fo they be good and in feafon and at j*d.* a pece or j*d.* ob. at the mofte.

MOUNETHLY.

MOUNETHLY.

Item it is thought good that STYNTES be hadde for my Lordes owne Mees and non other fo they be after vj a jd.

MOUNETHLY.

Item QUAYLLES in like wyfe to be hadde for my Lordes owne Mees and non other at Pryncipall Feeftes and at ijd. a pece at mofte.

MOUNETHLY.

Item SNYPES to be bought for my Lordes owne Mees at Pryncipall Feyftes fo they be good and after iij a jd.

MOUNETHLY.

Item PERTRYGES to be bought for my Lordes Mees and at ijd. a pece yff they be goode.

AT PRICIPALL FEESTES.

Item REDESHANKES to be bought at Principall Feeftes for my Lordes owne Mees after jd. ob. the pece.

AT PRINCIPALL FEESTS.

Item BYTTERS for my Lordes owne Mees at Principal Feeftes and to be at xijd. a pece fo they be good.

AT PRINCIPALL FEESTES.

Item FESAUNTES to be hade for my Lordes owne Mees at Principall Feeftes and to be at xijd. a pece.

AT PRINCIPALL FEESTS.

Item REYS to be hadde for my Lordes owne Mees at Princypall Feeftes and at ijd. a pece.

P   AT

AT PRINCIPALL FEESTES.

Item SHOLARDES to be hadde for my Lordes owne Mees at Pryncipall Feeftes and to be at vj *d.* a pece.

AT PRINCIPAL FEESTES.

Item KYRLEWES to be hadde for my Lordes owne Mees at Pryncipall Feeftes and to be at xij *d.* a pece.

AT PRINCIPAL FEESTES.

Item PACOKES to be hadde for my Lordes owne Mees at Principall Feeftes and at xij *d.* a pece and noo Payhennys to be bought.

MOUNETHLY.

Item it is thought good that all manar of WYLDFEWYLL be bought at the fyrft hand where they be gottyn and a Cator to be apoynted for the fame For it is thought that the Pulters of Hemmyngburghe and Clyf hathe great advauntage of my Lorde Yerely of Sellynge of Cunys and Wyldefewyll.

AT PRINCIPALL FEESTES.

Item SEE-PYES for my Lorde at Princypall Feeftes and non other tyme.

AT PRINCIPALL FEESTES.

Item WEGIONS for my Lorde at Principall Feeftes and no other tyme and at j *d.* ob. the pece except my Lordes comaundment be otherwyfe.

AT PRINCIPALL FEESTES.

Item KNOTTES for my Lorde at Principall Feeftes and no other tyme and at j *d.* a pece except my Lordes Comaundment be otherwife.

AT

AT PRINCIPAL FEESTES.

Item DOTTRELLS to be bought for my Lorde when thay ar in Seafon and to be at j d. a pece.

AT PRINCIPALL FEESTES.

Item BUSTARDES for my Lordes own Mees at Principal Feeftes and non other tyme except my Lordes comaundment be otherwyfe.

AT PRINCIPALL FEESTS.

Item TERNES for my Lordes Mees oonely at Principal Feeftes and non other tyme after iiij a j d. except my Lordes comaundement be otherwife.

MOUNTHLY.

Item GREAT BYRDES after iiij a j d. to ferve for my Lordes Mees Maifter Chambreleyn and the Stewardes Mees.

MOUNTHLY.

Item SMALE BYRDES for my Lordes owne Mees after xij a j d.

MOUNTHLY.

Item LARKYS for my Lordes owne Mees after xij for ij d.

MOUNTHLY.

Item BACON FLYKES for my Lordes owne Mees Mr. Chambrelayn and the Stewardes Mees bitwixt Candlemas and Shroftyde ells none except my Lordes comaundment be to the contrary.

YERELY.

YERELY.

Item that a Direccion be taken at Lekyngfeld with the Cator of the See what he fhall have for every SEAM of FYSCH thorowt the Yere to ferve my Lordes hous.

QUARTERLY.

Item that a Direccion be taken with my Lordes Tenauntes of Hergham and to be at a ferteyn with theme that they fhall ferve my Lordes hous thrugheowt the Yere of all manar of FRESH WAYTER FYSCHE.

YERELYE.

Item it is thought good that there be a counnt made with the Cator by great for EGGES and MYLK for the hoole Yere if it can be fo doyn what for a Gallon of Mylke and how many Egges for j d.

YERELY.

Item that from hensforth that theire be no HERBYS bought feinge that the Cookes may have herbes anewe in my Lordys Gardyns.

YERELYE.

Item a Warraunt to be fewed oute Yerely at Michaelmas for xx SWANNYS for th'expencez of my Lordes hous as too fay for Criftynmas Day v — Saynt Stephyns Day ij — Saynt John Day ij — Childremafs Day ij — Saynt Thomas Day ij — New Yere Day iij — ande for the xij^{th} Day of Criftynmas iiij Swannys.

XX. YERELY.

XX.

YERELY.

THE COPIES of the WARRUNTS to be fewed oute
Yerely for SWANNYS for th'expencez of my Loordes
hous after this forme followynge.

WELBILOVED I greete you well ande woll ande
charge you That ye delyver or caufe to be deliverd
unto my welbiloved Servauntes Richard Gowge Countroller
of my hous ande Gilbert Wedall Clarke of my Kitchinge for
the ufe and expencez of my faide hous nowe againſt the Feeſt of
Chriſtynmas next comynge Twenty SIGNETTS to be taken
of the breed of my Swannys within my Carre of Arrom within
my Loordeſhip of Lekingfeld within the Countie of Yorke
whereof ye have the kepinge Ande that ye caufe the fame to
be deliverd unto theme or too oone of theme furthwith upon
the fight hereof Ande this my writinge for the delyverey of the
fame fhal be unto you agenſt me and toffore myne Auditours
at youre next accompte in this bihalf fufficient Warrunt ande
Difcharge Geven undre my Signet and Signe Manuell at my
Manoure of Lekingfeld the xxij^d daye of Novembre in the
vth Yere of the reign of our Sovereign Loorde Kyng Henry
the viijth.

> To my welbiloved Servaunt the Balliff of
> my Lordeſhip of Lekingfeld afforeſaide
> ande Kepar of my feid Carre at Arrom
> ande to the Undre Kepars of the fame
> for the tyme beinge.

> YERELY.

YERELY.

The COPIES of the WARRAUNTS maide to the Receyvours Yerely for th'affignement of fuche MONEY as
they muft deliver for the kepinge af my Loordes hous.

WELBILOVED I Greete you well and woll ande ftrately
charge you withoute delay as ye intend to have me your goode
Loorde and well exchewe that at may enfewe unto you for
the contrary dooinge at your jeopardie Faill not 'to' content ande
pay too my welbiloved Servaunts Richard Gowge Coun-
trooller of my hous ande Gilbert Weddell Clarke of my
Kitchinge ftandinge charged with my hous for the furfte
payment of th'affignement affigned to theme for the kepinge of
my faide hous for this Yere beggynnynge at Michaelmas in the
vth Yere of the reigne of oure Sovereigne Lorde Kinge Henry
the viijth of the Revenus of my Landes within your receite
in the Countie of Northumberland of the Yere endynge at
the faide Michaelmas The Some of CLX *l.* of fuche Money as
is due unto me upon th'audicte at the faide Michaelmas Geven
undre my Signett at my Manor of Lekingfeld the xixth day
of Novembre in the vth Yere of the reign of our Sovereigne
Lorde Kinge Henry the viijth.

> To my Truftie and Welbiloved the Recey-
> vour of all my Lands within the Countie
> of Northumberland for the tyme beinge,

YERELY.

WELBILOVED I Greete you well and woll ande ftrately
charge you withoute delay as ye intend to have me your goode
Loorde ande woll exchewe that at may enfewe unto you for
the contrary dooinge at your jeopardie Faill not to content
ande pay to my Welbiloved Servaunts Richard Gowge
Countroller of my hous ande Gilbert Wedell Clarke of my
Kichinge

Kichinge ftandinge charged with my faide hous for the iiijth
payment of th'affignement affigned to theme for the kepinge
of my faide hous for this Yere begynnynge at Michaelmas
in the vth Yere of the reign of our Sovereign Lorde Kinge
Henry the viijth of the revenus of my Lands within your
receyte in the Countie of Yorke due unto me of the Martynmas Ferm payabill att Candlemas the Some of CCLviij *l.* xix *s.*
j *d.* — Geven undre my Signett at my Manor of Lekingfeld
the xixth day of Novembre the vth Yere of the reign of our
Soverain Lorde Kynge Henry the viijth.

> To my Truftie and Welbiloved the Recey-
> vor of all my Landes within the Countie
> of Yorke for the tyme beinge.

YERELY.

ITEM that vij Warrauntes be maide Yerele for th'affignement of fuche MONEY as is appointed to theme that
hayth the charge of my Lordes hous to be maid after the forme
of the Warraunts affore written that ys to fay THREE in the
Furfte Quarter bitwixt Michaelmas and Cryftynmas Viz. One
to the Receyvor of Northumbrelande for CLx *l.* One to the Receyvor of Cumbreland for C *l.* One to the Receyvor of Yorke-
fhyre for Lxxvij *l.* viij *s.* Whiche Money to be payd of the revenus
due uppon th'audits yerely TWO Warrunts in the Secounde
Quarter bitwixt Cryftynmas and our Lady day in Lentt Viz.
One Warrunt to the Receyvor of Yorkefhire for CCLviij *l.* xix *s.*
j *d.* Oone too the Receyvore of Northumbrelande for cvij *l.* iij *s.*
x *d.* Whiche Money too be payde of the Martynmas Ferm of
the faide Shires ONE Warrunt in the iij^d Quarter bitwixt our
Lady day and Midfomer to the Receyvor of Cumbreland Lx *l.*
of the Martynmas Ferm of the faide Shires whiche is payabill
bot than And OONE Warrunt in the quarter bitwixt Midfomer and Michaelmas to the Receyvor of Northumbrelande
for cxxj *l.* ix *d.* Whiche Money to be payde of the Whitfonday
Ferm

ferm of the faide Shires WHICHE is in full contentacion of the Some affigned for the kepinge of my Lordes hous Yerely.

YERELY.

ITEM xvijth WARRAUNTS for xxix DOES for th'expenfez of my Lordes hous bitwixt Ahhollowdey and Shraftide Yerely Viz. A Warraunt for ij Does at Spofforde for Alhallowday A Warraunt for iij Does at the Great Parke of Topclyff for the iij firfte Wekes bitwixt Alhallowday and Criftynmas A Warraunt for iij Does oute of the Litle Parke of Topclyff for the iij fecounde Wekes bitwixt Alhollowday and Chriftynmas ande A Warraunt for ij Does oute of Helagh Parke for the ij laft Wekes bitwixt Alhollowday and Criftynmas A Warraunt for ij Does oute of Lekingfeld Parc for Criftynmas day A Warraunt for oone Doe oute of Catton Parke for Sainte Stephyns day A Warraunt for ij Does oute of Newfeham Parke for the Hallydaies bitwixt the faide Saynt Stephyns day and Newyere day A Warraunt for ij Does oute of Helagh Parc for the Wark dayes bitwixt Newyere day and xijth day A Warraunt for ij Does oute of the Great Parke of Topclyff And a Warraunt for one Doe oute of the Litle Parc of Topclyff for the xijth day of Criftynmas A Warraunt for oone Do oute of Spofford for the firft week bitwixt xijth day of Criftynmas and Shroftide A Warraunt for one Doe oute of the Litle Parc of Topclyff for the ij^d week A Warraunt for one Doe oute of the Great Parc of Topclyff for the iij^d week A Warraunt for ij Does oute of Helagh Parc for the iiijth weke and vth week and A Warraunt for oone Doe oute of Lekingfeld Parc for the vjth Week Ande a Warraunt for oone Doe oute of Catton Parke for the vijth Week And a Warraunte for two Dofe out of Spofforth Parke for Newyer day.

The

The DERE appointed oute of every Parc in Winter as here
after folleyth.

WARRAUNTS for the hous in Winter is xvij

Spofford - - - - - - v
Great Parc of Topclyff - - vj
Litle Parc of Topclyff - - v
Helagh - - - - - - - vj
Lekingfoeld - - - - - iiij
Catton - - - - - - - ij
Newfeham - - - - - - ij

The Nombre of Does is — xxix.

YERELY.

ITEM xj WARRAUNTS for xxij BUKKES
for th'expenfez of my Lordes hous bitwixt May day ande
Hallyroode day next followynge Viz. A Warraunt for oone
Buk oute of the Great Parc of Wreffill for the firfte week
after May day A Warraunt for iij Bukkes oute of the
Great Parke of Topclyff for the ijth iijth and iiijth week after
May Day A Warraunt for ij Bukks oute of the Litle Parc of
Topclyff for Whitfonday ande the faide week whiche is the
vth week after May Day A Warraunt for ij Bukkes oute of
Spofford Park for the vjth and vijth Weeke after May day A
Warraunt for ij Bukkes oute of Helagh Parke for the viijth
ande ixth Weeke after May day A Warraunt for one Bukk
oute of Lekyngffeeld Parc for the xth week after May day A
Warraunt for ij Bukks oute of Catton Parc for the xjth ande
xijth week after May day A Warraunt for ij Bukks oute of
Newfeham Park for the xiijth ande xiiijth week after May day
A Warraunt for ij Bukks oute of the Great Parc of Topclyff
for the xvth and xvjth Week after May day A Warraunt for ij

Q   Bukks

Bukks oute of the Litle Parc of Topclyff for the xvijth and xviijth Week after May day Ande j Warraunt for oone Bukk of oute Spofforde Park for the xixth Week after May day.

The DERE appointed oute of every Parc in Somer as hereafter followith.

WARRAUNTS for the hous in Somer is xj

Great Park of Topclyff – –	v
Litle Park of Topcliff – –	iiij
Great Parc of Wreffill – –	j
Spofforde Park – – – – –	iij
Helagh Park – – – – –	ij
Lekyngfeeld Parc – – – –	j
Catton Parc – – – – –	ij
Newfham Parc – – – –	ij

The Nombre of Bukks is —— xx^{ti}.

XXI. DAILY.

XXI.

DAILY.

ITEM that the BREVEMENTES of th'EXPENSEZ of the HOUS be kept every day in the Countynghous at TWO TYMES on the DAY that is to fay FIRST tyme incontynent after the DYNNAR, Ande the SECOUNDE tyme at after SOPAR when Lyverys is ferved at hye tymes as principall Feeftes as Cryftynmas Eftre Saint-George-Tyde Whitfontide ande Alhallowtide ande at any other tymes when there is any great repaire of Straungers in the hous bicaus th'Officers fhall not forgett for long beringe of it in there myndes.

DAILY.

ITEM that the faide Clarkes of the Brevements breve every Straunger by name that commethe to my Loordes hous.

DAILY.

ITEM that the faide Clarkes of the Kechinge fee that the fervice that is appointed in the Booke of Direccions for th'Expenfez of my Loordes Hous be obferved and kept withoute inbrigementt ande to be examyned every day what lakks thereof to the ententt that the Officers fhall not parlune it to there prouffitt if there be any butt that it rynne oonely to my Loordes proufitt.

DAILY.

ITEM that the faide Clarkes of the Kechynge every day at vj of the Clok or vij in the Mornynge faill not too appoint the Larderer ande Cookes and to be with the faid Cookes att
the

the ftrikynge outte of the Meeffes of Beefs Mutons Veles
and Porkes that fhal be cutt oute for the fervice for my Loorde
and the Hous afwell for Braikefafts as for Dynnar ande Sopparr
Ande that they maik ande ftrike oute there Meeffes after the
quantite accordinge to the Order of the Direccions for th'expencez of my Loordes Hous to th'ententt that they fhall nather
maike it loffe nor more for excedinge Bott accordynge to the
Ordre of the Book.

WEEKELY.

ITEM that the faide Clarkes of the Kechynge fhall affore
they maik any Barganne for Provifion of any maner of grofs
Empcion for kepinge of my Loordes Hous that they maik my
Loorde privey theretoo affore the Barganne be concluded to
th'entent that they may knowe whether his Loordefhip will
agre to the faid prices or not if my faide Loorde be at home
ande if his Loordefhip be abfentt thanne to maik fuche of his
Lordefhip Counfaill or Servaunts that my faide Loorde leefs
in truft too fee which he haithe apointed prevey to the faide
Empcion affore the Barganne be concluded to th'ententt that
they may fee whether they have maide there Bargans in dewfull
tyme or nott.

MOUNTHLY.

ITEM that the faide Clarkes of the Kechinge at th'ende
of every Mouneth taik the Remaneth and fett the Price upon
the Heed of every thinge that Remaneth what it is worth And
to maik a Bill of all the clere expenfes of the faid Moneth and
to rate every man what he ftandes in a Meel 'the' Day ande
the Week and what th'hoole Mouneth drawith too in the
hous.

MOUNETHLY.

MOUNETHLY.

ITEM that the ſaide Clarkes of the Kechynge maike a Bill of the Deficyentts of every Officer ſingulerly by hym ſellf what Deficient he fallith in the Mouneth if any of theme ſo fall with the Price and Some Ande to maike a Bill what every Defficient of every Officer drawith too ande to preſent it to my ſaide Lord at every Mouneth end.

DAILY.

ITEM that the ſaide Clarkes of the Kechinge caſt up every day the Chequyrroll ande the Straungeours ande deduct the Vacauntes too ſee how th'Expenſes of the Brevementts woll wey togeder ande whanne they finde a Deffawtt too refforme it furthwith ande ſhew the ſaid Officers there Deffawtts in there myſbrevynge if they be ſoo founde.

YERELY.

ITEM that the ſaide Clarkes of the Keechinge ſee that whenſoever it ſhall fortune my Loorde to goo in the Kyngs Service beyonde the See that all his Loordeſhips Houſehold-Servaunts that goith over with his Lordeſhip the ſaide tyme that they have no Houſehold Wages from the day that they goo oute upon with his Loordeſhip to the day that they com home agayn Whiche haith the Kyngs Wages of my ſaide Loorde by the Day And thanne they to be entered into Wages in the Chequyrroull when they com home butt from that day that they com home on.

WEEKELIE.

ITEM it is Ordenede by my Loorde ande his Counſaill that whenſoever any of his Lordeſhip Servauntes be comaunded to ride on Meſſage in Winter Viz. from Michaelmas The which tyme Winter-Horſſemeat begynneth at To Saint Ellyn

day

day next after The which tyme the ſaide Winter-Horſſemeat goith oute at That every of theym be allowed for the tyme of his being furth in his Jornay within the ſaide ſpace ij d. for every Meall ande ob. for every his Baiting Ande for his Hors every day ande night of his ſaide Jornay iiij d. Viz. a penny for his baiting ande iij d. at night for his provounder The whiche is in all for a Man and his Hors in the daie in Winter viij d. if it be Etting-Daye Ande if it be Faſting-Daie than ij d. to be abaited The which is vj d. on a Faſting-Day within the ſaid ſpace from Michaelmas to Saint Elyns Daie ANDE whenſoever any his ſaide Lordeſhip Servauntes be comaunded to ride on Meſſage in Somer Viz. from Saint Ellyns daie the which tyme Somer-Horſmeet begynneth at unto Michaelmas next after The which tyme Somer-Horſhmet endeth at That every of theym for the tyme of his Jornay within the ſaid ſpace be allowed ij d. for every Meele ande ob. for his Baiting ande for his Hors every day of his ſaid Jornay within the ſaide ſpace to be allowed a penny ob. Viz. ob. for his baiting ande a penny at nyght for his greſſing The which is in all for a Man and his Hors on the daie in Somer v d. ob. if it be Etting-Daie And if it be Faſting-Daie than ij d. to be abaited for a Meall The which is but iij d. ob. on every Faſting-Day within the ſaid ſpace from Saint Elyns day to Michaelmas Provided alway that whenſoever any ſuche Parſonne the which is comaunded too ride and doth tarry at his Jornay end for ſuche cauſeth as he haith to doo in his Meſſage there than he to be allowed weekly for the tyme of his tarrying there xiiij d. for hymſelf Viz. ij d. a daie for hymſelf for his Mealls and xij d. for his Hors if it be in Winter Viz. j d. ob. quadr. a daie for his Hors Ande in Somer to be allowed Wekelie for the tyme that he ſo tarries at his jornay-ende conſernyng his buſynes xiiij d. for hym ſelf as is afforeſaid Viz. ij d. a Daie for hymſelf for his Mealls And viij d. for his Hors Viz. a penny the day for his Greſs Ande j d. more at all.

WEKELIE.

WEKELIE.

ITEM it is Ordeyned by my Loorde and his Counsaill that whensoever the Clarkes of the Keching Clarkes of the Brevements or any other Officers of Houfehold ar comaunded to ride furth confernyng the Provifion for th'Expenfes of his Lordefhipps Hous That every of theym be allowed viij *d.* on the daie for hymfelf and his Hors if it be in Winter Ande in Somer to be allowed ij *d.* for every Meall and ob. every Baiting And a penny for his Hors greffing on the daie and night for the tyme of his being furth confernyng the Provifion for the Hous And if it fortune any of the faid Clerkes or other Officers whiche ar comaunded to ride furth confernyng the Provifion for th'Expenfes of the hous foe that they muft tarry at any place where there provifion lies by the fpace of a Week or of a Mouneth that than they to tarry there ande to be allowed weeklie after xiiij *d.* a week for there Borde Wages And xij *d.* for there Hors if it be in Winter Ande in Somer after xiiij *d.* a Week for there Boord Wagies And viij *d.* for there. Hors after a penny the daie and night And a penny more at all.

YERELIE.

ITEM it is Ordeyned by my Loorde and his Counfaill at every Yeres ende that the Accompt of the Hous endes of That there fhal be at every fuch Yere ending of the faide houfeholde a Bill to be maide of the Remeineth of fuch Stuf as remeines unfpent provided and bought in the Yere afforefaide With the Names of the parcells every parcell by it felf With the price that it was bought fore Ande the daie of the moneth that it was bought on The faid Bill to be a Memorandum to be put in the Book of Houfeholde for th'Ordre of the hous of the New Yere thorrow the levis of the Book which is ordened for the hous Bicaus they fhall not have it written in the faid Book bicaus the Some of the Remeineth Yerely is not certayn and

therefore

therefore the Parcells thereof is thrawn in the Somes of the Parcells of the Somes of Money bicaus the Parcells of the Remaneth cannot keep alway a certayn Some but fome Yere more and fom Yere les as the cafe doth require nor alway one manner of Parcells to be the Remaneth nor of like valor as they be other Yeres bicaufe the Stuf that is beft cheep which muft be expended the moft of that ftuf is beft to be provided and bicaus that the faid Remaneth of the Stuf unfpent of the Yere affore ended fhal be the firft Som paid in partie of payment of the Some of th'Affignement apoineted for the keping of my Lordes hous for the New Yere Wherefore this faid Article is maide for the knowlege of th'ordre thereof bicaus it fhal be Yerelie the firft Som and Parcell paid for the hous.

YERELIE.

ITEM too be pajde too the Stiewarde Trefaurer Countroller ar Clarkes of the Keching whiche ftonds charged for to maike provifion for cclxvij Quarters and a Bufhell of Otes after xxd. the Quartar for th'expenfes of xxvij Hors of my Lordes ftanding in his Lordefhip Stabill at the charge of the Hous for one Hole Yere Viz. vj Gentle Hors——iiij Palfraies as to fay Oone for my Lady and iij for iij Gentlewomen ——Hobbies and Naggs iij as to fay Oone for my Lorde to ryde on Oone led for my Lord ande One fpare —— Sumpter Hors ande Maill Hors iij Viz. One for the Bedd One for the Coffurs ande One for the Maill —— vj Hors for thaym that ar at my Lordes horffing as to fay a Yong Gentleman Hors that is at my Lordes finding The Yoman of the Stabill Hors A Grome of the Chambre Hors at my Lordes finding A Grome of the Sterop Hors Ande ij Horfes for the Sumptermen that leedes the Sumpter Hors —— vij Chariot Hors to draw in the Charriot AFTER xj Quarters and iij Bufhells for every Hors in the faide Hoole Yere after j Peck on the daie for a Hors Which amountith to the Some for a Hors in the faide hoole Yere xviij s. xj d. ob. ANDE foo the hoole Some for the

faide

ſaide xxvij Hors for an Hole Yere is xxv*l*. xj*s*. x*d*. ob. if it be at xx*d*. a quartar.

HALF YERE.

ITEM that the ſaide Stieward Treſaurer Countroller or Clarkes of the Keching whiche dooth ſtonde charged provide for cxxxiij quarters iiij buſhels dimid. bz. of Otes after xx*d*. the quarter for the provaunder of the ſaide xxvij Hors for an half Yere after a Pek on the daie for a Hors Whiche comes to v quarters dimid. and a buſhell demid. for a Hors in the ſaid half Yere which amountith to the Some for a Hors in the ſaid half Yere to ix*s*. v*d*. ob. quadr. Ande ſo th'hoole Som for the ſaide xxvij Hors in the ſaide half Yere is xij*l*. xv*s*. xj*d*. quadr. if it be at xx*d*. the quartar.

QUARTARLY.

ITEM that the ſaide Stieward Treſaurer Countroller or Clarkes of the Kechinge which dooth ſtonde chargid provyde for Lxxvj Quarters vj Buſhells and a Pek of Otes after xx*d*. the Quarter for the Provaunder of the ſaide xxvij Hors for the ſpace of a Quarter of a Yere after j Pek on the daie for a Hors which comes to ij Quarters vj Buſhells and iij Peks for a Hors in the ſaide Quarter of the Yere which amounts to the Som for a Hors in the ſaide Quarter iiij*s*. viij*d*. ob. quadr. dimid. Ande ſo the Hoole Som for the ſaide xxvij Hors in the ſaide Quarter of the Yere is vj *l*. vij*s*. xj*d*. ob. dimid. quadr.

MOUNETHLY.

ITEM that the ſaide Stieward Treſaurer Countroller or Clarkes of the Keching which doeth ſtonde charged provyde for xxv Quarters ij bz. dimid. of Otes after xx*d*. the Quarter for the Provaunder of the ſaide xxvij Hors for the ſpace of a Mouneth after a Pek on the daie for a Hors which comys to vij bz. dimid. for a Hors in the ſaid Mouneth which amountith

R

to

to the Some for a Hors in the faide Mouneth xviij *d*. ob. quadr. Ande fo the Hoole Some for the faide xxvij Hors in the faide Mouneth is xLij*s*. ij*d*. quadr. if it be at xx*d*. the Quarter.

WEEKELIE.

ITEM that the faid Stieward Trefaurer Countroller or Clarkes of the Keching which doeth ftond charged· provide for v quarters vij bufhells and a pec of Ootes after xx*d*. the quarter for the Provaunder of the faide xxvij Hors for the fpace of a Week after a Pek on the daie for a Hors which comes to vij pekks for a Hors in the faide Weeke whiche amountith to the Some for a Hors in the faide Week iiij*d*. quadr. dimid. and foo the Hoole Some for the faide xxvij Hors in the faide Week is ix*s*. ix*d*. ob. if it be at xx*d*. the Quarter.

DAILY.

ITEM that the faide Stieward Trefaurer Countroller or Clarkes of the Keching whiche dooth ftond charged provyde for vj bufhell iij pekks of Otes after ij*d*. ob. the Bufhell for the Provaunder of the faide xxvij Hors for the fpace of a Daie after a Pek on the Daie to every Hors whiche comes to the Some for every Hors on the faide Daie ob. dimid. quadr. Ande foo th'hoole Some for the faide xxvij Hors on a Daie is xvj*d*. ob. quadr. dimid. if it be at ij*d*. ob. the Bufhell and after xx*d*. the Quarter.

DAILY.

ITEM to be paide to the faide Stieward Trefaurer Countroller or Clarkes of the Keching that dooth ftond charged 'to' provyd for cxxxiij Quarters dimid. and dimid. Bufhell of Beanys after ij*s*. the Quarter for Hors Breed to be maide of for th'Expenfes of xxvij Hors of my Lordes to ftond in his Stabill at

the

the charge of the Hous Viz. vj Gentle Hors — iiij Palfries as Oone for my Lady ande iij for my Ladys Gentlewomen — Hobbies and Naggs iij as to fay Oone for my Loorde to ride on One to leed and One fpare—Sumpter Hors ande Maill Hors iij Viz. One for the Bedd One for the Coffurs ande One for the Maill — vj Hors for theme that is at my Lordes horffing Viz. A Yong Gentleman Hors that is at my Loordes finding The Yoman of the Stabill Hors A Grome of the Chambre Hors at my Loordes finding A Grome of the Sterop Hors Ande ij Hors for the Sumptermen that leeds the Sumpter Hors—Ande vij Charriot Hors to draw in the Charriot After v Quarters v Bufhell and a Half of Beans for every of the faid Hors in the Yere Whereof to be maide DCCCCxij Loofs of Hors Breed Viz. of every Quarter CLxxij Loofs after viij Loofs j d. Ande thereof is allowed to be ferved iij Loofs on the Daie to a Hors for Provaunder As to fay Great Hors Palfraies Sumpter Hors Charriot Hors and Maill Hors And for every Nagg ij Loofs which amountith to the Some in th'hoole Yere xj s. iiij d. ob. for every Hors for Provaunder in Beanys after this faid price And fo th'hool Some of Provaunder for the faide xxvij Hors in the faid Hoole Yere xv l. vij s. j d. ob. If it be at ij s. the Quarter Alfo the faid Parfons to provyde for LXXvj Quarters dimid. and ij Bufhells j Pek of Beans after ij s. the Quarter for the Provaunder of the faid xxvij Hors by the fpace of Half a Yere after iij Loofs on the Daie for One Hors which comes to ij Quarters vj Bz. and iiij Peks for a Hors in the faid Half Yere Whereof to be maid CCCCLxvj Loofs after CLxxij Loofs of a Quarter Ande after viij Loofs a penny which amountith to the Some for a Hors in the faid Half Yere v s. viij d. quadr. And fo the hoole Some for the faid xxvij Hors for a Half Yere is vij l. xiij s. vj d. ob. quadr. if it be at ij s. the Quarter.

QUARTERLY.

QUARTERLY.

ITEM that the faide Stieward Trefaurer Countroller or Clarkes of the Keching that dooth ftond charged provyde for xxxviij Quarters iij Bufhell dimid. Pek of Beanys after ij *s.* the Quarter for the Provaunder of the faide xxvij Hors for the fpace of a Quarter of a Yere after iij Loofs on the Day for a Hors for Provaunder Which comes to a Quarter iij bz. and a Pek dimid. for a Hors in the faid Quarter Whereof to be maide ccxxxiiij Loofs after clxxij Loofs of a quarter and after viij Loofs j *d.* Which amountith to the Some for a Hors in the faid quarter ij *s.* x *d.* And foo th'hoole Some for the Provaunder of the faid xxvij Hors in the faid quarter is Lxxvj *s.* ix *d.* quadr. dimid. if it be at ij *s.* a Quarter.

MOUNETHLY.

ITEM that the faid Stieward Trefaurer Countroller or Clarkes of the Keching that dooth ftond charged provyde for xij Quarters of Beannys after ij *s.* the Quarter for the Provaunder of the faid xxvij Hors for the fpace of a Mouneth after iij Loofs on the Daie for a Hors for Provaunder Which comys to iij bufhell iij pekks for a Hors in the faid Mouneth Whereof to be maid iiij fcore x Loofs after viij Loofs a penny Whiche amountith to the Some for a Hors in the faid Mouneth xj *d.* quadr. and foe th'hoole Some for the Provaunder of the faid xxvij Hors in the faid Mouneth is xxiiij *s.* if it be at ij *s.* a Quarter.

WEEKELIE.

ITEM that the faid Stieward Trefaurer Countroller or Clarkes of the Kiching provyde for iij Quarters of Beans after ij *s.* the Quarter for the Provaunder of the faide xxvij Hors for the fpace of a Week after iij Loofs on the Daie to a Hors

for

for Provaunder which comes to iij pekks dimid. for a Hors in the Week after ob. quadr. the pek Whereof to be maid xxj Loofs after viij Loofs a penny Which comes to the Some for a Hors in the Week ij *d.* ob. Ande fo th'hoole Some for the Provaunder of the faid xxvij Hors in the faid Week is vj *s.* if it be at ij *s.* a quarter,

DAILY.

ITEM that the faide Stieward Trefaurer Countroller or Clarkes of the Keching provyde for iij bufhells dimid. of Beans after iij *d.* the Bufhell for the Provaunder of the faid xxvij Hors for a daie Whereof to be maide iiij fcore iiij Loofs after viij Looffes j *d.* Whiche comes to iij Looffes on the daie for a Hors for Provaunder and after quadr, dimid. for a Hors on the daie Ande fo th'hoole Some for the faid xxvij Hors for a Daie is x *d.* quadr. if it be at ij *s.* a quarter.

YERELIE.

ITEM that the faid Stieward Trefaurer Countroller or Clarkes of the Keching that doth ftond chargied provyde for Lxxvj quarters dimid. ij bufhells and a pek of Beans after ij *s.* viij *d.* the quarter for Hors Breed to be maid of for th'expenfes of my Loords Horffes in houfehold for a Hoole Yere Some of the Beans x *l.* iiij *s.* ix *d.* ob. Ande alfo to maike provifion for cxxxiij quarters dimid. and dimid. Bufhell of Otes after xvj *d.* the quarter for th'expenfes of my faid Lordes Horffes in houfehold for the faid Hoole Yere Some of the faid Otes x *l.* iiij *s.* viij *d.* Some xx *l.* ix *s.* vj *d.* Whereof x *l.* iiij *s.* ix *d.* ob. is appointed to be paide to the faide Stieward Trefaurer Countroller or Clarkes of the Kiching for the firft payment Viz. for the provifion of xxxviij quarters iij bufhell dimid. pek of Beans cij *s.* iiij *d.* to be provided at Alhallowtide Ande for provifion of Lxxvj quarters dimid. ij bufhells and a Pek

Pek of Ootes cij s. iiij d. to be provided at the said Alhallowtide to be paid at the saide Criftynmas which Beans and Ootes ar appoynted to serve fro the saide Michaelmas unto our Ladie daie next folloing Ande to be paide to the saide Parsons for the secound payment at Efter x l. iiij s. ix d. Viz. for the provision of xxxviij quarters iij bushells dimid. pek of Beans to be provided at Candlemes after Seed tyme cij s. iiij d. ob. for the provision of Lxxvj quarters dimid. ij bushells j Pek of Otes to be paide at the saide Efter cij s. iiij quadr. to be provided at the said Candlemes affore Seed tyme Which Beans and Otes provyded at the said tyme is appointed to serve from our said Ladye daie in Lent to Michaelmas next folloing And so th'hoole Some appointed for the provision of the said Beans and Ootes for th'expenses of the said Hors for oone hole Yere for the charge of the hous is xx l. ix s. vj d.

YERELIE.

ITEM to be paide to the saide Stieward Tresaurer Controller or Clarkes of the Keching for to provyde for iiij score Loode of Hay after ij s. viij d. the Loode for th'expenses of my Loordes Horsses standing in his Lordeship Stabill at the charge of the hous as to say vj Gentill Hors to stonde in the Stabill at Hay and Hard Meat by the space of the Hoole Yere which ar allowed after every Hors in the said hoole Yere iiij Lood of Hay xxiiij Lood — iiij Palfraies Whereof One for my Ladie ande iij for iij Gentlewomen to stond in the Stabill at Hay and Hard Meat by the space of Half a Yere after a Loode dimid. for every Hors in the said Half Yere vj Loodes — iij Hobbies and Naggs Viz. One for my Loorde to ride on One to be ledd and One to spare to stond in the Stabill at Hay and Hardmeat by the space of the Hoole Yere after ij Loode dimid. for every Nagg in the saide Yere vij Loode dimid. — iij Sumpter-hors ande Maill Hors Viz. One for the bedd One for the Coffurs and One for the Maill to stond in the Stabill at Hay

and

and Hardmeat by the fpace of th'hoole Yere after iij **Loode**
for every Hors in the faide Yere ix Loodes — vj Hors for theym
that is at his Lordefhip Horffing as to fay William **Worme**
Hors The Yoman of the Stabill Hors A Grome of the Stabill
Hors A Grome of the Sterop Hors Ande ij Horffes for the ij
Sumptermen that leedes the Sumpter Hors to ftonde in the
Stabill by the fpace of half a Yere after a Loode dimid. for
a Hors in the faid half Yere ix Loodes — vij Great Trotting
Hors to draw in the Charriot to ftand in the Stabill at Hay
and Hardemeat by the fpace of the hoole Yere after iij loode
dimid. for every Hors in the faid Yere xxiiij Loode dimid. —Ande
iij Myllne Hors as to fay ij to draw in the Milln and one to
carry Stuf to the Milln and fro the Milln to ftonde in the
Stabill by the fpace of the faid hoole Yere after iij loode dimid.
for every Hors in the faid Yere And Half a Loode les for
theym all in the faid Yere x loodes.

HALF YERE.

ITEM to be paide to the faide Stieward Trefaurer Countroller or Clarks of the Kiching that dooth ftond chargied
provide for iiij fcore xiij loods dimid. of Hay after ij *s*. viij *d*.
the Loode for th'expenfes of my Lordes Horffes ftanding in
his Lordefhip Stabill at the charge of the hous for one Halfe
Yere Some xij *l*. viij *s*. Which is appointed to be paide to the
faid Parfons at Michaelmas in th'end of the Yere And fo
th'hoole Some to be paid for full contentacion of the faid Hay
for my Lordes Horffes for an hoole Yere is . . . .

MOUNETHLY.

ITEM it is Ordeyned that thees Horffes folloing in the charge
of the hous be put to Grefs Yerely from Saint Elyn daie unto
Michaelmas next folloing as the names of theym hereafter
folloith

folloith Viz. iiij Palfrays Whereof one for my Ladie ande iij for iij Gentlewomen vj Hors for theme that ar at my Lordes Horffing Viz. A Yong Gentlman Hors at my Loordes finding The Yoman of the Stabill Hors A Grome of the Chambre Hors at my Lordes finding A Grome of the Sterop Hors And a Nagg for the Chariotmen to ride upon And ij Hors for the twoo Sumptermen that leedes the Sumpter Hors And at Michaelmas the faid Hors is to be taken up again to the Stabill and to ftond at hard meat to Saint Elyn daie next after being in the New Yere for th'accompt of the hous of the Yere folloing and fo to be ordeyned and kept Yerelie.

DAYLY.

ITEM it is Ordered that the Clarkes of the Keching whenfoever they taik Brevementes that th'Officers of Houfeholde doth breve in the Countinghous The faid Clarkes to write th'Officers Surname to th'entent whenfoever the Deficients be drawyn and caftyn by th'audit in th'Officers necks of houfehold that he fhall not thraw the faid deficients in an Officer neck whiche occupieth whiche Deficient was in the tyme of hym that is departed but that he fhall maik it knowne in whoos tyme the faid Deficients was in.

AT every REMEVING of my Lordes Hous.

ITEM a Chequirroll to be maide at all fuch tymes when his Lordefhip brekith up Hous of the Names of the Parfons that fhall be within at meat ande drink with my Lorde ande to gif attendaunce uppon his Lordefhip To be Signed with my Lordes hand.

AT

AT every REMEVING of my Lordes Hous.

ITEM a Chequirroull to be maide of the Names of the Parfons that fhall goo to Borde Wagies in the Town where his Lordefhip lieth to his Lordefhip remeve and fettes up hous agayn To be figned with my Lordes hande.

AT every REMEVING of my Lords Hous.

ITEM a Chequirroull to be maide of the Names of the Parfons that fhall go affore unto the place where his Lordefhipp remeves unto for the preparing of all thing there To be fignyd with my Lordes hand.

AT every REMEVING of my Lordys Hous.

ITEM a Chequirroull to be maide of the Names of my Lordes Houfhold Servaunts that be abfent afwell aboute his Lordefhip bufynes as there owne bufynes Ande to have no Borde Wagies allowed theym for the faid Caufe To be fignyd with my Lordes hande.

AT every REMEVING of my Lords Houfe.

ITEM a Chequirrooll to be maide of the Names of my Lordes Houfhold Servauntes appointed to bide ftill in any place by my Lordes comaundment Ande for what caufes they be left there behind Ande the faid Chequirroull to be fignyd with my Lordes hande.

S   AT

AT every REMEVING of my Lordes Hous.

ITEM a Chequirroll to be maide at all fuch tymes when my Loorde breks upp hous of the Names of the Parfons that be at Borde Wagies at the charge of the Hous by my Lordes Comaundment Whiche my Lord giffeth theym for there Frendes faiks notwithftanding that they ar not entered in the Chequirroll Ande to be figned with my Lordes hande.

MOUNETHLY.

ITEM a bill to be made at th'ende of every Mouneth of the clere Expenfes of my Lordes Hous for the faide Mouneth Ande every Man to be rated what he ftandes in the meall the Day the Weeke ande the Mouneth.

YERELY.

ITEM that the Clarkes of the Kechyn or of the Brevements every Yere bring my Lorde a Bill of the Remaneth takyn at the faide Michaelmas be looked uppon Ande if if amount to a more Some than the Remaneth whiche is fet in the begynnyng of Orders of Houfehold than fo much as it amountith to more to be abated in the Fyrfte Warraunt for the Affignement of the houfe in the firft quarter bitwixt Michaelmas ande Criftynmas Yerely Ande if the Remaneth fortune to be lefs than is appointed in the begynnyng of the Booke of Orders that than the Fyrft Warraunt for the Affignement of the hous in the fyrft quarter bitwixt Michaelmas ande Criftynmas be made fo muche more as the money wanting of the faide Remeneth bicaus of making oute of the hoole Affignementt.

YERELY.

YERELY.

ITEM that the Clarks of the Kitchyng or of the Count-
yng Hous make my Lorde a Bill Yerely at Michaelmas at
th'ende of the Yere what Remaneth of the Monay affigned
for the kepyng of the hous for that Yere to there hands
comyng As to fay remanyng of the Houfehold Wagies of
the Chapell Wagies of the Wynter Horfsmeat Yerely of the
Totiell Some of the Remaneth remanynge unfpent of the
faide Yere or any other Empcions that ar bought better
cheep then the prices appointed in the Booke of Orders of
the Houfe That my Lorde may fe what remaned fpared for
thees forefaid caufes.

YERELY.

THE COPY of the FYRSTE WARRAUNT for
th'Affignement of my Lordes Houfe When the Remaneth is more than is rated in this Booke.

WELBILOVIDE I grete you wele ande wol ande charge
you (all excufes and delayes laide aparte) as ye intende to
have me youre goode Lorde ande wol exchew that at may
enfewe unto you for the contrary doyng Ye faill not furthwith
uppon the fight hereof to content ande pay to my welbilovid
Servaunts Robart Percy Countrolher of my houfe ande Gilbert
Weddell Chief Clark of my Kytchyn ftandyng charged with
my faide houfe this Yere in full contentacion for the firft
payment of th'affignement affignide unto theym for kepyng
of my faide houfe for this Yere begynnyng at Michaelmas
in the vjᵗʰ Yere of the reign of our Soverain Lorde King
Henry the viijᵗʰ of the Revenus of all my Lands within
Yorkefhire whiche fhal be dew unto me at this Audiet to your
hands

hands comyng to my Coffers where is feen by me ande my Counfaill that ye do pay but the Some of cxLj *l.* xj *s.* vj *d.* ob. quadr. in full contentacion of there Some affignede for there Fyrft Payment at this tyme of ccxxxvj *l.* x *s.* iij *d.* quadr. Seyng that they have receyvede in the price of divers Victualls in there laft Remaneth remanyng of the Yere ended at Michaelmas the Some of Lxxvj *l.* x *s.* iij *d.* quadr. Which makith up the forefaide Some affigned theme for the Fyrft Payment of the Fyrft Quarter Whiche Remaneth amountith to more than the Remaneth accuftumed in the Booke of Orders by the Some of xviij *l.* viij *s.* v *d.* quadr. For whiche concideracion there is clere payd unto theym at this tyme bot the Som of cxLj *l.* xj *s.* vj *d.* ob. quadr. bicaus of the batement of the forefaide xviij *l.* viij *s.* v *d.* quadr. whiche they have more in the Remaneth of this Yere than they hadd the laft Yere GEVEN at my Caftell of Wrefill the xiiij^th day of October in the vj^th Yere of the reign of our Sovereign Lorde King Henry the viij^th.

> TO my Trufty Servaunt WILLIAM WORM Gentleman Ufharr of my Chambre my Coffurer ande Generall Receyvour of all my Landys in the North Parties for this Yere.

YERELY.

THE COPY of the LAST WARRAUNT for th'Affignement of my Lords Hous.

WELBILOVYD I grete you wele ande wol ande ftrately charge you without delay as ye intende to have me your good Lorde ande wol exchew that at may infew unto you

for

for the contrary doyng at your jeopardy Faill not to content ande pay to my welbiloved Servaunts Robart Percy
Countroller of my Hous ande Gilbert Weddell Cheef Clarke
of my Kichyng ftandyng charged with my faide Houfe for
the vijth and laft payment of th'Affignement affigned unto
theym for the kepyng of my faide Hous for this Yere begynnyng at Michaelmas in the vjth Yere of the reign of
our Sovereign Lorde Kyng Henry the viijth and fhall ende
at Michaelmas next following of the Revenus of all my
Landes in Northumbrelande to your handes comyng dewe
to my Coffers of the Whitfonday Ferm payabill at Lambmes
Ye content and pay the Some of ciiij $l.$ xiiij$s.$ ix$d.$ in redy
Monay over ande befids that they have xv $l.$ vj$s.$ charged
upon theym the faide tyme as parcell of there Affignement
as in the Fermes of divers Meddowes ande Paftures at
Lekyngfeld ande Wrefill as it appereth more playnly in the
Booke of Orders of my faide Hous for the makyng up of
cxxj $l.$ ix$d.$ affigned unto theym in the iiijth quarter bitwixt
Midfommer and Michaelmas Whiche is in full payment
of there Hole Affignement for this Hoole Yere endyng
at the faid Michaelmas next for to come GEVEN under my
Signet and Sign Manuell at my Manour of Lekynfeld the
xxjth day of Novembre in the vjth Yere of the reign of our
Soverayn Lorde Kyng Henry the viijth.

> TO my Trufty Servaunt WILLIAM
> WORME Gentleman Ufhar of my
> Chambre my Coffurer ande my Re-
> ceyvoure Generall of all my Lands in
> the North Parties for this Yere.

YERELY.

YERELY.

ITEM that the Clarks of the Kitchyng or of the Countynghous make my Lorde a Bill Yerely at Michaelmas at th'ende of the Yere of every grofs Empcion bought that Yere for th'expenfes of my Lords Hous What it doth excede if any be above the prices appointed in the Booke of Orders of the Hous That my Lorde may fee wherein he is charged more for that caus in the faide grofs Empciens.

WEEKLY.

ITEM it is Ordered ande Agreide by my Lorde his Heed Officers ande Counfaill that the Baker fhall Aunfwarr my Lorde of every Quarter of Wheet in Manchetts DCXL after ij Maunchetts to a Loof of houfehold Breed Of Houfehold Breed cciiij fcore ande of Trenchor Breed cciiij fcore bicaus the Loofs of the Trenchor Breed be larger than the Loofs of Houfeholde Breed.

MOUNTHLY.

ITEM it is Ordered ande Agreed by my Lorde his Heed Officers of Houfehold and Counfaill that there fhal be vj Quarters of Malt brewed at every Brewynge in his Houfe thrughoute the Yere Whereof to be maide at every Brewing of every Quarter of Malte whiche is brewed in my Lords Hous in Winter xij Hoggefheds after ij Hoggefhedes to a Quarter And in Somer xj Hoggefheds after ij Hoggefheds of a Quarter Some a Hoggefhed les at all Bicaus the faid Beere muft be maide bygger in Somer than in Winter for turnynge.

DAILY.

DAILY.

ITEM it is Ordered by my Lorde his Heed Officers of Houſeholde and Counſaill that there ſhal be ſtrikkyn of every Carcaſs of Beef Lxiiij Stroks whiche is after xvj Stroks of every Quarter and after iiij Tilde in every Quarter and after iiij Stroks in every Tylde.

DAILY.

ITEM it is Ordered by my Lords Heed Officers of Houſehold and Counſaill that there ſhal be ſtrikkyn of every Carcaſs of Muton xij Stroks after iij Stroks in every Quarter.

DAILY.

ITEM it is Orderede by my Lords Heede Officers of Houſehold and Counſaill that there ſhal be ſtrikkyn of every Veell xvj Stroks after iiij Stroks of every Quarter.

DAILY.

ITEM it is Orderede by my Lords Heed Officers of Houſehold and Counſaill that there ſhal be ſtrikkyn of every Pork xxꝰ Strokes after v Strooks in every Quarter.

WEEKELEY.

ITEM it is Ordered by my Lordes Heedes Officers of Houſehold ande Counſaill that there ſhal be ſtrikkyn of every Saltfiſche called a Lyng Fiſche vj Stroks after iij Strooks in a Side.

WEEKELY.

WEEKELY.

ITEM it is Orderede by my Lords Heede Officers of Householde and Counſaill that there ſhal be ſtrikkyn of every Saltfiſhe callede a Habberdyn Fiſche iiij Stroks after ij Stroks in ather Syde.

WEEKELY.

ITEM it is Ordered by my Lordes Heede Officers of Houſeholde and Counſaill that there ſhal be ſtrikkyn of every Salt Salmon xij Stroks after 'iij Stroks *' in every Quarter.

WEEKELY.

ITEM it is Ordered by my Lords Heed Officers of Houſehold ande Counſaill that there ſhal be ſtrikkyn of every Stokfiſhe iiij Stroks after ij Stroks in every Side.

* The MS. read 'iiij Stroks': but this muſt be a Miſtake.

XXII.

XXII.

A BREWYING at WRESILL.

FYRSTE paide at Wrefill for vi quarters of Malte after v s. the quartir — xxx s.

Item paide for vl lb. Hopps for the faide Brewynge after j d. ob. the lb. — ix d.

Item paide for v fcore Faggitis for the faide Brewynge, after v Fagotts j d. ande after ij s. the c. — xx d.

SUMMA xxxij s. v d.

Wherof is made xij Hoggeshedes of Beyr Every Hoges- hede contenyng xlviij Gallons Which is in all cccciiij^{xx} xvj gall. aftir ob. qu. the Gall. Save iij s. vij d. les at all — xxxij s. v d.

A BREWYNG at WRESILL and carryede to TOPCLIF.

Fyrfte paide for vj quarters Malte at Wrefill after v s. the quarter — xxx s.

Item paide for vj lb. Hopps for the faid Brewyng after j d. ob. the lb. — jx d.

Item paide for v fcore Faggots for the faid Brewyng after v faggotts j d. — xx d.

T

Item

Item paide for Carriage of the said Brewyng from Wresill to Borrow - brigg by watir Viz. xij Hogeshedes whiche makith iij Tonns after iiij s. v d. the Tonne and a penny more at all — xiij s. iiij d.

Item paide for the Hire of iij Wanys for carrying of the said iij Tonne from Borrow-brigg to Topclyf after viij d. for the Hyer of every Wayne — ij s.

SUMMA xlvij s. ix d.

Wherof is made xij Hoggeshedes of Beyr Every Hogges-hede contenyng xlviij gallons Whiche is in all cccciiij ˣˣ xvj gallons after a Penny the Gallon and iij d. les at all Which is derer by qu. in every gallon Save iij s. iiij d. les at all — xlvij s. ix d.

MALTE bought at WRESILL ande carried to TOPCLIF to be brewed there.

Fyrste paide for vj quarters of Malte bought at Wresill aftir v s. the quarter — xxx s.

Item paide for Carryage of the said Malte from Wresill to Borrow-brigg by watier aftir viij d. the Carriage of every quartir — iiij s.

Item paid for the Hire of a Wayn for Carriage of the said Malte from Borrow-brig to Topclyf — viij d.

Item paid for vj lb. Hopps for the saide Brewynge aftir j d. ob. the lb. — jx.

Item paid for v ˣˣ Fagotts for the said Brewyng after v Fagotts j d. and after ij s. c. — xx d.

SUMMA xxxvij s. j d.

Wherof

Wherof is made xij Hoggesheds of Beyr Every Hoggs. contenyng xlviij Gallons Which is in all cccciiij^{xx} xvj Gallons aftir ob. qu. the Gallon Ande xiij d. more at all Whiche is better cheep by qu. in every gallon Save x d. more at all — xxxvij s. j d.

MALTE bought at TOPCLIF ande Brewede there.

Fyrfte paide for vj quarters Malt bought at Topclif after vj s. viij d. the quarter — xl s.

Item paide for vj lb. Hopps for the faid Brewyng aftir j d. ob. the lb. — jx d.

Item paide for v^{xx} Fagotts for the faide Brewyng after v fagotts a penny ande aftir ij s. c. — xx d.

SUMMA — xlij s. v d.

Wherof is made xij Hoggeshades of Beyr every Hoggs-heed contenyng xlviij Gallons Whiche is in all cccciiij fcore xvj Gallons aftir ob. qu. dimid. the Gallon And v d. more at all Which is derrer by dimid. quad. in every Gallon fave vij d. more at all — xlij s. v d.

BEYR brewyd at REPONNE.

ITEM paide for xxiiij Barrells of Beyr bought at Reponne Which maketh xij Hoggefhedes Every Hoggefheed contenyng xlviij Gallons Whiche is in alle cccciiii^{xx} xvj Gallons aftir ij d. the Gallon Whiche is deerer by j d. dim. quad. in every Gallon fave vij d. les at all Than any of the other Wayes — iiij l. xvj s.

XXIII. THE

XXIII.

THE NAMES OF ALL MANER OF BILLIS that muſt be made the Houſhold at DIUERS TYMES of the Yeir as hereafter followith Ande at whatte TYMES they ſhal be maide.

THEES BILLIS following to be maid Yeirly at MI-CHAELMES for the ful fyniſhing of all maner of Billes for the OLDE YEIR ending at the ſaid Michaelmes for the Hous As the names of theim hereaftir followith.

FURSTE a Bill of the Remaneth of all the Stuf Remanyng unſpente provided for th'exſpencis of my Lordes Hous endid at Michaelmes Yeirely.

I T E M a Bille of Paymente of Quartir Wagies to the Gentlemen of my Lordes Chapell from Midſomer to Mi-chaelmes.

ITEM a Bille of Chekke of Paymente of Borde Waigies of my Lords Servauntes from Midſomer to Michaelmes.

Item a Bille of Payment of Somer Horſſemete to my Lordes Servauntes of the Riding Houſhold from Sainte Elynne Day to Michaelmes to be made at Michaelmes.

Item a Bille of the Chekke of the ſaim.

Item

Item a Bill of Paymente of Wagies to my Lordes Houſhold Servauntes for the Half Yeir begynnyng at our Lady daye in Lente ande ending at Michaelmes.

Item a Bill of Chek of the ſaim.

Item a Bill of the Naimes of all maner of Creditours with the Names of all maner of Stuf taiken of them for th'exſpences of my Lordes Hous for the Yeir ending at this Michaelmes whiche be unpaide foir.

Item a Bille of the Names of the Parſons that been abſente as well aboute my Lordes buſineſs as their owne buſines in the ſaide Quarter from Midſomer to Michaelmes.

Item a Bill of Chekk of the Quartir Waiges of the Gentle-men of my Lordes Chappell from Midſomer to Michalmes.

THEIS BILLIS folloing to be made Yeirly at MI-CHAELMES for the NEW YEIR begynnyng at the ſaide Michaelmes for the Hous As the Names of theme hereaftir followeth.

FYRST the Hoole Chequirroill of the Noumbre of this Yeir.

Item a Quartir Chequirroill of all my Lordes Servauntes to be in Hous from Michaelmes to Criſtenmes.

Item a Bill of my Lordes Servauntes that haithe no Borde Waiges allowid bicaus they have Licens to go about their owne buſines from Michaelmes to Sainte Androw-tyde.

Item

Item a Bill of my Lordes Houſhold Servauntes that ſhal be within at Meat and Drinke wheir my Lord ande my Laidy lieth to my Lord ſet upp his Houſs again.

Item a Bill of the Names of my Lordes Servauntes that ſhall gif their Attendaunce upon my Lord and my Laidy Ande to be at Bourde in the Towne wheir my Lord lieth.

Item a Bill of the Names of the Parſonnes appointed Yeirly at Michaelmes by my Lord and his Counſaill to be of the Riding Houſhold ande to have Winter Horſſemeat allowed theime.

Item a Bill of the Naimes of my Lordes Ordinary Offycers and Servauntes appointid to be Quartir Waiters in every of the iiij Quartirs of the Yeir.

Item a Bill of the Noumbre of all the Horſſis of my Lordes ande my Laidies that ar apointid to be at the charge of the Hous for the Hoole Yeir.

Item a Bill of the Names of the Parſonnes that ar mo in the Rowmes of the Chequirroil thanne ar apointed in the Booke of Orders of the Hous abidyng in the Hous at Michaelmes.

Item a Bill of the Names of the Parſonnes that wantis in the Rowmes of the Noumbre appointed in the Booke of Orders to be in the Chequirroill at the ſaide Michaelmes.

Item a Bill of the Names of the Perſonnes that ar daly in the Houſs and ſhal be at Meat and Drinke this ſaide Quartir from Michaelmes to Chriſtenmes which be not in the Chequirroill at this ſaide Michaelmes.

Item ·

Item a Bill of the Names of the Parſonnes that ar in the Chequirroil ande Ordeignid to go to Borde Waigies in the Towne from Michaelmes to Chriſtenmes ande not to be at Meat and Drink in the Houſs.

Item a Bill of all ſuche Stuf as is to be provided for th'expences of my Lordes Houſs for the Quarter from Michaelmes to Criſtenmes.

Item a Bill to be made in the Quartir from Michaelmes too Criſtenmes yf my Lorde braike up Houſs of the Naimes of the Parſonnes that ſhal be at Bord Waigies at the charge of the Houſs by my Lordes Comaundemente whiche be not in the Chequirroill the ſaide Quartir.

Item a Warraunte for taïkyng upp of Swannes for th'exſpences of my Lordes Houſs for the Quartir from Michaelmes too Chriſtenmes.

Item vij Warrauntes for the Hoole Aſſignemente for keaping of my Lordes Houſs the ſaide Yeir begynnyng at Michaelmes.

Item xvij Warrauntes for xxix Dois for th'expences of my Lords Houſs for this Wynter of this Yeir begynnyng at Michaelmes.

Item a Bill of Cheke of the Payment of Quartir Waiges to the Gentilmen of my Lordes Chapell for the Quarter bitwix Michaelmes and Criſtynmes.

Item a Bill to be maide Yerely at Mychaelmes of the Namys of the Parſons which ſhal be within at Meat and Drink wher my Lord kepith his Secrete Houſe and to brevid at Strangers.

THEIS

THEIS BILLYS following to be made Yerly at CRIS-TYNMAS for that Quarter as the Namys of theim hereafter folloith.

FIRSTE a Quartar Chequirroill off my Lordes Housholde Servaunts to be in Hous from Cristynmas to oure Lady day in Lentt.

Item a Bill of the paymente of the Quartar Wages too the Gentillmen of my Lordys Chapell from Michalmas to Chriftynmas.

Item a Bill of the Namys of the Parfonnys of the Chequirroill appointed to goo to Borde Wages the faide Quartar from Criftynmas to oure Lady day in Lente.

Item a Bill of the Chekk of Paymente of Borde Wages to my Lords Servaunts from Michalmas to Criftynmas.

Item a Bill of the Chekk of the Parfonnys abfence of the names of theym that wente to Borde Wages the faide Quartar from Michalmas to Criftynmas.

Item a Bill of the Parfonnys that arr mo in the Rowmys in the Chequirroill than ar appointed in the Booke of Orders in the Hous abiding in the Hous at Criftynmas.

Item a Bill of the Namys of the Parfonnys that wants in the Rowmys of the Noumbre appointed in the Booke of Ordours to be in the Chequirroill now at the faide Criftynmas.

Item

Item a Bill of the Namys of the Parſonnys that ar daily in the Hous ande ſhal be at Meat and Drynke in the Hous this ſaide Quartar from Criſtynmas to oure Lady day in Lente whiche be not in the Chequirroill at the ſaide Criſtynmas.

Item a Bill of alle the Creditours that haith any Monay owing unto theym for Stuf takyn for th'expenſes of my Lordys Hous for the ſaide Quartar from Michaelmas to Criſ-tynmas.

Item a Bill of the Namys of alle ſuch Stuf as is to be provided for the ſaide Quartar.

Item a Bill to be made in the ſaide Quartar from Criſtyn-mas to oure Lady day if my Lorde breake up Hous of the Namys of the Parſonnys that ſhal be at Borde Wages at the Charge of the Hous by my Lords Comandment whiche be not in the Chequirroill.

Item a Bill of Chek of Quarter Waigeth * to the Gentil-men of my Lordes Chapell for the Quarter bitwix Criſtynmes and our Ladie Daie in Lent.

THEIS BILLES following to be made Yerely at our LADY DAYE in Lente for that Quarter as the Namys of them hereafter followith.

FIRSTE a Chequirroill of all my Lordys Houſhold Ser-vaunts to be in Hous from our Lady Day in Lente to Mid-ſommer.

U   Item

* So in the MS. for ' Quarter Wages.'

Item a Bill of Payment of Quarter Wages to the Gentlemen of my Lords Chappell from Criftynmas to oure Lady Day.

Item a Bill of Paymente of Wages to my Lordes Houfeholde Servaunts for T'half Yere begynnyng at Michaelmas ande ending at our Lady Day.

Item a Bill of the Chekk of T'half Yere Wages to my Lordys Houfehold Servaunts from Michaelmas to our Lady Day.

Item a Bill of the Namys of the Parfonnys appointed Yerely at Saynt Elyn day to be of the Riding Houfeholde ande to have Somer Horffemeat allowid them.

Item a Bill of the Parfonnys of the Chequirroill appointed to go to Borde Wages from our Lady Day to Midfommer.

Item a Bill of the Namys of the Parfonnys that ar mo in the Rowmys in the Chequirroill thanne ar appointed in the Booke of Ordours of the Hous abiding in the Hous at our Lady Day.

Item a Bill of the Namys of the Parfonnys that wants in the Rowmys of the Noumbre appointed in the Booke of Ordours to be in the Chequirroill at our Lady Day.

Item a Bill of the Namys of the Parfons that ar daily in the Hous at Meat ande Drinke from oure Lady Day too Midfommer whiche be not in the Chequirroill at our faid Lady Day.

Item a Bill of the Namys of all manar of Creditours that haith any Monay owing unto them for Stuf takynne for th'expences th'expences of my Lords Hous for the faide Quarter from Criftynmas to our Lady Day.

Item a Bill of the Namys of all fuche Stuf as is to be provided for the Hous for this faide Quarter from our faide Lady Daye to Midfommer.

Item a Bill of the Namys of the Parfonnys that been abfent as well aboute there own Bufinefs as my Lordes Bufynefs the faide Quarter from Criftynmas to our Lady Day.

Item a Bill to be made in the faide Quarter from our Lady Daye to Midfommar if my Lorde breake up Hous of the Namys of the Parfonnys that fhal be at Borde Wages at the Charge of the Hous by my Lords Comaundemente whiche be not in the Chequirroill the faid Quarter.

Item a Bill of Chek of the Payment of Quarter Wages to the Gentilmen of my Lordes Chapell from our Lady Daye in Lent to Mydfomer.

THEIS BILLYS folloing to be made Yerely at MID-SOMMER for that Quartar as the Namys of them hereafter followith.

FIRSTE a Quartar Chequirroill of alle my Lordes Houfholde Servaunts to be in Hous from Midfommer to Michaelmas.

Item a Bill of the Payment of the Quarter Wages to the Gentlemen of my Lords Chappell from our Lady Day to Midfommer.

Item

Item a Bill of the Parſonnys of the Chequirroill appointed to goo to Borde Wages the ſaide Quarter from our Lady Day to Midſommer.

Item a Bill of the Namys of the Parſonnys that ar mo in the Rowmys in the Chequirroill thanne ar appointed in the Boke of Ordours of the Hous abiding in the Hous at Midſomar.

Item a Bill of the Namys of the Parſonnys that wants in the Rowmys of the Noumbre appointed in the Booke of Ordors to be in the Chequirroill at the ſaide Midſommar.

Item a Bill of the Chekk of Payment of Borde Wages to my Lords Servaunts in the Chequirroill the ſaide Quarter from our Lady Day to Midſommar.

Item a Bill of Paymente of Winter Horſſemeat to my Lords Servaunts of the Riding Houſchold from Michalmas to Saint Elyn Daye to be made at Midſommar.

Item A Bill of Chekk of Payment of the Winter Horſſemet to my Lords Servaunts of the Riding Houſehold to be made at the ſaide Midſommar.

Item a Bill of the Namys af the Parſonnys that ar daily in the Hous at Meat and Drinke from Midſommar to Michaelmas whiche be not in the Chequirroill at the ſaid Midſomar.

Item a Bill of alle the Creditours that haith any Monay owing unto theym for Stuf takyn for th'expences of my Lords Hous for the ſaide Quarter from oure Lady Day to Midſommar.

Item

Item a Bill of the Namys of all fuche Stuf as is to be provided for the Hous this faide Quarter.

Item a Bill of the Namys of the Perfonnys that been abfent as well aboute my Lords Bufinefs as there own Bufinefs this faide Quarter from our Lady Day too Midfommar.

Item a Bill to be made in the faide Quarter from Midfommar to Michalmas if my Lorde breake up Hous of the Namys of the Parfonnys that fhal be at Borde Wages at the Charge of the Hous by my Lords Commandment Which be not in the Chequirroill the faide Quarter.

Item a Bill of Chek of the Payment of Quarter Wagies to the Gentilmen of my Lords Chapell from Mydfomer to Mychelmes.

*XXIIII.

XXIIII.

THEIS BE THE BILLS that muſt be made
MOUNETHLY every Mouneth thurrewte the
Yere.

ITEM Billys of the Remaneth to be made at the ende of
every Mouneth.

Item that a Bill of the Deficients of every Officer be made
at th'ende of every Mouneth.

Item a Bill to be made to my Lorde for a Pye at the
ende of every Mouneth of the clere Expenſes of my Lords
Houſe for the ſaide Mouneth Ande every Man to be ratidd
what he ſtandys in the Meall the Daye the Weke ande
the Mouneth.

Item to make my Lorde a Bill at th'ende of every Moneth
what Monay is Receyvide for th'expenſis of my ſaid Lordys
Hous.

Item to make my Lorde a Bill at th'ende of every Moneth
what Monay is laide oute for Stuf bought for the Expenſis of
my Lordys Hous the ſaide Mouneth.

Item to make my Lorde a Bill at th'ende of every Mouneth
what Stuf is provided for the ſaide Hous ande unpaide fore.

XXV.

XXV.

THEIS BE THE BILLS that muſt be made at every **RENEWALLE** when my Lorde braks up Hous.

FIRSTE a Chequirroil of the Parſonnes that ſchal be within at Meat and Drinke where my Lorde is and gif there Atendaunce upon my Lorde.

Item a Chequirroil of the Parſons that ſchal goo to Borde Wagies in the Towne where my Lorde lieth to my Lorde Set up his Hous agayn.

Item a Chequirroill of the Parſonnes that ſhal go afore unto the Place where my Lorde remevith unto and make reddy for my Lorde there.

Item a Chequirroil of the Parſonnes that be abſent as well by Licence as about there owne Buſines ande to have no Bordewages alowid theme for that cauſe.

Item a Chequirroil of the Parſonnes appointedde to abide ſtill in any place by my Lords Comandement ande for what cauſe.

Item a Chequirroil of the Parſonnes that be atte Borde Wages at the charge of the Hous ande not in the Chequirroil whiche my Lorde giffith theme for there Frends ſaike.

Item

Item a Chequirroil too be made of fuche Parfonnes as fhal be at Meate and Drinke daily wheir my Lord fhall keap his Hous at fuche tymes as he brakithe up his Houf-hold Ande how they fhall ferve at Mealls ande outhir tymes.

XXVI.

XXVI.

A SHORTE DRAUGHT made of TH'ORDER of my Lordes SERVAUNTES of the RIDING HOUS-HOLDE As well Winter as Somer How they fhal be appointed to gif their Attendaunce daily at every tyme when my Lorde rides As hereaftir followith.

THE NAMES of all fuyche PARSONS that RIDES befoir with hym that goith to taike up my Lordes Lodginges when his Lordefchipp rides — v.

FYRSTE A Yoman Ufcher of the Chamber for taking of my Lordes Lodginges.

ITEM A Clarke of the Keching to go befoire to fe all thinges takyn in for the Offices againft th'Officers cuming.

ITEM A Yoman Ufcher of the Hall for Herbigiours for my Lordes Servauntes.

ITEM A Groim of the Chaumbere for keping of my Lordes Chaumbere.

ITEM A Yoman or Groim Cooke to go befoire for making redy for my Lorde.

X   THE

THE NAMES of the **PARSONNES** that goith before daily with the **CLOITHSAKKE** — iiij.

FIRSTE a Yoman or Groim Porter for keping the Yaites.

ITEM a Grome Sumpterman for the Clothſakke with
the Bedde.

ITEM a Grome Sumpterman for the Clothſakke with
the Coffurs.

ITEM All Gentlemen Servauntes too awaite uppon the
Cloithſakkes.

THIES BE THE NAMES of the **PARSONNES**
that ſhal ride befoir my Lorde when His Lordſchip
rides. — jx.

FIRST A Yoman of the Seller to ride befoire with
the Cup.

ITEM Marſchalles of the Hall.

ITEM an Officer of Armes.

ITEM all outher Gentlemen being their to ride befoire
my Lorde in like caaſe.

ITEM a Gentleman Uſchere of the Chambere.

ITEM

ITEM a Sewar for my Lorde.

ITEM a Carver for my Lorde.

ITEM a Cupberer for my Lorde.

ITEM a Chaplayn for my Lorde.

THIES BE THE NAMES of the PARSONNES
That fhal attende ande com bihind my Lorde when his Lordefchip rides — xviij.

FYRST The Yoman of the Robes.

ITEM the Yoman of the Horfs.

ITEM Yomen of the Chaumbere.

ITEM the Yoman of the Pantry.

ITEM the Yoman of the Buttery.

ITEM Yomen Waiters.

ITEM a Groim of the Chaumbere.

ITEM the Groim of th'Ewry.

ITEM A Clarke of the Signet.

ITEM A Clarke of the Forein Expences.

ITEM

ITEM A Groim of the Waredrobe.

ITEM A Groim of the Steropp.

ITEM all outher Yomen being with my Lorde to ride bibinde my Lorde in like caas.

XXVII.

XXVII.

THIS IS THE DRAUGHT of TH'ASSYGNE-MENT of my Lords HOUS How it is thought good that it fhal be orderid and aplied ande kept at this STYNTE following for a YERE With the DEUDUC-TIONS not expended to be abaited oute of the faid Somme.

THE ASSIGNEMENT now is Dcccccxxxiii *l*. vj *s*. viii *d*. Whiche mufte be more in MEAT and DRINKE ande WAGES if it be kept according to the Che-quiroill As to faye — in WAGES xLv *l*. xiiij *s*. — Ande in METE and DRINKE cxxxv *l*. xvij *s*. — SUMMA of both the faid Summes is more by c. iiij fcore j *l*. xj *s*. And fo T'hoole Some With the fore-faide Some of Dcccccxxxiij *l*. vj *s*. viij *d*. for the HOUS to be kepte aftir this rate appointed in the Booke mufte be — Mcxiiij *l*. xvij *s*. viij *d*.

THEIS AR THE PARCELLYS that ar Deducted oute of the forefaid Some for every maner of thing with the Va-lour of it that muft be provided for the Keping of the faid Hous the faid Year.

FIRSTE for Lynnon Cloth to be bought — xLvj *s*. viij *d*.

ITEM for Hyer of Pewter Veffell — xL *s*.

ITEM

ITEM for Counterfete Veffell ande Rughe Veffell to be bought — cx *s.*

ITEM for Brafs Potts to be bought — xxvj *s.* viij *d.* †

ITEM for Stoon Crucis to be bought — x *s.*

ITEM for Se-colls to be bought — xix *l.* iij *s.* iiij *d.*

ITEM for Charcoole to be bought — xx *s.*

ITEM for Fewell of Wodd to be bought — vij *l.* xvj *s.* ij *d.*

ITEM for Provaunder for my Lords Horffes — x *l.*

ITEM for Shoing of my Lords Horffes — xx *l.* †

ITEM for Rewards to Players in Criftynmas — Lxxij *s.* †

ITEM for Cofts neceffary — xLvj *s.* viij *d.* †

ITEM for Chappell Wages — xxxv *l.* xv *s.*

ITEM for Houfhold Wages — cLiij *l.* vj *s.* viij *d.*

ITEM for Winter Horffe-meat — xxiiij *l.*

ITEM for Somer Horffe-meat — viij *l.*

Summa totalis of
alle the faid De-
duCtions * is — cccxviij *l.* vj *s.* vj *d.*

ANDE

* This Sum Total does not correfpond with the Particulars, which amount but to 296 *l.* 13 *s.* 2 *d.* This makes it probable that fome Article is omitted above in the Original Copy amounting to 21 *l.* 13 *s.*

ANDE ſo T'HOOLE ASSIGNEMENT for the Hoole Yere alle the Deuductions abaited as is aforſaide oute of t'hoole Some of мcxiiij *l.* xvij *s.* viij *d.* is clere remanyng for Mete and Drinke — ᴅcciiij˟˟ xvj *l.* xj *s.*

THE HOOLE EXPENSES of viij˟˟ vj Parſonnys whiche is now the full Noumber appointed in the Chequirroille aftir ij *d.* ob. a man a Meal and aftir xvij *d.* ob. a man a Weke And aftir ʟxxj *s.* vj *d.* a man for the Hoole Yere without any Vacants amountith to the ·Hoole Some for the fore- ſaide viij ſcore vj Parſonnys for the ſaide Hoole Yere — ᴅ. iiij˟˟ xiij *l.* xj *s.* ij *d.*

ANDE ſo ther lacks off the foreſaide ᴅcc. iiij˟˟ xvj *l.* xj *s.* ij *d.* affigned for Meat and Drinke for t'hoole Yere cciij *l.* xj *s.* ij *d.* whiche is apointed for ʟvij Straungers Daily thurrow- oute the Yere oon with anouther aftir ij *d.* ob. a man a Day ande aftir xvij *d.* ob. a man a Weke and aftir ʟxxj *s.* vj *d.* a man a Yere for the full Stynte of Straungers to be allowed for t'hoole Yere — cciij *l.* xj *s.* ij *d.*

13 *s.* 4 *d.* — By comparing the ſeveral Articles marked above with a Dagger †, with the correſpondent Articles in Pag. 17, 22, 23, 24, it will be ſeen, that the Sums here are wrong : As are alſo ſome of the following Calculations. They are given however exactly as they occur in the Original Copy.

XXVIII.

XXVIII.

THE ARTICLES DAYLY.

DAILY.

FYRSTE that the faide Clerke be daily at the BREVING every daie by vij of the clokke in the Mornynge ande there to breve every Officer accordinge as the cuftome is unto halfe hour after viij of the clokke Ande that there be no Brakefaftis delivert unto the tyme that all th'Officers have brevidd.

DAILY.

ITEM that the faide Clarks of the Brevements ALLOWE nather Brede Aile Bere Wyne Flefche Fyfche nor noone outher things that are Brevedde Except they fe a goode caufe why And if they think th'Expenfes be to much Thann they to reafon with th'Officers why it is fo And if they fe not a goode concideracion why it fhulde be fo Then they not to Allowe it upon them But att a Deficient.

DAILY.

ITEM that the faide Clarks of the Brevements Allowe no WYNE for Drinkings to the Yoman or Grome of the Seller Excepte it be by Recorde of an Ufcher Nor Wyne to be alowid that is fervid for Mealis in the Great Chambere or in the Halle Excepte it be by Recorde of an Ufcher of the Chambere or of the Halle And they to be at the Brevements.

DAILY.

DAILY.

ÍTEM that the ſaide Clarks of the Brevements Allowe no BRAIKEFASTS that ar ſervid by any Officer But ſuich as ar appointed in the Bille of Braikefaſts Excepte it be by the Comaundement of an Heade Officer an Uſher of the Chaumber or of the Hall.

DAILY.

ÍTEM that the ſaide Clarks of the Brevements allowe no LYVEREIS that ar ſervide by any Officer Excepte it be appointed in the Bille of Lyvereis Or elles by Commaundment of an Heed Officer an Uſcher of the Chaumber or of the Hall.

DAILY.

ÍTEM that the ſaide Clarks of the Brevements BREVE every Officer after outher in Ordre As to ſay Furſte The Grome of the Halle The Pantry The Seller The Buttery The Keching Th'Ewry And The Grome or the Kepar of the Wodyard.

DAILY.

ÍTEM that the ſaid Clarks of the Brevements ſee all maner of GROSS EMPCIONS that ar bought To be entred furthwith in the Journalle Booke when they ar bought.

DAILY.

ÍTEM that the ſaide Clarks of the Brevements SEE furely that every Groſs Empcion that is boughte for th'Ex-

Y   pence

pence of my Lords Hous be broughte in And ſe Suerely whether it be abill Stuf or not (aftir the Price that is ſet upon it or not) or it be entred or occupied.

DAILY.

ITEM that the ſaide Clarks of the Brevements ſee the CATOURER enter the Parcells every mornyng at the Breving time of the Officers And if he ſo doo not Thanne they to ſhewe it to the Heed Officers for to be reformed or elles to be entred over nighte every day.

DAILY.

ITEM that Oon of the Clarks of the Counting Hous looke daily upon the CATOURE STUF that he * bringith And that it be brought upp into the Countinghous And if it be not able Stuf nor Worth the price that he ſettith upon yt to deliver it hym agayne And not to be deteynidde ne occupied for my Lords uſe.

DAILY.

ITEM that if the ſaide Clarks of the Brevements ſe the Catoure raiſe His PRICE of his Stuf outherwiſe thanne he was wont to doo Thanne they to reaſonne with hym upon it And if they ſe gudd caus why it ſhuld be raiſidd ſo to allowe it And if not to abaite his Price accordinge as it is worthe.

DAILY.

ITEM that the ſaide Clarks of the Brevements have an OVERSIGHTE to every Office And if they ſe th'Officers

* i. e. the Catourer bringeth.

ficers of the fame have any Reforte of Perfons into there faid Office Thanne they to fhewe it to the Heed Officers for reformacion of itt.

DAILY.

ITEM that every Daie at the Brevinge an USCHER of the Chamber to be theire to Breve for the Chaumbre what Comaundement is there.

DAILY.

ITEM that the Ufchers of the Chaumbre ande of the Halle fe whether the POTTES be fillid as they ought to be when the Officers bringith them or notte And if they be not Than they to fhewe it to the faide Clarks at the Breving And they to refourme yt.

DAILY.

ITEM that the faide Clarkes of the Brevements enquire every Daie of the Usfhers at the Breving what DEFAL-TEIS they finde with the Officers Ande the faide Clarks to refourme the fame.

DAILY.

ITEM that all the Officers of Houfehold bring upp there KEIS of ther Offices every night when my Lorde is fervid for alle nighte into the Counting-hous AND that they have them not down unto the tyme that they have Brevidde in the mornying Withoute an Ufher A Yoman of the Chaumber or an Heed Officer Servaunte com for them ANDE alfo that the faide Officers bryng up there faide
KEIS

KEIS into the Counting-hous every day when the Latter Dynner is doon And to fetche theim agayn at iij of the Clock to ferve for Drinkings.

DAILY.

ITEM that the Brevements of th'Expenſs of the Hous be kept every Daye in the Counting-hous at TWO TYMES of the Daie That is to faye Furſt Tyme incontinent aftir the Dynner Ande the Second Tyme at Aftur Supper when Lyverys is fervid at Highe Tymes as Principal Feeſts as Criſtynmas Eſtur Sainte-George-Tide Whitſontide ande Alhallowtide And at any outher tymes when ther is any great Repaire of Straungers in the Hous Bicaus the Officers fhalle not forget for long bering of it in ther mynds.

DAILY.

ITEM that the faide Clarks of the Brevements breve every STRAUNGER by Name that commeth to my Lords Houſe.

DAILY.

ITEM that the faide Clarks of the Keching fe that the SERVICE appointed in the Book of Directions for th'Expences of my Lords Hous be obfervid ande kept withoute Imbrigemente And to be examyned every Day what Lacks therof To th'entente that th'Officers fhal not perluine it to there proufit if there be any But that it rymaine onely to my Lords Proufit.

DAILY.

DAILY.

ITEM that the ſaide Clarks of the Kechinge every daye at vj of the Clock or vij in the Mornynge faile not to appoint the LARDERER ande COOKS And to be with the ſaide Cooks at the Strikinge oute of the Meeſſes of Beffs Muttons Vealls ande Porks that ſhal be cut oute for the Service for my Lord ande the Hous As welle for Braike-faſtes as for Dynnar and Sopar ANDE that they make ande ſtrike oute the Meeſſes aftir the Qwantite accordinge to th'Ordre of the Direcciouns for th'Expences of my Lords Hous To th'entent that they ſhalle nather make it leſs nor more for Exceding but according to the Ordre of the Booke.

DAILY.

ITEM that the ſaide Clarks of the Kechinge caſt up every daie the Chequirroille ande the Straungers And Deduct the VACANTS to ſe Howe th'Expences of the Breve-ments wool wey togedre And when they finde a Defalte to Refourme it furthwith Ande ſhewe the ſaid Officers ther Defalts in there mysbreving if they be ſo found.

DAILY.

ITEM that the Steward Treſourer Countroller or Clarks of the Keching (which Doith ſtand chargid) Provide for vj Buſſhell and iij Pekks of Otes aftir ij d. ob. the Buſſhell for the Provaundre of xxvij HORS for the Space of a Daie aftir a Pekk on the Day for every Horfs — Whiche com-meth to the Somme for every Hors by the ſaide Daie ob. dim. quad. — Ande ſo t'hoole Somme for the ſaid xxvij Hors
on

on a Daie is xvj*d*. ob. quad. dim.   yf it be aftir ij*d*. ob.
the Bufhill And after xx*d*. the Quarter. '

DAILY.

ITEM to be paide to the faid Steward Trefaurer Comptroller
or Clarks of the Keching that doith ftonde chargid to
provide for cxxxiiij Quarters dim. and Demy Busfhell of
Beanes (aftir ij*s*. the Quarter) for HORSBREADE to be
made of for th'Expences of xxvij Hors of my Lords to
ftonde in his Stable at the Charge of the Hous Viz. —
vj Gentle Hors — iiij Palfreis (as Oon for my Lady Ande
Thre for my Ladies Gentlewomen) — Hobbies and Naggs iij
(As to fay Oon for my Lord to ride upon Oone to leed
Ande Oon Spayr) — Sumpter Hors And Mail-hors iij (Viz.
One for the Bedde Oon for the Coffure And Oon for the
Mail) — vj Hors for them that is at my Lords Horfinge
(As to fay a Young Gentleman Horffe that is at my Lords
Horffing Fyndinge The Yoman of the Stabille Hors A Groim
of the Chaumber Hors at my Lords finding A Groime of
the Stirop Hors And two Hors for the Sumptermen that
ledes the Sumptir-hors) — And vij Charriot-hors to drawe in
the Charriot — AFTER v Quarters v Busfhell and A half
of Beanes for every of the faid Hors in the Yere Whereof
to be made Dccccvij Looffs of Horfbread — Viz. of every
Quarter cLxxij Looffs aftir viij Loofs a penny And therof
is allowid to be fervid iij Looffs on the Daie to a Hors
for Provaunder As to fay Great Hors Palfreis Sumpter-hors
Charriot-hors and Mail-Hors Ande for every Nag two Looffs
— Which amounteth to the Somme in T'hoole Yere xj*s*. iiij*d*.
ob. for every Hors for Provaunder in Beanes aftir this faide price
ANDE foo T'hoole Somme of Provaunder for the faid xxvij
Horffes in the faide Hoole Yere is xv*l*. vij*s*. j*d*. ob. if
it be at ij*s*. the Quarter ALSO the faid Perfonnes to provide

vide for Lxxvj Quarters dim. ij Bush. ande a Pekk of Beanes
after ijs. the Quarter for the Provaundre of the said xxvij
Hors by the space of Half a Yere After iij Looffs uppon
the Daie for Oon Hors Whiche cometh to ij Quarters vj
Bush. and iij Pekks an Hors in the said half Yere Wherof
to be made cccccLxvj Looffs after cLxxij Looffs of a Quarter
And after viij Loofs a penny Whiche amountith to the
Somme for Oone Hors in the said Half Yere vs. viijd. dim.
quad. AND so t'hoole Somme for the said xxvij Hors for
an Half Yere is vij l. xiijs. ob. quad. if it be at ijs. the
Quarter.

DAILY.

ITEM that the Steward Tresaurer Countroller or Clarks
of the Kechinge provide for iij Bush. dim. of Beanes aftir
iijd. the Bush. for the PROVAUNDER of the said xxvij
Hors for a Daie Wherof to be made iiij score iiij Looffs
Aftir viij Looffs a Penny Which cometh to iij Loofs on
the Daie for a Hors for Provaunder And after quad. dim. for
a Hors on the daie — AND so t'hoole Somme for the said
xxvij Hors for a Daie is xd. quad. if it be at ijs. the
Quarter.

DAILY.

ITEM it is Ordred that the saide Clarks of the Kechinge
whensomevir they taike the Brevements that th'Officers
of Householde doith breve in the Countinghous The said
Clarks to write th'Officers SURNAYMS to th'Entente
whensomevir the Deficients be drawen and castyne by th'Auditor in th'Officers Weike of Houshold That he shalle not
thraw the said Deficients in an Officer Weke which occupieth Whiche Deficient was in the tyme of hyme that is
                                                    departed

departed but that he fhall maik it knowyn in whois tyme the faide Deficients was in.

DAILY.

ITEM it is Orderedde by my Lord His Hede Officers of Houfehold and Counfaille that there fhal be ftrikken of every Carcafs of BEIF Lxiiij STROKS Whiche is after xvj Stroks of every Quarter Ande aftir iiij Tilde in every Quarter Ande aftir iiij ftroks in every Tylde.

DAILY.

ITEM it is Ordredde by my Lords Hede Officers of Houfcholde and Counfail that there fhal be ftrikken of every Carcafs of MUTTON xij Strokes aftir iij Strokes in every Quartir.

DAILY.

ITEM it is Ordred by my Lordes Hede Officers of Houfcholde ande Counfaile that there fhal be ftrikken of every VEAL xvj Strokes after iiij Stroks of every Quarter.

DAILY.

ITEM it is Ordride by my Lords Hede Officers of Houfholde and Counfail that there fhal be ftrikken of Every PORKE Twenty Stroks aftir v Stroks in every Quarter.

DAILY.

DAILY.

ITEM it is Ordained that the faide Clarks of the Kitching fhall maike a mencion in the BREVING BOOKS at every Tyme or Tymes that my Lorde or my Laidy removes oute of his Standing Houfhold ande is at the charge of his Coffurs And alfo of his Lordfhip Hoim Riding agayn to his Hous With the Noumber of the Parfonnes of the Chequirroil of Houfhold that awaited uppon his Lordefhip at every fuche tyme And the Naims of the plaices that his Lordfhip roid unto.

DAILY.

ITEM it is ordeynid by my Lord and his Counfaille that the CATOURE fhalle enter noone of his Percellies into the Journalle Booke at no tyme nor tymes Excepte They be by Or at the leefte Oon of them that ftondeth chargid with th'Expences of the keapynge of my Lordes Houfe Except fomme of my Lordes Counfaille be their prefente AND that the faide Catoure be daily in the Counting-hous for the faide caus at the houre of Oon of the Clok at After Noon to enter his Empcions in the Journalle Booke befoire fomme of my Lordes Counfaille or befoire fomme of theim that ftondeth chargid with the keping of my faide Lordes Houfe ANDE the Clarks of the Keching to fee this Houre kept daily and this Article executyd As they wolle advoide my Lords defpleafure and ftonde at theire Jeoparty for the contrary doing.

Z   DAILY.

DAILY.

ITEM it is ordered by my Lord ande his Counſaille
That the BAIKERS the BRUERS ande the BUCHERS
ſhall enter noon of theire Furninnters Braſiantours nor Ne-
canters into the Journaille Booke with noone of the Clarkes
of the Counting-hous at no day tyme nor tymes Excepte
They be by Or at the leeſt Oon of theme that ſo ſtondeth
charged with th'Expences of my Lordes Houſe Excepte
ſomme of my Lordes Counſaille be preſent AND that the
foreſaide Baiker Brewer ande Boucher be daily in the Coun-
ting-houſe at the Houre of Oone of the Clok at After Noone
yf the cais ſo requires that they have any thing to enter
That they may enter their Fornintors Braſianturs and Necantours in the Journalle Booke Ande to taille with th'Officers befoire ſomme of theime that ſtondeth chargid with
th'Expences of my Lordes Hous ANDE that the Clarkes
of the Keching ſee this Houre kepte daily and this article executyd As they wolle advoide my Lordes deſ-
pleaſure ande ſtonde at theire Jeopardy for the contrary
doyinge.

DAILY.

ITEM it is Ordenyde by my Lorde and his Counfell to have a MOROWE MASSE - PREIST dailly now
in his Lordeſhipes Hous to ſay Maſſe Dailly at vj of the
Clok in the mornynge thoroweowte the Yere that the Officers of his Lordeſhipes Houſholde may ryſe at a dew Hower
and to here Maſſe dailly To th'entent that they may com to
receyve their Keys of their Offices at the Hower apoynted
                                                    That

That they fhall not nede to come to no Service afterwarde
for tendynge of their Offices By reafon whirof my Lorde
nor Straungers fhall not be unfervyde at no howre nor tyme
when Ufhers fhall comaunde.

XXIX.

XXIX.

TH' ARTYCLES WEKELY.

WEKELY.

FIRSTE if that any th'OFFICERS of th'OFFICES be not at the Counting-houfe by vij of the Clock in the Mornynge for to BREVE Thanne the faide Clarks of the Brevements to fchew it to the Hede Officers for reformacion thereof.

WEKELY.

ITEM that the faide Clarks of the Brevements Entre alle the Tailles of the FURNIUNTERS in the Journal Booke in the Counting-hous every Daie furthwith aftir the Brede be delivert to the Pantre And thenne the ftok of the Tail to be delivert to the Baker and the Swatche to the Paunteler.

WEKELY.

ITEM that the faid Clarks of the Brevements Entre al the BRASIANTURS in the Victual Booke in the Counting-hous at every Tyme furthwith after the Bere be deliverte into the Buttery And the ftok of the Tail to be delivert to the Brewar ande the Swaiche to the Butler.

WEKELY.

WEKELY.

ITEM that the Clarks of the Brevements Entre al the NECANTOURS at every Wekes End in the Journal Book in the Counting-hous AND when they ar Entridd the Yoman or Grome of the Larder ande the Slaugh-terman be boithe prefente when they fo entre.

WEKELY.

ITEM that the faid Clarks of the Brevements by th'advice of the Countroller ande the Hede Clarke of the Kechinge caufe the CATOUR to go abrode in the Countrey Weke-ly for Byinge of Stuf in fuche places as is thoughte it fchal be beft cheip Ande to By it feldomeft aboute where my Lorde liethe Excepte it maye be hadde as goodde cheip their as outher where.

WEKELY.

ITEM whereas MUSTERDE haith been boughte of the Sawcemaker affore tyme That nowe it be made within my Lordes Houfe Ande that Oone be provided to be Grome of the Squillary that canne make it.

WEKELY.

ITEM that the POTTS of the Seller ande the CAN-NES of the Buttery be meafured And if th'Officers afk more Alowance thanne they be of Thanne it to be fet as a Deficiente upon there Hedes.

WEKELY.

WEKELY.

ITEM it is devised that from hensforthe no CAPON-NES to be boughte but oonelie for my Lords owne Mees Ande that the saide Capons schal be boughte for ij *d.* a pece leyne and fedd in the Pultrye Ande the Maifter Chambreleyn ande the Stewarde be servidde with Capounnes if there be Straungeres fitting with theme.

WEKELY.

ITEM It is thoughte goode that CHEKINS be boughte for my Lords owne Meafs onely Ande Maifter Chamberleyne ande the Stewardes Meas So that they be at an ob. a pece.

WEKELY.

ITEM it is thoughte goode HENNES be boughte from Criftynmas to Shroftide fo they be good and at ij *d.* a pece Ande my Lorde Maifter Chamberleyne and the Stewards Meas to be fyrved with theme and noon outher.

WEKELY.

ITEM it is thoughte goode to By PIDGIONS for my Lords Meas Maifter Chambreleyne ande the Stewardes Meas So they be boughte after iij for a penny.

WEKELY.

WEKELY.

ITEM it is thoughte goode that CONYES be boughte for my Lorde and Maifter Chaumbreleyne ande the Steuwardes Meas if there be Straungers fittynge with theim So they be boughte after ij*d.* a pece ande be goode.

WEKELY.

ITEM that the Clarks of the Kechinge fchal afore they maike any Berganne for Provifion of any manir of GROSS EMPCION for kepinge of my Lords Hous That they maike my Lorde privey therto afore the Berganne be concludedde To th'entent that they may know whether his Lordefchip wool agre to faide Price or not If my faid Lorde be at Home ANDE if his Lordefchipp be Abfente Thanne to maike fuche of his Lordefchip Counfail or Servaunts (that my Lorde leiffs in truft to fee whiche he haith appointed) privey to the faid Empcion afore the Berganne be concludedde To th'entente that they may fe whether they have made there Bergannes in dewfulle tyme or not.

WEKELY.

ITEM it is Ordeynidde by my Lorde ande his Coun-faile thanne whenfomevir any of his Lordefchip Servaunts be comaunded to ride on meffage in WINTER (Viz. from Michaelmes whiche tyme Winter Horffemeat begynneth at To Sainte Elynne daie nexte after the whiche tyme the faid Winter Horffemeat goith oute at) That Every of theime be allowid for the tyme of his being furth in his Journey within the faid fpace ij*d.* for every Meal And ob. for every

his

his Baitinge Ande for his Horfe every daie ande nighte
of his faide Journey iiij *d.* Viz. a Penny for his Baitinge
Ande iij *d.* at nighte for his Provendour The whiche is in
alle for A Man ande his Hors in Winter on the daie viij *d.*
If it be Ettynge Daie Ande if it be Faftinge Daie Thanne
ij *d.* to be abaited The whiche is vj *d.* on a Faftinge Daie
within the faide fpace from Michaelmas to Sainte Elynns
Daie ANDE whenfomever any of his faid Lordefhip Servaunts be commaunded to ride on Meffage in SOMER
(Viz. from Sainte Elyne Day The which tyme the Somer-
Horffemeat begynneth at Ande Michaelmas nexte after the
whiche tyme Somer-Horffmeate endith at) That Every of
theme for the tyme of his Journey within the faid fpace
be allowidde ij *d.* for every meal and ob. for his Baitynge
Ande for his Hors every daie of the faid Journey within
the faid fpace to be allowidde j *d.* ob. Viz. j *d.* at nyghte
for his Greffinge Ande ob. for his Baitinge The whiche is
in alle for a Man ande his Hors on the Daie in Somer
v *d.* ob. If it be Etting Daie Ande if it be Fafting Daie
thanne ij *d.* to be abaitedde for a Meal The whiche is in alle
but iij *d.* ob. ordeinary Faftinge Daie within the faide fpace
from Sainte Elyne Daye to Michaelmas PROVIDED
alwais that whenfomever any fuche Perfonne the whiche is
commaunded to ride ande doith tarry at his Journey Ende
for fuche caufes as he haithe to doo in his Meffage theire
Thanne he to be Allowid Wekelie for the tyme of his
tarryinge there xiiij *d.* for hym felf Viz. ij *d.* a Daie for
hyme felf for his Mealls Ande xij *d.* for his Hors If it be
in Winter Viz. j *d.* ob. quad. a Daie for his Hors Ande in
Somer to be alowidd Wekelie for the tyme that he fo
tarrieth at his Journey ende confernynge his bufinefs xiiij *d.*
for hym felf as is aforefaid As to faye ij *d.* a Daie for
hyme felf for his Mealls Ande viij *d.* for his Hors Viz. a
penny the Daie for his Grefs Ande j *d.* more at alle.

WEKELY.

WEKELY.

ITEM It is Ordeynidde by my Lord ande his Counceil that whenfoever the Clarks of the Kechinge Clarks of the Brevements or any outher Officers of Houfehold ar commaundede to ride furthe confernynge the PROVICION for th'Expens of his Lordefchipps Hous That every of theim be allowidd viij *d.* on the daie for hym felf ande his Hors If it be in Winter Ande in Somer to be allowidde ij *d.* for every Meal Ande ob. every Baitinge Ande j *d.* for his Hors Greffinge upon the Daie and Nighte for the tyme of his beinge furthe confernynge the Provicion for the Hous ANDE if it fortune that any of the faide Clarks or outher Officers whiche ar commaunded to ride furth concernynge the Provicion for th'Expence of the Hous for that they mufte tarry at any plaee where there Provicion liethe by the fpace of a Weke or of a Mounithe That thanne they to tarrye there Ande be allowed Weklie aftir xiiij *d.* a weke for theire Borde Wages Ande xij *d.* for theire Hors If it be in Winter Ande in Somer aftir xiiij *d.* a weke for their Borde Wages Ande viij *d.* for theire Hors aftir a Penny the daie, and night Ande a penny more at al.

WEKELY.

ITEM that the faide Stewarde Trefaurer Comptroller or Clarks of the Kytching (which doith ftonde chargedde) provide for v Quarters vij Busfhells ande a Peck of OOTS aftir xx *d.* a Quarter for the Provaundre of xxvij Hors for the fpace of a Weke Aftir a Pekke on the Daie for a Hors Whiche commethe to vij Pecks for a Hors in the

A a   faide

ſaide Weke Whiche amountithe to the Somme for a Hors
in the ſaide Weke iiij *d.* qu. dim. Ande ſo th'oole Somme
for the ſaid xxvij Hors in the ſaide Weke is ix *s.* ix *d.* ob.
If it be at xx *d.* the Quarter.

WEKELY.

ITEM that the ſaide Steward Treſaurer Comptroller or
Clarks of the Kitchinge provide for iij Quarters of BEANYS
aftir ij *s.* the Quarter for Provaunder for the xxvij Hors for
the ſpace of a Weke Aftir iij Looffs on the daie to a Hors
for Provaundre Whiche cometh to iij Pecks dim. for an Horſs
in the Weeke aftir ob. quad. the Pecke WHEROF to be
made xxj Looffs After viij Looffs a Penny Whiche cometh
to the Somme for ane Hors in the Weik ij *d.* ob. AND ſo
th'oole Somme for the Provaundre of the ſaid xxvij Hors
in the ſaide Weike is vj *s.* if it be at ij *s.* the Quarter.

WEKELY.

ITEM It is Orderide ande agreide by my Lords Heede
Officers ande Counceil that the BAKER ſchal aunſwere
my Lorde of every Quarter of WHEIT in Maunchettes
cxl — aftir ij Maunchetts to a Loof of Houſhold Breade
— Of Houſehold Breade cc iiij Score Ande of Trencher
Breade cc iiij Score bicauſe the Looffs of the Trencher Breade
be larger thanne the Looffs of the Houſhold Breade.

WEKELY.

ITEM It is ordered by my Lordes Heede Officers of
Houſeholde and Counceil that there ſhal be ſtrikken of
every Salte Fiſche callidd A LYNGE - fiſche vj Strookes
Aftir iij Stroiks in a Side.

WEKELY.

WEKELY.

ITEM It is Ordred by my Lords Heede Officers of Houfehold and Counceil that theire fchal be Strykkyne of every Saltfifche calledde A HABBERDYNE Fifche iiij Stroiks After ij Stroiks on aither Side.

WEKELY.

ITEM It is ordered by my Lordes Heede Officers of Houfeholde and Counceile that there fchal be ftrikkynne of every Salt SALMOUNE xij ftroiks After iiij Stroiks in every Quarter.

XXX.

XXX.

TH'ARTICLES MOUNETHLY.

MOUNETHLY.

FIRST that the faide Clarkes of the Counting-hous or Brevements fe the Reconyinge made every Mouneth before theme in the Counting-hous bitwixte the Tanner ande the Slaughterman of alle the HIDES of the Beiffs that ar flayne for th'Expence of my Lordes Hous.

MOUNETHLY.

ITEM that the faide Clarks of the Brevements fe the Reconynge made every Mounethe before them in the Counting-hous bitwixte the Glover ande the Slaughtirman of the FELLIS or SKYNNES of the Muttouns that ar flayne for th'Expence of my Lords Hous.

MOUNEHELY.

ITEM that the faide Clarks of the Brevements fe the Reconynge made every Mouneth before theim in the Counting-hous bitwix the Tallow Chaundeler ande the Slaughterman of alle the TALLOWE that cometh of the Beiffs ande Muttons that ar flayne for th'Expence of my Lords Hous.

MOUNETHLYE.

MOUNETHLYE.

ITEM that the faide Clarks of the Brevements fe the Brevynge made every Mouneth before theime in the Counting-hous bitwixt the Yoman or Grome of Paiftry ande the Baker of alle fuche FLOURE as is Delivert oute of the Bakhous to the Kechinge.

MOUNETHELY.

ITEM that the faide Clarks of Brevements entre in the Counting-hous Mounethlie alle the PRETEREAS in the title of Cofts Neceffary where they were wonte to be entridde before tyme aftir the Catour Parcelles of every Mounethe.

MOUNETHLY.

ITEM that the CATOUR PARCELLIS be caft every Mouneth up to knowe whether they do Lack of the Somme that is affigned for theim or ellis they excede above the faid Somme.

MOUNETHLY.

ITEM that the faide Clarks of the Brevements maike up the Pies of all th'expenduntours at every mouneths ende.

MOUNETHLY.

ITEM that the faide Clarks of the Brevements taike the REMAINES at every Mounethes ende Ande a Bille to be made of the Parcellis what remanethe Ande to be broughte to my Lorde to fee.

MOUNETHLYE.

MOUNETHLYE.

ITEM that the faide Clarks of the Kechinge or of the Brevements maike my Lorde at every Mounethis ende a Bill of the Names of the PERSONNES That ar Daily in Hous Ande ar not in the Chequeroll Ande for what Caufis they fo continewe in the Hous That my Lorde ande his Conceil may taike Direccion outher to put theim in Rowmes or ellis to caus theme to departe oute of the Hous ANDE the faide Bille to be fignedde with my Lords Hands.

MOUNETHLY.

ITEM It is thoughte goode that PIGGIS be boughte fo they be goodde Ande at iij d. or iiij d. a pece For of a Pig there may be made to ferve iiij Meas,

MOUNETHLYE.

ITEM It is thoughte goode to bye GEIS fo that they be goode Ande for iij d. or iiij d. at the moifte Seing that thre or iiij Meas may be ferved therof.

MOUNETHLYE.

ITEM It is thoughte goode as that no PLOVERS be bought at No Seafon but onelie in Criftynmas ande at Principal Feefts Ande my Lorde to be fervide therwith ande his Borde End Ande none outher ANDE to be boughte for a penny a pece or j d. ob. at moifte.

MOUNETHELY.

MOUNETHELY.

ITEM It is thought goode that MALLARDS be bought onelie for my Lords owne Meas So they be goode Ande bought for ij*d*. a pece.

MOUNETHELY.

ITEM It is thought goode that no TEALLIS be bought but if so be that outher Wilde Fowel cannot be gotten Ande to be at a penny a pece.

MOUNETHLY.

ITEM It is thought goode that WODCOKKS be hadde for my Lordes owne Meas ande noon outher And to be at j*d*. a pece or j*d*. ob. at the moiste.

MOUNETHLY.

ITEM It is thought goode that WIPIS be hadde for my Lords own Meas onelie And to be at j*d*. a pece.

MOUNETHLYE.

ITEM It is thought goode that SEE GULLIS Be hadde for my Lords owne Meas And noone outher So they be good ande in Seafon And at j*d*. a pece or j*d*. ob. at the moiste.

MOUNETHLYE.

MOUNETHLYE.

ITEM It is thought goode that STYNTS be hadde for my Lords owne Meas and noone outher So they be after vj for a penny.

MOUNETHLY.

ITEM QUAILLIS in like caas to be hadd for my Lords owne Meas and noone outher at Principal Feaftes And at ij *d.* a pece at moifte.

MOUNETHLY.

ITEM SNYPES to be bought for my Lords owne Meas at Principal Feefts So they be goode Ande after iij a penny.

MOUNTHLY.

ITEM PERTRIGES to be bought for my Lords Meas Ande at ij *d.* a pece If they be goode.

MOUNETHLY.

ITEM It is thoughte goode that Al Maner of WILDE FOWEL be bought at the firfte hand where they be gotten And a Catour to be Appointed for the fame For it is thought that the Pulters of Hemmyngburghe and Clif haithe great Advauntage of my Lorde Yerelie of felling of Cunyes and Wilde Fowel.

MOUNETHLY.

MOUNETHLY.

Item GRATE BIRDES after iiij a pennye to ferve for my Lords Meas Maifter Chaumbreleyne ande the Stewards Meas.

MOUNETHLY.

Item SMALLE BIRDS for my Lords owne Meas Ande after xij a penny.

MOUNETHLYE.

Item LARKS for my Lords owne Meas after xij for ij d.

MOUNETHLY.

Item BACON FLIKKES for my Lords owne Meas Maifter Chaumbreleyne ande the Stewardes Meas bitwixt Candlemas and Shroftide ellis noone Except my Lords comaundement be to the contrary.

MOUNETHLY.

ITEM That the Clarks of the Kechinge at th'Ende of every Mouneth taike the REMANETH And fet the price uppon the hede of every thing that Remanethe what it is worthe Ande to make a Bille of alle the clere Expences of the faid Mounethe Ande to raite every Man what he ftands in a Meal Daye ande Weeke Ande what th'oole Mounethe drawith to in the Hous.

B b   MOUNETHLY.

MOUNETHLY.

ITEM that the said Clarks of the Kechinge make a Bill of the DEFICIENTS of every Officer singularlie by it self what Deficient he fallethe in the Mounethe If any of them so falle With the price ande Somme ANDE to make a Bill what every Deficiente of every Officer drawith too Ande to present it to my saide Lord at every Mounethis ende.

MOUNETHLY.

ITEM that the Tresaurer Comptroller or Clarks of the Kechinge (whiche doith stonde chargidd) provide for xxv Quarters ij Busshells Demy of O O T I S aftir xx d. the Quarter for the Provaunder of the said xxvij Hors for the space of a Mouneth after a Pekke on the Daie for an Hors W H I C H E comythe to vij Bush. Demy for an Hors in the said Mounethe Whiche amounteth to the Somme for an Hors in the said Mouneth xviij d. ob. qu. A N D E so th'oole Somme for the saide xxvij Hors in the said mouneth is xLij s. ij d. quad. If jt be at xx d. the Quarter.

MOUNETHLIE.

ITEM that the said Steward Tresaurer Comptroller or Clarks of the Kechynge (that doith stonde chargid) provide for xij Quarters of B E A N E S aftir ij s. the Quarter for the Provaunder of the saide xxvij Hors for the space of a Mouneth also iij Looffs on the Daie for a Hors for Provaunder W H I C H E cometh to iij Bush. ande iij
Pckks

Pekks for a Hors in the said Mouneth Wherof to be made iiij score x Looffs after viij Looffs a penny Whiche amountithe to the Somme for a Hors in the said Mounethe xj *d.* qu. ANDE so th'oole Somme for the Provaundre of the said xxvij Hors in the saide Mounethe is xxiiij *s.* if it be at ij *s.* the Quarter.

MOUNETHLY.

ITEM It is ordeined that theis Horssis followinge in the Charge of the Hous be put to GRESS Yerelie from Sainte Elyn Daie unto Michaelmas next following As the naimes of them hereafter folloith Viz. iiij Palfreis (wherof Oone for my Ladie Ande iij for iij Gentlewomen) vj Hors for them that ar at my Lordes Horssinge (Viz. a Yong Gentleman Hors at my Lords findynge the Yoman of the Stabill Hors a Grome of the Chaumbre Hors at my Lords findynge a Grome of the Steropp Hors And a Nag for the Charriotmen to ride upon Ande ij Hors * for the ij Sumptermen that ledith the Sumptir Hors) ANDE at Michaelmas the said Hors is to be takyn up agayne to the Stabill Ande to stonde at Harde Meat to Sainte Elynne Daie nexte aftir being in the Newyere for th'accompte of the Hous of the Yere followinge ande so to be Ordeyned and kepte Yerelie.

MOUNETHLIE.

ITEM a Bill to be made at the ende of every Mouneth of the Clere Expencis of my Lords Hous for the said Mouneth And every MANNE to be ratidde what he stands in the Meal the Daie the Weke ande the Mounethe.

MOUNETHLIE.

* Thefe Two Horfes are accounted in the reckoning but as One; having Each but half the ufual allowance.

MOUNETHLIE.

ITEM It is ordred ande agreede by my Lorde his Hede Officers of Houſeholde ande Counceil that there fchal be vj Quarters of MALT brewidd at every Brewinge in his Houſe througheoute the Yere WHEROF to be made at every Brewinge of every Quarter of Malte whiche is brewidde in my Lords Hous in Winter xij Hoggeſhedes after ij Hoggeſhedes to a Quarter And in Some xj Hoggeſheds after ij Hoggeſheds of a Quarter (ſave a Hoggeſhede les at alle) bicaus the ſaid Bere muſt be made bigger * in Somer thanne in Winter for Tunnynge.

MOUNETHLY.

ITEM It is ordeyned by my Lorde ande agreade That thois Parſons that ſtandes chargid with the Keaping of my Lordes Houſs for the hoole Yeir ſhall every Mouneth in the Yeir maike my Lord a Bill of all the GROSS EMPCIONS bought in the ſaide Mouneth With the Prices of every thing Ande to declair in the ſaid Bill what the ſaide Parcells bought in the ſaide Mouneths cometh to Ande alſo what it doithe amounte above the Prices in the Booke of Orders Or what it cumis to les thanne the Prices in the Book of Orders That my Lorde may ſe Mounethly what it is deerer thanne the Prices in the Booke of Orders Or what it is better cheip than is in the ſaide Booke of Orders.

MOUNETHLY.

* So the Ancient MS. but a modern Hand has altered it to 'Bitterer'.

MOUNETHLY.

ITEM it is ordeynid by my Lorde ande his Coun-faille That the Clarks of the Kitching or of the Brevements faile not at every moneths ende to ENTER and INGROSS in the Booke that is Ingroſſid mounethly of the clere Ex-penduntur of the Houſ the Totall Somme of all the Expen-duntors of all maner of HORSSE MEAT expendede the ſaide mointhe at the Charge of the Houſs.

MOUNTHLY.

ITEM It is ordeynde by my Lorde ande his Counſaill That the Clarke of the Kitching or of the Counting-houſs faill not at th'Engroſſinge up of every half Yere to enter into the Booke that is ingroſſid upp of the Mounethe that the Half Yeir endes in the Totall Somme of WAIGIES paide to my Lords Houſhold Servaunts for the ſaide Half Yeir.

XXXI.

XXXI.

THE ARTICLES FOR PRINCIPALLE FEISTES.

AT PRINCIPAL FEISTS.

FIRSTE It is thoughte that C R A N Y S muſte be hadde at Criſtynmas ande outher Principall Feiſts for my Lords owne Meas. So they be bought at xvj d. the pece.

AT PRINCIPAL FEISTS.

Item It is thoughte in-like-wies that HEARONSEWIS be boughte for my Lordes owne Meas So they be at xij d. the pece.

AT PRINCIPAL FEISTS.

Item R E D E S C H A N K S to be boughte at Principalle Feiſts for my Lords owne Meas after j d. ob. the pece.

AT PRINCIPAL FEISTS.

Item BITTERS for my Lordes owne Meas at Principal Feiſts Ande to be at xij d. a pece ſo they be goode.

AT

AT PRINCIPAL FEISTS.

Item FESSAUNTIS for my Lordes owne Meas to be hadde at Principalle Feiftis Ande to be at xij *d.* a pece.

AT PRINCIPAL FEISTS.

Item REIS to be hadde for my Lordes owne Meas at Principal Feifts Ande at ij *d.* a pece.

AT PRINCIPAL FEISTS.

Item SHOLARDIS to be hadde for my Lords owne Meas at Principal Feifts Ande to be at vj *d.* a pece.

AT PRINCIPAL FEISTS.

Item KIRLEWIS to be hadde for my Lords owne Meas at Principal Feifts Ande to be at xij *d.* a pece.

AT PRINCIPAL FEISTS.

Item PACOKKS to be hadde for my Lordes owne Meas at Principal Feiftes and at xij *d.* a pece And no PAY-HENNES to be bowght.

AT PRINCIPAL FEISTS.

Item SEEPIES for my Lorde at Principal Feifts Ande noone outher tyme.

AT

AT PRINCIPAL FEISTS.

Item WEGIONNES for my Lorde at Principal Feiſtes ande noone outher tyme Ande j*d*. ob. the pece Excepte my Lordes comandement be outherwis.

AT PRINCIPAL FEISTS.

Item KNOTTIS for my Lorde at Principalle Feiſts Ande noone outher tyme Ande at j*d*. a pece Except my Lords comaundement be otherwis.

AT PRINCIPAL FEISTS.

Item DOTTREELIS to be bought for my Lorde when they ar in Seaſonne Ande to be at a penny a pece.

AT PRINCIPAL FEISTS.

Item BUSTARDES for my Lords owne Meas at Principall Feiſts Ande noon outher tyme Except my Lords comaundement be otherwis.

AT PRINCIPAL FEISTS.

Item TEARNES for my Lordes owne Meas oonelie at Principalle Feiſts ande noon outher tyme aftir iiij a penny Excepte my Lordes comaundemente be outherwis.

XXXII.

XXXII.

THE ARTICLES QUARTERLY.

QUARTERLY.

FIRSTE that the Clarks of the Brevements make a Copye of the CHEQUIROIL a Sennet afore every Quartre Daie That it may be fhewide to my Lorde to be correct Ande made upp and fignidde affore the next Quartre begynne ANDE alle the Names of the Perfons that fchal be in my Lordis Hous the faide Quartre.

QUARTERLY.

ITEM That the faide Clarks of the Kitching or the Brevements whenfoever my Lorde braikth up Hous They fchal make my Lorde a CHEQUIRROIL of the Naims of the Perfonnes that fchal gif their Attendaunce wheire my Lorde doith abide ande fchal be at meallis at meat ande drinke within wheir his Lordefchipp is With the nams of theim Ande in what Rowmes they fhal ferve ANDE at every fuche tyme as my Lorde fo doith braike up his Hous A Bille to be made ande to be fignidde with my Lorde Hande.

QUARTERLY.

ITEM That the faide Clarks of the Kitchinge or of the Brevements maike my Lorde a Bill of the Perfouns

that

that fchal remayne ftille at BORDE-WAGES where my
Lorde didd kepe Hous unto the tyme that his Lordefchipp
fet up Hous agayne ANDE that every Perfoune fo goinge
to Borde-Wagies fchall have allowidde xij d. a Weike for
the tyme of his Borde-Wages ANDE the faid Bille to be
fignedd with my Lordes Handde.

QUARTERLIE.

ITEM that the faid Clarks of the Kitchinge or of the
Brevements make my Lorde a BILLE of the Names of
alle fuche Perfonnes that defierith to have Licence and haithe
Leif of my faid Lorde or of his Counfail to go home aboute
theire owne bufines when my Lord doith breake up Hous
at any tyme Unto the tyme that his Lordefchip fet up Hous
agayne WHICHE Perfounes ar not ordeynide to have
Borde-Wages allowid theme the faid tyme bicaufe they go
aboute theire owne bufines ande giffeth noon attendaunce
upon my Lorde ande doithe not continew theie where ony
their fellowis doithe abide ANDE at every tyme that my
Lorde doithe breake up Hous A Bille to be made of the
Naims of fuch Perfonnes Ande what Rowme they lon-
gidde to That haith Licence fo to departe ANDE to be
Signidde with my Lords hande Bicaus they fchal have none
allowance of Bord-Wages for the faid caufis.

QUARTERLIE.

ITEM That the faid Clarkis of the Kitchinge or of
the Brevements make my Lord a BILL of the Names of the
Gentlemen of the Chapel at every Quarter Bicaus they ar
accuftumed to be paide theire Houfhold Wages Quarterlie
WITH the names of the Perfonnes Ande the Somes that
they

they take by Yere With the Somes that every of theme fchal be paid the faid Quarter for their Houfhold Wages AND the faid Bill to be figned with my Lords Hand.

QUARTERLIE.

ITEM that the faide Clarks of the Kitchinge or of the Brevements make my Lorde a BILLE at every Quarter of the Naimes of the Gentlemen of the Chapel that ar departidd from my Lords Servis without licence And alfo the Abfence how long every of theme abfentidd theim felf in the faid Quarter without leve Ande how muche their fhal be abaited of theire Quarter-Wages or Half Yere after the rate that they taike by the Quarter for the tyme of theire abfence AND to declare unto theme in the faid Bille why they be fo abaited of their Wages AND at every quarter or tyme that they fchal be paid The faid Bill to be made and fignid with my Lords Hand.

QUARTERLIE.

ITEM that the faid Clarks of the Kitching or of the Brevements maike my Lorde at every Quarter ande Half Yere a BILL of the Naymes of the Perfonnes in the Che-quirroil that departidde oute of my Lordes Service WITH the Titles of the Rowmes that they Servidde in Ande what Wagies they tooke To th'Entent that my Lorde ande his Counfail may provide for Perfonnes agayne for the faid Roumes ANDE the faide Bill to be fignide with my Lords Hande.

QUARTERLIE.

QUARTERLIE.

ITEM that the faide Clarks of the Kitchinge or of the Brevements maike my Lorde at every Quarter ande Half Yere a BILL of the Rowmys in the Chequirroil that lackith Perfonnes in them Accordinge to th'Ordre of the Chequirroil in this Booke of Ordres ANDE to bring the faid Bill to my Lorde when the Chequirroil of the Houfholde for the faid Quartre fchal be fignedde To th'entent that my Lorde may fhew his pleafure whether his Lordefchip wol have Perfonnes in the faide Rowmys that ar vacante according to the Booke of Ordris or not.

QUARTERLIE.

ITEM that the faide Clarks of the Kitching or of the Brevements calle of my Lordes Couferer or Clarke of the Trefaurye every Quarter and Half Yere (when Houfeholde Wagies fchal be paide) for the Bille of alle fuche PRESTS of WAGIES as he haithe paide by my Lordis Comaundement to any of my Lordis Houfeholde Servauntis in partie of Paymente of theire Wagies That it may be abaitidde in theire faide Wagies when they fchal be paide at every Quarter or Half Yere ANDE the faid bill to be fignede with my Lordis Hande.

QUARTIRLIE.

ITEM That a Direccion be takynne with my Lordis Tenauntis of AROME Ande to be at a certein with theim That they fchal ferve my Lordis Hous throughcoute the Yere of all maner of Frefche Watter FISCHE.

QUARTIRLIE.

QUARTIRLIE.

ITEM that the Steward Trefaurer Comptroller or Clarkis of the Kitchinge (whiche doith ftonde chargidde) provide for Lxxvj Quartris vj Busfhellis ande a Pecke of OOTES after xx *d.* the Quarter for the Provaundre of the faide xxvij Hors for the fpace of a Yere after a Pekke on the Daie for a Hors WHICHE comes to ij Quarters vj Busfhellis ande iij Pekks for a Hors in the faid Quartre of the Yere Whiche amountithe to the Somme for a Hors in the faid Quartre iiij*s.* viij*d.* ob. qu. dim. ANDE fo Th'oole Somme for the faide xxvij Hors in the faide Quartre of a Yere is vj *l.* vij*s.* xj*d.* ob. dim. qu.

QUARTIRLIE.

ITEM that the faide Stewarde Treaforer Comptroller or Clarks of the Kitching (that doith ftonde chargidde) provide for xxxviij Quarters iij Busfhellis Dim. Peck of BEANYS after ij*s.* the Quartre for the Provaundre of the faide xxvij Hors for the Space of a Quarter of a Yere aftir iij Looffs on the Daie for a Hors for Provaundre WHICHE cometh to a Quartre iij Busfhellis ande a Pekke dim. for a Hors in the faide Quarter Wherof to be made ccxxxiiij Looffs after cLxxij Looffs of a Quartre Ande after viij Looffis j*d.* WHICHE amountith to the Somme for an Hors in the faide Quarter ij*s.* x*d.* ANDE fo th'oole Some for the faide xxvij Hors in the faide Quartre is Lxxvj*s.* ix*d.* qu. dim. If it be at ij*s.* the Quarter.

QUARTERLY.

QUARTERLY.

ITEM it is ordeynid by my Lord ande his Counfaill That the Clarks of the Kitching or of the Counting-hous faill not at th'Engroffing up of every Quarter to enter in the Booke (that is ingroffidd up of the Mounthe that the Quarter endes in) the totall Some of the HOUSHOLD WAIGES paide Quarterly to the Gentlemen of my Lords Chapell.

QUARTERLY.

ITEM it is thought by my Lorde and his Counfell that there fhall be Yerely ij Gentillmen of the Chappell COUNTER-TENORS more than the Ordynary appoynted in the Book of Orders of Houfholde Bicaufe it is now perceyvid there was to fewe Gentillmen before in nomber appoynted in the Booke of Orders to kepe both Mattyns Lady Maffe Highe Maffe and Evyn - Songe to ferve the Queare And to kepe the iiij Rector Choryes upon Pryncipall Feefts who 'are' ordeynyde to be had for that caufe.

QUARTERLY.

ITEM it is ordeyned by my Lorde and his Counfaill that at the ende of every Quarter when the Bill of the faid Quarters fhal be brought unto my Lord to correct The Clarks of the Kechinge Or thois that ftandes charget with th'Expences of my Lordis Hous fhall bringe my Lord a BILL in with the Billis of the faid Quarter of the Naymes off all the Parcellis of all manner of Groiffe Empcions that

haith

haith benne providet in the faid Quarter With the Pricis
and the Sommes as well the Parcellis providet and paid for
in the faid Quarter As the Parcellis providet and owing for
in this Quarter Ande to whome And what dayis is taikynne
for the Payment of the fame AND alfo to bryng under a
little Stille † in th'Ende of the faid Bill the Naymes of all
Manner of Creditoures that is owing for anny manner of
Provicion of anny former Quarters which is providet and
not paied forr in the faid former Quarter for this Yere
And a Still † on the Hede of every Quarter of the Parcellis
that is provided forre.

† † i. e. A Stile, or a Style : viz. a Tide, Rubric or Summary.

XXXIII.

THE ARTICLES FOR HALFE YERES.

HALF YERE.

FIRSTE that the Clarks of the Ketchinge or of the Brevements maike my Lorde a BILLE at every Half Yere (Viz. at our Lady Daie in Lente Ande Michaelmas next following) of the Names of my Lordis Householde Servauntis that are accuſtomed to be paide the Householde Wagies at the ſaid Half Yere WITH the Titles of the Rowmes that every man ſerveth in With the Sommes that they taike by Yere With the Sommes that every of them ſchal be paide the ſaide Half Year for their Wagies ANDE the ſaid bill to be ſignedde with my Lordis Hand.

HALF YERE.

ITEM that the ſaide Clarks of ·the Kechinge or of the Brevementis ſchalle make my Lorde a BILLE at every Half Yere when Half Yere Wagies ſchal be paide (As to ſaye at our Ladye Daie in Lent and Michaelmas next followinge) of the names of my Lords Servaunts that abſentidde theim ſelf from my Lordes Service without Licence in the ſaide Half Yere Ande what ſpace they were abſente Ande for what Cauſis WITH the Sommes that they ſhal be abaitedde of there Half Yere Wagies Aftir the Rate of the tyme of there abſence ANDE the ſaide Bille to be ſigned with my Lords Hande.

HALF

HALFE YERE.

ITEM that the Stewarde Trefaurer Comptroller or Clarks of the Kechinge (whiche doithe ftonde chargidde) provide for cxxxiij Quartres iiij Busfhels Demy of O O T I S aftir xx d. the Quartre for the Provaunder of the faide xxvij Hors for an Half Yere Aftir a Pek on the Daie for an Hors W H I C H E comethe to v Quarters Demy ande a Buf-fhell Demy for an Hors in the faide Half Yere Whiche amountithe to the Somme for an Hors in the faid Halfe Yere to ix s. v d. ob. qu. ANDE fo th'oole Somme for the faide xxvij Hors in the faide Halfe Yere is xij l. xv s. xj d. qu. if it be at xx d. the Quarter.

HALFE YERE.

ITEM to be paide to the faide Stewarde Treaforer or Comptroller or Clarks of the Kitchinge that doithe ftonde chargidde 'to' provide for iiij fcore xiij Loodes Dim. of HAYE after ij s. viij d. the Loode for the Expences of my Lordis Horffes ftanding in his Lordefchip Stable at the charge of the Hous for an Half Yere — Somme xij l. viij s. W H I C H E is appointed to be paide to the faide Per-fonnes at Michaelmas in th'ende of the Yere ANDE fo th'oole Somme to be paide for fulle contentacion of the faide Haye for my Lordes Horffes for an hoole Yere is. . . .

HALF

HALF YEIR.

ITEM it is ordeynide by my Lord and his Counſaill That the Clarks of the Kitching or of the Counting-hous faille not at th'Engroſſing upp of every Half Yeire to enter into the Booke that is ingroſſed upp of the Monethe that the Half Yeire endes in The totalle Somme of WAIGIES paide to my Lords Houſhold Servaunts for the ſaide Half Yere.

XX XIIII.

XXXIIII.

TH'ARTICLES YERELY.

YERELIE.

FIRSTE that the Clarks of the Kitchinge or of the Brevements maike my Lorde a Bille Yerelie at Michael-mas of the Naimes of my Lordis HOUSEHOLDE SERVAUNTIS that was put to Borde Wagies and abfentedde themfelf without Licence frome the placis where they wer appointede to be at Bordewagies ande to gif theire Attendaunce there ANDE what fpace they were Abfent ande for what caufis With the Sommes of the money that they fchal be abaitidd of theire Borde Wagies after the date of the tyme of their Abfence ANDE the faid Bille to be figned with my Lordis Hand BICAUS they were not. redy there to attende · or ride where my Lorde woulde co-maunde theme.

YERELIE.

ITEM that the faide Clarks of the Kitchinge or of the Brevements make my Lord Yerelie at Sainte Elyns Daie (when the Perfonnes fhal be paid that ar appointed in the Chequirroile of WINTER HORSSEMETE) a Bill of the Names of his Servaunts that fchal be paide for theire faid Winter Horffemet at the faid Sainte Elyn daie WITH the Titles in what Rowme every man ferveth With the
Sommes

Sommes that every of theme fhal be paide for theire faide Winter Horffemeate at the faid tyme ANDE the faide Bill to be figned with my Lordis Hande.

YERELYE.

ITEM that the faide Clarks of the Kitchinge or of the Brevements make my Lorde Yerelie at Sainte Elyne daie (when the Perfonnes fhal be paid that ar appointed in the Bille of Winter Horffemeate) A Bill of the names of my Lordis SERVAUNTS that were ABSENT ande gaf not Attendaunce uppon my Lorde the faide Winter and were appointed in the faid Bille AS wel thois that abfentidde themfelf from Attendaunce uppon my Lorde (that was appointed in the faide Winter Horffemeate) withoute Licence As thois that was at my Lordis Bufinefs ande had allowance by the daie As thois that were at my Lordis Lyverey If his Lordefchip continued at a place They to be abaitid for their Abfence of the Somme allowidde for there faid Winter Horffemeat aftir the rate of the Weiks ande Mounethes accordinge to the rate of the valor allowid for theire faid Winter Horffemeate AND the faid Bill to be figned with my Lordes Hande.

YERELIE.

ITEM that the faid Clarks of the Kichinge or of the Brevements maike my Lorde Yerelie at Michaelmas (when the Perfons fhal be paide that ar appointed in the Bille of SOMMER HORSSEMEATE) a Bill of the Naimes of my Lordis Servauntis that fchal be paide for theire faide Somer Horffemeate at the faid Michaelmas WITH the Sommes that every of theme fhal be paid for theire faid

Sommer

Sommer Horſſemeat at the ſaid tyme With the Titles of the Rowmes that every Manne ſerveth in ANDE the ſaide Bill to be ſigned with my Lordis Hande.

YERELYE.

ITEM That the ſaid Clarks of the Kitchinge or of the Brevements maike my Lorde Yerelie at Michaelmas (when the Perſons ſhal be paide that ar appointed in the Che-quirroil of Somer-Horſſemete) a Bill of the Names of my Lordis SERVAUNTES that were ABSENT ande gaf not their Attendaunce uppon my Lorde the ſaid Sommer ande were appointed in the ſaid Bill of Somer Horſſemeate AS wel thois that abſented theime ſelf from Attendaunce upon my Lorde withoute Licence As thois that were in my Lordes Buſines ande hadde Allowance by the Daie As thois that were att my Lordes Lyverey IF his Lordeſchip contynude at a place They to be abaited for their abſence of the Some allowidde for the ſaid Sommer Horſſemeat aftir the Rate of the Weiks or Mounethes Accordinge to the rate of the vaillour allowid for their ſaid Somer Horſſemeat ANDE the ſaid bill to be ſigned with my Lordis Hande.

YERELIE.

ITEM It is thoughte goode That my Lordis SWANNES be taken and fedde to ſerve my Lordis Hous Ande to be paide fore as they may be boughte in the Countrey Seing that my Lorde haithe Swannys enoughe of his Owne.

YERELIE.

YERELIE.

ITEM it is thought goode that theire be a Covenaunte made with the Catoure by great for EGGIS ande MILKE for th'oole Yere if it canne be fo doone What for a Galloune of Milke Ande howe many Eggis for a Penny.

YERELIE.

ITEM That a direccion be takynne at Lekinfeld with the Catour of the See what he fchal have for every SEAIME of FISCHE thurrowt the Yere to ferve my Lordis Hous.

YERELIE.

ITEM That frome hensfurthe there be no HERBIS bought Seinge that the Cooks may have Herbis inewe in my Lordis Gardins.

YERELYE.

ITEM a Warraunte to be fervide oute Yerelie at Michal-mes for twentie SWANNIS for th'Expencis of my Lordis Houfe As to faye for Criftynmas daie v — Sainte Stephins daie two — Sainte John daie two — Childremas daie ij — Sainte Thomas daie ij — Newyere daie iij — Ande for the xijth daie of Criftynmas iiij Swannes.

YERELY.

YERELY.

THE COPIES of the WARRAUNTIS to be fervide oute Yerelie for SWANNES for the Expencis of my Lordis Hous aftir this Fourme followinge.

WELBILOVIDE I grete youe wele Ande wof ande charge youe that ye deliver of caus to be delivert unto my welbilovide Servaunts Richerd Gowge Comptroller of my Hous Ande Gilbert Wedal Clarke of my Kitchinge For th'ufe ande expencis of my faide Hous nowe againfte the Feeft of Criftynmas next comynge Twentie SIGNETTES To be takenne of the Breide of my Swannes within my Carre of Aromme within my Lordefchip of Lekinfeld within the Countie of Yorke Whereof ye have the kepinge ANDE that ye caus the fame to be delivert unto theme or to Oone of theme furthwith uppon the Sight herof ANDE this my Writinge for the Delyverie of the fame fhal be unto youe anempft me ande tofore myn Auditours at youre nexte accompte in this bihalve Sufficiaunte Warraunte ande Difcharge GEVEN under my Signet and Signe Manuel at my Manoure of Lekinfeld the xxijth daie of Novembre In the vth Yere of the Reigne of our Soverigne Lorde Kinge Henry the viijth.

> To my Welbiloved Servaunte the Baillif of my Lordefchipp of Lekinfeld aforefaid and Kepar of my faid Carre at Arome Ande to the Under-Kepres of the fame for the tyme beynge.

> YERELIE.

YERELIE.

THE COPIES of the **WARRAUNTS** made to the Receyvours Yerely for th'Affignemente of fuche **MONEY** as they muft deliver for the Kepinge of my Lordis Hous.

WELBILOVIDE I grete youe wele Ande wooł ande ftraitely charge youe withoute Delaye as ye entende to have me your goode Lorde ande woll Exchewe youe that at maye enfieu unto youe for the contrarie doinge at your Jeopardy Faile not to content ande paye unto my Welbilovid Servauntie Richerde Gowge Comptroller of my Hous ande Gilberte Wedal Clarke of my Kitchinge ftanding chargid with my hous (for the Firfte Payment of th'Affignement affignede to theim for Kepinge of my faide Hous for this Yere begynnynge at Michaelmas in the vth Yere of the Reigne of our Sovreign Lorde king Henry the viijth) of the Revenues of my Landes within your Receit in the Countie of Northumbreland of the Yere endyng at the faid Michaelmas The Somme of an **HUNDRETH** ande **THRESCORE POUNDS** of fuche Money as is due unto me uppon th'Auditte at the faid Michaelmas **YEVEN** under my Signet at my Manour of Lekinfeld the xixth daie of Novembre In the vth Yere of the Reigne of our faid Sovereigne Lord Kinge Henry the viijth.

To my Truftie and Welbilovide the Receyvoure of my Landis within the Countie of Northumbrelande for the tyme beinge.

YERELIE.

YERELIE.

WELBELOVIDE I grate youe wele Ande wol ande ftraitelie charge you withoute delaye as ye intende to have me your goode Lorde ande wol exchew that at maye enfiew unto you for the contrarye doinge at your Jeopardie Faile not to content ande paye unto my welbilovide Servauntis Richard Gowge Comptroller of my Hous ande Gilbert Wedal Clarke of my Kitchinge ftanding chargidde with my faid Hous For the iiijth Payment of the Affignemente affignid to theme for Keping of my faide Hous for this Yere (begynnynge at Michaelmas in the vth Yere of the Reigne of our Sovereign Lorde King Henry the viijth) of the Revenues of my Lands within your Receite in the Countie of York Due unto me of the Martynmas Ferme payable at Candlemas The SOME of ecɭviij *l.* xix *s.* j *d.* — YEVEN undre my Signet at my Manour of Lekinfeld the xixth daie of Novembre In the vth Yere of the Reigne of our Sovereigne Lorde King Henry the viijth.

Too my Truftie and Welbelovide the Receyvours of al my Landis within the Countie of Yorke for the tyme beinge.

E o   YERELIE.

YERELIE.

ITEM that vij WARRAUNTIS be made Yerelie for th'Affignement of fuche MONEY As is appointed to them that haithe the Charge of my Lordis Hous To be made aftir the Forme of the Warraunts afore writtyn That is to faye iij in the Firſt Quartre bitwixt Michaelmas and Chriſtynmas Viz. Oone to the Receyvour of Northumbreland for cLx l. One to the Receyvour of Cumbrelande for c l. One to the Receyvour of Yorkeſhire for Lxxvij l. viij s. Whiche Money to be paide of the Revenues due uppon th'Audiċts Yerelye. TWO Warraunts in the Seconde Quarter bitwixt Criſtynmas ande oure Ladie Daie in Lent Viz. Oone Warraunte to the Receyvour of Yorkeſhire for ccLviij l. xix s. j d. One to the Receyvoure of Northumberlande for cvij l. iij s. x d. Whiche Money to be paide of the Martynmas Ferme of the ſaide Shires OONE Warraunte in the iij d Quarter bitwixt our Ladie Daie ande Midſommer to the Receyvour of Cumbrelande for Lx l. of the Martynmas Ferme of the ſaide Shires Whiche 'is' payable but thanne AND OONE Warraunte bitwix Midſommer ande Michaelmas to the Receyvour of Northumbreland for cxxj l. ix d. Whiche Money to be paide of the Whitſondaie Ferme of the Said Shires WHICHE is in full contentacion of the Some aſſignedde for the Keping of my Lordis Hous Yerelie.

YERELY.

ITEM it is ordeiyinde by my Lorde and his Counſaill That the Lxvj l. xiij s. iiij d. Whiche is aſſignyd now more thanne the old Aſſignemente for Keapyng of the Houſs Be lefte in the REMAYNETHE of the Parcellis of Stuf remaynynge Yerely at the Yeires Ende Too th'Entente that
the

the fame Remaynethe that fhal be left unfpent fhal be grater in valloure by the forefaide Some in theis Parcells of Grofs Empcions followinge AS to fay Wheat Malte Beefe Muttons Wyne Wax ANDE to be lefte in fuche Parcells of the afoyrnamyde Empcions as may be provydid befte cheep the faide Yeir for my Lords Profit and Advantauge.

YERELIE.

ITEM xvij Warraunts for xxix DOIS for th'Expencis of my Lordis Hous bitwixt Alhallowdaye ande Shroftide Yerelie Viz. Oone Warraunte for Two Dois at Spofforde for Alhallodaie A Warraunte for Thre Dois at the Great Parke of Topcliff for the iij Firft Weiks bitwixt Alhallowday and Criftynmas A Warraunte for Thre Dois out of the Litle Parke of Topcliff for the iij Secounde Weiks bitwixt Alhallowdaie ande Criftynmas Ande A Warraunte for Two Dois out of Helaghe Parke for the Two Laft Weeks bitwixt Alhallowdaie ande Criftynmas A Warrauntt for Two Dois out of Lekinfeld Parke for Chriftynmas daie. A Warraunte for Oon Doo out of Catton Parke for Sainte Stephins Daie A Warraunte for Two Dois oute of Newfham Parke for the Hallidaies bitwixt the faide Sainte Stephins Daie and Newyeres Daie A Warraunte for Two Dois oute of Helaghe Parke for the Worke-daies bitwixt Newyeres Daie and xijth Daie A Warraunt for Two Dois oute of the Great Parke of Topcliff Ande A Warraunt for Oon Doo oute of the Litle Parke of Topcliff for the xijth Daie of Criftynmas A Warraunt for Oon Doo oute of Spofforde for the Firft Weike bitwixt the xijth Daie of Chriftynmas ande Shroftide A Warraunte for Oone Doo oute of the Litle Parke of Topclif for the Secounde Weke A Warraunte for Oon Doo oute of the Greate Parke of Topclif for the iij^d Weike A Warraunt for Two Dois out of Helaghe Parke for the iiijth
Weike

Weike and v^{th} Weike A Warraunte for Oon Doo oute of Lekinfeld Parke for the vj^{th} Weike A Warraunte for Two Dois oute of Spofforde Parke for Newyeres Daie Ande A Warraunte for Oone Doo out of Catton Parke for the vij^{th} Weike.

The D E R E appointed oute of every Parc in Winter as hereaftir followithe.

WARRAUNTE for the Hous in Winter is xvij.

Spofforde – – – –	v.
Great Parke of Topcliff	vj.
Litle Parc of Topcliff	v.
Helaughe – – – –	vj.
Lekinfeld – – – –	iij.
Catton – – – – –	ij.
Newfechame – – –	ij.

The Noumbre of Dois is — xxix.

YERELIE.

ITEM xj WARRAUNTS for Twenty BUCKS for th'Expenfis of my Lords Hous bitwixt May Daie ande Halliroode Daie nexte following Viz. A Warraunte for Oone Buck oute of the Great Parke of Wrefil for the Firft Weik aftir May Daie A Warraunte for Thre Bucks oute of the Great Parke of Topcliff for the Second Thirde ande iiij^{th} Weike aftir May Daie A Warraunte for Two Bucks oute of the Litle Parke of Topcliff for Whitfondaie and that Weke whiche is the vth Weike

Weike after May Daie A Warraunt for Two Bucks oute of Spofforde Parke for the vjth ande vijth Weike aftir May Daie A Warraunt for Two Bucks oute of Helaghe Park for the viijth Weeke ande ixth aftir May Daie A Warraunt for Oone Bucke oute of Lekinfeld Parke for the xth Weeke aftir May Daie A Warraunte for Two Bucks oute of Catton Parke for the xjth and xijth Weke aftir May Daie A Warraunte for ij Bucks oute of Newſam Parc for the xiijth ande xiiijth Weeke aftir May Daie A Warraunte for Two Bucks oute of the Great Parke of Topcliff for the xvth and xvjth Weke aftir May Daie A Warraunte for ij Bucks out of the Litle Parc of Topcliff for the xvijth and xviijth Weike aftir May Daie Ande a Warraunte for Oon Buck oute of Spofford Parke for the xixth Weike aftir May Daie.

The D E R E appointid oute of every Parc in Sommer as hereaftir followithe.

WARRAUNTES for the Hous in Sommer is xj.

Great Parc of Topcliff	v.
Litle Parc of Topcliff	iiij.
Great Parc of Wreſelle	j.
Spofforde Parc – – –	iij.
Helaughe Parke – –	ij.
Lekenfelde Parke – –	j.
Catton Parke – – –	ij.
Neweſham Parke – –	ij.

The Noumbre of Bucks is — xx.

YERELIE.

YERELYE.

ITEM That the faide Clarks of the Kitchinge fee that whenfomevre it fhal fortune my Lorde to go in the KINGIS SERVICE beyonde the See That alle his Lordefchip Servaunts of Houfhold That goith ovir with his Lordefchip the faide tyme That they have no Houfehold Wagies from the Daie that they go oute uppon with his Lordefchip To the Daie that they come home agayne Which haith the Kingis Wagies of my faide Lorde by the daie And Thanne they to entre into Wagies in the Chequirroil whenne they com home but from that Daie at they come Home on.

YERELYE.

ITEM It is ordeynidde by my Lorde ande his Counceil at every Yeres Ende that th'Accompte of the Hous endis of That theire fhal be at every fuche Yere endynge of the faide Houfeholde A Bille to be made of the REMAINETHE of fuche Stuf as remainith unfpent provided ande boughte in the Yere afforefaide WITH the Namys of the parcellis every parcel by it felf With the price that it was bought fore Ande the daie of the mouneth that it was bought on THE faide Bill to be a Memorandum to be put in the Booke of Hous- hold for th'Ordre of the Hous of the Newyerefe thorrow the Levis of the Booke whiche is ordeynidde for the houfe Bicaufe they fhal not have it written in the faide Booke Bicaus the Some of the Remaneth yerelie is not certein Ande therefore the Parcellis therof is thrawyn in the Sommes of the Parcellis of the Sommes of Money Bicaus the Parcells of the Remanith cannot keip alwaie a certeigne Some but fome Yere more and fome Yere lefs as the cafe doith require Nor alway oone

maner

maner of Parcellis to be the Remaneth nor of like Valoure as they be outher Yeris Bicaus the Stuf that is beſt cheipe whiche muſt be expendidde the moiſt of that Stuf is beſt to be provided Ande bicaus that the ſaid Romaineth of the Stuf unſpent of the Yere afore ended ſchal be the firſte Some paide in partie of Paymente of the Somme of th'Aſſignemente appointed for the Keping of my Lords Hous for the Newyere W H E R- F O R E this ſaide article is made for the knowlege of th'Ordre therof Bicaus it ſchal be yerely the firſt Some ande Parcell paide for the Hous.

Y E R E L I E.

ITEM to be paide to the Stewarde Treſaurer Comptroller or Clarks of the Kitchinge Whiche ſtondeth chargidde for to make provicion for cclxvij Quarters and a Buſſel of OITS after xx d. the Quartre for th'Expens of xxvij Hors of my Lordis ſtanding in his Lordeſchip Stabille at the charge of the Houſe for oone whole Yere Viz. vj gentle Hors iiij Palfreis (as to ſay Oone for my Ladie and iij for iij Gentillwomen) Hobbies ande Naggis iij (Viz. Oone for my Lorde to ride uppon Oone ledd for my Lorde and Oone ſpaire) Sumpter Hors ande Mail Hors iij (Viz. Oone for the Bedde Oon for the Coffurs ande Oone for the Maille) vj Hors for theim that ar at my Lordis Horſſinge (as to ſay A Yong Gentillman Hors that is at my Lordis fyndinge The Yoman of the Stabill Hors A Grome of the Chaumbre Hors at my Lordis findinge A Grome of the Steropp Hors Ande Two Horſſis for the Sumptermen that ledith the Sumpter-Hors) vij Charriot Hors to draw in the Charriot A F T I R xj Quarters ande iij Busſhellis for every Hors in the ſaid Hoole Yere aftir a Pekke upon the Daie for an Hors Whiche amountithe to the Somme for an Hors in the ſaid Hoole Yere xxviij s. xj d. ob. ANDE ſo th'oole Somme

for

for the faid xxvij Hors for an Hoole Yere is xxv *l.* xj *s.* x *d.* ob,
If it be at xx *d.* a Quarter.

YERELIE.

I T E M that the faide Stewarde Treafaurer Comptroller
or Clarks of the Kitchinge (that doith ftonde chargidde)
provyde for Lxxvj Quartres Dim. ij Buffells ande a Pekke of
BEANYS aftir ij *s.* viij *d.* the Quartre for HORS-BREADE
to be made of for th'Expencis of my Lordis Horffis in Housholde for an Hoole Yere — Somme of the Beanes x *l.* iiij *s.*
ix *d.* ob. ANDE alfo to make Provicion for cxxxiij Quartres Dim. and Dim. Busfhel of O I T E S after xvj *d.* the
Quartre for th'Expens of my faid Lordis Horffis in Houfeholde for the faid Hoole Yere — Somme of the faide OITES
x *l.* iiij *s.* viij *d.* ═ SOMME xx *l.* ix *s.* vj *d.* Wherof x *l.* iiij *s.* ix *d.*
ob. is appointed to be paide to the faide Stewarde Treafaurer
Comptroller or Clarks of the Kitchinge for the Firft Paymente Viz. for the Provicion of xxxviij Quartres iij Buf-
fhel Dim. Pek of Beanys cij *s.* iiij *d.* to be provided at Alhallowtide Ande for Provicion of Lxxvj Quarters Dim. ij Buf-
fhel ande a Pekke of Otes cij *s.* iiij *d.* to be provided at
the faide Alhallowtide to be paide at the faide Criftynmas
Whiche Beanes ande Oites is appointidd to ferve from the
faide Michaelmas unto our Ladie Daie next followinge AND
to be paide to the faide Perfonnes for the Secounde Paymente at Eftur x *l.* iiij *s.* ix *d.* Viz. for the Provicion of
xxxviij Quarters iij Busfhells Dim. Pekke of Beanys to be
providedde at Candlemas after Seede Tyme cij *s.* iiij *d.* ob.
Ande for the Provicion of Lxxvj Quarters Dim. ij Buf-
fhellis and a Pekke of Ootis to be paide at the faid Efture
cij *s.* iiij *d* qu. to be provided at the faide Candlemas affore
Seede Tyme Whiche Beanes ande Oites providedde at the
faide tyme is appointed to ferve from oure faide Ladye
Daye

Daye in Lente to Michaelmas next followinge A N D fo
th'oole Somme appointed for the Provicion of the faide Beenys
ande Oites for th'Expencis of the faid Hors for an Hoole Yere
for the charge of the Hous is xx *l.* ix *s.* vj *d.*

Y E R E L I E.

ITEM To be paide to the faide Stewarde Trefaurer
Comptroller or Clarks of the Kitchinge for to provide for
iiij^{xx} Loode of HAYE after ij *s.* viij *d.* the Loode for th'Expencis of my Lordis Horffis ftanding in his Lordefchip Stable
at the charge of the Houfe — Viz. vj Gentil Hors to ftonde
in the Stable at Haye and Harde-meate by the fpace of the
Hoole Yere whiche are alowide aftir every Hors in the faid
Hoole Yere iiij Loide of Haye $=$ xxiiij Loide.   Four Palfraies
Wherof Oone for my Ladye and iij for iij Gentlewomen to
ftonde in the Stabill at Haye and Harde-meat by the fpace of
half a Yere Aftir a Loode Dim. for every Hors in the faide
half yere $=$ vj Loids.   Thre Hobbies ande Naggis Viz. Oone
for my Lorde to ride on Oone to be ledde Ande Oone to
fpaire to ftonde in the Stable at Haye ande Harde-meate by
the fpace of th'oole yere Aftir ij Loids Dim. for every Nagge
in the faid yere $=$ vij Loides Dim.   Thre Sumpterhors ande
Mail Hors Viz. Oone for the Bedde Oone for the Coffres
ande Oone for the Mail to ftonde in the Stable at Haye ande
Harde-meate by the fpace of th'oole Yere after iij Loide for
every Hors in the faid yere $=$ ix Loides.   Six Hors for theme
that is at his Lordefhip Horffinge As to faye William Worm
Hors The Yoman of the Stable Hors A Grome of the Sterop
Hors ij Hors for the ij Sumptermen that ledith the Sumpter-
Hors To ftonde in the Stable by the fpace of half a yere Aftir
a Loode Dim. for an Hors in the faide half yere $=$ ix Loodes.
Seven Great Trotting Hors to drawe in the Charriot To
ftonde in the Stable at Haye ande Harde-meate by the fpace

of

of th'oole yere Aftir iij Loids Dim. for every Hors in the faide
Yere = xxiiij Loide Dim. — AND iij Mylne Hors As to faye
Two to drawe in the Mylne Ande Oone to carry Stuf to the
Mylne ande from the Mylne To ftonde in the Stabille by the
fpace of the faide Hoole yere aftir iij Loide Dim. for every
Hors in the faide yere Ande half a Loide lefs at all in the
faide yere.

YERELY.

ITEM that the Clarks of the Kitchinge or of the Breve-
ments every Yere bring my Lord a Bille of the REMA-
NETH takyn at the faide Michaelmas to be lookedde uppon
Ande if it amounte to a more Some thanne the Remaneth
whiche is fet in the begynnyng of Ordres of Houfehold
Thanne fomuche as it amountithe to more to be abaited in
the Firfte Warraunte for the Affignement of the Houfe in the
Firfte Quarter bitwixte Michaelmas ande Criftynmas yerelie
ANDE if the Remaineth fortune to be leffe thanne is appointedde in the Begynnynge of the Booke of Ordres That
thanne the Firfte Warraunte for th'Affignemente of the Hous
in the Firfte Quarter bitwixte Michaelmas and Criftynmas
be made fomuche more as the Money wantinge of the
faide Remaineth Bicaus of makinge oute of th'oole Affignemente.

YERELY.

ITEM that the faide Clarks of the Kytchinge or of the
Counting-hous maike my Lorde a Bille yerely at Michaelmas
at th'ende of the yere what Remaineth of the MONEY
affignede for the Kepinge of the Houfe for that yere to
theire handes comynge As to faye Remanynge of the Houfehold

hold Wages Of the Chappel Wages Of the Winter Horſe-meat Of the Total Some of the Remaineth remanyng unſpent of the ſaide yere OR any outher Empciouns that ar bought better cheipe thanne the Prices appointedde in the Booke of Ordres of the Hous THAT my Lorde may ſe what Remained ſpared for thies foreſaide cauſis.

YERELY.

ITEM that the Clarks of the Kitchinge or of the Coun-ting-hous make my Lorde a Bill yerely at Michaelmas at th'ende of the yere of every GROSS EMPCION bought that yere for th'Expens of my Lords Houſe What it doith excede if any be above the Prices appointedde in the Booke of Ordres of the Hous That my Lorde may ſe wherin he is chargidde more for that cauſe in the ſaide Groſs Empcions.

YERELYE.

THE COPY of the Firſte WARRAUNTE for th'Aſſignement of my Lordes Hous When the Re-manethe is more thanne is ratidde in this Booke.

WELBELOVIDE I grete youe wele Ande wol ande charge youe Al Excuſis ande Delaies laide aparte As ye intende to have me your goode Lorde Ande wol Exchew that at may enſieu unto youe for the contrarye doying YE fail not furthwith uppon the ſight herof to content ande paye unto my Welbylovid Servaunts Robert Percy Comptroller of my Hous and Gilbert Wedal Chief Clarks of my Kitch-inge ſtanding chargydde with my ſaide Hous this Yere in
fulle

fulle contentacion of the Firſt Paymente of th'Aſſignement aſſignedde unto theyme for kepinge of my ſaide Hous for this Yere (begynnyny at Michaelmas in the vj[th] yere of the Reigne of oure Soverigne Lorde Kyng Henry the viij[th]) of the Revenus of al my Lands within Yorkeſchire whiche ſhal be dew unto me at this Audite to your hands commyng to my Coffurs Wheire is ſeen by me and my Counſail that ye doo paye but the Some of cxꞮj *l.* xj*s.* vj*d.* ob. qu. in ful Contentacion of their Some aſſigned for their Firſt Paymente at this tyme ccxxxvj *l.* x*s.* iij*d.* qu. Seynge that they have receyvidde in the price of Divers Victuallis in ther laſte Remaneth remanynge of the yere ended at Michaelmas the Some of ꞁxxvj *l.* x*s.* iij*d.* qu. Whiche makith upp the foreſaid Some aſſigned theim for the Firſt Paymente of the Firſte Quarter Whiche Remaneth amountithe to more than the Remaineth accuſtumedde in the Booke of Ordris by the Some of xviij *l.* viij*s.* v*d.* qu. For whiche Conſideration their is clere paid unto theim at this tyme but the Some of cxꞮj *l.* xj*s.* vj*d.* ob. qu. bicaus of the Batement of the foreſaid xviij *l.* viij*s.* v*d.* qu. whiche they have more in the Remaineth of this yere thanne they hadde the Laſt Yere YEVEN at my Caſtel of Wreſſil the xiiij[th] Daie of Octobre in the vj[th] Yere of the Reigne of our Soverigne Lorde King Henry the viij[th].

> Too my Truſty Servaunte William Worme Gentillmen Uſher of my Chambre my Coffurer and General Receyvour of alle my Landes in the Northe Parties.

YERELY.

YERELY.

COPY of the Laſt WARRAUNTE for th'Aſſignemente of my Lords Houſe.

WELBELOVIDE I grete Youe wele And wol and ſtraitelie charge youe withoute delaye As ye entend to have me your good Lorde ande wool exchew that at maye enſieu unto youe for the contrary doynge at your Jeopardye Fail not to content ande paye unto my Welbelovide Servauntes Robert Percy Comptroller of my Hous ande Gilbert Wedal Cheif Clarke of my Kitchinge ſtandyng Chargidde with my ſaide Hous for the vijth and Laſte Payment of th'Aſſignement aſſigned unto theim for the Kepinge of my ſaide Houſe for this Yere (begynnyng at Michaelmas in the vjth Yere of the Reigne of our Soverigne Lorde King Henry the viijth ande ſchal 'be' ended at Michaelmas next followinge) of the Revenues of alle my Landis in Northumbrelainde to your hands cuminge dewe to my Coffures of the Whitſondaie Ferme payable at Lambmas YE content and paye the Some of eiiij $l.$ xiiij $s.$ ix $d.$ in Redy Money ovre ande beſides that they haive xvj $l.$ vj $s.$ chargidde uppon theim the ſaide tyme as Parcel of theire Aſſignemente as in the Fermes of Diverſe Medowis ande Paſturs at Lekinfeld ande Wreſſil As it apperith more plainly in the Booke of Ordreis of my ſaide Hous for the making up of cxxj $l.$ ix $d.$ aſſigned unto theim in the iiijth Quartre bitwixt Midſommer and Michaelmas Which is in fu!l Paymente of their Hoole Aſſignement for this Hoole Yere Ending at the ſaide Michaelmas next for to come YEVEN undre my Signet ande Signe Manuil at my Manour of Lekinfeld the xx^a Daie

Daie of Novembre in the vjth Yere of the Reigne of our Soverigne Lorde King Henry the viijth.

To my Truftie Servaunte William Worme Gentilmen Ufhar of my Chambre my Coffurer ande General Receyvour of all my Landis in the North Parties.

YERELY.

COPY of the Firfte **WARRAUNTE** for Keaping of my Lordes Hous When the Affignemente is M *l.* Ande the **REMANETH** no Parcell therof.

WELBILOVID I grete you weall And woll and charge you All excufis ande delaies laide aparte As ye intende to have me youre goode Lorde Ande wol exchewe that at may infew unto you for the contrary doing at your Jeopartie Y E faile not furthwith uppon the fight hereof to contente and pay unto my Welbilovid Servauntes William Worm Gentillman Ufcher of my Chaumbre Gilbert Wedal Chief Clark of my Kitching ande Thomas Hurwod Yoman Ufher of my Chaumbre (ftanding chargid with my Hous this Yeir) in partie of Paymente of M *l.* affigned unto theim now for th'Expens of my Hous this faide yeir Whiche is above the old affignement appointed for keaping of my faid Hous by LXVj *l.* xiij *s.* iiij *d.* for the yeres by paft Ande to be paid to theim in full Paymente for theire Firft Paymente of their faid Affignemente affigned unto them for Keaping of my faide Hous this Yere (begynnyng at Michaelmas in the Nyente Yere of our
Sovvereigne

Sovvereigne Lord King Henry th'eight) the Some of cc *l.*
To be takin of the Revenuis of all my Landes within Yorke-
shire whiche shal be due unto me at this Audicte to your
handes cuming to my Coffires WHICHE Some is moir by
Lxvj *L* xiij *s.* iiij *d.* than haith been accustomed afore tyme
assigned for keaping of my Hous For th'entente that they shall
leive remanyng at the yeres ende of divers Victuallis unspent
paide for as mooche as amountithe to the Some of Lxvj *L* xiij *s.*
iiij *d.* cleir paide fore ovir ande above alle outher Creditours
full paid for the saide Yeir Ande also bicause they schall haive
no Parcell of the Remanethe of the former Yeir ended at
Michaelmas last past Whiche shall stande charged this Yeir
with my saide Hous But that they shall pay Redy Money
fore Of this cc *l.* of their Fyrst Paymente of their saide
Assignement to theim that was chargid the last Yeir So that
they have no Creditours owing of that former yeir And the
Money paid for the Remanethe ovir and above all Creditoures paide that remaynes to be paid to my Coffers as
Money spared of th'Assignement of the former. YEVEN
under my Signet and Signe Maneuell at my Manour of
Leckynfealde iiij^te Die Octobris Anno Regni Regis Henrici
Octavi nono.

   To my Trusty Servaunte William Worme my
    Coffurer Gentillman Uscher of my Chamber and
    my Receyvour Generall of all my Landes in the
    North Parties this Yeir.

                  YERELY.

YERELY.

COPY of the Laſt WARRAUNTE for Keaping of my Lordes Hous When th'Aſſignement is M *l.* Ande the PASTURES no Parcell of it.

WELBELOVIDE I grete you weal And wol and ſtraitely charge you without deley As ye intende to have me your good Lord And wol exchew that at may enſieu unto you for the contrary doing at your Jeopartie Faile not to contente and paye to my Welbelovide Servauntes William Worme Gentillman Uſcher of my Chaumbre Gilbert Wedall chief Clarke of my Kitching ande Thomas Horwod Yoman Uſchre of my Chaumbre ſtanding chargid with my Hous this Yeir (begynnynge at Michaelmas in the Nyente Yeir of the Reigne of our Soverigne Lord Kinge Henry th'eight Ande ſchall ende at Michaelmas next following) the Some of Oon Hundreth and Fifty Poundes in full contentacion of the vijth and laſt Paymente of th'Aſſignement aſſigned unto theim for keaping of my ſaide Houſe Of the Revenues of all my Landes in Northumberland to your hands cumming dew to my Coffers of the Whitſonday Fermes paiabill at Candelmas ' and ' Lambmas To th'entente that they ſhall contente and paye in redy money at the Yeirs ende for all ſuche Medowes ande Paſtures as ſhal be occupied for th'Expens of my ſaide Hous the ſaide Yeire As well at Leckynfeald as at Wreſill YEVIN under my Signet and Signe-Mannuell at my Mannour of Leckynfealde the xviijth Daie of October in the Nyente Yere of the Reign of our Souvereign Lord King Henry the viijth.

> Too my Truſty Servaunte William Worm my Coffurer Gentillman Uſcher of my Chaumbre Ande my Receyvour Generall of all my Landes in the North Parties this Yeir.

> ### YERELY.

YERELY.

ITEM It is Ordeynide by my Lord and his Counſaill that the Clarks of the Kitching or of the Counting-hous ſhall write the vij Warraunts cler upp in Parchemente that be made Yeirely for th'Aſſignemente of the Money for Keaping of my Lordes Houſ of ſuche Money as is appointed to theim that haith the charge for Keaping of my ſaide Lords Hous for the Recept of Money.

YERELY.

WELBELOVIDE I grete You wele And wol and ſtraitly charge youe withoute deley As ye intende to have me your good Lord and wol exchew that at may enſieu unto you for the contrary doing at your Jeopardy Faill ye not to Content and Pay to my Welbilovyd Servaunts William Worme and Thomas Horwod Gentlemen Uſhers of my Chaumbre. And Gilbert Wedall Chief Clark of my Kytching ſtanding char- gid with my Houſ this Yeir in full Payment of the vij^th ande laſt Paymente of the ſaide Aſſignemente aſſignid unto theim for keaping of my ſaide Houſ this Yeir of Revenues of my Landes in Cumbreland by You receyvid of my Coffurer William Worme to your handes cuming That ye content and pay the Some of c l. of ſuche Money as is dew unto me of the Whitſonday Ferme payable at Lambmes Too th'entent that they ſhall content and pay now at the Yeres end for the Fer- mis of all ſuche Meddowes ande Paſtures in ther Handes as is occupied for th'Expenſes of my Houſ this ſaide Yeir That is to ſay to the Baillyf of Leckynfeald for the Ferm of My- dewes ande Paſtures ther xij l. xs. To the Grave of Newſham for the Ferme of Middowes ande Paſters ther Lxxvjs. Ande to

the

the Baillyf of Topclif for the Ferme of Middowes and Pasters their xxxvj*s*. viij*d*. Somme of all xviij *l*. ij*s*. viij*d*. YEVEN under my Signet and Signe Manuell at my Maynour of Leckingfield the ixth day of December The tenth Yeir of the Reign of our Sovrain Lord King Henry the viijth.

YERELY.

ITEM A Bill to be made of the Names Yerlie to my Lord at Michaelmas at th'end of every Yeare of all the Percelles of STUFFE providede and remainynge Unspente for the Keapinge of my Lordes House for the former Yeare With the Namis of every Percell and what Quantitie remaineth of every Parcell that so doth remayn unspent of the Provicion for Keapinge of my Lordes House for the said formere Yeare endet at the said Michaelmas which is fullie paid for and remaneth in the Remaneth of the said Yeare endit at the said Michaelmas.

YERELY.

ITEM It is ordeind by my Lord and his Counsaill That thoes that standeth charged with my Lordes House shall maik my Lord a Bill Yearlie at Michaelmas at th'ende of the Yeare of the Names of all such MONNEY as is savid of th'Assignmente of the House As to saie in the Checkes of all mannere of Bordwaiges thoroughoute the Yeare The Checks of al mannere of Paymente of Waiges for my Lord Houshold-Servaunts for the ij Halfe Yeres Alsoo the Checkes of all mannere of Payments of Waigies to the Gentilmen of my Lords Chapell of the iiij Quarters of the Yeare And also the Checkes of the Absence of the Parsonnes assigned in the Winter and Somare Horsmeate.

YERELY.

YERELY.

ITEM It is ordynyde by my Lorde and his Counfail Yerly at Mychaelmas at th'end of the Yere That thois Parfons that ftandeth chargede with th'Expenfes for Kepyng of my Lordes Hous for the former Yere fhall caus yerely at th'ende of the Yere when the Remaneth is takyn of the Provicion of the VICTUALLS of unfpent remanyng of the former Yere Provifion The Clerks of the Keching or of the Counting-houfe to make his Lordfhipe a Bill of the Namys of every Empcion with the Quantitie and Totall Some of the fame which is to be ordynede providet for th'Expenfes of my Lordes Hous according to the Booke of Ordres AND to expreffe in the faid Bille what is fpared of the fame of every Empcion apojnted in the Booke of Ordres to be provided for the Hole Yere With the Nayme Price and Quantitie and alfo what Empcions doth excede above the fam Price and Quantitie apointid in the faid Booke of Ordres to be provided for the Hole Yere And to name the Empcion with Price and Quantitie what is fpared or what it dothe excede in every of the faid Empcions in Quantitie or Price.

XXXV.

XXXV.

THE NEW WARRANTS devifid by my Lord That fhal be made YERELY for the DAIES OF PAYMENT for the SOMES affignid for Keapyng of my Lordes Houfs Yerely.

YERELY.

WELBELOVED I grete Youe wele Ande woll ande ftrately charge Yowe without deley As ye intende to have me Your Good Lord Ande wol exchew that at may enfiew unto you for the contrary doing at your Jeopardy Fail ye not furthwitth uppon the fyght herof To content and pay out of my Coffers unto my Welbilovid Servauntes William Worme and Thomas Horwod Gentlemen Ufhirs of my Chaumbre ande Gilbert Wedall Cheif Clark of my Kitchinge ftanding chargid with the Keaping of my Houfs theis Yeir (begynnyng at Michaelmes laft paft befoir the dait hereof) In party of Payment of Oon Thoufande Powndes affignid unto theim now for th'Expences of and Keaping of my faide Houfs for this faide Yeir Whiche is above the old Affignement ap-pointid in my Booke of Orders for Keaping of my faide Houfs in Yeirs by paft by Lxvj *l.* xiij *s.* iiij *d.* Ande to be paide unto theim now uppon Monday the furft daye of the Moneth of November Whiche fhal be Alhallowday next cuming aftir the Daite hereof For their FURST PAYMENT of their faid Affignement affignid unto theim for Keaping of my faide Houfs this Yeir begynnyng at Machaelmes in the Tenthe

Yeir

Yeir of the Reigne of our Sovvereigne Lord King Henry the
viijth In full contentacion for the Payment of their furſt Warraunte of their Aſſignement for Keaping of my ſaide Hous this
ſaide Yeir the SOMME of Two Hundreth Powndes Whiche
is the Furſt Warraunte paide unto theim in this Quarter
bitwixte Michaelmes and Criſtenmes THE ſaid Some to be taken
of the Revenues of all my Landes within Yorkeſhir Whiche
ſhal be dew unto me of my ſaid Landes uppon this Audicte
of Michaelmes laſt for the Yeir ending at the ſaid Michaelmes
to your handes cuming by my Receyvours for the tyme being
Of all my ſaid Landes The ſaide Some to be reteynid by
th'andes of every of theim befoir named now ſtanding chargid with my Houſ for this Yeir of You my Coffurer for the
tyme being Whiche Some is moir by the foreſaid ʟxvj l. xiij s.
iiij d. thanne the old Aſſignemente appointed in the Booke of
Orders for th'entente that they ſhall leef remanyng at the
Yeres ende of Divers Victualls unſpent and paide fore as
muche as amountithe to the foreſaide Some of ʟxvj l. xiij s.
iiij d. clear paide fore Ovir and above all outher Creditors and
Stuf taiken for the full Expences ande Keaping of my ſaide
Houſ for the ſaide hoole Yeir Whiche Yeir ſhall ende at Michaelmas next to come aftir the Dait herof Ande alſo bicauſe
they ſhal have no Parcell of the Remaneth of no Maner of
Stuf provided for the Expences of my ſaide Houſ whatſom-
evir they be Whiche remaneth unſpent of the former Yeir ending at Michaelmes laſt paſt Whiche ſhall ſtande chargid this
Yeir with my ſaid Houſ But that they ſhall pay redy money
fore of that c l. of their Furſte Payment of their ſaide Aſſignement to theime that was chargid the laſt Yeir So that they
leef no Creditours uncontente nor unpaid of the former Yeir
Ande the reſt of the Money remanyng the Remaneth paide
fore Ande all outher Creditours paide of that Yeir Thanne
that at remaynes They whiche ſtood chargid with my Houſ
for that Yeir to paye the ſame to my Coffers As Money ſavid

and

and unſpent of the Aſſignement for keaping of my ſaide Houſe for the foreſaide Yeir YEVEN undir my Signet and Signe Mannuill at my Maynour of Leck the laſt day of Septembre the Tenth Yeir of the Reign of our Souvereigne Lorde King Henry the viijth.

To my truſty ande Welbilovid Counſaillour Maiſter John Hobſon Bachellir of Devinity Ande chargid with the Receiptes and Payments of my Bookes of Foren Expeins and Reparacions this Yeir.

YERELY.

WELBELOVED I grete Youe wele Ande woll and ſtraitly charge Yow without delay As ye entende to baive me your good Lord Ande woll exchew that at may enſiew unto Youe for the contrary dooing at Your Jeopardy Faill ye not to content and pay out of my Coffers unto my Welbilovid Servaunts William Worm and Thomas Horwood Gentilemen Uſhers of my Chaumbr Ande Gilbert Wedall Cheef Clarke of my Kitchinge ſtanding chargid with my Hous this Yeir begynnyng at Michaelmes laſt paſt for the ij^e PAYMENT to be payd unto theyme now uppon Teuſday the laſt day of the Moneth of Novembre whiche ſhal be Sainte Andrew day nexte cuming aftir the Dait herof befoir Criſtenmes nexte to com For their ſaide Paymente of their Aſſignement aſſignid unto theim for Keaping of my ſaide Houſs this ſaide Yeir In full contentacion for the Paymente of their ſaide Warraunte of their Aſſignemente for Keaping of my ſaide Houſs this ſaide Yeir Begynnyng at Michaelmes laſte in the Tenth Yeir of the
Reigne

Reigne of our Souvereign Lord King Henry the viijth THE SOME of Oone Hundrith ande Thirty Powndes Whiche is the ij^{de} Warraunte paide unto theime in this Quarter bitwixt Michaelmes ande Criftenmes THE faide Some of cxxx *l.* to be taiken of the Revenues of all my Lands within the Countie of Cumbrelande whiche fhal be dew unto me of my faide. Landes uppon this Audicte of Michaelmes laft pafte for the Yeir ending at the faide Michaelmes to your handes cuming by my Receyvour for the tyme beinge of my faide Landes THE faide Some to be receyvid by th'aundes of every of theime befoir named nowe ftanding chargid with my Hous for this Yeir of Yow my Coffurir for the tyme beynge YEVEN under my Signet and Signe Manuell at my Maynour of Leckinfeld the – – – daye of Novembre The Tenthe Yeir of the Reigne of our Souvereigne Lorde King Henry the viijth.

To my trufty ande Welbilovyd Counfaillour Mr. John Hobfon Bachellr of Devinitie And chargid with all the Receptes and Payments of my Bookes of Foren Expences and Reparacions this Yeir.

YERELY.

YERELY.

WELBELOVID I grete yow wele And woll and ſtrately charge yow without deley as ye entende to have me your good Lord Ande woll exchew that at may enſiew unto yow for the contrary doing at your Jeopardy Faill ye not to contente and paye oute of my Coffers uuto my Welbilovid Servauntes William Worme and Thomas Horwodde Gentlemen Uſhers of my Chambre Ande Gilbert Wedall Cheef Clarke of my Kitching ſtanding chargid with my ſaide Houſs this Yeir begynnyng at Michaelmes laſt paſt For the iij^d PAYMENT to be paide unto theime uppon Thurſday the xxiiij day of the Monethe of Decembre whiche ſhal be Criſtenmes Evyn For their third Paymente of their Aſſignemente aſſignide unto theim for keaping of my ſaide Hous this ſaide Yeir In full contentacion for the Payment of their Thirde Warraunte of their Aſſignement for Keaping of my ſaide Hous this Yeir begynnyng at Michaelmes laſt In the Tenthe Yeir of the Reign of our Souvrayn Lord King Henry the viijth THE SOME of Foure ſcore Ten Powndes Whiche is the iij^d Warraunt and Laſt to be paid unto theim in this Quarter bitwixt Michaelmes and Criſtenmas in full Contentacion of their laſte Warraunte of that Quarter THE ſaide Some of iiij^{xx} x l. to be taken of the Revenues of all my Landes within the Countye of Northumbrelande Whiche ſhal be founde dew unto me of my ſaide Landes uppon this Audicte of Michaelmes laſt for the Yeir ending at the ſaid Michaelmes To your handes cuming by my Receyvour for the tyme being of my ſaide Landes The ſaid Soumne to be receyvid by t'handes of every of theim befoir namid now ſtanding chargid with my Houſs for this Yeir of yow my Coffurer for the tyme being YEVEN under my Signet and Signe Manuell at

my

my Maynour of Leckynfeld the xxij daie of Decembre The tenthe Yeir of the Reigne of our Sovereigne Lord King Henry the viij^th.

To my Trufty ande Welbelovid Counfaillor Maifter John Hobfon Bacheller of Divinitie Ande chargid with all the Recepts and Payments of my Bookes of Foren Expences ande Reparacions this Yeir.

YERELY.

WELBILOVYD I grete you wele Ande woll and ftraitly Charge Yowe without deley As ye entend to have me your good Lord Ande woll exchew that at may enfiew unto you for the contrary doyng at your Jeopardy Fayll ye not to content ande pay oute of my Coffers unto my Welby-lovyd Servaunts William Worme and Thomas Horwodde Gentlemen Ufhers of my Chaumbre And Gilbert Wedall Cheef Clark of my Kitchyng ftandyng chargid with my Hous this Yeir begynnynge at Michaelmas laft paft For the iiij^th PAYMENT to be paid unto theym uppon Wedinfday the fecond Day of February whiche fhal be Candellmas day next to com For their iiij^th Payment of theyr Affygnement affygnyd unto theym for keapyng of my fayd Hous this faid Yeir Yn full contentacion for the Payment of their iiij^th Warraunte of their Affygnement for keapyng of my fayd Hous this Yeyr begynnyng at Mychaelmes laft in the tenthe Yeir of the Reigne of our Souvereyn Lord King Henry the viij^th THE SOMME of Two Hundryth and Fourty Powndes Whiche is the iiij^th Warraunte paide unto theym for theyr fayd Af-

H h   fignement

fignement for kepyng of my fayd Hous this Yeir Ande the
Fyrft and Laft Warraunte payable unto theym in this Quarter
bytwixt Cryftenmes and our Lady Daye in Lent THE faide
Somme to be taikyn of my Revenues of all my Landes withyn
the County of York to your handes cumyng whiche ys founde
dew unto me of all my faide Landes within the fayd fhyre of
York of thys Yeyr Begynnyng at Michaelmes Of the Martynmes Ferme now dew ande payable to me of my faide Landes
of this faid fhyr at this fayd Candellmes to your handes
cumynge by my Receyour of the faym for the tyme beyng
of my faide Landes THE faid Somme to be receyvid by
th'aundys of every of theym befoir namyd now ftandynge chargid
with my Hous for this Yeir of Yow my Coffurer for the
tyme beynge YEVEN under my Signet and Signe Manuell
at my Caftell of Wrefill the furft day of February the Tenthe
Yeyr of the Reygne of our Souvrayne Lord King Henry
the viij^th.

Too my Trufty ande Welbilovyd Counfaillour Maifter John Hobfon Bachellir of Divinity And
chargid with all the Recepts and Payments of
my Bookys of Foren Expences and Reparacions
this Yeyr.

YERELY.

WELBELOVIDE I grete You wele And woll and
ftraitly charge youe without deley As ye entend to have me
Your good Lord And woll exchew that at may enfiew unto
You for the contrary doyng at your Jeopardy Faill ye not to
content and paye oute of my Coffers unto my Welbiloved
Servauntes William Worme ande Thomas Harwod Gentlemen.

men Ushers of my Chaumbre And Gilbert Wedall Cheef
Clark of my Kitching standyng chargid with my Hous
this Yeir begynnyng at Michaelmes last past For the vth
PAYMENT to be paide unto theim uppon Friday the xxv
Daie of the Mouneth of Marche whiche shal be our Lady Day
in Lent next to com For their v. Payment of their Assigne-
mente assignid unto theym for keaping of my said Hous this
said Yeir in full contentacion for the Payment of their vth
Warraunt of their Assignement for keaping of my said Hous
this Yeir Begynnyng at Michaelmes in the teuthe Yeir of the
Reigne of our Souvereigne Lord King Henry the viijth THE
SOMME of Oon Hundrith and Ten Powndes Whiche is
the vth Warraunte paid unto theym for their said assignement
for keaping of my saide Hous this said Yeir Ande the Fyrst
Warraunt payable unto theym in this Quarter bitwixte
our Lady Daye in Lent and Midsommer AND the said
Somme of cx $l.$ to be taiken of my Revenues of all my Landes
within the County of Northumbreland to your handis cuming which is found dew unto me of all my said Landes
within the said County of Northumbrelande of this Yeir
Begynnyng at Michaellmes of the Martynmes Ferm now dew
and payable to me of my said Landes of this said shyer at
this said Lady Daye to your handes cuming by my Receyvour
for the tyme beyng of my said Landes THE said Somme to
be receyvid by the handes of every of theym befoir namyd
now standyng chargid with my Hous for this Yeir of Yow
my Coffurer for the tyme beynge YEVEN at my Castell of
Wresill the xxiij^d daye of Marche the Tenthe Yeir of the
Reigne of our Sovaryn Lorde King Henry the viijth.

Too my Trusty ande Welbilovyd Counsaillour Maistir
John Dobson Bacheller of Devinity And charged with
all the Receptes ande Payments of my Bookes of Foren
Exspences ande Reparacions this Yeir.

YERELY.

YERELY.

WELBILOVID I grete Youe wele And woll and ſtraitly
charge You without deley As ye entend to have me your
good Lord Ande woll exchew that at may enſiew unto you
for the contrary doyng at your Jeopardy Faill not to content
and pay out of my Coffers to my Welbilovid Servaunts William Worm ande Thomas Horwod Gentlemen Uſhers of my
Chaumber Ande Gilberte Wedall Cheef Clark of my Kitchyng
ſtandyng chargid with my Houſs this Yeir Begynnyng at Michaelmes laſt paſt For the vjᵗʰ PAYMENT to be paid unto
theym uppon Satturdaye the xxvijᵗʰ Day of the Monnethe of
Aprill whiche ſhal be Eſtur Evyn next too com For their vjᵗʰ
Payment of their Aſſignement aſſignid unto theym for keaping
of my ſaid Hous this ſaide Yeir In full contentacion of the
Payment of their vjᵗʰ Warraunte of their Aſſignement for
Keaping of my ſaid Houſs this Yeir Begynnyng at Mychaelmes in the Tenth Yeir of the Reigne of our Souvereigne
Lord King Henry the viijᵗʰ THE SOMME of iiijˣˣ l. whiche
is the vjᵗʰ Warraunte paid to theym for their ſaid Aſſignement
for the keaping of my ſaid Hous this ſaid Yeir And the ijᵈ and
Laſt Warraunte payable unto theim in this Quarter bytwyxt
our Lady Day in Lent and Midſomer In full contentacion of
their laſt Warraunte of that Quarter THE ſaid Somme of
Foureſcor Poundes to be takyn of my Revenues of all my
Landes within the County of Cumbreland to your handes cuming Whiche is dew unto me of all my ſaide Landes within
the ſaid County of Cumberland of this Yeir Begynnyng at
Michaelmes of the Martynmes Ferme now dew and payable
to me of my ſaid Lands of the ſaid Shier at our Lady Day in
Lent laſt paſt To your handes cuming by my Receyvour for
the tyme being of my ſaid Landes THE ſaid Somme to be
Receyvid by th'aundes of every of theym befoir named now
ſtondyng

ftondyng chargid with my Houfs for this Yeir of Yow my Coffuerer for the tyme being YEVEN under my Signet and Signe Manuell at my Caftell of Wreffill the xvj Day of Aprill the Tenthe Yeir of the Reigne of our Souvreigne Lorde King Henry the viijth.

Too my Trufty and Welbilovid Counfaillour Maifter John Hobfon Bacheller of Devinity And chargid with all the Recepts and Payments of my Books of Foren Exfpenfis and Reparacions this Yeir.

YERELY.

WELBELOVED I grete you wele And wol and ftraitly charge You without deley As ye entend to have me Your Good Lord And wol exchew that at may enfiew unto You for the contrary doing at your Jeopardy Faill not to content ande paye oute of my Coffers to my Welbiloved Servauntes William Worme and Thomas Horwod Gentlemen Ufhers of my Chaumbre And Gilbert Wedall Cheef Clark of my Kitching ftonding chargid with my Hous this Yeir Begynnyng at Michaelmes laft paft for the vijth and laft Payment to be paid unto theym uppon Monday the furft Day of the Moneth of Auguft Whiche fhal be Lambmes Day next to com For their vijth and Laft PAYMENT In full contentacion and full payment for the Somme of their Hoole Affignement of Oon Thoufand Powndes affignid unto theym for keping of my faid Houfs for an Hoole Yeir Begynnyng at Michaelmes laft paft and endyng at Michaelmes next to com aftir the date herof In full payment of their vijth and Laft Warraunte in full contentacion of their hoole Somme of Affignement for keaping of
my

my said Hous this Yeir Begynnyng at Michaelmes in the
Tenthe Yeir of the Reigne of our Sovereigne Lord King
Henry the viijth THE SOMME of Oon Hundrith and Fyfty
Poundes whiche is the vijth Warraunte and Laſt paid unto
theim in full contentation of their ſaid Aſſignement for keaping of my ſaid Hous this ſaide Yeir And the firſt and Laſt
Warraunte payable unto theim in this Quarter bitwyxt Lambmes and Michaelmes for keaping of my ſaid Hous for this
boole Yeir whiche ſhall end at Michaelmes next to com THE
ſaid Some of Oon Hundreth and Fifty Poundes to be taiken
of my Revenues of all my Landes within the County of York
to your Handes cuming Whiche is dew unto me of all my
ſaid Landes within the ſaid County of York of this Yeir
begynnyng at Michaelmes of the Whitſonday Ferm now dew
and payable unto me of my ſaid Landes of the ſaid Shier at
this ſaid Lambmes to your Hands cuming by my Receyvour
for the tyme beinge of my ſaid Landes of the ſaid Shier The
ſaid Some to be receyvid by th'aundes of every of theym
befoir namid now ſtanding chargid with my Houſs for this
Yeir of You my Coffuerer for the tyme being To th'entent
that they ſhall content and pay now at the Yeires end for the
Fermes of all ſuche Meddowes and Paſtures that they have
occupyid in their Handes for th'exſpences of my Hous this
ſaide Yeir Above the Some of their Aſſignement paid to theym
for Keaping of my ſaide Houſs as is befoir ſaid As to ſay
to the Collectour of Leckynfeld for the Fermes of Meddowes
and Paſtures their that they have occupyid for the uſe of my
ſaid Houſs this Yeir Twelf Poundes and Ten Shillinges And
to the Grave of Newſham for the Ferme of Meddowes ande
Paſtures at Wreſill that they have occupied for the uſe of my
ſaid Houſs this Yeir Thre Powndes Sexteen Shillings And to
the Grave of Topeclif for the Ferme of Meddowes and Paſtures their that they have occupied for the uſe of my ſaide Houſs
this Yeir Twenty Shillinges Sex and Eight Pens In all xviij *l.*
ij *s.*

ij*s.* viij*d.* whiche they have occupied in their handes this faide
Yeir Ovir ande above the forefaid M *l.* affigned unto theim in
full contentacion for keaping of my faid Hous for this faid
Hoole Yeir endyng at Michaelmes next to com after the
Daite herof YEVEN &c. the Laft Day of July An° Regni
Regis Henrici viij^vi xj^no.

     Too my Trufty and Welbilovid Counfaillour Maifter
     John Hobfon Bacheller of Devinity And chargid
     with all the Recepts and Payments of my Books
     of Foren Exfpences and Reparacions this Yeir.

A NEWE

A NEWE DRAUGHT drawyn of the FYRSTE WARRAUNTE for the FYRST PAYMENTE of the Affignemente for Keapping of my Lordes Hous Yeirly WHEREIN is nowe Naymyd- the Quantities of VICTUALLES Remaynyng unfpent to the Vaillour of Oon Hundrethe Marks WHICHE fhal be favyd at the Yeires end of the Hoole Affignemente appoyntyd for Keapyng of my Lordes Hous of the VICTUALLES Provydid the former Yeirs.

YERELY.

WELBELOVYD I grete Youe welle Ande wolle ande ftrately charge Youe without deley As ye entende to have me Your Goode Lorde Ande wolle exchew that at may enfieu unto You for the contrary doyng at your Jeoparty Faille not furthwith uppon the fight herof too contente ande pay out of my Coffurs unto my Welbilovyd Servauntes William Worme and Thomas Horwod Gentlemen Ufhers of my Chaumbre Ande Gilbert Wedall Cheef Clarke of my Kitchen ftanding chargid with the Kepyng of my Hous this Yeir Begynnyng at Michaelmes laft pafte befoir the dait herof In pairty of Payment of Oone Thoufand Poundes affignyd unto theim nowe for th'Exfpences and Kepyng of my faide Hous for this faide Yeire Whiche is above the old Affignemente appoyntid in my Booke of Orders for Keaping of my faide Hous in Yeres by paft by Threfcore Poundes ande Sex, Thirteen Shillings ande Foure Pens Ande to be paide theime now uppon Wednefday the Fyrft Day of Novembre whiche fhal be Alhallow

Day

Day next cummyng after the daite herof For the FYRSTE
PAYMENTE of their Affignemente affignyd unto theim for
Keapyng of my faide Hous this Yere Begynnyng at Michaelmes In the xij[th] Yeire of the Reigne of our Souverain Lord
King Henry the viij[th] In full contentacion for the Paymente
of their Fyrft Warraunte of their Affignemente for Keaping
of my faide Hous this Yeir THE SOMME of cc l. Whiche
is the Fyrfte Warraunte paide unto theime in this Quarter
bitwixte Michaelmes ande Criftenmes THE faide Somme
to be taikynne of the Revenues of all my Landes within
Yorkfhire Whiche fhal be due unto me of my faide Landes
uppon this Audicte at Michaelmes laft for the Yeire endinge
at the faide Michaelmes to your handes commynge by my
Receyvour for the tyme being of my faide Landes THE
faide Some to be receyvyd by the haundes of every of theime
befoyr naymed now ftandyng chargid with my Hous for this
Yeire of Youe my Coffurer for the tyme being Whiche Some
is more by the forefaide Lxvj l. xiij s. iiij d. thanne th'old
Affignemente appoynted in the Booke of Orders FOR th'Entente that they fhalle leefe remaynyng at the Yeires ende
of divers Victualles unfpente ande paide fore as moche as
amountethe to the forefaide Somme of Lxvj l. xiij s. iiij d.
cleare paide fore in thees Victualles followinge as to faye in
Whete in Malte in Beeffes in Muttons in Wyne ande in Wax
OVER ande above alle Creditoures and Stuf taikyn for the
fulle Exfpences ande Keapyng of my faide Hous for the faide
hoole Yeir Whiche Yeir fhalle ende at Michaelmes nexte to
com after the daite herof ANDE alfo bicaus they fhal haive no
Parcell of the Remayneth of no mayner of Stuf provided for
th'Exfpences of my faide Hous whatfoever they bee that remayneth unfpente of the former Yeire ending at Michaelmes
lafte pafte whiche fhalle ftonde chargid this Yeire with my
faide Hous But that they fhalle pay Redy Money fore of this
Two Hundreth Poundes of their Fyrft Paymente of there

I i   faide

ſaide Aſſignemente to theime that was chargid the laſt Yeir
Soo that they leef no Creditoures uncontentid nor unpaide of
the former Yeire AND the Reſte of the Reſidue of the
money remaynyng The remayneth paide fore And alle Creditoures paide of that Yeir Thanne that at remayneth They
whiche ſtandes chargid with my Hous for that Yeire to pay
the ſame to my Coffurers As money ſavyd ande unſpente of
th'Aſſignemente for Keaping of my Hous for the foreſaide
Yeir. YOVEN under my Signet and Signe Manuell at my
Caſtelle of Wreſille the iiijth Day of Octobre In the xijth
Yeir of the Reigne of oure Souvereygne Lorde King Henry
the viijth.

Too my Truſty ande Welbilovid Servaunte Gilbert
Wedalle Cheef Clarke of my Kiching My Coffurer ſtanding chargid with all the Receptes ande
Paymentes of my Bookes of Foren Exſpences
and Reparacions.

YERELY.

ITEM It is Ordynyde by my Lorde and his Counſeill that
ther ſhal be paide fore the Holl WESHING of all mannar of
LYNNON belonging my Lordes Chapell for an Holl Yere but
xvij$s$. iiij$d$. And to be weſhid for Every Penny iij Surpleſes
or iij Albes And the ſaid Surpleſſes to be Weſhide in the
Yere xvj tymes aganſt thees Feeſts following Viz. Furſt aganſt
Mychelmes Evyn xviij Surpleſſes for Men 'and' vj for Children—
And aganſt Alhallow Evyn xviij Surpleſſes for Men and vj for
Children — And aganſt Criſtynmas Evyn xviij Surpleſſes
for Men and vj for Children — And aganſt New Yere
Evyn xviij Surpleſſes for Men and vj for Children — Aganſt
Twolfte Evyn xviij Surpleſſes for Men and vj for Children
— Aganſt

— Aganſt Candlemas Evyn xviij Surpleſſes for Men and vj for Children — Aganſt Shrafte Evyn xviij Surpleſſes for Men and vj for Children — Aganſt our Lady Evyn in Lent xviij Surpleſſes for Men and vj for Children — Aganſt Tenable Wedinſday xviij Surpleſſes for Men and vj Children — Aganſt Eſter Evyn xviij Surpleſſes for Men and vj for Children — Aganſt the Aſſenſion Evyn xviij Surpleſſes for Men and vj for Children — Aganſt Whitſon Evyn xviij Surpleſſes for Men and vj for Children — Aganſt Corpus Criſti Evyn xviij Surpleſſes for Men and vj Children — Aganſt Trynyte Sondaye xviij Surpleſſes for Men and vj for Children — Aganſt Midſomar Evyn xviij Surpleſſes for Men and vj for Children — And aganſt Lambmes Evyn xviij Surpleſſes for Men and vj for Children WHICH is iiij tymes to be weſhid in every Quarter of the Yere WHICH the Weſhing of the ſaid SUR-PLESSES for the foreſaid Chapell for an holl Yere amountith to the Som of x ſ. viij d. AND vij ALBES for Veſtments to be weſhid xvj tymes in the Yere at thees Feeſts following Viz. iij Albes for a Sute and iiij Albes for iiij ſingle Veſtments for the iiij Alters Viz. Aganſt Mychaelmes vij Albes to be weſhid — In lik cais aganſt Alhallow Evyn other vij Albes to be weſhide — Aganſt Criſtynmes Evyn vij Albes to be weſhide — Aganſt New Yere Evyn vij Albes to be weſhide — Aganſt Twoltfe Evyn vij Albes to be weſhide — Againſt Candlemes Evyn vij Albes to be weſhide — Aganſt Shrafte Evyn vij Albes to be weſhide — Aganſt our Lady Day in Lent vij Albes to be weſhide — Aganſt Tenable Wedinſday vij Albes to be weſhide — Againſt Eſter Evyn vij Albes to be weſhid — Aganſt the Aſſenſion Evyn vij Albes to be weſhide — Aganſt Whitſon Evyn vij Albes to be weſhide — Aganſt Corpus Criſti Evyn vij Albes to be weſhide — Aganſt Trynyte Sonday vij Albes to be weſhide — Aganſt Mydſomar Evyn vij Albes to be weſhide — And vij Albes to be weſhide Lambmes Evyn WHICH Albes is iiij tymes to be weſhid in every

Quarter

Quarer WHICH amountith to the Som of (in the holl Yere) iij *s.* j*d.* FOUR ALBES for Children for bering of Candilftiks and Cenfoures to be wefhid xij tymes in the Yere at thes Feefts following Viz. iiij Albes for Children aganft Mychaelmes Evyn — iiij Albes fore Children aganft Alhallowetyid — iiij Albes for Children aganft Criftmes Evyn — iiij Albes for Children aganft New Yer Even — iiij Albes for Children aganft xij¹ʰ Evyn — iiij Albes for Children aganft Candilmes Evyn — iiij Albes for Children aganft our Lady-Day in Lent — iiij Albes for Chidren aganft Efter Evyn — iiij Albes for Children aganft the Affencion Evyn — iiij Albes for iiij Children aganft Witfon Evyn — iiij Albes for Children aganft Corpus Crifti Evyn — And iiij Albes for Children aganft Trynyte Sonday WHICH Albes for Children is iij tymes to be wefhid in every Quarter WHICH amountith to the Some of in the holl Yere xvj *d.* AND FIVE AULTER-CLOTHES for covering of the v Alters to be wefhid xvj tymes in the Yere Viz. Aganft Mychelmes v — Aganft Alhallowmes v — Aganft Criftynmes v — Aganft New Yer Evyn v — Aganft xij¹ʰ Evyn v — Aganft Candilmas Evyn v — Aganft Shraft Evyn v — Aganft our Lady Day in Lent v — Aganft Tenable Wedinfday v — Aganft Efter Evyn v — Aganft the Affencion Evyn v — Aganft Whitfon Evyn v — Aganft Corpus Crifti Evyn v — Aganft Trynyte Sonday v — Aganft Mydfomar Evyn v — And aganft Lambemes Evyn v WHICH Alter-Clothes is to be wefhid iiij tymys in every Quarter WHICH amontith to the Som of ij*s.* iij*d.* AND SO TH'OLLE SOM for the WESHING of all the forefaid Lynnon Stuf belonging my Lords Chapell for an hole Yere to be wefhid after the Rait aforefaid after iij Pecis j*d.* Amountith to the Some of - - - - - -

XXXVI.

XXXVI.

THE ORDER OF THE CREDITOURIS of the HOUSEHOLD if any bee Yeirly for the Houfe Howe my Lord will have the Hoole Bill of the Creditouris of the Houfehold caſt upp at Michaelmes at th'End of every Yeire And at the Half Yeir Quairterly and Mounethly in the Yeir WHEN the Remanith is taikin and my Lord commaund to haive it doone By the Clarkis of the Keching for the tyme beyng by the fight of Th'auditours TO fee how th'Expenduntur for the Houfehold for the Yeire weyth with th'Affignemente of the faide Year Too bee caſt up aftir the Fourme and Ordre hereaftir following WANTS deduct and not fpokkyn of in the Mounethis and in the Quairters And at the Half Yeiris to be fpokkyn of.

FIRST the HOOLE BILL of CREDITOURIS FOR THE HOUSEHOLD of every Yeire endid at Michaellmes is - - - - †

WHEROF

IN Houfehold Waiges for the Houfehold Servauntes for the Laſt Half Yeire owing is - - - -

In

† No particular Sums are fpecified here or below : It being only intended to fhow in what order the Bills are to be kept.

IN Chapell Waiges for the Gentillmen of my Lordis Chapel for their Laſt Quairtir Waigis of the Yeir owing is – – – –

IN Winter Horſſemeat of my Lordis Houſehold Servauntis (if it be owing for at this tyme) is – – – –

IN Somer Horſſemeat of my Lordis Houſehold Servauntis (if it be owing for at this tyme) is – – – –

IN Fermes of Medues ande Paſtures at Lekynfeld Wreſill and Topclif (As Percell of th'oole Somme aſſignyd to the Houſcholde for Keaping of my Lordis Hous for th'oole Yeir payable at Michaelmes) is – – – –

IN Money owing for the Borde-waiges of my Lordis Houſehold Servauntes put to Bord-waiges this ſaid Yeir and notte aſſigned to be at Meat and Drynk in my Lordis Houſe (if any bee owing for) is – – – –

IN Wheat owing for (if any bee) – – – –

IN Malt owing for (if any bee) – – – –

IN Beeffe owing for (if any bee) – – – –

IN Muttons owyng for (if any bee) – – – –

IN Wyne owing (for if any bee) – – – –

IN Wax owing for (if any bee) – – – –

IN Horſſe Bread owing for (if any bee) – – – –

IN Horſſe Shoing owyng for (if any bee) – – – –

IN Fewell owing for (if any bee) – – – –

In

IN Hier of Pewtir Veffell (if any bee) - - - -

IN the Waigis of the Paftur-Keapars for the laft Half Yeir (if any bee) - - - -

IN the Waigis of the Laundeirs of Houfe for the laft Half Yeir or laft Quairter (if any bee) - - - -

IN Seamys of Fifhe owing for (if any bee) - - - -

IN Wylde Fewle owing for (if any bee) - - - -

IN Catour Percellis owing for (if any bee) - - - -

SUM TOTAILLIS of all the foirefaide Creditouris as is afoirefaide amountithe in th'oole too - - - -

WHEREOF they have receyvid toward the Payment of the foirefaide Creditours, As to fay,

FIRST their is owing in full Contentacion of th'Affignemente for the Hoole Yeir toward the Payment of the Foirfaide Creditours of the Houfehold For their Laft Warraunt for this Yeir endinge at Michaelmes in fulle Contentacion of their Hoolle Affignement affignid to theym for Keapyng of my Lordis Hous for the faid Hole Yeir ending at this faide Michalmes - - - -

ITEM they muft have of theym that ftandis chargid with the Houfeholde this New Yere for the Remaineth delivred theim of the Stufs remainynge ande not fpent Whiche was provided in the former Yeire ande paid for and
left

left remainyng and delivered to the forefaid Perfons ftanding chargid this Yeir as Percell of ther Firft Somme of their Firft Warraunt As to fay Fyrft in Brede- - -In Beare- - -In Aille - - -In Wyne- - -In Beeffs - - -In Muttons - - -In Saltfifhe - - -In Verjous- - -In Vinacre - - -In Oille - - -In Hony - - - In All Maner of Spices - - - In Wax- - -In Quarrions - - -In Tapers- - -In Torches - - -In Roffyn - - -In Weke - - - In Parifhe Candell- - -In Hoppis- - -In White Salt - - -In Bay Salt- - -In Se-coill- - -In Charcoille - - -In Shids - - -In Fagotts- - -In Hay - - - In Wheat- - -In Malt - - -In Ootes- - -SUM of all the forefaid Stufs remanyng is - - - - .

ANDE fo their lackith yet for fulle Contenta-cion and Payment of their faide Creditors Which the houfhold haith fpent cleare aboive th'olle Somme affignid for the keping of my Lordis Hous - - - - - - WHICH is in full Con-tentacion of all Manner of Things for the Hoole Keaping of my Lordis Hous the foirfaide Hoole Yeire to the Parfons whiche ftandith chargid with the Keaping of my Lordis Hous this faide Yeire.

ITEM IT is ordeignid by my Lord and his Counfaill Yeirly at theis DAIES following OF PAYMENT The Daies of Payment of th'Affignement of the Som affignid for Keap-yng of my Lordis Houfe As to fay Alhallowtide - - - Saint Androw-Day - - -Criftenmes - - -Candlemes- - - Our Lady-Day in Lent- - -Eftur - - -and Lambmes YF the Mouneth or Quairter be caft upp For the Cleare Expenduntur fpent in my Lordes Houfe for the faid tyme To know what is owing

to

to Creditouris for Stuf taiken of theyme for th'Expeinces of my Lordes Houſe and, owing for, That the Som of Monay taiken for the Fell Hide and Tallowe of the Beeffs and Multons * ſpent in my Lordes Houſe be caſt upp That my Lord may know what that Some of Money drawis to moir that they have in their handes for the ſaide Fell Hide and Tallow at every Daye of Payment moir in Money thanne their Som of Money that they receyve for the Daies of Payment of theire Affignement for Keapyng of my Lordes Houſe.

* So in the MS. paſſim.

K k   XXXVII.

XXXVII.

TH'ARTICLES FOR EVERY REMEVYNG OF MY LORDS HOUS.

AT every REMEVINGE of my Lords Hous.

FIRST A Chequiroil to be made at alle fuche Tymes as his Lordefhip brekith up Houfe of the NAMES of the Perfons that fchal be within at Meat and Drinke with my Lorde and to gif attendaunce upon his Lordefhip AND to be figned with my Lordes hand.

AT every REMEVYNGE of my Lords Hous.

ITEM A Chequirroil to be made of the Names of the Perfons that fhial go to BORDEWAGES in the Towne wheir his Lordefchip lieth To his Lordefchip Remeve and fet up his Hous agayn TO be Signed with my Lords Hande.

AT every REMEVINGE of my Lords Houfe.

ITEM A Chequirroil to be made of the Names of the PERSONS that fchal go afore unto the place wheir his Lordefchip remevith unto For prepairinge of al thinge ther TO be Signed with my Lords Hande.

AT

AT every REMEVYING of my Lords Hous.

ITEM A Chequirroil to be made of the Names of my Lords Houſeholde Servaunts that be **ABSENT** As wel about his Lordſhip buſines as their owne buſines Ande to have no Bordewages allowid them for the ſaid cauſe TO be Signid with my Lords Hand.

AT every REMEVYING of my Lords Hous.

ITEM A Chequirroil to be made of the Names of my Lordes Houſholde Servaunts appointed to **ABIDE STIL** in every Place by my Lords Commaundement Ande for what Cauſes they be left ther behinde ANDE the ſaide Chequirroil to be Signed with my Lords Hande.

AT every REMEVINGE of my Lords Hous.

ITEM A Chequirroil to be made at alle ſuche Tymes when my Lorde brakithe up Hous of the Names of the Perſons that be at **BORDWAGES** at the Charge of the Hous by my Lordes Commaundement Whiche my Lord giffeth theim for their frends ſaike Notwithſtanding that they ar not enterd in the Chequirroil ANDE to be ſigned with my Lordes Hand.

XXXVIII.

XXXVIII.

HERE BEGYNNETH THE BOOKE of All Manner of STILES concernyng my Lordes Houſe to be made for BOOKES BILLES or any outher WRITINGES whiche ſchal be made at any tyme or tymes from Yeir to Yeir for th'Order of my ſaide Lordes Houſeholde HOW the ſaide Stiles ſchall begyn AND for what Cauſis they doo concerne TO BE MADE Wekely Mounethly Quarterly Or at any Princi-pall Feiſts Or at any Remevalles or Breaking at any Tyme or Tymes my Lordes Hous AS HEREAFTIR FOL-LOWETH the ſaide Stiles Oon after Anouther How they ſchall be made at any Tyme or Tymes in the Yeir when it is requiſite for any to be made.

THE STILE OF THE REMANETH how it ſchal be writtyn Yerely at Michaelmes of all the STUFS remanyng unſpent of the former Yeir ended at the ſaide Michaelmas.

THIS is the BILL of the REMANETH Takyn at the place where my Lorde lieth Yerely uppon xxxth Daye of Sep-tember which is the morrow after Michaelmes-Daye By the Sight of the Stewarde or Treaſorer or Comptroller or Sur-vieur or Dean of his Lordeſchip Chappell or Oon of his Lordeſchip Counſaill or a Chaplayn a Gentleman or Yoman—Uſcher

Uſcher of the Chaumber or a Clarke of the Kechinge Of all
Maner of STUF remanynge unſpent at the ſaide Michaelmas
Whiche was provided for th'Exſpences for the Kepinge of my
Lordes Houſe the former Yeir ended at the ſaid Michaelmas AS
the Names of the Parcells of the ſaide Stuf with their Prices
that remaned unſpent provided in the ſaide Yeir HEREAFTIR
FOLLOWITH in this Bill ſigned with my Lordes Hande.

THE STILE OF THE HOOLE CHEQUIRROILL

how it ſhal be writtyn YERELY at Michaelmes of
the PARSONNES that ſchal abide in my Lords Hous
for the Hoole Yere.

THE KALENDER BEGYNNYNGE at Michaelmes in
the   Yeir of the Reigne of our Sovereigne Lorde King
Henry the viij th Of the NOUMBRE of all my Lordes SER-
VAUNTES in his Chequirroil Daily Abiding in his Houſ-
holde AS the Names of theim hereafter followithe FIRST my
Lorde j — my Lady j — my yong Lorde and his Bredren
iij — Ande their Servauntes ij (As to ſay a Yoman ande a
Groim) — The Nurſy iij (as to ſay two Rokkers ande a
Childe to attende in the Nurcy) — Gentlewomen for my
Lady iij — Chaumberers for my Lady ij — my Lordes Breder
every of theim with their Servauntes iij (As to ſaye if they
be Preiſts his Chaplayn his Childe ande his Horſkepar) — my
Lordes Hede Officers of Houſholde iiij — fyrſt the Chambre-
layn ande his Servauntes vij (As to ſay his Chaplayn his
Clarke two Yomen a Childe of his Chaumber ande his Horſ-
kepar) — The Stewarde ande his Servauntes iiij Chargid
(As

(As to fay his Clark his Childe ande his Horfkepar) Ande
Unchargide iij (As to fay his Clarke ande his Horfkepar) —
The Treafaurer and his Servaunts iij (As to fay his Clarke
ande his Horfkepars) — The Comptroller ande his Servaunts iij
(As to fay chargide his Clarke ande his Horfkepar Ande
unchargide bot his Horfkepar) — The Dean of the Chapell
and his Servaunte ij — The Surviour ande his Servaunte ij —
Two of my Lordes Counfail and aither of theim a Servaunte
iiij — The Secreatary ande his Servaunte ij — my Lordes Chap-
laynes in Houfholde vj (As to fay the Aumer Ande if he be a
maker of Interludes Than he to have a Servaunte to th'entente
for writing of the parties Ande ellis to have noon — The
Maifter of Graimer j — A Chaplain to ride with my Lorde j
— The Subdean j — The Gofpeller j — The Lady Meffe Preifte
j — Two Gentlemen Ufchers and a Servaunte theim iij —
Two Carvers for my Lorde ande a Servaunte bitwixt theim
iij (Except they be at their Fryndes fynding And than aither of
theim to have a Servaunte) — Two Sewars for my Lorde ande
a Servaunte bitwixt theim iij (Except they be at their Fryndes
fynding and than aither of theim to have a Servaunte) — Two
Cup-berers for my Lorde and a Servaunte bitwyxt theim iij
(Except they be at their Frindes fynding ande than aither of
theim to have a Servaunte) — Two Gentlemen Waiters for
the Bordes Ende and a Servaunte bitwixt theim iij — Haunf-
men ande Yong Gentlemen at their Fryndes fynding v (As
to fay Hanfhmen iij And Yong Gentlemen iij) — Officers of
Armes j — Yomen Ufhers of the Chaumbre ij — Gentlemen
of the Chappell ix (Viz. The Maifter of the Childer j Tenours
ij Countertenors iiij The Piftoler j Ande ij for the Organes)
— Childer of the Chapell vj — Two Marfchallis of the Hall
ande a Servaunte bitwixt theim iij — Yomen of the Chaumbre
vj — Yomen Ufchers of the Hall j — Yomen Waiters v —
Yomen Officers of Houfholde xj (Viz. The Yoman of the
Robes j Yoman of the Horfs j Yoman of tho Veftry j Yoman
of

of th'Ewry j Yoman of the Pauntry j Yoman of the Sellar j
Yoman of the Buttery j Yoman Cooke for the Mouthe j
Yoman of the Bak-hous j Yoman of the Brew-hous j Ande
Yoman Porter j) — Gromes ande Gromes Officers of Houf-
hold xx As to faye Gromes of the Chaumbre v (That is to
fay iij to ride with my Lorde, ij to abide at home ande Oone
for my Lady) — Gromes of the Waredrob iij (As to faye
Groim of the Robys j Groim of the Beddes j Groim of the
Waredrob for my Lady j) Groim of Th'ewry j — Grome
of the Pantry j — Groime of the Sellar j — Groim of the
Buttery j — Gromes of the Kitching ij (Viz. a Groim for the
Mouthe ande a Groime for the Larder) — Groim of the
Hall j — Groime Portar j — Groim of the Sterop j — Groim
of the Palfrays j — Groim Sumpterman j — Ande Groim of
the Chariot j — Childer for Offices in Houfholde vj (As to
faye The Waredrob j The Kitching j The Squillary j The
Stable j The Chariot j Ande the Bakhous j) — The Arifmen-
der j — The Bochery j — The Catoury j — The Armory j —
Mynftrallis iij (As to fay A Taberet A Lute and A Rebekk)
— Footeman j — Falconers ij — Painter j — Joyner j —
Hunte j — Gardynner in Houfe j (Viz. The Gardyner of
the Place where my Lorde lieth for the tyme to have Mate
ande Drinke within) — Under Allmoner of the Hall j Ande
'he' to ferve the Groimes of the Chaumbre with Wodde —
My Lordes Clarkes in Houfholde x (Viz. A Clarke of the
Kitchinge j — Clarke of the Signet j — Clarkes of the Foren
Expenfis ij — Clarke of the Brevements j — Clarke Avenar j —
Clarke of the Warks j — Clarke to breve under the Clarke of
the foren Expenfis j) — Milners ij — THE HOOLE NOUM-
BER of al the faide Parfons in Houfholde is cLxvj Whiche is or-
deigned by my Lorde and his Counfail and fhal not be excedid
but kept ALWAIES provided how they fhall entre to their
Wagies at their Quarter Daies (That is to faye Michaelmas
Criftenmas our Lady Daye in Lent and Midfoimmer) aftir the

ufe

ufe and maner as is accuftomed That is to fay Whofomevir cummeth to my Lordes Service in Houfholde within
a Mouneth befoir any of the faide iiij Quarter Daies or within
a Mouneth after Than they to entre Wagies at the faide
Quarter Daye And if they com not within a Mouneth befoir
or a Mouneth after any of the faide iiij Quarter daies Than they
to tarry ande not to entre Wagies too the next Quarter-daye
that fhal com after Without it fhall pleas my Lorde to rewarde
theim any thing for it at his pleafure ALSO when-foevir the
faide Noumber is not fulle Than my Lorde to be infourm-
ed by his Hede Officers That his Lordfhip may taike in
fuche as his Lordefchip fhall think befte for the fulfilling of
the faide Noumbre if the caife fo require Alwaes provided
the Wagies accuftomede of my Lordes Hous That every
Parfon bilonging to every Roome accuftomede in this foirfaide Bill fhall have by Yeir after this Some following Yf
they be paied by th'Affignement of the Hous FYRST every
Rokker in the Nurcy xxs. — Every Gentlewoman attending
uppon my Lady ande not at my Ladies finding v Marks —
Every Chamberer to my Ladye ande not at my Ladies
fynding xls. — The Hede Officers of Houfholde as to faye
Fyrfte The Chaumbrelayn to have x l. fee in Houfhold If
he have it not by Patente — The Stewarde chargide in Houfholde xx l. Ande unchargid x l. And cumming ande going
x Markes — The Treafurer of the Houfe abiding in Houfholde ftanding chargide xx l. ande chargide with his Fellow
x l. ande unchargide x Markes — The Comptroller of Hous
abiding in Houfeholde ftanding chargid xx l. Ande chargide with his Fellowe or a Clarke of the Kiching x l. Ande
unchargide x Marks — The Survior in Houfholde x Markes
if he be not promotede by Patent — The Dean of the Chappell iiij l. If he have it in Houfholde ande not by Patente
— Every Oon of my Lords Counfaill to have cs. fee If he
have it in Houfholde ande not by Patente — The Secreatarye

in

in Houſholde if he be not promoted cs. — The Clarke of the Signet iiij Markes — Every Scolemaiſter teching Gramer cs. — Every Chaplayn Graduate v Markes — Every Chapleyn not Graduate xls. — Preiſts of the Chappell iij As to ſaye Oon at cs. The Seconde v Marks Ande the Thirde at iiij Markes (Alwaies provided That the moiſt Diſcreat Parſon of the ſaide iij Preiſts of the Chappell be appointed to be Sub-dean Ande to have no more Wagies than he hadd) — Every Gentleman Uſcher v Marks — Every Carver Sewar and Cup-berer for my Lorde and my Lady v Marks — Every Gentle-man Waiter for the Bordes End iiij Marks — Every Yoman Uſcher of the Chaumber iiij Marks — The Haunſhmen to be at the finding of my Lorde — Every Officer of Armes if he be Harolde x Marks Ande if he be Purſivaunte v Marks if he be paide in Houſholde ande not by Patente — Gentil-men of the Chappell x (As to ſaye Two at x Marks a pece — iij at iiij l. a pece — Two at v Marks a pece — Oon at iiij Marks — Oon at xls. — ande Oon at xxs. — Viz. ij Baſſis — ij Tenors — ande vj Countertenors) — Childeryn of the Chappell vj After xxvs. a pece — Yoman of the Veſtry xls. ande if he be chargide with an outher Office than to have but xxs. — Every Marſhall of the Hall v Marks — Every Mynſtral if he be Taberet iiij Marks Every Lute and Re-bekke xxxiijs. iiijd. Ande to be paide in Houſhold if they have it not by Patente or Warraunte — Every Yoman of the Chamber xls. — Every Yoman Officer xxxiijs. iiijd. — Every Yoman Water xxxiijs. iiijd. — Every Groim of the Chamber xxs. — Every Armorere to have iiij Markes for Keping of my Lordes Stuf As well his Armory in his Hous as outher where He finding al maner of Stuf for clenſinge of the ſaide Stuf — Every Arreſmendar If he be Yoman xxxiijs. iiijd. for his Wagies And xxs. for finding of all maner of Stuf bilonging to his Facultye Except Silke and Golde Ande if he be Groim xxs. for his Wagies And xxs. for finding of his

Stuf

Stuf in like caas — Every Faloconer If he be Yoman xl s.
Ande if he be Groim xx s. — Every Hunte xx s. — Every
Groim Officer of Housholde xx s. — Every Childe in every
Office xiij s. iiij d. — Every Warkeman in Householde xl s.
Ande cuming and going xx s. — Every Footeman xl s. bicaus
of muche wering of his Stuf with Labour — Every Borser If
he be Yoman to have xxxiij s. iiij d. Ande if he be Groim xx s.
Ande to be oute of Meat and Drinke ande all outher char-
gies of the Hous — Every Under Almoner of the Hall xx s.
bicaus he shal hew Wodde for the Gromes of the Chamber
ande bring it to theim — Every Clarke of the Kitching v
Marks — Every Clarke of the Brevements xl s. — Every
Clarke of the Warks v Marks — Every Clarke of the Foren
Expensis iiij Mark — Every Clarke Avener xx s. — Every Clarke
of the Wering Booke xl s. — Every Clarke that writes under
the Clarkes of the Foren Expensis iiij Noblis Without they be
outherwis agreade with. THE KALENDAR ENDING at
Michalmes next for to com after the date herof With the
Wagies accustomed for the Housholde Servauntes that be not
promoted ALWAIES providede that what Parsons somevir
they be that haith Promocion Excepte the foiresaide Hede
Officers shall have no Wagies in Housholde after they be promotede without the concideracion of his Lordeschippis pleasure be further shewid theim in the said Chequirroil AL-
WAIES PROVIDED that what Person somevir he be that
cummeth to my Lordes Service That incontinent after he
be enterede in the Chequirroill that he be sworne in the
Counting-hous by a Gentleman Usher or a Yoman Usher
in the presence of a Hede Officer Ande in their absence
befoire the Clarke of the Kitching Aither by suche an Oithe
as in the Booke of Oithes if any suche be Or ellis by suche
an Oithe as they schall seam best by their Discreffions.

THE

THE STILE OF THE QUARTIR CHEQUIR-ROILL how it fhall be writtyn QUARTERLY every Quarter in the Yeir Of the PARSONNES that fhall abide in my Lordes Hous every Quarter.

THE KALENDIR BEGYNNYNG at Michaelmes in th'Eight Yeir of the Reigne of our Sovereigne Lorde King Henry the viijth of all my Lordes SERVAUNTES in the Chequirroill daily abidinge in his Houfholde AS the Names of theim hereafter followith Ande how they fhall entre to their Wagies in Houfholde at their Quarter Dayes AS to fay Michaelmas Criftenmes Eftur and Midfomer ALWAIES provided by my Lorde and his Counfaill after the ufe and maner befoir accuftomed That is to fay Whofomevir cummeth to my Lordes Service in Houfholde within a monneth befoir or after any of the iiij Quarter Daies befoirfaid Than they to enter Wagies at the faide Quarter Daies Ande if they com not within a Mouneth befoir any of the faide iiij Quarter Daies or within a Mouneth after Than they to tarry and not to entre to Wagies to the next Quarter Daye that fhall com after Without it fhall pleafe my Lord to rewarde theim any thing for it at his pleafure THE NOMBRE of theim that fchall be kept daily in Houfholde this Quarter is the Noumbre of Whiche Noumbre is appointed by my Lorde and his Counfail whiche fhall not be exceded but kept ALWAIES PRO-VIDED that whenfomevir the faide Noumbre is not full my Lorde to be infourmide to taike in fuche as his Lordefchip fhall thinke befte for fulfilling of the faido Noumbre yf the caife fo require ALWAIES provided that the Wagies accuftomed of my Lordes Servauntes that every Parfone bilonging 'to' every Rowme accuftomed in this foirfaide Roil fhal have by Yeir after this Some following FYRSTE the Hede Officers of Houfhold ftanding chargide xx *l*. Ande with his Fellows x *l*. Ande unchargid cuminge ande and going x Marks — The Comptroller of the Hous abiding in Houfhold Standinge chargid xx *l*. ande with his Fellow or a Clarke of the Kitching x *l*. And unchargid cuming and going x Marks If he be not promoted — The Surviour in Houfhold x Marks If he be not promoted by Patent — The Secreatary in Houfhold If he be not promoted c*s*. — The Clarke of the Signet iiij Marks — The Dean of the Chappell iiij *l*. If he have it in Houfholde ande not by Patent — Every Scolemaifter teching Gramer in the Hous c*s*. — Every Chaplain Graduate v Marke Every Chaplein not Graduate xl*s*. — Every Gentleman Ufcher v Marks — Every Cup-berer Carver and Sewar v Marks — Every Gentleman Waiter and Yomen Ufchers of the Chaumbre iiij Markes — Every Yoman of the Chaumbre xl*s*. — Every Yoman Waiter xxxiij*s*. iiij *d*. — Every Yoman Officer of Houfholde xxxiij*s*. iiij *d*. — Every Groime of the Chaumbre Groim Officer of Houfholde and Groimes of the Stable xx*s*. — Every Hede Clarke of the Kitching v Marks — Every Under Clarke xl*s*. — Every Childe in Offices that be no Groim xiij*s*. iiij *d*. THE KALENDAR begynnynge at Michaelmes and ending at Criftenmes next following in the viij^th Yeir of the Reigne of our Sovereigne Lorde Kinge Henry the viij^th afoirefaide Whiche be Wagies appointed for the Houfeholde Servauntes whiche be not officed ALWAIES PROVIDED that what Parfoine fomevir they be Except the foir-faide Hede Officers after the fourme befoirfaide have no Waigies in Houfeholde Whiche haith any Promocion by my Lorde Without the concideracion of his Lordefchippes pleafure be further fchewid in this forefaide Chequirroill.

THE

THE STILE OF THE BILL How it fhal be written of my Lordes Houfholde Servauntes which
haithe LICENSE to go aboute their own Bufines
in the Quarters When my Lorde breakithe up
Hous Ande haithe noo Bordewagies allowide theim
for that caufe.

THE CHEQUIRROIL of the Noumber of my Lordes
Houfhold Servauntes That haithe LEVE of my Lorde and his
Counfail to go about their owne Bufines ande hadd no Borde-
Wagies allowid theim for that caus in the Quarter bittwixte
Michaelmes ande Criftenmas Viz. from xxixth Daye of Sep-
tember whiche was Michalmes-Daye in th'Eight Yeir of the
Reigne of our Sovercigne Lorde King Henry the viijth Unto
Thurfdaye xxvth Daye of December next following Whiche
was Criftenmas Daye in th'Eight Yeir of our faide Sove-
raigne Lorde King Henry the viijth AS the Names of the
Parfounes And what Parfounes they be Ande for what caufis
the faide Parfounes haithe no Bordewagies allowed theim
Hereafter followeth in this Bill (Signid with my Lordes Hande)
That went aboute their owne bufines.

THE

THE STILE OF THE BILL How it fhal be
wryttin of my Lordes SERVAUNTES that
fhal be within at MEAT ande DRINKE where
my Lorde lieth when he brakes upp Hous.

THIS IS THE CHEQUIRROILL of all my Lordes
SERVAUNTES in Houfeholde apointid by my Lorde and
his Counfail to be within at MEAT and DRINKE at
Wrefil And yef their attendaunce daily upon my Lorde and
my Lady wheir they remayn at the charge of the Standing
Hous from the firfte Daye of Octobre in th'Eight Yeir
of the Reigne of our Sovereign Lorde King Henry the viij^th
Whiche daie his Lordefhip brak up his Hous upon at after
Michalmes Unto Thurfdaye xx^th daie of December next
following Whiche fhal be Sainte Thomas-Evyn befoir Criftenmes in th'Eight Yeire aforefaide Whiche daie his Lordefchip
fet up his Hous again at Wrefill AS the Names of the faide
Parfounes that was appointed to gif their attendaunce uppon
my faide Lorde and Lady ande remaned there to be within at
Meat and Drinke in the Hous all the faide tyme Ande in
what Rowmes every Man fervid in Hereafter followith in this
Bill Signid with my Lordes Hand.

THE

THE STILE OF THE BILL How it fhall be
written of my Lordes SERVAUNTES whiche
fhall goo too BORDEWAGIES in the TOWN
wheir my Lorde lieth Ande not departe when my
Lord brakith Hous Ande to gef their attendaunce
upon my Lorde bitwixt Meallis.

THIS IS THE CHEQUIRROILL of the Noumbre of
all my Lordes SERVAUNTES in Houfeholde appointede by
my Lorde and his Counfail to be at BORDEWAGIES in
the Towne at Wrefill ande remayn their wheir my Lorde and
my Lady liethe at the charge of the Stonding Hous Ande to gif
their attendaunce upon my faid Lorde and Ladye dailly bitwixt
Meallis from Wedinfdaye the fyrft daye of October whiche is
the ijde Daye after Michaelmas-Daye whiche Daye my Lord
brak up his Hous on at Wrefill in th'Eight Yeir of the Reigne
of our Sovereigne Lorde King Henry the viijth Unto Thurfdaie
xxth daye of Decembre nexte following whiche fhal be Sainte
Thomas Evyn befoir Criftenmes in th'Eight Yeir of our faid
Sovereigne Lorde whiche Daie his Lordefchip fet up his Hous
again at Wrefill AS the Names of the faide Parfounes that
was appointed to Bordewagies at Wrefil the faide tyme ande
remayn their Hereafter followithe in this Bill Signede with
my Lordes Hande.

THE

THE STILE OF THE BILL How it fhal be written of my Lordes SERVAUNTES That is appointed to have WINTER HORSSEMETE Yerely And fhall ride wheir my Lorde rydeth at Michaelmas.

THIS IS THE BILL of the Noumbre of my Lordes SERVAUNTES affignid by my Lord and his Counfail to be of my Lordes RIDING HOUSHOLDE And to have WINTER HORSSEMET allowid th'eim this Yeir As to faye from Mondaye xxixth Daie of Septembre which was Michaelmas-Daie lafte pafte in th'Eight Yeir of the Reigne of our Sovereigne Lorde King Henry the viijth Unto Thurf-daye iij^{de} Daye of May Whiche fhal be Saint Elyn-Daie next following in the ixth Yeir of our faid Souvereigne Lorde Whiche daie the faide Winter Horffemeat goithe oute on ANDE the faid Parfonnes to be paid for their faid Winter Horffemeat at the faid Sainte Elyn-Daie ALWAIES provi-ded that the Bill of Winter Horffemeat be appointed and made redy for my Lorde to Signe yerely uppon Michaelmas Daie AND every Parfoine to be allowid for his Winter Horffemeate xs. AS the Naimes of the Parfounes Ande What Parfounes they be Ande in what Rowmes every Man fhall ferve And for what caufe every Man fhal be allowid Winter Horffemete Hereafter followith in this Bill Signide with my Lordes Hande.

THE

THE STYLE OF THE BILL How it fhal be writtyn of my Lordes ORDINARY OFFICERS and SERVAUNTES for every Quarter Whiche of theim be appointed to awaite in every Quarter of the Yeir.

THIS IS THE CHEQUIRROILL of the Noumbre of my Lordes Ordinarye Officers ande Servauntes whiche ar appointed to be QUARTER-WAITERS Ande haithe no Houfholde-Wagies bicaufe they have promociones ande is officed AS the Naimes of the faid Parfonnes Ande in what Quarter every Man fhall awaite in Houfhold upon my faid Lord Ande in what Rowmes every Man fhall doo Service in Hereafter followethe in this Bill maide at Michaelmas in th'Eight Yeir of the Reigne of our Sovereigne Lorde King Henry the viij^{th} And Signed with my Lordes Hand.

M m

THE

THE STILE OF THE BILL How it ſhall be
writtyn of all the HORSSES of my Lordes and
my Ladyes that ſhall be at the Charge of the
Hous AS well thois that ſtandes at Harde Meate
as thois that goith to Greſs bitwixte Michaelmes
and Sainte Elyn Daye.

THIS IS THE BILL of all the HORSSES of my Lordes
and my Laidies That is appointed to be at the charge of the
Hous this Yeir As to ſaye Gentle Horſſes Palfraies Hobbies
Naggs Cloithſak-Hors ande Mail Hors As wel thois that
goith at Greſs this Winter As thois that ſhal ſtand in the
Stable at Harde Meat ANDE what every Hors ſhal be
allowid that ſtandes at Harde Meat by the Daye As to ſaye
every Hors a Pekke of Ootes Or ellis 4ᵈ in Breade after iiij
Loiſſes 4ᵈ for Provaunder uppon the Daye Begynnyng uppon
Mondaye xxixᵗʰ Daye of Septembre laſte paſte in th'Eight
Yeir of the Reigne of our Sovereigne Lord King Henry the
viijᵗʰ whiche was Michaelmas-Daie Ande ſhall end upon the
iijᵈᵉ Daie of May Whiche ſhal be Sainte Elyn Daie nexte
following AS the Naimes of the Horſſis and what Horſſes they
be Ande where to they bilonge Hereafter followithe in this
Bill Signed withe my Lordes Hande.

THE

THE STILE OF THE BILL How it fchal be writtin every Quarter of all the PERSSONNES that ar in the Chequirroill above the Noumbre appointed in the Booke of Orders of Houfholde As the Concideracion why apperith in the faide Bill moir at large.

THIS IS THE BILL of the Names of the PARSONNES That ar in the Chequirroill Above the Noumbre appointed in the Booke of Ordres of Houfholde to be in the Chequirroill Whiche my Lorde yeffith Mete and Drinke unto Being in his Hous at this Michaelmes in th'Eight Yeir of the Reigne of our Sovereigne Lorde King Henry the viijth WHICHE was thought by my Lorde and his Counfail mufte contynue ovir the Noumber affignidd in the Booke of Ordres AS the concideracion why heraftir followith in this Bill Signide with my Lordes Hande.

THE STILE OF THE BILL How it fhal be writtyn every Quarter of the Yeir of all the PARSONNES that wantes in the ROWMES in the Chequirroil That fhulde fulfill th'oole Nomber appointed in the Booke of Orders That my Lorde fhulde keep for an Hoole Yeir in his Hous.

THIS IS THE BILL of the Names of the PARSONNES That wantes in the ROWMES in the Chequirroill made at Michaelmas in th'Eight Yeir of the Reigne of our Sovereigne Lorde

Lorde Kinge Henry the viij^th That fhulde fulfill the Hoole
Noumbre appointed that my Lorde fhulde keip in his Hous
for an Hoole Yeir AS the Names of the faide Parfonnes
Ande what Parfonnes they be Ande in what Rowmes they
waite in my faide Lordes Hous Hereaftir followithe in this
Bill Signide with my Lordes Hande.

THE STILE OF THE BILL How it fhal be
writtyn every Quarter in the Yeyr Of al the PAR-
SONNES daily abiding in my Lordes Hous And
ar not in the Chequirroil Whiche my Lord giffithe
MEAT ande DRINKE unto And as the Concideracion why apparith moir playnly in the faide
Bill.

THIS IS THE BILL of the Names of the PARSONNES
that ar daily abiding in my Lordes Hous Ande ar not in the
Chequirroil That my Lorde giffithe MEAT and DRINKE
unto being in his Houfe Made at Michaelmae in th'Eight
Yeire of the Reigne of our Sovereigne Lorde Kinge Henry
the viij^th For that Quarter to Criftenmas nexte followinge
AS the Naimes of the Parfonnes Ande what Parfonnes they
be Ande for what Caus Hereaftir followith in this Bill Signide
withe my Lordes Hande That be daily in the Hous ande not
in the Chequirroill.

THE

THE STILE OF THE BILL How it fchal be writtyn Quarterly every Quarter in the Yeir of the PAYMENT of WAGIES to the Gentlemen of my Lordes CHAPPELL every Quarter.

THIS IS THE BILL of full Contentacion of Paymente of Wagyes to the GENTLEMEN of my Lordes CHAP-PELL from the Quarter begynyng at Michaelmas in th'Eight Yeir of the Reigne of our Sovereigne Lorde King Henry the viij^th Ande ending at Criftenmas next followinge in the faide viij^th Yeire of our faide Sovereigne Lorde King Henry the viij^th AS the Names of the Parfonnes Ande what every Man takith by Yeir for his Wagies Ande what he is paide for the faide Quarter Hereafter followith in this Bill Signid with my Lordes Hande.

THE STILE OF THE BILL How it fhall be writtyn Quarterly every Quarter in the Yeir of the PARSONNES that fchal be at BORDE-WAGIES in the Towne wheir my Lorde lieth And to continew their AS the Concideracion why apperith moir planely in the faide Bill.

THIS IS THE CHEQUIRROILL of the Names of my Lordes Servauntes that fchal de at BORDE-WAGIES at Lekynfelde or Wrefill ande lefte their ftil Ande for what caus they be ordeignide to remayn their in this Quarter Videlit from Mondaye xxix^th Daie of September which was Michaelmas Daie

Daie lafte pafte in th'Eight Yeir of the Reigne of our Sove-
reigne Lorde King Henry the viij^th Unto the xxv^th Day of
December next following Whiche fchal be Criftenmas Daie
in the Eight Yoir afoinfaide AS the Names of the Parfonnes
Ande what Parfonnes they be And for what Caus they were
lefte their to remayn this faide Quarter at Borde Wages
Hereafter followethe in this Bill Signed with my Lordes
Hand.

THE STILE OF THE BILL How it fchal be
writtyn Quarterly every Quarter in the Yeir of
the CHEKKE of BORDEWAGIES of my
Lordes Servauntes Whiche be appointed to go
to Borde Wagies every Quarter That kepith not
where they be appointed.

THIS IS THE BILL of Chekk of my Lordes Servauntes appointed to goo to BORDEWAGIES Quarterly As to
faye from Mondaye xxix^th Daie of Septembre in th'Eight
Yeir of the Reigne of our Sovereigne Lorde Kinge Henry
the viij^th Unto Thurfdaye xxv^th Daye Decembre next following whiche was Criftenmes Deie in the viij^th Yeir aforefaide AS the Names of the Parfonnes that went to Bordewagies all the faide Quarter Ande for what Caus they were
Chekkedde of their Bordewagies Hereafter followith in this
Bill Signid with my Lordes Hand.

THE

THE STILE OF THE BILL How it fchal be written Quarterly every Quarter in the Yeir of all fuche **PARCELLIS** of **STUF** takyn of any Parfon for th'Expens of my Lordes Hous Whiche is owing ande not paide for in the faide Quarter.

THIES BE THE NAYMES of the Parfonnes That haith any **STUF** takin of theim for the Expences of my Lordes Hous from Midfomer lafte pafte in the vij^{th} Yeir of the Reigne of our Sovereigne Lorde King Henry the viij^{th} Unto Michaelmas nextte followinge in the viij^{th} Yere of the Reigne of our faide Sovereigne Lord AS the Names of the Parfonnes With the Names of the **PARCELLIS** of Stuf takyn of theim With the Prices of the faide Stuf Ande to whom it is owing that is unpaid fore that haith byn takyn for th'Expence of my faide Lordes Hous Hereafter followith in this Bill Signide with my Lordes Hand In full Contentacion of all maner of **VICTUALLIS** bought ande owinge foir That was takyn in the foirfaid Quarter from Midfomer to Michelmes aforefaide In full Contentacion of all maner of Creditoures owinge for any maner of Stuf takyn for the Hous in the foirfaide Quarter.

THE

THE STILE OF THE BILL How it fchal be writtin Quarterly every Quarter in the Yeire of al fuche GROSS EMPCIONS CATOUR-PARCELLIS ande outher neceſſary STUF that fchal be providede for th'Expence of my Lordes Hous for every Quarter.

THE BILL of all fuche Groſs Empciones ande Catour-Parcellis ande outher neceſſary Stuf That fchal be provided for th'Expence of my Lordes Hous the Firſte Quarter bitwixte Michaelmas ande Criſtenmas in th'Eight Yeir of the Reigne of our Sovereigne Lorde Kinge Henry the viij^{th} Here-after followethe.

THE STILE OF THE BILL How it fchal be writtyn at every REMEVALL of my Lordes Hous Of my Lordes SERVAUNTS that goith befoir to the Place wheir my Lorde fchal com For providing and preparing of th'Offices their againſte my Lordes cuming theyr.

THIS IS THE BILL of the Names of my Lordes Houſe-holde Servauntes appointed by my Lord and his Counſaill to go befoir to Lekinfeld or Wrefill alwaies at my Lordes REMEVALL wheir my Lorde fchall keip his Criſtenmas For preparing ande ordering of th'Offices and making redy of theim Ande to be at Borde Wagies in the Towne alwaies

From

From Thursdaye xiiijth Daie of December before Sainte Thomas-Daie befoir Criftenmas in the viijth Yere of the Reigne of our Sovereigne Lorde King Henry the viijth Unto Saint Thomas-Evyn the xxth Daye of the faim Mounethe Which Daie his Lordefchip fet up his Hous again befoire Criftenmas AS the Names of the faide Officers Ande what Officers they be that be appointedde to go befoir Yerely for preparing of my Lordes Lodgings wheir his Lordefchip fchall keip his faide Criftenmas Ande 'to' what Rowmes every Man belongithe Ande wherefoir they be fent befoir Hereafter followith in this Bill Signide with my Lordes Hande.

    THE STILE OF THE BILL How it fchal be writtyn at the BREAKING up of my Lordes HOUS Yerely at Michaelmas when my Lorde goith about the taking of his Accompts of his Servauntes in Hous Of the PARSONNES that fchal be at Bordwages TO my Lorde fet up his Hous uppon Sainte Thomas-Evyn.

    THIS IS THE CHEQUIRROILL of the Names of my Lords Servaunts that fhal be at BORDE-WAGIES at Lekynfeld or Wrefill ande left their ftill And for what Caus they be ordeignide to remayn their AS to faye from the fyrft Daie of October Which Daie my Lord brake up his Hous at Wrefill at after Michaelmes in th'Eight Yeir of the Reigne of our Sovereigne Lorde Kinge Henry the viijth Unto xxth Daie of December next following Whiche fchal be Sainte Thomas-Evyn befoir Criftenmas Whiche Daye my Lorde fet up his Hous again at Wrefill AS the Names of the Parfonnes Ande what Parfonnes they be Ande for what Caus they be

left

lefte thier behinde all the faide tyme at Bordewagies Hereafter followith in this Bill Signide with my Lordes Hand.

THE STYLE OF THE BILL How it fhal be
Writtyn at every Breaking up of my Lordes Hous
of the PARSONNES that fhal be at BORDE-
WAGIES at the Charge of the Hous Ande not
in the Chequirroill AS apperith moir playnly in
the faid Bill.

THIS IS THE BILL of the Naymes of the Parfonnes
That be at BORDEWAGIES now at the Charge of the
Hous Ande ar not in the Chequirroil Viz. from Wedinfday
the fyrfte Daie of October Whiche Daie my Lordes Hous
brak up uppon at Wrefil at after Michaelmes in th'Eight Yeir of
the Reigne of our Sovereign Lord King Henry the viijᵗʰ Unto
Thurfday xx Daie of Decembre next following Which fchal
be Saint Thomas – Evyn afoir Criftenmas in th'Eight Yeire
afoirfaid Which day his Lordefchip fet up his Hous on again
at Wrefill AS the Names of the Parfons And what Parfonnes
they be that ar fo allowid Whiche my Lord giffeth Mete and
Drinke unto Whiche be daily in the Hous and not in the
Chequirroill AS the Names of theim hereafter followeth in
this Bill Signid with my Lordes Hand.

THE

THE STILE OF THE BILL How it fhal be wryttyn of the HALF-YEIR WAGIES too the HOUSEHOLD SERVAUNTS befides the CHAPPELL.

THIS IS THE BILL of Payment of Waigies to my Lordes Houfholde SERVAUNTES in his Chequirroill That ar to be paide at the HALF YEIR begynnyg at our Lady-Daye in Eftur-Weke lafte pafte in the vij Yeir of the Reigne of our Sovereign Lorde King Henry the viijth Ande the faide Half Yeir ending at Michaelmes nexte following in th'Eight Yeir of our faide Sovercigne Lorde King Henry the viijth AS the Names of the faide Parfonnes And what every of theim fhall taike for their faide Half-Yeir Wagies that haith Houfholde Wagies allowed theim As appereth in the Chequirroil of Houfeholde Hereafter followeth in this Bill Ande what every of theim ar paide for their faide Half Yeir Wagies in full Contentacion of their faide half Yeir that ought to be paid at this tyme ovir ande befides the Wagies of the Gentlemen of the Chappell accuftomed to be paide Quarterly As it appereth by a Bill Signed with my Lordes Hand for the faide Half Yeir.

THE

THE STILE OF THE BILL How itte fchal be writtyn every Half Yeir of the CHEK of HOUSEHOLDE WAGIES to my Lordes Servaunts Ande for what Caufe they be fo abaited Apperith more plainely in the faide Bill.

THIS IS THE NAMES of my Lordes Houfeholde Servauntes Who my Lorde and his Counfaill thinkes reafonable fchall be abaited of their HALF-YEIR WAGIES From our Lady-Daie in Lent in the vijth Yeir of the Reigne of our Sovereigne Lord King Henry the viijth Unto Michaelmes next following in th'Eight Year of the Reigne of our faide Sovereigne Lorde King Henry the viijth WHICHE is abaited of their Half-Yeir Wagies With the Names of the Parfonnes And what Parfonnes they were Ande what Rowmes they ferved in Ande what they be abaited Ande wherin Ande what they take by Yeir Ande for what Caufe Hereafter followith in this Bill Signid with my Lordes Hand.

THE STILE OF THE BILL How it fchal be writtyn at every Saint-Elyn Daie of the Payment of WINTER-HORSSEMEATE to my Lordes Servauntes Begynnyng at Michaelmas ande paide at Sainte-Elyn Daie.

THIES AR THE NAIMES of my Lordes Houfeholde Servauntes that haithe their WINTER HORSSEMEAT paid theim

theim now at Sainte Elyn - Daie in th'Eight Yeir of the Reigne of our Sovereigne Lorde King Henry the viijth Whiche wer appointed in the Bill of my Lordes Riding Houfholde of this Yeir made at Michaelmas lafte pafte in the vijth Yeir of Reigne of our faide Sovereigne Lord King Henry the viijth Who kept in their Horffis at Harde Mete And roide with my Lorde and Where His Lordefchip comaunded theim the faide Winter AS the Names of the faide Parfonnes Ande in what Rowmes every Man Servide Ande what every Man is allowed for his faide Winter Horffe-Meat Hereafter followeth in this Bill Signed with my Lordes Hand According th'Orders of the Houfeholde Booke.

THE STILE OF THE BILL How it fhal be writtyn at every Saint-Elyn Daie When they be paide Of the CHEK of my Lordes HOUS-HOLDE SERVAUNTES in the WINTER-HORSSEMEATE.

THIES BE THE NAMES of my Lordes Houfeholde Servauntes that were appointed in the Bill of WINTER-HORSSEMEAT to be of the Riding Houfholde Begynnyng at Michaelmes lafte pafte in the vijth Yeir of the Reigne of our Sovereigne Lorde King Henry the viijth Ande what was Diffallowed the faide Parfonnes of their faide Winter Horffe-Meate Ande what they were that hadd noon allowed Ande for what Caus they were Diffalowid Hereafter followith in this Bill Signide with my Lordes Hand.

THE

THE STILE OF THE BILL How it fchal be
writtyn at Sainte - Elyn Daie Of my Lordes
SERVAUNTES appointede to have SOMER-
HORSSE-MEATE Ande to be paide at Michaelmas Yerely.

THIS IS THE BILL of the Noumbre of my Lordes
Servauntes Affignid by my Lorde and his Counfaill to be
of my Lordes Riding Houfeholde Ande to have SOMER
HORSSE METE allowid theim this Yeir AS to faye from
Satturdaye iij^d Daye of May Whiche was Sainte Elyn
Daye lafte pafte in th'Eight Yeir of the Reigne of our
Sovereigne Lorde King Henry the viijth Unto Mondaie
xxixth Daie of Septembre Whiche fchal be Michalmes Daie
next following in the faide viijth Yeir Whiche Daie the faide
Somer Horffe Meat goith out on Ande the faide Parfonnes to
be paid their Somer Horffe Meate at the faide Michaelmas
Daie next following ALWAIES providede that the faide Bill
of Somer Horffe Meate be appointed ande made redy for my
Lorde to Signe Yerely upon the faide Sainte-Elyn Daye Ande
every Man to be allowid for his Somer Horffe-Meat iij$s$ iiij$d$.
AS the names of the faide Parfonnes Ande what Parfonnes
they be Ande in what Rowme every Man fhal Serve Ande for
what Caus every Man fchal be allowid Somer Horffe Meat
Hereafter followith in this Bill Signede with my Lordes
Hande,

THE

THE STILE OF THE BILL How it fchal be Writtyn of my Lordes Servauntes that is appointed to have SOMER HORSSE METE Yerely That fchall ride where my Lorde Rideth atte Sainte - Elyn Daye.

THEIS BE THE NAMES of my Lordes Houfeholde Servauntes That haithe SOMER HORSSEMEAT paide theim now at Michaelmas in th'Eight Yeir of the Reigne of our Sovereigne Lorde King Henry the viij^th Whiche wer appointed in the Bill of my Lordes Riding Houfeholde made at Sainte Elyn Daye lafte pafte in the viij^th Yeir of our faide Sovereign Lorde Who kepte their Horfes at Grefs Ande rode when they were comaunded all the faide Somer AS the Naimes of the faide Parfonnes Ande in what Rowmes every Man Servide Ande what every Man is allowide for his faide Somer Horffe - Meat Hereafter followeth in this Bill Signid with my Lordes Hand according to the order of the Houfeholde Booke.

THE STILE OF THE BILL How it fchal be writtyn at Michaelmas when they be paied Of the CHEKK of my Lordes Houfholde Servauntes in the SOMER-HORSSEMEATE.

THIES AR THE NAMES of my Lordes Houfeholde Servauntes That wer appointedde in the Bill of SOMER-HORSSE

HORSSE MEAT to be of the Riding Householde Begynnyng
uppon Satturdaye the iij^d Daie of May Whiche was Sainte-
Elyn Daye laſte paſte in th'Eight Yeir of the Reigne of our
Sovereigne. Lorde King Henry the viijth ANDE what was
Diſſalowede the ſaide Parſonnes of their ſaide Somer Horſſe
Meate Ande what they were that hadd noon allowed Ande
for what Caus they were diſſalowede Hereafter followeth in
this Bill Signid with my Lordes Hande.

THE STILE OF THE BOOKE callid TYPES
PENDUNTUR Howe it ſchal be writtyn every
Mouneth Off all maner of thinges expended in
my Lordes Hous for the ſaide Mouneth.

THIS IS THE BILL of th'Expences of all Maner of
VICTUALLIS Expended in a Mounethe in my Lordes Hous
Beggynnyng uppon Satturdaye the fyrſte Daye of Novembre
in th'Eight Yeir of the Reigne of our Sovereigne Lorde King
Henry the viijth Ande ending uppon Sondaie at night the laſte
Daye of the ſame Moneth Whiche is by the ſpace of iiij
Wekes ande two Daies AS to ſaye in Breade Wyne Beyr
Ale Beif Multounes Catoure-Parcellis Wax White-Lights
Spices Salte Otemeal Sawſes Fewell Coſts-Neceſſary Horſſe-
Meat and all Maner of Outher Thinges Expendede for
the Houſeholde Ande what was cletely expended of every
of theim in my Lordes Hous As the Noumbre of the Che-
quirroill with the Straungers (all the Vaicants deducted)
Ande what every Parſone ſtandes in a meal a Daie a Weke
ande a Mouneth As Hereafter followeth in this Booke.

THE

THE STILE OF THE BILL How it fhal be
writtyn every Mouneth in the Yeir of all the
DEFICIENTES of every Officer in my Lordes
Hous With the VALOR.

THIS IS THE BILL of Deficients of all th'OFFI-
CERS bilonging to my Lordes Houfhold in the Mounethe
of November With the Names of the PARCELLIS Ande
in what Office they ar in Ande how muche every Officere
ar in Deficient With the Prices of the Parcellis that they ar
in deficient of Hereafter followeth in this Bill Signid with
my Lordes Hande.

THE COPY of the FIRST WARRAUNTE of
TH'ASSIGNEMENT How it fchal be writtyn
Yerely for the FIRST PAYMENTE in Yorke-
fchir For Kepirg of my Lordes Hous To theim
that ftandes chargid —

WELBELOVIDE I grete You well Ande wol ande ftrately charge you Al excufis laide aparte As ye intende to have
me your goode Lorde Ande wol exchiew that at may enfieu
unto you for the contrary doing Ye fail not furthwith uppon
the Sight herof to content and paye to my Welbiloved Servants
William Worme Gentleman Ufcher of my Chaumber and
Gilbert Wedall Cheif Clarke of my Kitchirge and Thomas
Hurwod Yoman Ufcher of my Chaumbre ftanding chargid
with my faide Hous this Yeir In full Contentacion for the

O e   FYRSTE

FYRSTE PAYMENT of th'Affignement affignid unto theim for the the Keping of my faide Hous this Yeir Begynnyng at Michaelmes in th'Eight Yeir of the Reigne of our Sovereigne Lorde King Henry the viij^th of the Revenues of all my Landes within Yorkefhir whiche fchall be dew unto me at this Audicte To your handes cuming to my. Coffurs Wheir is fcan by me and my Counfaill that ye doo pay but the Some of cxxx *l.* iij *s.* xi *d.* qu. in full Contentation of their Some affignid for there Firfte Payment at this tyme of ccxviij *l.* ix *d.* Being that they have receyved in the Price of Diverfe Victuallis in the lafte Remaneth remanyng of the Yeir ending at Michaelmas the SOME of iiij^xx xij *l.* iiij *s.* viij *d.* ob. qu. Whiche makithe up the forefaid Some affigned to theim for the Firfte Payment of the Fyrfte Quarter Whiche Remanith amountith to moir than the Remaneth accuftomed in the Booke of Orders by the Some of xxxiiij *l.* ij *s.* x *d.* ob. qu. For whiche Concideracion their is cleir paide unto theim at this tyme but the Some of cxxx *l.* iij *s.* xj *d.* qu. Bicaus of the Baitement of the foirfaide xxxiiij *l.* ij *s.* x *d.* ob. qu. Whiche they have more in the Remaneth of this Yeir than they hadde the Laft Yeir YEVYN under my Signet ande Signe Manuell at my Caftell of Wrefill the iiij^th Daie of October in th'Eight Yeir of the Reigne of our Sovereigne Lorde King Henry the viij^th.

Too my Truftye Servaunte William Worme Gentleman Ufcher of my Chaumber my Coffurer ande Generall Receyvour of all my Landes in the Northe Parties this Yeir.

THE

THE COPY of the **SECOND WARRAUNTE** of th'ASSIGNEMENT How it fehal be writtyn yearly for the **SECOND PAYMENTE** in Cumbreland TO be paied of the Revenues diew upon th'Audicte of the Yere ending at Michalmes For Keping of my Lordes Hous To theim that ftundithe chargid.

WELBELOVIDE I great you well Ande woll and ftrately charge you without delay As ye intende to have me your goode Lorde Ande woll exchiew that at may enfiew unto you for the contrary dooing at your Jeopardy Fail not to content ande pay to my Welbilovid Servauntes William Worme Gentleman Ufcher of my Chambre Gilbert Wedal Chief Clarke of my Kitching and Thomas Hurwod Yoman Ufcher of my Chaumbre Standing chargid with my Hous for the 11ᵈ PAYMENTE bitwixt Michaelmas and Criftenmas in th'Eight Yeir of the Reigne of our Sovereigne Lorde King Henry the viij'ᵗʰ Of the Revenues of my Lands of Cumberland to your handes cuming to my Coffurs the SOME of c *l.* Cf fuche Money as is dew unto me upon th'Audict at Michaelmas YEVEN under my Signet and Signe Manuell at my &c.

Too my Truftye Servaunte William Worme Gentleman Ufcher of my Chaumbre my Officer and General Receyvour of all my Landes in the Northe Parties this Yeir.

THE

THE COPY of the iii^d WARAUNT of th'AS-
SIGNEMENTE How it fchal be writtyn Yerely
for iii^d PAYMENT in Yorkefchire TO be paid
of the Revenues dew upon th'Audicte of the Yeir
ending at Michalmes For Keping of my Lords
Hous To theim that Standeth chargid.

WELBILOVIDE I grete you well Ande wol and ftrate-
ly charge You without delay As ye intend to have me
Your Goode Lorde And wol exchiew that at may enfieu unto
you for the contrary doing at your Jeopardye Fail not to con-
tent and pay to my Welbilovid Servauntes William Worme
Gentleman Ufcher of my Chaumbre Gilbert Wedal Chief
Clarke of the Kitching and Thomas Hurwood Yoman Ufcher
of my Chamber Standing chargid with my Hous for the iii^d
PAYMENT bitwixe Michaelmes and Criftenmas in th'Eight
Yeir of the Reigne of our Sovereigne Lorde King Henry viijth
Of the Revenues of my Landes of Yorkefchire to your handes
cuming to my Coffurs the SOME of Lxxvij l. viij s. Of fuche
Money as is dew unto me uppon th'Audicte at Michalmes
YEVEN under my Signet and Signe Manuell at my Caftell
of Wrefill iiijth Daie of Octobre in th'Eight Yeir of the
Reigne of our Sovereigne Lorde King Henry the viijth.

Too my Truftye Servaunte William Worme Gentle-
man Ufcher of my Chaumbre my Coffurer and
General Receyvor of al my Landes in the North
Parties this Yeir.

THE

THE COPY of the ivth WARRAUNTE of th'ASSIGNEMENT How it fchal be writtyn Yerely for the ivth PAYMENT in Yorkefchire TO be paide of the Revenus of Martynmas Fermes dew and payable at Candelmas For Keping of my Lordes Hous To theim that ftandes chargid.

WELBILOVIDE I grete you well Ande woll ande ftrately charge you Without delaye As ye intende to have me your goode Lord Ande wol exchew that at may infew unto you for the contrary doing at your Jeopardye That ye fail not too contente and paye unto my Welbiloved Servauntes William Worme Gentleman Ufcher of my Chaumbre Gilbert Wedal Chief Clarke of the Kitching ande Thomas Hurwod Yoman Ufcher of my Chaumbre Standing chargid with my Hous this Yeir for the FIRSTE PAYMENT and LASTE bitwixte Criftenmas ande our Lady-Daye in Lent in th'Eight Yeir of the Reigne of our Sovereigne Lorde King Henry the viijth Of the Revenues of my Landes of Yorkefchire to your handes cuming to my Coffurs the SOME of ccxLv *l*. v *s*. v *d*. Cf fuche Money as is dew unto me of the Martynmas Ferme dew ande payable at Candelmas YEVEN under my Signet ande Signe Manuell at my Caftell of Wrefill iiijth Daie of Octobre th'Eight Yeir of the Reigne of our Sovereigne Lorde King Henry viijth.

> Too my Trufty Servaunte William Worme Gentleman Ufcher of my Chaumbre my Coffurer ande General Receyvor of al my Landes in the North Parties this Yeir.

THE

THE COPY of the vth WARRAUNTE of th'ASSIGNEMENT How it fchal be writtyn Yerely for the vth PAYMENT in Northumbreland TO be paide of the Revenus of Martynmas Fermes payable at our Lady-Daie in Lent For Keping of my Lordes Hous To theim that ftonds chargid.

WELBELOVIDE I grete you well Ande woll ande ftrately charge you without delay As ye intende to have me your good Lorde Ande wol exchew that at may infiew unto you for the contrary doing at your Jeopardye Fail not to content and paye unto my Welbilovid Servauntes William Worme Gentleman Ufcher of my Chaumbre Gilbert Wedall Cheif Clarke of my Kitching Ande Thomas Hurwodd Yoman Ufcher of my Chaumbre Standing chargid with my Hous this Yeir For the FIRSTE PAYMENT of th'Affignement of my Hous bitwixt our Lady-Daye in Lent ande Midfomer Of the Revenues of my Landes of Northumbreland to your handes cuming to my Coffurs the SOME of cvij *l.* iiij *s.* x *d.* Of fuche Money as is dew unto me of the Martynmes Fermes Dew and payable at our Lady-Day in Lente YEVEN under my Signet and Signe Manuell at my &c.

Too my Truftye Servaunte William Worme Gen-tlemen Ufcher of my Chambre my Coffurer ande General Receyvor of al my Landes in the North Parties this Yeir.

THE

THE COPY of the vi^th WARRAUNTE of th'Affignement How it fchal be writtyn Yerely for the
vi^th PAYMENT in Cumbreland TO be paied of
the Revenus of Martynmas Fermes payable at our
Lady - Daie in Lent For Keping of my Lordes
Hous To theim that ftondeth chargid.

WELBILOVIDE I grete you well Ande woll ande
ftrately charge you without delay As ye intende to have me
your Goode Lorde Ande wol exchew that at may enfieu unto
you for the contrary doing at your Jeopardye Fail not to content and paye unto my Welbeloved Servauntes William
Worme Gentleman Ufcher of my Chaumbre Gilbert Wedal
Cheif Clarke of my Kitching ande Thomas Horwod Yoman
Ufcher of my Chaumbre Standing chargide with my Hous
this Yeir for the 11de PAYMENT bitwixt our Lady - Daie
in Lent ande Midfomer in the ix^th Yeir of the Reigne of our
Sovereigne Lorde King Henry the viij^th Of the Revenus of
my Landes of Cumberlande to your Handes cuming to my
Coffurs the SOME of Lx l. Of the Martynmes Fermes Dew
and payable at our Lady-Daye in Lente YEVEN under my
Signet ande Signe Manuel at my &c.

Too my Truftye Servaunte William Worme Gen-
tleman Ufcher of my Chambre my Coffurer and
General Receyvor of al my Lands in the North
Partics this Yeir.

THE

THE COPY of the viith WARRAUNTE for
th'ASSIGNEMENT How it fchal be writtyn
Yerely for the viith PAYMENT and LASTE
in full payment of th'oole Some of th'Affignement for th'ole Yeir in Northumbrelande TO
be paide of the Revenus of Whitfonday Fermes
payable at Lambmes For keping of my Lordes
Hous To theim that ftondeth chargide.

WELBILOVIDE I grete you well Ande woll and ftrately
charge you without delay As ye intende to have me your
goode Lorde Ande wol exchew that at may enfiew unto You
for the contrary doing at your Jeopardye Fail not to content
and paye to my Welbilovide Servauntes William Worme
Gentleman Ufcher of my Chaumbre Gilbert Wedall Chief
Clarke of my Kitching ande Thomas Hurwodde Yoman
Ufcher of my Chaumber Stonding chargide with my Hous
this Yeir In full Contentacion of the viith WARRAUNTE
ande LAST PAYMENT of th'Affignement affignede unto
theim for Keping of my faide Hous for this Yeir Begynnynge
at Michaelmes in th'Eight Yeir of the Reigne of our Sovereigne Lorde King Henry the viijth Ande fchall ende at
Michaelmas next following Of the Revenus of all my Landes
in Northumbreland to your handes cuming Dew to my Coffurs
of the Whitfonday Fermes payable at Lambmes YE content
and paye the SOME of ciiij *l.* xiij *s.* ix *d.* in redy Money
Ovir ande befides that they have xvj *l.* vj *s.* chargide upon
theim the faide tyme As Parcell of their Affignement affigned
unto theim As in the Fermes of Divers Medowis ande Paftures
at Lekynfelde ande Wrefill AS to faye LXXvj *s.* at Wrefill

Ande

Ande xij *l*. xs. at Lekinfelde As it appereth more plainly in the Booke of Orders of my Lordes Hous FOR the making up of the Some of cxxj *l.* ix *d.* assignide vnto theim in the IIIIth Quarter bitwixt Midsomer ande Michalmas Whiche is in full Payment of their hoole assignement for this hoole Yeir ended at the saide Michaelmes next for to com YEIVEN under my Signet ande Signe Manuell at my &c.

Too my Trustye Servaunte William Worme Gen-
tleman Uscher of my Chaumbre my Coffurer and
General Receyvor of all my Landes in the North
Parties this Yeir.

THE COPY OF THE WARRAUNTE How it
shall be writtyn Yerely of the DELIVERY of the
SIGNETTS for th'Expences of my Lordes Hous
To be takyn in suche places as my Lorde haith
Breders.

WELBELOVIDE I grete you well Ande wol ande strately charge you that ye deliver or caus to be delivered unto my Welbelovede Servauntes William Worme Gentleman Uscher of my Chaumbre Gilberte Wedal Chief Clarke of my Kitching And Thomas Horwod Yoman Uscher of my Chaumbre Stonding chargide with my Hous For th'Use and Expens of my saide Hous now againste the Feiste of Cris-tenmas next to com xxx SIGNETTS To be takyn of my Brode of my Swannys within my Carre of Arom within my Lordeschip of Lekinfeld within the countie of Yorke Wherof ye have the kepinge Ande that ye cause the saim to be delivert unto theim or to oone of theim furthwith uppon the Sight

P p   hereof

hereof Ande this my Writing fchal be unto you anempfte me and tofore myn Auditours at your next accompte in this bihalve fufficiante Warraunte and Difcharge YEVEN under my Signet ande Signe Manuell at my Caftell of Wrefill the iiij^th Daye of Octobre in th'Eight Yeir of the Reigne of our Sovereigne Lorde King Henry the viij^th.

Too my Welbilovide Servaunte Rauf Swinburne Yoman Ufcher of my Chambre ande Baillif of my Lordefchip of Lekynfelde aforefaide Ande Kepar of my faide Carr at Arom Ande to the Under Kepars of the faim for the tyme beinge.

THE FOURM OF A DRAUGHT How it fchal be for TOTALLING of the Noumbre of the Chequirroil with the Noumbre of the Straungers the Vacants Deducted For a Mouneth When they cafte up the Parfonnes at the Mounethes end.

FIRSTE To cafte ovir the Parfonnes of the Chequirroill Double every Etting Daie Ande upon the Fafting Daies but Single the Parfons Ande than to Deducte all the Parfons that be Vacante of the Chequirroill in the faide Mouneth Ande make that the Nombre of the Chequirroill The Parfons that ar Vacant Deducted.

ITEM Than to cafte ovir all your Straungers in the faide Mouneth.

ITEM Than to cafte ovir all your Vacantes of the Parfonnes of the Chequirroill wanting in the faide Mouneth.

ANDE

ANDE than to caste the Fyrste Noumbre in the whiche the Vacants of the Perfonnes of your Chequirroil are deducted and laye to theim your Straungers daily in the faide Mouneth to the faid Noumber Ande than to take half of it uppon the Fafting Daie and Double the Etting Daye And than to make the Nombre of the fame.

THIS IS THE CHEQUIRROILL of the Noumbre of my Lordes SERVAUNTES in Houfhold appointed by my Lorde and his Counfaill to be at BORDE - WAIGIES in the Towne at Leckynfelde Ande to remayne their at all tymes whenne my Lorde and my Lady lieth at the New Lodge in Leckynfeld Pare at the charge of the Standing Hous Ande to yef their attendaunce uppon my faide Lord and Lady daily bitwixte Meallis Notwithftonding that they be at Borde-Waigies in the Towne their At all fuche tymes as my Lorde fo liethe at the faide Lodge And brakith upp his Hous For taiking th'Accomptis of all th'Offices in his Lorde-fhippis Houfs AS TO SAY from Sondaye the iiij^th daye of Sep-tember in the Leventh Yeir of the Reign of our Sovereign Lorde King Henry the viij^th Whiche daye his Lordefhip brack up his Hous on at Wrefill this Yeir afoir Michaelmes Bicaus his Lordefhip wol have th'Accompte of th'Offices of Houfholde takyn befoir his going to London concerning his Dormount Book ande Wering Booke Bicaus his Lordefhip muft be at London befoir Alhallowtide nexte UNTO Wedinf-daye the xxviij^th Daye of Septembre nexte following whiche is Michaelmes - Evyn in the Leventh Yeir afoirfaid Whiche day th'Accompte of the olde Yeir goith oute uppon Ande the New Yeir begynnes uppon AS the Naimes of the Per-fonnes

Somes And what Parsonnes they be Ande what Rowmes they belong too Hereaftir followith in this Bill Signed with my Lordes Hande Which wente to Bordewaigies their at this tyme WHICHE Bill was made now befoir Michaelmas afoir the daie accustomed in the Booke of Orders of the Hous Bicaus of my Lordes going up to London so soon.

THIS IS THE CHEQUIRROILL of the Noumbre of my Lordes SERVAUNTES of Houshold appointid by my Lorde and his Counsaill to be at Bordewaigies in the Towne at Wresill Ande to remayne their still FROM Teusday the vjth daye of Septembr in the Leventh Yeir of the Reigne of our Sovereigne Lorde King Henry the viijth Whiche daie his Lordship brack up his Hous at Wresill befoir this Michaelmes next cuming and roide to Leckynfeld for taiking th'accompte of all th'Officesse in his Lordeshipps Hous concernyng his Dormount Booke ande Wering Booke UNTO Wedinsdaye the xxviijth Daie of September Whiche is Michaelmes-Even next following in the Leventh Yeir of the Reigne of our saide Sovereigne Lord Whiche day the Olde Yeir endes upon ande the New Yeir begynnes on AS the Naimes of the Parsonnes Ande what Parsonns they be that weir apointed to remayne their at Bordwaigies this saide tyme Ande for what caufis they weir left behinde Hereafter followeth in this Bill Signid with my Lordes Hande WHICH Bill was made now befoir Michaelmes befoir the Daie accustomed in the Booke of Orders of the Hous Bicaus of my Lords going up to London befoir Alballowtide next cuminge.

THIS

THIS IS THE BILL of the Naimes of my Lordes HOUSHOLD SERVAUNTES appointid by my Lord and his Counsaill to go befoir to Leckynfeld for providing and ordering of the Offices their when my Lord fhall Lye at the New Lodge in the Park their at this tyme Whenne my Lord brack up his Hous at Wrefill uppon Sonday the iiij^th daye of Septembre befoir this Michaelmes next cuming in the Leventh Yeir of the Reigne of our Sovereigne Lord King Henry the viij^th And roide to Leckynfelde for taiking th'Accomptes of all th'Offices in his Lordfhipps Hous concerning his Dormount Booke and Wering Booke Unto Wedinfdaye the xxviij^th Daie of Septembre next following in the Leventh Yeir of the Reigne of our Sovereigne Lord King Henry the viij^th Whiche Daie th'Accompte of the Olde Yeire for the Houfholde went out uppon Ande the New Yeir begynnes upon AS the Names of the faid Officers and what Officers they be that were appointed to go befoir for preparing of my faide Lordes Lodginges this faide tyme at the New Lodge in Leckynfeld Park And what Rowme every Man belongith too Ande wheirfoir they weir fente afoir Hereaftir followith in this Bill Signed with my Lordes Hande.

THIS IS THE CHEQUIRROILL of the Noumbre of my Lordes SERVAUNTES in Houfhold That haithe Licens of my Lorde and his Counfaill to go about their owne Bufines or my Lordes Bufinefs And haithe no Bordewaigies allowid theim for that Caus at this tyme AS to fay frome Teufday the vj^th Daye of September in the Leventhe Yeir of the Reigne of our Sovrain Lorde King Henry the viij^th Whiche Daie his Lordfhip brack up his Houfs on at Wrefill befoir this

Michaelmes

Michaelmes next cuming Ande roide to Leckynfeld for taiking th'Accomptes of all th'Offices of Houfhold concernyng his Dormount Booke and Wering Booke Unto Wedinfday the xxviij Daie of September Whiche is Michaelmes-Evyn next following in the Leventhe Yeir of the Reigne of our Sovrain Lorde King Henry the viij^{th} aforrfaide Whiche Daie the Olde Yeir goith oute uppon Ande the New Yeire begynnes upon AS the Names of the Parfonnes Ande what Parfonnes they be Ande for what caus the faide Parfonnes had no Bordewaigies allowid theim Hereafter followith in this Bill Signid with my Lordes Hande That wente abowte my Lordes bufines or their Owne the faide tyme.

* THIS IS THE BILL of the REMANETH of all Man- noure of STUFFE remainynge unfpent of the Provifion made for the Keapinge of my Lordes Houfe for the Yeare endet at Michaelmes laft paft Anno xiiij^{mo} R. H. viij AS well the Remaineth taiken at the place where my Lord lieth Yearlie As at all outher places where anny Stuff remanneth of the Provifion of the faid former Yeare The faid Remanneth to be taikyn Yearlie upon the xxix Daie of Septembr whiche is Michaelmas-Daie THE faid Remaneth to be taikyn by the Sight of the Stewerde Trefourer or Coumptroulere Survioure or Deane of his Lordfhip Chapell Or one of his Lordfhip Counfaill Or a Chaplane Or by the . . . . of Gentle- men Or a Yoman Ufchere of the Chaumbre Or a Clarke of the Kytchyn Or by fuch outhere Perfonnes as my Lord fhall name and appointe to taike the faid Remanneth of all Manor off Stuffe remannynge unfpente As well Parcelles paid for As the Parcelles off Stuffe remannynge providet for the faid Houfe

* The remaining Articles in this Chapter are of a later Date, and appear in the MS. to be written by a different hand from the former.

Houfe and unpaid for Which was providet for th'Expenfes for
Kepinge of my faid Lordes Houfe for the faid former Yere Endet
at the faid Michaelmas lafte AS the Names of the Parcelles
of the faide Stuffe With there Prices That remaned unfpente
And what Quantitie remanede of every Parcell And what
Mannoure of Stuffe it was providet the faid Yere and un-
fpente Hereafer followeth in this Bill Signed with my Lordes
Hande,

THE STILE OF THE BILLS for Braking upe of
    my Lordes Hous at after the xijth Day of Criftenmes
    Or aney outher tyme.

THYS YS THE CHEQUIROULL of all my Lordes
SERVAUNTES in Houfholde apontide by my Lorde ande
his Counfaill to be within at Mete ande Drinke to gyf ther
attendance upon my Lorde and myLady at Wrefill Wher they
remayn at the charge of the Standing Hous nowe to attende
upon my Lorde and my Lady within now of the Braking up
of my Lordes Hous at after this xijth Day of Criftynmes As
to fay from Wedinfday the vijth Day of January Which was
the morow after the faid xijth day in the xiiijth Yer of the
Reign of our Sovereign Lorde King Henry the viij h Which
day his Lordfhipis Hous was broken uppe at Wrefill as is
accuftomyde Yerely Unto Sonday next following the xjth day
of the fame Monnyth Which day his Lordfhipe fett upe his
Hous on agayn at Wrefill AS the Namys of the Parfonnes that
was apontide to gif ther Attendaunce upon my faide Lorde
and Lady Ande to be within at Mete and Drinke in the Hous
Ande in what Rowmys every Man ferved yn Herafter followith
in this Bill Signede with my Lordes Hande,

THIS

THIS IS THE BILL of my Lordes SERVAUNTES Which be apontide of the Holl Nombr of the Chequiroull by my Lord and his Counfail And to be at Bordwages in the Town at Wrefill And to remayn ther at the Charge of the Standing Hous Ande not to be within at Mete and Drink in the Hous wherin my Lorde lieth Ande is apontid to gif ther Attendance upon my Lorde and my Lady daly bitwix Meills within wher his Lordfhipe lyeth now at this tyme of the Breking up of my Lordes Hous at Wrefill at after this xij^{th} day of Criftynmes By the fpace of iiij Dais Viz. From Wedinfday at morn the vij^{th} day of January Which was the morow after the faid xij^{th} day of Criftynmes Anno xiiij° Which day his Lord-fhipes Hous was brokyn up on at Wrefill as is accuftomyde yerely Unto Sonday at Morne next following the xj^{th} day of the fame Mounyth Which day his Lordfhipe fett up his Hous on agayn at Wrefill AS the Namys of the faide Parfons Ande what Parfons they bee that was apontide to go to Bordwages in the Town at Wrefill this fayd tyme And to gif ther Atten-dance daly upon my Lorde and my Lady bitwix Meills Here-after followith in this Bill Signed with my Lordis Hande.

THIS YS THE CHEQUIROULL of the Noumbr of my Lordes SERVAUNTES Apontid of the Holl Noumbr of the Chequiroull by my Lorde and his Counfaill That hath Licens to goe as well about my Lordes Bufynes as their own And haith no Bordwages allowide theym at this Tym for that Caus As to fay from Wedinfday the vij^{th} day of January Which was the morow after the xij^{th} day of Criftynmes
Anno

Anno xiiij° Which Day his Lordſhipe brak up his Hous on ſt Wreſill As is accuſtomyde yerly. Unto Sonday at morne next following the xjth day of the ſaid Monnythe Which day his Lordſhipe ſett up his Hous on agayn at Wreſill AS the Namys of the Parſonnes And what Parſons they be And for what Caus they had no Bordwages allowid theym And for what Caus they hadde Licens to go about my Lordes Buſynes or ther own Hereafter followith in this Bill Signed with my Lordes Hande.

THE STILE OF THE BILL How it ſhal be maide yerly at Mychelmes Of the NAMYS of the PAR-SONS Whiche ſhal be within at Mete and Drinke Wher my Lord kepith his SECREAT HOUS And to be brevid as Strauingers.

THES YS THE BILL of the Namys of the PARSON-NES which be Warkmen and ſhal be within at Mete and Drinke in my Lordes Hous Wher my Lord lieth and kepith his SECREAT HOUS Whiche be not in the Chequiroll of the Nombre apontide to be within Who my Lorde hathe promyſide Mete and Drinke unto as longe as they ar in his Lordſhipes Houſe - Warkes Who my Lord hath ordynyd for ſpede of ther Warks to be at Mete and Drink within wher his Lordſhip kepis his Secreat Hous And to be Brevid as Strauingers at this tyme Viz. From Thurſday the xxixth day of Septembre Which was Mychelmes-day laſt paſt Anno xvj° Which day th'Old Yer ends and the New Yer begyns on Unto Thurſday the xxth day of Decembre next follo-wing Which ſhal be Saint Thomas-Evyn afore Criſtynmes Which day my Lord ſetts up his Hous on agayne at Wreſill

Q q   AS

A S the Namys of the Parfons And what Parfons they be Hereafter followith in this Bill Signed with my Lords Hande.

THE STILE OFF THE BILL to be maide in the REMANETH When ther is any Stuff delyvert to the Houfehold for the New Yere providet by the Boke of my Lordys Foren Expenfes and nott by the Howfe-holde.

THIS IS THE BILL, of the Namys off all fuche EMPCIONS if any be bought by my Lordys Coffurer Clerke of his Foren Expenfes Or by hym that doith pay the Booke of my Lordis Foren Expenfes Which is providet fore at Avauntage For the Keaping of my Lordys Houfe And delyvert at Michaelmes at the Begynnynge of the Yere to thoys Parfons Which fhall ftand chargid with my Lordys Houfe for the Newe Yere Begynnynge at the faide Michael-mes With the Remaneth of Stuff payed fore remayninge fpared and unfpent of the former yere As in party of Payment off the Fyrft Waraunt for this faid Newe Yere Begynnynge at Michaelmes For the Affignment for Keapinge of my faid Lordys Howfe Begynnynge for this faid Yere AS the Namys of the Parcels of the faid Stuff With the Prices And whatt Manner off Stuff it is Hereafter followith.

XXXIX.

XXXIX.

A SHORT DRAUGHT MADE OF TH'ORDER of my Lordes SERVAUNTES that fhal be at Meat ande Drinke daily in my Lordes Hous Wheir my Lord kepith his SECRET HOUSS Whenne his Lordfhip BRAKETH his Houfhold AND how they fhall attende of his Lordfhip at MEALLIS Ande be orderid HEREAFTIR followith in this BILL How they fhal be orderid at euery fuche tyme.

TO SITT at my LORDES BOURD ENDE.

MY Lordes Eldeft Sonne

MY Lordes Secounde Son

MY Lordes Third Sonne

MY Lordes Broither

FOUR —— A Meas.

THE

THE PARSONNES to AWAIT at Meallis in my LORDES CHAMBRE ande to have the REVERCION

THE Aumer

THE Carver

THE Sewar

THE Cupbearer to my Lorde

THE Cupberer to my Lady

THE Gentleman Waiter for the Bordes Ende

A Haunsheman to await upon the Cuppis at the Bordes Ende

A Yoman Usher to awaite

A Yoman of the Chaumbre to awaite

ANoither Yoman of the Chaumbre to awaite

A Yoman Officer to await uppon the Cupbord and to serve Pauntry Buttery ande Seller

A Groim of the Chaimbre to keep the Doore

TWELVE —— iij Meas

THE

THE PARSONS to SIT in the GREAT CHAUMBRE at the KNIGHTES BOORD.

A Gentlewoman for my Lady

A Chaumberer for my Lady

ANoither Chaumberer for my Lady

A Gentlman Uſher

A Yoman Uſher to awayt at Aftir-dynner

THE Cheef Clarke of the Keching that cummes upp with my Lordes Service.

MY Lordes Coffurer.

SEVEN ——— ij Meas

THE PARSONS that ſhall SIT in the HALL at DYN-NER in my Lordes Dynner-Tyme Ande to AWAITE at AFTER DYNNER.

A Yoman of the Chaumbre

ANoither Yoman of the Chaumbre

A Groim of the Chaumbre to my Lorde

A Groim of the Chaumbre to my Lady

A

A Groim of the Wardrob

A Clark of my Lordes Foren Exſpences

A Clark of the Brevementes

A Clark Avener

A Porter

A Groim of my Lorde PERCES Chaumbre

TEN —— ij Meas.

THE BORD for TH'OFFICERS to SIT at That doithe ATTENDE.

A Clark of the Kechyng.

A Groim of the Ewry

A Yoman Cooke to ſerve at the Dreſſer

A Groim Cooke to ſerve in the Keching

A Child of the Keching for the Broches

A Child of the Squillary.

SIX —— A Meas Dimid.

XL.

XL.

THE HOOL NOUMBER OF ALL THE PARSONS Whiche is Alwaies thought meat by my Lord and his Counfaill Ande no mo in noumber To be ABOUT MY LORD at fuch tymes whenne his Lordfhip kepith his SECRAT HOUSS at the New Lodge or outerwheir Whenne his Lordefhip BRAIKITH UP HIS HOUSS Ande taikes the ACCOMPTIS of all TH'OFFICES in his Lordefhipps 'houfehold' AS the NAIMES of the ROWMES whereunto they fhall parteigne Hereaftir followith.

MY Lord

MY Lady

THE NOUMBRE ij.

MY LORDES CHILDRYNNE.

MY Lordes Eldeft Sonne

MY Lordes Secounde Sonne

MY

MY Lordes Thirde Sonne

MY Lordes Doughter.

THE NOUMBR — iiij.

MY LORDES COUNSAILL

ONE of my Lordes Counsaill for Aunswering ande Ridyng of Causis whenne Suters cumeth to my Lorde.

THE NOUMBRE —j.

TH'OOLE NOMBRE of the PARSONNES thought enoughe to serve ande await upon my Lorde in his Chambr at Meills at DYNNER ande SOPAR daly Whenne he kepith a SECRET HOUSS Ande to be at MEAT and DRINKE wheir my Lord lieth Ande to have my Lordes Revercion Ande to sit at the LATTER DYNNER.

A Preste as a Chaplein Ande to await as Aumer at the Borde

A Carver for the Bourde to serve my Lord

A Sewar for the Bourd to serve my Lord

A Cupberer for my Lorde

A Cupberer for my Lady

A

A Gentlemen Waiter to ferve ande await uppon the Cuppis for my Lordes Bourd-End.

A Yoman Ufher to keep the Chaumbre Doore at Meallis wheir my Lord ande my Lady dyneth ande fopps

A Yoman of the Chaumbre to bear the Furft Dyfhe to the Bourd

ANoither Yoman of the Chaumbre to bear the Secounde Dyfhe to the Bourde

ANoithir Yoman of the Chaumbre to bear the Third Difche to the Bourde

ANoithir Yoman of the Chaumbre to bear the iiijth Difhe to the Bourd.

A Officer of an Office to await upon the Cupbourd ande to ferve as Pauntler Butteller ande for the Seller

A Groim of the Chaumbre to keep the Chaumbre-Door under the Yoman Ufher.

THE NOUMBER ——— xiij.

THE PARSONNES THAT BE ORDEYGNID to be in the HOUSS to ATTENDE upon my Lord and my Lady at all tymes for SERVYNG of my Lorde and my Laidy Whenne his Lordfhip kepith a SECRET HOUSS Ande to fit at the FIRST DYNNER at the
R r   KNIGHTS

KNIGHTS BORD in the Great Chambre Ande to attende at AFTER - MEALLIS.

A Gentlewoman to attende upon my Laidy in hir Chaumbre.

A Chaumbererer to attend upon my Lady in hir Chambre.

Anoithir Chaumberer to attend upon my Lady in hir Chambre

A Gentleman Usher to kepe my Lordes Great Chambre at all tymes bitwixt Meallis

A Yoman Usher to attende upon my Ladies Chaumbre and to go for all thingis that She comawndeth

A Head Clark of the Keching to com upp with my Lordes Shirt.

MY Lordes Coffurer for receyvying of all maner of Receptes of Lordes Landes

THE NOUMBRE —— vij.

THE NAMYS OF ALL MANER of PARSONNES that must ferve for all OFFICES Wheir my Lord lieth whenne his Lordefhip kepith his SECREAT HOUSS Whiche must DYNE in the HALL daily at the FURST DYNNER.

A Groim of the Chaumbre to my Lord to waite in my Lords Chaumbre bitwixte Meallis Ande for keping of it clean.

A

A Groim of the Chaumbre for my Lady to await upon my Ladies Chaumbre bitwixt Meallis Ande for keaping and dreſſing of it clean

A Groim of the Wardrob for kepinge of the Wardrob And for dreſſing of my Lord ande my Ladies Stuf in it.

A Clark of my Lordes Foren Exſpences for writing daily the Booke of my Lordes Foren Exſpences for delyvery of Moncy oute of my Lordes Coffers.

A Clark of the Brevementes to breve daily in the Counting-Houſs for the Houſhold.

A Clark Avener for breving daily of Horſſemate and Livereis of Fewell.

A Porter to keep my Lordes Gaites.

A Groim to my Lorde PERCY for keaping of my Lord PERCIS Garments clean daily.

A Under Clark of the Keching to ſee the Countinhous daily orderde ande kepte

A Yoman or a Groim of the Hall to ſet the Hall And to breve daily for the Hall Ande to Delyve rFewell.

A Groim of th'Ewry to keep the Stuf in the Buttery Pauntry ande Seller And to ſerve at Latter Dynnir

A Yoman Cooke to have the Ovirſight of the Keching ande to ſerve at the Dreſſer.

A Groim Cooke to ſerve in the Keching ande Larder and as Haiſtiller at the Raingo

A

A Child of the Keching for turnynge of the Broches Ande for maiking clean ande fweping of the Kiching

Anoither Child of the Keching for keping of the Veffell Ande for maiking clean of the faide Veffell in the Squillary.

THE NOMBRE —— xv.

THE HOLLE NOMBRE is —— XLII,

XLI.

XLI.

THE ORDER OF THE BILL of all my Lordis SER-VAUNTIS in Houfhold appointid to awaite in the GREATE CHAUMBRE daily thurrowte the WEKE Ande to what ROWMES they doo perteign in Houfhold That fo fhall awaite daily Ande at what HOURIS every man fhall awaite in the faide Greate Chaumbre uppon my Lorde Ande Howe long As well AFOIR NOON As AFTIR NOON As to fay Gentlemen - Ufchers Gentlemen of Houfhold Yomen - Ufchers Marfhallis of the Halle Yomen of the Chaumbre Yomen Officers Yomen Waiters Groimes of the Chaumbre And Groim Officers of Houfhold HEREAFTIR FOLLOWITH the Order of theim How every of the faide Parfons fhall attende Ande how long Ande at what Houris.

THE NAMES of my Lordes Servauntes appointid too awaite BEFOIR NOONES daily thurrowte the Weke Ande at what HOURIS AS the NAIMES of theim Ande too what ROWMES they doo perteign that fo fhalle awaite HERE-AFTIR FOLLOWITH Who may at AFTIR-DYNNER go aboute their own bufinefs.

THE

THE NAIMES of the Gentlemen-Ufchers Gentlemen of Houfholde Yomen-Ufchers Ande Marchallis of the Hall That fhall awaite in the GREATE CHAUMBRE Daily thurreowte the Weke uppon FLESCH-DAIES on the FOORE NOONES From vij of the Clock in the Mornyng to x of the Clock that my Lorde gons to Dynner WHYCHE PAR-SONNES for their waiting Befoir Noon haith Licence at Aftir-Noon to go about their own bufinefs from the faide Noon to iij of the Clocke that Evin-Song begin Which is by the fpaice of iij houris Ande they not to faill than to com in again And raithir yf any Straungers cum.

THE GENTLEMEN to awaite BEFOIR NOON daily thrughoute the WEKE That haith Licence to go aboute their own Bufinifs at AFTIR NOON.

FIRSTE A Gentlemen Ufcher to my Lorde.

ITEM A Carver to my Lorde

ITEM A Sewar to my Lorde

ITEM A Cupbearer too my Lorde

ITEM A Gentleman Waiter for the Borde Ende

ITEM A Marfhall of the Hall

THE NOUMBRE of the PARSONS as GENTLE-MEN ar ——— vj.

THE

THE NAIMES of the Yomen of the Chaumbre Yomen-Waiters ande Groimes of the Chaumbre that fhall awaite in the GREAT CHAUMBRE Daily BEFOIR NOON in the Mornyng thrugheoute the Weke on FLESCH-DAIES From vij of the Clock in the Mornyng To x of the Clocke that my Lorde go to Dynner WHICHE PARSONS for theire waiting Before Noon haith Licence at Aftir-Noon to go aboute their own Bufinefs From the faid Noon to iij of the Clok That Evin-Song begyn Which is by the fpaice of iij howeris Ande they not to fail than to com in again Ande raithir if any Straungers com.

THE YOMEN of the Chaumbre Yomen-Walters and Gromes of the Chaumbre to awaite BEFOIR NOON thrughoute the WEKE Daily That haith Licence to goo about their own Bufinefs at AFTIR-NOON.

FURSTE THE Yoman of the Roibis Yoman of the Chaumbre

ITEM The Yoman of the Chaumbre that attendith uppon my Lordis maikyng redy

ITEM The Yoman of the Chaumbre that attends uppon my Laidy.

ITEM A Yoman Waiter

ITEM An outhir Yoman Waiter

ITEM An outhir Yoman Waiter

ITEM

ITEM An outhir Yoman Waiter

ITEM A Groim of the Chaumbre to my Lorde

ITEM An outher Groim o'th Chambre too my Lorde

ITEM A Child to awaite under the Groimes of the Chaumbre.

THE NOMBRE of the PARSONS as YOMEN Ande GROIMES of the CHAUMBRE ar ——— x.

THE NAIMES of th'OFFICERS OF HOUSHOLDE that ſhall awaite in the GREAT CHAMBRE Daily BEFOIR NOON thrughoute the Weke on FLESCH-DAIES From vj of the Clock in the Mornyng Unto viijᵗʰ of the Clock next following That they ſhall go to theire OFFICES for ſervyng of BRAIKEFASTS Which is by the ſpace of two Houris Ande the ſaide Officers to yef like atten-dance in the Greate Chaumbre Daily thurrowte the Weke upon the Fleſch-daies From ix of the clock that Braikefaſts be don Unto x of the Clock that they go to ſerve in their Offices for DYNNER by the ſpaice of an houre WHICH OFFICERS for their waiting Befoir Noon the ſaide iij Houris haith Licence at Aftir-Noon to go aboute their owne Buſineſs from the ſaide Noon unto iij of the clok That they ſhall com in again for ſervyng of DRYNKYNGS Whiche is iij Houris And they not to faile than to com in again for ſervyng of Drynkyngs Ande rathir if any Straungers com.

THE

THE YOMEN OFFICERS Groim Officers of
Houſholde to awaite BEFOIR NOON thurrowte
the Weke daily That haith Licence to go aboute
their own buſineſs at AFTIR-NOON.

FURSTE A Yoman Uſcher of the Halle

ITEM The Yoman of the Pauntry

ITEM The Groim of the Buttery

ITEM The Groim of the Ewry

THE NOMBRE of the PARSONS as YOMEN OFFI-
CERS and GROIM OFFICERS ar —— iiij

THE NOUMBRE OF ALL MY LORDIS SER-
VAUNTIS appointid to awaite in the GREATE
CHAUMBRE every Day in the morning DAILY
THRUGHOUTE THE WEKE from vj of the
clock to x of the Clok ar —— xx.

S s.   XLII.

XLII.

THE ORDER OF ALL MY LORDIS SERVAUN-
TIS in Houſholde appointid to await in the GREATE
CHAUMBRE daily thrughout the WEKE Ande to what
ROWMIS they doo perteign in Houſholde that ſo ſhall
awaite daily Ande at what HOURIS Every Man ſhall awaite
in the ſaide Great Chaumbre upon my Lorde Ande at what
houre at AFTIR-NOON As to ſay Gentlemen Uſchars
Gentlmen of Houſhold Yomen Uſchers Marſchallis of the
Hall Yomen of the Chaumbre Yomen Waiters Groimes of
the Chaumbre Ande Groim Officers of Houſhold AS HERE-
AFTIR followith the Order of theim How every of the
foireſaide PARSONES ſchall attende And how long And at
what houris at AFTIR-NOON.

THE NAIMES of the Gentlemen Uſchers Gentlemen of Houſholde Yomen Uſchers Ande Marſchallis
of the Hall that ſhall awaite in the GREAT
CHAMBRE Daily uppon FLESCHE-DAIS
at AFTIR-NOONES Which doith not await
BEFORE NOON Viz. From Oon of the Clock
aftir Dynnar be Doon at AFTIR NOON Unto
iiij of the Clocke that that they go to SUPAR
Whiche Parſonnes for their waiting at Aftir-noon
hadde Licence to go aboute their own Buſineſs the
FORE NOON.

THE

THE GENTLEMEN to awaite at AFTIR-
NOON daily thrughout the Weke Whiche had
Licence to goo aboute their own bufinefs the
FOIR-NOON.

FYRSTE A Gentleman Ufcher too my Laidy

ITEM A Carver to my Laidy

ITEM A Sewar to my Laidy

ITEM A Cupbearer to my Laidy

ITEM A Gentlemen Waiter for the Bord-ende

ITEM Yoman Ufcher of the Chaumbre to my Lady.

ITEM A Marfhall of the Hall.

THE NOUMBRE of the PERSONES as GENTLE-
MEN ar ———— vij.

THE NAIMES OF THE Yomen of the Chaumbre
Yoman Waiters Ande Groimes of Chaumbre That fhall
await in the GREAT CHAUMBRE Daily at AFTIR-
NOON From Oon of the clock that Dynner be doon Unto
thre of the Clock that they ryng to Even-Songe WHICH
PARSONES for their waiting Aftir Noon the faide iij
Houris haith Licence Befoir Noon to go aboute their own
Bufinefs From vij of the Clock in the Mornyng Unto x of
the

the Clok that they ſhall com in again to awaite for DYN-
NER Which is iij houris Ande they not to faill than to com
in again Ande raithir if any Straungers com.

THE YOMEN OF THE Chaumbre Yomen
Waiters Ande Groimes of the Chaumbre to await
at AFTIR-NOON Daily thrughoute the Weke
Which had Licence to go aboute their owne
Buſineſs BEFOIR NOON.

FYRSTE The Yoman of the Horſs.

ITEM A Yoman of the Chaumbre

ITEM A Yoman Waiter

ITEM A Yoman Waiter

ITEM Anouthir Yoman Waiter

ITEM A Groim of the Chaumbre too my Lorde

ITEM A Groim of the Chaumbre to my Laidy.

THE NOUMBRE of the PARSONS as YOMEN and
GROIMES of the CHAUMBRE ar ——— vij.

THE NAIMES OF TH'OFFICERS OF HOUS-
HOLDE that ſhall awaite in the GREAT CHAUMBRE
Daly

Daly at AFTIR NOON thrughout the Weke upon FLESCH-DAIES From Oon of the Clock at Aftir-Noon To iij of the Clock That they goo to ferve in their offices for DRYNKYNGS Which is by the fpaice of iij Houris Ande alfo the faide Parfons to yef like attendance in the Great Chaumbre daly thurrowte the Weke uppon Flefch – Daies From iij of the Clock that they have fervid Drynkyngs Unto iiij of the clock that go to ferve in their offices for SUPAR by the fpaice of an Houre WHICHE PARSONS for their waiting at Aftir-Noon the faide iiij houris haith Licence Befoir Noon to go aboute their own Bufinefs From vij of the Clock in the Mornyng Unto x of the Clock that they fhall com in again to ferve for DYNNAR Which is iij Houris Ande they not to faill than to com in again And raithir if any Straungers com.

THE YOMEN OFFICERS ande Groim Offi-cers of Houfhold to awaite at AFTIR NOON thrughoute the Weke Daily Which haith Licen-ce to go aboute their own Bufinefs BEFOIR NOON.

FURSTE a Yoman of the Beddes

ITEM a Yoman of the Buttery

ITEM a Groim of the Pauntry

ITEM a Groym Ufcher of the Hall.

THE NAIMES of theis PERSONES as YOMEN and GROIM-OFFICERS ——— iiij.

THE

THE NAMES OF THE Gentlemen Ufchers Gentlemen of Houfholde Yomen Ufchers ande Marfchallis of the Halle that fhall attende in the GREAT CHAUMBRE Daly thrughoute the Weke uppon FLESCH-DAIES From vij of the Clock at AFTIR SOPAR Unto Nyen of the Clok at Night That my Lordes Lyverey be Servid for All Night and all outher Lyvereys Bicaus the GAITS is Ordeignid to be fhette alwaies at the faid hour To th'Entente that no Servaunte fhall com in at the faid Gaite that ought to be within Whiche ar oute of the Hous at that hour.

THE GENTILLMEN to awaite at AFTIR SO-PAR Daily thrughoute the Weke To the CUP-BOURD be made for my Lordes Lyverey for All Nyght.

FYRSTE A Gentleman Ufcher too my Lord

ITEM A Gentleman Ufcher to my Lady

ITEM A Carver to my Lord

ITEM A Carver to my Lady

ITEM A Sewar to my Lorde

ITEM A Sewar to my Lady

ITEM A Cupbearer to my Lord

ITEM A Cupbearer to my Laidy

ITEM

ITEM A Gentleman Waiter for the Bord-Ende

ITEM Anouthir Gentleman Waiter for the Bord-Ende

ITEM A Yoman Ufcher to my Laidy

ITEM A Marfhall of the Hall

ITEM An outhir Marfhall of the Hall

THE NOUMBRE of the PARSONS as GENTLEMEN
ar ——— xiij.

THE NAIMES OF THE Yomen of the Chaumbre Yomen Waiters ande Gromes of the Chaumbre That fhall awaite in the GREAT CHAUMBRE Daily uppon FLESCH DAIES From vij of the Clok at Night AFTIR SOPAR be doon To Nyen of the Clock at night That my Lordis Lyverey be fervid for All Night And all outhir Livereys Bicaus the GAITS ar orderd to be fhet alwaies at the faide hour To th'entente that no Servaunte of my Lordis fhall com in at the faide Gaits that ought to be within Whiche ar oute of the hous at that hour.

THE YOMEN OF THE Chambre Yomen Waiters and Gromes of the Chaumbre to awaite at AFTIR SOPAR Daily thrughoute the Wek To the CUPBORDE be maide for my Lordis Lyverey for All Night.

FYRSTE A Yoman of the Roobis

ITEM

ITEM A Yoman of the Horſs

ITEM A Yoman of the Chaumbre that attendis uppon my Lordis maikyng redy

ITEM A Yoman of the Chaumbre that attendis uppon my Laidy

ITEM An outhir Yoman of the Chaumbre

ITEM A Yoman Waiter

ITEM An outhir Yoman Waiter

ITEM An outher Yoman Waiter

ITEM An outher Yoman Waiter

ITEM A Mynſtrell Yoman Waiter

ITEM An outher Mynſtrall Yoman Waiter

ITEM A Footeman Yoman Waiter

ITEM A Groim of the Chaumbre to my Lord

ITEM An outher Groim of the Chaumbre to my Lord

ITEM An outher Groym of the Chaumbre to my Lord

ITEM A Groim of the Chaumbre to my Laidy

ITEM A Child to awaite under the Groimes of the Chaumbre.

THE NOMBRE of thies PARSONES as Yomen and GROMES of the CHAUMBRE ar ——— xvij.

THE

THE NAMES OF TH'OFFICERS OF HOUSHOLD that shall yef NOON ATTENDAUNCE in the GREAT CHAUMBRE No Day thurrowte the Weke naither upon FLESH-DAIES nor FYSH-DAIES From vij of the Clock that Sopar be doon Unto ix of the Clock at Night that my Lord be Servid for ALL NIGHT Bicaus they must goo and gif their attendance in the Countinghous for their Brevements expendid the said day.

THE YOMEN OFFICERS of Houshold and Groim Officers of Houshold that shall gif NOON ATTENDAUNCE in the Great Chaumbre No Day in the Weke from Sopar be doon for going to the Countinghous for their Brevements.

FURSTE Gilbert Swinborn Yoman of the Beddes

ITEM A Yoman Uscher of the Hall

ITEM A Yoman of the Pauntry

ITEM A Yoman of the Buttery

ITEM A Groim of the Pauntry

ITEM A Groim of the Buttery

ITEM A Groim of the Ewry

ITEM A Groim Usher of the Hall

THE NOMBRE of thies PARSONES as YOMEN and GROIM OFFICERS of Houshold whiche shall NOT attende at AFTER SOPAR is —— viij.

T t   THE

THE NOMBRE of all my Lordis SERVAUNTIS that ar appointid to await in my Lordis GREATE CHAMBRE every Day at AFTIR NOON daily thurrowt the Weke ar.....

AND SO THOOLE NOUMBRE OF PARSONS afoirſaid my Lordis SERVAUNTIS THAT AR appointid as well to await BEFOIR NOON as to await at AFTER NOON daily thrughout the Weke is.....

THE NAIMES OE ALL SUCH MY LORDIS SERVAUNTIS As Preiſts Chapleines and outhir Servauntis in Houſhold That ar NOT appointid to gif attendaunce nor thought meat to awaite in the GRET CHAUMBRE uppon my Lord DALY thurrowt the Weke Whiche is not thought conveinent to be DAILY WAITERS about my Lord Bicaus of outher their Offices and Buſineſs concernying their ſaide ROWMES in my Lordis Houſ AS the Naumes of thois Parſonnes With the Rowmes that every of theim belongith to Whiches be not thought conveniente to attend in the GREAT CHAUMBRE But in the HALL at ſuche tymes Befoir Noon and After Noon if STRAUNGERS com For furniſhyng the Hall If they have no Buſineſs in their ſaide Offices ande Rowmes in my ſaide Lordis Houſ HEREAFTIR FOLLOWETHE.

MY

MY LORDIS CHAPLEINS ande PREISTS in Houfhold Whiche be NOT appointid to attend at NO tymes but at SERVICE TYMES and MEALLIS.

FURSTE A Preift a Doctour of Devinity a Doctour of Law or a Bachelor of Devinitie to be Dean of my Lords Chapell.

ITEM A Preift for to be Surveyour of my Lordes Landis

ITEM A Preift for to be Secretary to my Lorde

ITEM A Preift for to be Aumer to my Lorde

ITEM A Preift for to be Sub-Dean for ordering ande keaping the Queir in my Lordis Chappell daily

ITEM A Preift for a Riding Chaplein for my Lorde

ITEM A Preift for a Chaplein for my Lordis Eldeft Son to awaite uppon him daily

ITEM A Preift for my Lordis Clark of the Clofet

IYEM A Preift for a Maifter of Gramer in my Lords Hous

ITEM A Preift for Reading the Gofpell in the Chapell daily

ITEM A Preift for Singing of our Ladies Mafs in the Chappell daily

THE NOUMBRE of thois PERSONS as CHAPLEINS and PREISTS IN HOUSHOULD ar —— xj.

THE

THE GENTLEMEN ande CHILDRIN of my Lordis CHAPPELL Whiche be not appointid to uttend at no tyme but oonely in excerciſing of GODDIS SERVICE in the CHAPELL Daily at Mattins Lady-Maſs Highe-Maſs Even-Long ande Complynge.

GENTLEMEN of my Lordis CHAPPELL

FURST A Baſs

ITEM A Seconde Baſs

ITEM The Thirde Baſs

ITEM A Maiſter of the Childer A Countertenor

ITEM A Seconde Countertenour

ITEM A Thirde Countertenour

ITEM A iiijth Countertenor

ITEM A Standing Tenour

ITEM A Second Standing Tenour

ITEM A iij^d Standyng Tenour

ITEM A Fourth Standing Tenour

THE NOMBRE of thois PARSONS as GENTLEMEN of my Lordis CHAPPELL —— xj.

CHILDRIN

CHILDRIN of my Lordis CHAPPELL

ITEM The Fyrſt Child a Trible

ITEM The ij^d Child a Trible

ITEM The iij^d Child a Trible

ITEM The iiij^th Child a Second Trible

ITEM The vth Child a Second Trible

ITEM The vj^th Child a Second Trible.

THE NOUMBRE of thois PARSONS as CHILDRIN of my Lordis CHAPPELL —— vj.

YOMEN OFFICERS Groim Officers and Groimes in Houſhold Whiche be NOT appointid to attend Bicaus of outhir their Buſineſs Which they attend DAILY in their Officis in my Lordis Hous But oonely in the HALL at the tymes befoir namyd.

FURST A Yoman Cooke for the Mouth Who doith hourely attend in the Kitching at the Haiſtry for roiſting of Meat at Braikefeſtis and Meallis.

ITEM

ITEM A Groim Cooke for the Mouthe Who hourely attends in the Kiching for dreſſing of Meat at Braikefaſts
and Meallis.

ITEM A Groim of the Larder Who hourely attendis in
the Larder for receyvyng of Victuallis Ande delyvering
of Victuallis to the Kechyng for Expenſis.

ITEM A Child of the Squillery for delyvering of Veſſell
at Mealis Ande receyvyng and dreſſing of theim up
agayn

ITEM The Yoman Baiker Who doith hourely attende in
the Bakhous for Moilding and Baiking daily when they
baike.

ITEM A Child of the Bakhous Who doith hourely attende
in the Bakhous for Muylding and Baikinge daily when
they baike

ITEM The Yoman Brewer Who doith attend in the
Brewhous for Brewing daily when they Brew.

ITEM A Child of the Brewhous Who doith attende in
the Brewhous for Brewing daily when they brew

ITEM An Arriſmender Who is hourely in the Waredrob
for Wyrking uppon my Lordis Arres and Tapſtry

ITEM The Furſt Groim of the Waredrob for the Robes
Who is hourely in the Waredrob for Sewing and Amend-
ing of Stuf.

ITEM The ij^d Groim of the Waredrob for the Beddis
Who is hourely in the Waredrob for Lyring Sowing and
Jouning of Stuf.

ITEM

ITEM The iij^d Groim of the Waredrob Who is hourely in the Waredrob for Sewing and Mending of Stuf in like caus.

ITEM A Child of the Waredrob Who is hourely in the Waredrob for Sewing and Mending of Stuf concerning At my Lordis finding.

ITEM The Armorer Who is hourely in th'Armory for Dreffing of his Harnefs

ITEM A Groim of the Chaumbre to my Lord PERCY Who waits hourely uppon my Lord PERCIS Chaumbre.

ITEM The Second Groim to my Lord PERCY Who waitith hourly in my Lord PERCIS Chaumbre For Brufhing and Dreffing of his Stuf.

ITEM A Groim of the Chaumbre to my Lord ij Sonnes who be togeader Who awaitis hourely uppon their Chambre for Brufhing and Dreffing of their ftuf

ITEM A Groim of the Sterop Who attendis hourely in the ftabill for Dreffing and Wattering my Lordis Horffis.

ITEM A Groim Sumpterman Who attendis daily in the Stabill for helping to drefs his Sumpter – horffes and my Laidis Palfraies.

ITEM A Groim of the Hakneys Who attendis daily in the Stabill for helping to drefs my Lordis Hobbies and Naggis.

ITEM A Groim of the Stable Who attendis in the Stable for maiking clean of the faid Stabill hourely and daly.

ITEM

ITEM A Gardynner Who attendis hourely in the Garden for Setting of Erbis and Clipping of Knottis and Sweping the said Garden clean hourely.

ITEM A Groim Hunte Who keapis my Lordis Houndis and Huntith with theim daily

ITEM A Groim Mylner Who attendis hourely in the Mylne for Grynding of Corn for Baiking and Brewing for my Lordis Houss.

ITEM A Groim - Porter Who contynueth Hourely and Daily for Keaping the Gait.

ITEM A Groim for Dryving of my Lordis Charriot

ITEM A Keaper for Keaping of the said Charriot Horsses.

THE NOMBRE of thois PARSONS as YOMEN OFFICERS GROME OFFICERS and GROMES IN HOUSHOLD —— xxvij.

CLARKS IN MY LORDIS HOUS Whiche are NOT appointid Daily to attend Bicaus of maiking of their BOOKIS Which they ar chargid with to write hourely uppon.

FURSTE A Clark of the Signet Who writes Daily under my Lorde All maner of Writing and Letters whiche doe go daily from my Lord.

ITEM

ITEM A Cheif Clark of the Keching Who daily keapith the Counting Hous And feis the Breving daily and Service fervid of Meate and Drynk.

ITEM A Clark of my Lordis Foren Expenfis Who doith attend the Groffing up of my Lordis Bookis of his Foren Expenfis daily.

ITEM An Under-Clark of the Keching Who feis all maner of Victuallis delyvert to every Office and the Victuallis ftrickkyn owt for fervice.

ITEM A Clarke of the Garners Who writes the Breving Booke daily And receyves the Granys and delivers the Granys daily.

ITEM A Clarke Avener of the Counting - Hous Who Keapith the Brevyng Book of Horffemete and Fewell daily And enters the Parcellis into the Jornall Booke that ar daily bought.

ITEM A Clarke for my Lordis Everyng Booke Who enters all maner of Parcells into my faide Lordis Booke daily Whiche is bought for the ufe of my faide Lorde.

THE NOMBRE of thois PARSONNES as CLARKIS in my Lordis HOUS —— vij.

U u
XLIII.

XLIII.

THE NAIMES of all maner of PARSONNES in my Lordis CHEQUIRROILL that my Lord alloweth to haive SERVAUNTS in his Hous Whiche ar not appointid to attend But to go about their own Businefs all the Day But onely at MEALLIS TYMES.

FURSTE A Clarke to my Lordis Broider

. ITEM A Hors Keapar to my faid Lordis Broider

ITEM A Servaunte to the Surveyor of my Lords Landes

ITEM A Servaunte to the Secreatary.

ITEM A Servaunte to the Maifter of Gramer For to be Ufher of the Scole

ITEM A Servaunte to the Doctour or Bacheler of Devinitie

ITEM A Servaunte to the Furft Gentleman Ufher

ITEM A Servaunte to the ij^d Gentleman Ufher

ITEM A Servaunte bitwixt a Carver ande a Sewar

ITEM A Servaunte bitwixt ij Gentleman Waiters

THE NOMBRE of thois PARSONNES as SERVAUNTES to GENTLEMEN in my Lords HOUS — x.

THE HOOLE NOMBRE of all my Lordis SERVAUNTIS ande GENTLEMEN SERVAUNTES that ar NOT APPOINTID to awaite bicaus of outher their BUSINESS Whiche they attend DAILY for my Lorde —— XLIIII.

XLIIII.

XLIIII.

ALMANER OF REWARDES CUSTOMABLE ufede YERLY by my Lorde to be YEVEN ande PAIDE by his Lordifchipe From Michaelmas To Michaelmas Yerely AS it doith appeire in the BOOKE of his Lordfhipe FOREN EXPENCES of every Yere what CUSTOMABLE PAY-MENTS they be that my Lorde ufith Yerely Ande for what Caufes they be YEVEN Ande wherfor every SOME is paide Ande for what Confideracion As well for Waiges ande FEES paide owt Yerely of his Lordefchippe Coffures 'as' RE-WARDIS CUSTOMABLE ufed Yerly by my Lorde at New Yers Day Ande other tymes of the Yere HIS Lordfchipe ande my Ladies Offerings at Principall Feifts Yerly accuftomed Ande REWARDS ufede Cuftomable to be Yeven Yerely to STRANGERS As PLAYERS MYNSTRALLS ande others AS the Some of every Rewarde particulerly With the Confideracion why ande wherefore it is Yeven With the names of the PARSONES to whom the faide Rewards be Yeven More Playnly Hereafter Folowith ande Apperith in this Booke WHICH be Ordynary and Accuftomable Payments by my Lorde ufede Yerly if the tymes fo requier.

ALL MANER OF OFFERINGS for my Lorde ande my Lady ande my Lordis Childeren CUS-TOMABLE ufed Yerly at PRINCIPALL FEASTS

FEASTS ande other OFFERINGE-DAYES in
the Yere As the Confideracion WHYE more
playnly Hereafter followith.

FURST My Lordis Offerringe accuftomede upon Alhallow-
Day Yerely When his Lordfhippe is at home At the Highe
Mas If he kepe Chapell ―――― xij. *d.*

ITEM My Ladis Offerringe accuftomede upon Alhallowe-
Day Yerely If fche offer at the Highe Maffe If my Lorde
kepe Chapell TO be paid owt of my Lords Coffures If
fche be at my Lordis Fyndinge ande not at hir owen
―――― viij *d.*

ITEM My Lordes Offerringe accuftomed upon Criftynmas-
Day Yerely When his Lordfhipe is at home At the Highe
Mas If he kepe Chapell ―――― xij *d.*

ITEM My Ladies Offeringe upon Criftynmas-Day Yerly at
the Highe Mas If my Lorde kepe Chapell To be paide owt
of my Lordis Coffures If fche be at my Lordis fyndynge
ande not at hir even ―――― viij *d.*

ITEM My Lordis Offeringe upon Saynt Stephyns Daye
When his Lordfchipp his at home a Groit to bow at a
Lawe Mas in his Clofett ―――― iiij *d.*

ITEM My Lordis Offeringe accuftomede upon New-Yers-
Day Yerely When his Lordefchip is at home At the High
Mas If he kepe Chapell ―――― xij *d.*

ITEM My Ladies Offeringe accuftomede upon New-Yers-
Day Yerely at the High Mas If my Lorde kepe Chapell To
be

be paid owt of my Lordis Coffures If sche be at my Lords fyndynge and not at hir owen ------ viij d.

ITEM My Lords Offeringe accustomede uppon the xijth Day Yerely When his Lordschipe is at home At the High Mas if he kepe Chapell ------ xij.

ITEM My Ladies Offeringe accustomed uppon the xijth Day Yerely at the High Mas If my Lorde kepe Chapell To be paide owt of my Lords Coffures If sche be at my Lordis fyndinge and not at hir owen ------ viij d.

ITEM My Lordis Offerynge accustomede uppon Candilmas-Day Yerely To be sett in his Lordschippis Candill to offer at the High Mas when his Lordschipp is at home v Groits for the v Joyes of our Lady ------ xx d.

ITEM My Laidis Offerynge uppon Candilmas-Daie Yerely To be sett in hir Candill to offer at the High Mas iij Groitts To be paid owt of my Lordis Coffures If sche be at my Lordis fyndynge and not at hir owen ------ xij d.

ITEM My Lorde useth and accustomyth Yerely upon Candilmas-Day to caus to be Delyveride for the Offeringe of my Lords Son and Heire the Lorde Percy To be sett in his Candill ij^d Ande for every of my Yonge Masters my Lords Yonge Sonnes to be sett in the Candills affore the Offeringe j d. for aither of them ------ iiij d.

ITEM My Lordis Offeringe accustomede Yerly upon Saint Blayes Day to be sett in his Lordschipps Candill to offer at Hye Mas if his Lordschyp kepe Chapell ------ iiij d.

ITEM My Laidis Offeringe accustomede Yerely upon Saint Blayes Day to be sett in hir Candill to offer at the Hye
Mas

Mas To be paid owt of my Lordis Coffures if fche be at my Lordis fyndynge ande not at hir owen ——— iiij *d.*

ITEM My Lorde ufeth and accuftomyth Yerly upon Saynt Blays Days to caufe to be delyveride for the Offerynge of my Lordis Sone and Heire the Lorde Percy to fett in his Candill j *d.* Ande for every of my Yonge Mafters my Lords Yonger Sonnes to fett in ther Candills after j *d.* for every of them for ther Offerings this faid day ——— iij *d.*

ITEM My Lordis Offeringe accuftomede uppon Goode-Friday Yerely if his Lordfchipp be at Home and kepe Chapell when his Lordfchipe crepith the Cros ——— iiij *d.*

ITEM My Ladis Offerringe accuftomede Yerely upon Good-Friday When fhe crepith the Croffe To be paide owt of my Lordis Coffures if fche is at my Lordis fyndinge and not at hir own ——— iiij *d.*

ITEM My Lorde ufeth and accuftomoth yerely when his Lordfchip is at home to caus to be delyveride for the Offerrings of my Lordis Sone and Heire the Lord Percy upon the faid Good-Friday When he crepith the Crofe ij *d.* Ande for every of my Yonge Maifters my Lords Yonger Sonnes after j *d.* to every of them for ther Offeringes when they Crepe the Cros the faid Good-Friday ——— iiij *d.*

ITEM My Lordis Offeringe accuftomede Yerely uppon Efter-Evyn when his Lordfhipp takyth his Rights — iiij *d.*

ITEM My Ladis Offeringe accuftomede Yerely uppon Eftur-Evyn when hir Ladifchipe taketh hir Rights if fche be at my Lords fyndynge and not at hir owen ——— iiij *d.*

ITEM My Lorde ufith and accuftomyth yerly to caus to be delyverid to his Lordfchippis Childeren that be of Aige to

take

take there Rights For them to offer upon Efters Even After ij*d.* to every of them —— .

ITEM My Lorde ufith and accuftometh yerely to caus to be delyvrede to every of his Lordfchipps Wardis or Hanfman or Anny other Yonge Gentilmen that be at his Lordfchipes fyndyinge Ande be of Aige to take ther Rights After ij *d.* a pece to every fuch Parfon ——

ITEM My Lords Offerynge accuftomede yerely upon Efter-Day in the mornyng when his Lordfhipe Crepith the Cros after the Refurreccion If his Lordfchippe be at home and kepe Chapell —— iiij*d.*

ITEM My Ladis Offering accuftomede yerly upon Efter-Daye in the mornynge when hir Ladyfchip Crepith the Cros after the Refurreccion To be paide owt of my Lordis Coffures if fhe be at my Lordis findinge and not at hir owen —— iiij*d.*

ITEM My Lord ufeth and accuftomethe upon Efter-Day in the mornynge to caus to be delyverid to my Lords Eldeft Son the Lord Percy and to every of my Yonge Mafters my Lords yonger Sones after j*d.* to every of them to offer when they Creep the Cros the faid day after the Refurreccion —— iij*d.*

ITEM My Lords Offeringe accuftomede upon Efter - Day Yerely when his Lordfchip is at home at the High Mas if my Lorde kepe Chapell —— xij *d.*

ITEM My Ladis Offerenge accuftomide uppon Eftir - Day yerely at the High Mas If my Lorde kepe Chapell To be paid owt of my Lords Coffures if fhe be at my Lords fyndinge and not at hir owen —— viij*d.*

ITEM

ITEM My Lorde ufith and accuftomyth upon Efter-Day
Yerely when his Lordfchip is at home If my Lorde kepe
Chapell To caus to be delyvered to my Lords Eldeft Sone
the Lord Percy Ande to every of my Yonge Mafters
my Lords Yonger Sonnes After ȝd. every of them for
them to offer the faid Efter-Day in the Chapell at the
Hye Mas ——— lij d.

ITEM My Lordis Offirynge accuftomede upon Saynt George-Day Yerly at the Hye Mas When his Lordfchyppe is at
home And kepith Saynt George-Feaft ——— x d.

ITEM My Lordis Offeringe accuftomyde at the Mes of Requiem uppon the morowe after Saynt George-Day When his
Lordfchip is at home and kepith Saynt George-Feaft Which
is accuftomede yerely to be don for the Saullis of all the
Knightes of th'Order of the Garter Departede to the Mercy
of God ——— iiij d.

ITEM My Lorde ufeth and accuftomyth When he is at home
Ande kipith Dergen over Nyght And Mes of requiem
uppon the morowe my Lord his Father xij Month Mynde
To offer at the Mas of Requiem ——— iiȝ d.

ITEM My Lorde ufith and accuftomyth yerely when his
Lordfchip is at home To caus to be delyvered to my Lordis
Eldeft Sone and Heyre the Lorde Percy Ande to every of
my Yonge Mafters my Lords Yonger Sons after ȝd. to
every of them for them to offer this faid daye at the faid
Mes of Requiem Done for my Lords Father xij Month
Mynde ——— iij d.

ITEM My Lordis Offerynge accuftomed uppon the Affencion Day yerly when his Lordefchip is at home at the High
Mas if he kepe Chapell ——— xij d.

ITEM

ITEM My Ladies Offeringe accuſtomede upon the Aſſen-cion-Day yerly at the Hy Mas in the Chapell To be paid owt of my Lordis Coffures if ſhe be at my Lordis fyndynge and not at hir owne —— viij *d.*

ITEM My Lords Offeringe accuſtomede upon Whitſonday yerely at the Hye Mas in the Chapell when his Lordſchip is at home —— xij *d.*

ITEM My Ladis Offeringe accuſtomede uppon Whitſonday yerely at the High Mas in the Chapell To be paid owt of my Lords Coffures if ſche be at my Lords fyndynge and not at hir own —— viij *d.*

ITEM My Lord uſith and accuſtomyth yerly when his Lord-ſchipp is at home if he kepe Chapell to caus to be delyvered unto my Lords eldeſt Sone and heir the Lorde Percy Ande to every of my Yonge Maſters my Lords Yonger Sonnes after j *d.* every of them For them to offer at the Hye Mas yerly the ſaid Witſonday —— iij *d.*

ITEM My Lordis Offeringe accuſtomede upon Trinite Son-Day yerly when his Lordſchyp is at home at the Highe Mas if he kepe Chapell —— xij *d.*

ITEM My Ladis Offerynge accuſtomede yerely uppon Tri-nite-Sonday at the High Mas if my Lorde kepe Chapell To be paid owt of my Lords Coffures if ſhe be at my Lords fyndyng and not at hir owen —— viij *d.*

ITEM My Lorde uſith yerely to ſende afor Mychealmas for his Lordſchipe Offering to the Holy Blode of Haillis — iiij *d.*

ITEM My Lorde uſith yerly to ſend afor Michealmas for his Lordſchips Offerynge to our Lady of Walſyngcham — iiij *d.*

X x   ITEM

ITEM My Lord uſith yerely to ſende afor Michealmas for his Lordſchipe Offeringe to Saynt Margarets in Lyncolin-ſchire —— iiij *d.*

ITEM My Lord uſith and accouſtomyth to ſende yerely for the Upholdynge of the Light of Waxe which his Lord-ſchip fyndis byrnynge yerely befor the Holy Bloude of Haillis Containing xvj lb. Wax in it aftir vij *d.* ob. for the fyndynge of every lb. if redy wrought By a Covenaunt maide by gret with the Mounk for the hole Yere for fynding of the ſaid Light byrnynge —— x *s.*

ITEM My Lorde uſith ande accuſtumyth to ſende yerely for the Upholdynge of the Light of Wax which his Lord-ſchip fyndith birnynge yerly befor our Lady of Walſyng-ham contenynge xj lb. of Wax in it after vij *d.* ob. for the fyndynge of every lb. redy wrought By a Covenaunt maid with the Channon by great for the hole Yere for the fynd-inge of the ſaid Light byrnning —— vj *s.* viij *d.*

ITEM My Lord uſith ande accuſtomyth to ſende yerely for the Upholdynge of the Light of Wax which his Lordſhipe fyndith byrnynge yerely before Saynt Margret in Lyncolen-ſhire conteyning xvj *l.* Waxe in it After vij *d.* ob. for the fyndynge of every lb. rydy wrought by a Covenant maid by gret with the Preſt † ther for the hole Yere for fyndynge of the ſaid Light byrnynge —— x *s.*

ITEM My Lord uſeth and accuſtomyth to paye yerly for the fyndynge of a Light of Wax to birne befor our Lady in the Whit-Frers of Doncaſter of my Lordis foundacion at every Mas-tyme daily thorowout the Yere ſett before our ſaid Lady there To be paid to the Prior of the ſaid Hous for the hole Yere for fyndynge ot the ſaid Light To be paid ounes a Yere —— xiij *s.* iiij *d.*

AL

† Perhaps it ſhould be ' Provoſt.'

AL MANER OF REWARDIS Cuftomable ufede
yerely To be Yeven by my Lorde to STRAN-
GERS as PLAYERS MYNSTRAILLS or any
other Strangers whatfomever they be As the Confideracion WHY more playnly hereafter folowith.

FURST My Lorde ufith and accuftomyth To gyf to the
Kings Jugler if he have wone When they cuftome to
come unto hym yerely —— vj s. viiij d.

ITEM My Lord ufith and accuftomyth to gyf yerely the
Kynge or the Queenes Barwarde If they have one When
they cuftom to com unto hym yerely —— vj s. viij d.

ITEM My Lorde ufith and accuftomyth to gyfe yerly to
every Erlis Mynftrellis when they cuftome to come to hym
yerely iij s. iiij d. Ande if they come to my Lord feldome
ones in ij or iij yeres than vj s. viij d. —— vi s. viij d.

ITEM My Lorde ufith and accuftomedeth to gife yerely to
an Erls Mynftrall If he be his fpeciall Lorde Frende or
Kynfman If they come yerely to his Lordfchipe . . . . .
Ande if they come feldom ones in ij or iij Yeres —vj s. viij d.

ITEM My Lorde ufith and accuftomedeth When he rewardis them To gyf the Prior of the Whit-Frers of Doncafter
of my Lordis Foundacion toward the byeynge of ther Store
agaynft the Advent befor Criftynmas —— xx s.

ITEM My Lord ufeth and accuftomyth if his Lordfchip ly
at Leknfeld to gyf yerely to the Servaunts that comyth to
his Lordfchip thetheir from the Prior of Watton Th'abbot of
Mefx

Mefx * or the Proveſt of Beverlay And bringeth his Lordſchip iiij Pykes ij Crannes and ij Signetts Than my Lord to gyfe in rewarde to the faide Servaunts that foe fendes my Lorde —— x s.

ITEM My Lorde uſith and accuſtomyth yerly when his Lordſhip is at home to gif to the Kings Servaunt that bryngith his Lordſhip his Newe Yers Gyft from the Kinge uppon the New-Yers-day If he be a Speciall Frende of my Lordis vj l. xiij s. iiij d. And if he be a Servaunt of the Kings and bot a Particulare Parſon —— c s.

ITEM My Lord uſith and accuſtomyth yerely when his Lordſchip is at home to yef unto the Barne-Biſhop of Beverlay when he comith to my Lorde in Criſtmas Hally-Dayes when my Lord kepith his Hous at Lekynfeld — xx s.

ITEM My Lorde uſeth and accuſtomyth to gif yerely when his Lordſhip is at home to the Barne - Biſhop of Yorke when he comes over to my Lord in Criſtynmaſe-Hally-Dayes as he is accuſtomede yerely —— xx s.

ITEM My Lorde uſith ande accuſtomyth when his Lord-ſhip is at home to gyfe the Quenes Servaunt that bryngeth hir Graces Newe-Yers-Gyft to my Lorde after the xij th Day As ſche is accuſtomede to fende it yerly —— Lxvj s. viij d.

ITEM My Lorde uſith and accuſtometh to gif yerely when his Lordſhipp is at home to every Erlis Players that comes to his Lordſhipe bitwixt Criſtynmas ande Candelmas If he be his ſpeciall Lorde and Frende ande Kynſman —— xx s.

ITEM My Lorde uſith ande accuſtomyth to gyf yerely when his Lordſhip is at home to every Lordis Players that

* This word is obſcurely written in the MS. It may perhaps be ' Meſr,' i. e. ' Miſrule.' See below p. 344.

that comyth to his Lordfchipe betwixt Criftynmas and
Candilmas —— x s.

ITEM My Lordy ufeth ande accuftomyth to gyf yerely to
the Servaunt of his Sone-Lawe that hath marrede his
Lordfhipis Doughter if he be upon New-Yeres-Day with
his Lordfhip ande Sendis his Lordfchip a New-Yeres-Gyft
Then in rewarde to his Servaunt that bryngis the faid
New-Yers-Gyft —— xiij s iiij d.

ITEM My Lorde ufith ande accuftomyth to gyf yerely to
the Servaunt of my Lady his Lordfhips Doughter if fche be
maryede ande be on Newe-Yeres-Day with his Lordfhip
ande fende his Lordefhip a New-Yeres-Gyft the faid New-
Yers-day Than in rewarde to hir Servaunte that bryngs the
faid New-Yeres-Gyft to my Lorde —— vj s. viij d.

ITEM My Lorde ufith ande accuftomyth to gyf yesly unto
the Servaunt of his Lordfchipis Sone and heire the Lorde
Percy if he be Marrede ande be in Hous with his Lordfchip and Sendis his Lordfhip a New-Yeres-Gyft uppon
New-Yers-day Than in rewarde to his Servaunt that bryngis the faid Newe Yeres-Gyft —— xij d.

ITEM My Lorde ufeth ande accuftomyth to gyf yerely a
Dookes or Erlis Trumpetts if they com vj together to his
Lordfhipp Viz. if they come yerly vj s. viij d. ande if they
come but in ij or iij Yeres than —— x s.

ITEM My Lorde ufeth and accuftometh Yerly when his
Lordfhip is at home to gyf to iij of the Kyngs Shames
when they com to my Lorde Yerely —— x s.

ITEM My Lorde ufeth ande accuftomyth to fende yerely to
the Monk that kepyth the Light afor the Holy Bloode of
Haillis

Haillis for his rewarde for the hole Yere for kepinge of the said Light Lightynge of it at all Service Tymes daily thorowt the Yere ———— iij s. iiij d.

ITEM My Lord useth and accustomith to syende yerely to the Channon that kepith the Light before our Lady of Walsyngham for his reward for the hole Yere for kepynge of the said Light Lightynge of it at all Service-Tymes dayly thorowt the Yere ———— xij d.

ITEM My Lord usith and accustomyth yerely to send to the Prest that kepith the Light Lightynge of it at all Service-tymes daily thorowt the Yere ———— iij s. iiij d.

AL MANER OF REWARDIS Customably usede to be Yeven by my Lorde to his Lordshipis SER-VAUNTS As the Consideracion WHY more playnly hereafter followith.

FURST My Lorde useth and accustomyth to gyf his Lord-shippis Barbor at all such tymes as he shavith my Lorde and my Lorde comaundith hym or them rewarde for shaving of his Lordshippe ———— xij d.

IEEM My Lord useth and accustomyth if he kepe Chapell to gife yerely in reward when his Lordschip is at home to the Childeren of his Chapell when they doo synge the Res-ponde callede *Exaudivi* at the Matyns-tyme for xj M. Virgyns uppon Alhallow-day ———— vj s. viij d.

ITEM

ITEM My Lorde ufith and accuftomyth yerly to gyf to the Yoman or Grom of the Veftry uppon All Salls ‡ Evyn if his Lordfchip kepe Chapell and be at home for ryngynge all the faid night for all Criftyn Salls and for hayvynge his Lorde and father and his Lady and mother Salls moft Specialle in memory and for all Criften Salls —— xx *d.*

ITEM My Lord ufeth and accuftomyth to gyfe yerly upon Saynt Nicolas-Even if he kepe Chapell for Saynt Nicolas to the Mafter of his Childeren of his Chapell for one of the Childeren of his Chapell yerely vj *s.* viij *d.* And if Saynt Nicolas com owt of the Towne wher my Lord lyeth and my Lord kepe no Chapell than to have yerely iij *s.* iiij *d.* —— vj *s.* viij *d.*

ITEM My Lord ufeth and accuftomyth to gyfe yerely if his Lordfhip kepe a Chapell and be at home them of his Lordfchipes Chapell if they doo play the Play of the Nativite uppon Criftynmes - Day in the mornnynge in my Lords Chapell befor his Lordfhip —— xx *s.*

ITEM My Lord ufith and accuftomyth if he keepe Chapell to gyfe yerly in reward when his Lordfchip is at home to the Childeren of my Lordis Chapell for fynginge of *Gloria in Excelfis* at the Mattyns-tyme upon Criftynmas-Day in the mornynge —— vj *s.* viij *d.*

ITEM My Lorde ufith and accuftomyth to gyfe yerly when his Lordfhipe is at home to his Barward when he comyth to my Lorde in Criftmas with his Lordfhippes Beefts for makynge of his Lordfchip paftyme the faid xij days —— xx *s.*

ITEM My Lorde ufith ande accuftomyth to gyf yerly when his Lordfchipp is at home to his Mynftraills that be daly in his

‡ It is here, and below, erroneoufly written in the MS 'Pfalls.'

his Houfhold as his Tabret Lute ande Rebek upon New-Yeres-Day in the moenynge when they doo play at my Lordis Chambre doure for his Lordfchipe and my Lady xx s. Viz. xiij s. iiij d. for my Lorde and vj s. viij d. for my Lady if fche be at my Lords fyndynge and not at hir owen And for playing at my Lordis fome and heir Chaumbre doure the Lord Percy ij s. And for playinge at the Chaumbre doures of my Lords Yonger Sonnes my Yonge Maifters after viij d. the pece for every of them —— xxiij s. iiij d.

ITEM My Lorde ufith and accuftomyth to gyfe Yerely when his Lordfhipe is at hom to his iij Hamfhman uppon New-Yers-Day when they doo gyfe his Lordfchip Glovis to his New-Yers-gyft And in rewarde after vj s. viij d. to every of them —— xx s.

ITEM My Lorde ufith ande accuftomyth to gyfe yerely when his Lordfhip is at Home to the Gromes of his Lordschipp Chambre uppon New-yers-day to put in their Box as his Lordfchip is accuftomede Yerly —— xx s.

ITEM My Lorde ufeth and accuftomyth to gyf yerely when his Lordfhipe is home and hath an Abbot of Miferewll ‡ in Criftynmas in his Lordfchippis Hous uppon New-Yersday in rewarde —— xx s.

ITEM My Lorde ufeth ande accuftomyth to gyf yerly when his Lordfchip 'is at home' upon New-yers-day to his Lordfhips Officer of Armes Arrold or Purfyvaunt for Cryinge *Larges* befor his Lordfchip the faid New-yers-day as upon the xijth Day folowinge after x s. for an day —— xx s.

ITEM My Lorde ufeth ande accuftomyth to gyf yerely when his Lordfhipe is at hom upon New-yeres-day to his Lordfhipis

‡ i. e. Mifrule}

ſhipis vj Trompettes when they doo play at my Lords Chaumbre Dour the ſaid Newe-yers-day in the mornynge xx s. Viz. xiij s. iiij d. for my Lord vj s. viij d. for my Lady if ſche be at my Lords fyndynge and not at hir owen —— xx s.

ITEM My Lord uſeth ande accuſtomyth to yɛfe yerely upon New-yers-day to every of his Lordſchipis Foot-men when they doo gyf his Lordſhip Gloves for his New-yers-gyft the ſaid New-yers-day in the mornnynge And in reward as his Lorſhip is acuſtomede yerely iij s. iiij d. to every of them —— iij s. iiij d.

ITEM My Lorde uſeth to gif yerely accuſtomede to the Yoman or Groim of the Veſtry that doith ſerve the Rowme upon Candilmas - Day and bryngith my Lord the Taper that is haloyd that the Roundletts of Smale Lights goth aboute With one of Smalleſt Roundletts that goth obowt the ſaid Taper of the hallowed Lights In reward — iij s. iiij d.

ITEM My Lorde uſeth and accuſtomyth to gyf Yerely when his Lordſhipp is at home in reward to them of his Lordſhip Chappell and other his Lordſhipis Servaunts that doith play the Play befor his Lordſhip uppon Shroftewſday at night yerely in reward —— x s.

ITEM My Lord uſith and accuſtomedith to gyfe yerely if his Lordſhip kepe a Chapell and is at home in rewarde to them of his Lordſhipe Chapell and other his Lorſhipis Servauntes that playth the Play of Reſurrection upon Eſtur-Day in the Mornnynge in my Lordis 'Chapell' befor his Lordſhipe —— xx s.

ITEM My Lord uſith and acuſtomyth yerly upon Eſtur-Day when his Lordſhip is at hom to gyf to the and the Yoman Cook and Coks of his Lordſchips Kçchyng xx s.

Y y   Viz.

Viz. xiij *s*. iiij *d*. for my Lord and vj *s*. viij *d*. for my Lady if fche bee at my Lords fyndynge and not at hir owen — xx *s*.

ITEM My Lorde ufith and accuftomyth to gvf yerely upon Saynt George-Day if his Lordfhip be at home To his Offi-cer of Armes Arrold or Purfyvaunt for Cryeinge of *Largis* befor my Lorde the faide day at Dynar if his Lordfhip kepe Saynt George Feeft at hom In rewarde —— x *s*.

ITEM My Lord ufith and accuftomyth yerly To gyf to hym which fytts in his Lordfhippis hous as my Lords Auditor at Michaelmas uppon all his Lordfhips Servauntes that be Officers which ftandith charged with the Kepinge of anny Stuf of my Lords in his Dormount Booke ande Weringe Book And for the makinge up of the Books of all the Stuf that is fownde faltie how it fhal be Amendit Alfo for the entre of all the Stuf into indentors founde more at the faid accompt in the handis of the faid Officers And alfo for the makyng up the booke of the Deficiens of the Officers of fuch ftuf as is founde wantynge at the faid accompt —— lxvj *s*. viij *d*.

ITEM My Lorde ufeth and accuftomyth yerly to gyf hym which is ordynede to be the Mafter of the Revells yerly in my Lordis Hous in Criftmas for the overfeyinge and or-deringe of his Lordfchips Playes Interludes and Drefinge that is plaid befor his Lordfhip in his Hous in the .xij^th Dayes of Criftenmas And they to have in rewarde for that caus yerly —— xx *s*.

ITEM My Lorde ufeth and accuftometh yerly to gyff to the Yoman or Grome of the Veftre if his Lordfhip kep Chapell of Alhallowe - Day at nyght which is alwayes All - Salls Evyn for Ryngynge for all Criftynne Salls the faide nyghte to it be paft Mydnyght —— iij *s*. iiij *d*.

AL

AL MANNER OF REWARDIS cuſtomable uſede to
be Yeven by my Lorde for his Lordſhipe ande my
Ladis BROTHERHEDE Ande alſo for my Lorde
PERCYS Brotherhede To anny GILDE or HOUS
OF RELIGION As the Conſideracion WHY
mor playnly hereafter folowith.

FURST My Lorde uſeth and accuſtomyth to pay yerely ta
the Maſters of Saynt Criſtofer-gilde of Yorke if my Lorde
be Brother and my Lady Syſter ther For ther Brotherhede
for an hole Yere to the ſaid Saynt Criſtofer-Gild xiij s. iiij d.
after vj s. viij d. for ather of them vj s. viij d. Viz vj s. viij d.
for my Lorde and vj s. viij d. for my Lady if ſche be at my
Lords fyndynge and not at hir owen At ſuch tyme as the
Maſters of the ſaid Saynt Criſtofer Gild of York bringis my
Lord and my Lady for their Lyverays a Yarde of Narrow
Violette Cloth and a Yerde of Narow Rayd Cloth ——
xiij s. iiij d.

ITEM My Lorde uſeth ande accuſtomyth to pay yerely to
the Maſters of the ſayd Saynt Criſtofer-Gilde of Yorke if
my Lordis Son ande heire the Lord Percy be Brother ther
For his Brotherhede for an hole Yere to the ſaid Saynt
Criſtofer - Gilde at ſuch tymes as the Maſters of the ſaid
Gild bryngith to my ſaid Lorde Percy for his Lyvery a
Yerde of Narowe Violett Cloth and a Yerde of Narow
Rayd Cloth —— vj s. viij d.

ITEM My Lorde uſeth and accuſtomyth yerly to pay the
Proctor of Saynt Roberts of Knaſbrughe Wher my ſaide
Lord

Lord and my Laidy ar Breder For ther Broderhede for an hole Yere after iij *s*. iiij *d*. for my Lorde and iij *s*. iiij *d*. for my Lady if fhe be at my Lordis fyndynge and not at hir owen vj *s*. viij *d*.

AL MANIR OF FEES and WAIGES Cuftomably ufede to be paid yerly owt of my Lords COF-FURES As the Confideracion WHY more playnly hereafter folowith.

FURSTE My Lorde ufeth and accuftomyth to pay to hym that ftandith chargide | for all | to accompt for all his Lord-fhipis Fyfch wher his Lordefhipe lyeith and hath the Ke-pinge of his Lordfhips Dikis ther with the Fyfch in them Which my Lord gyffyth hym yerly for his kepynge of the fame for his Fee to be paide at ij tymes in the Yere Viz. at our Lady-Day in Lent and Michealmes after x *s*. at ather day ——— xx *s*.

ITEM My Lorde ufith and accuftomyth to gife one yerely for the kepinge of his Lordfhipis Mayzes at Semer and for takynge owt of the Reydis ande Wedis from tyme to tyme as they grow in it Ande for feeyng to his Lordfhipis Swannes that goith uppon the faid Maze In full contentacion for his hole yere Fee to be paid ones a Yere at Michealmes — x *s*.

ITEM My Lorde ufeth ande accuftomyth to pay yerely owt of his Lordfchipis Coffures to one or ij Parfones of his Lordfhip Servaunts that ftands chargede with the Kepinge of all my Lordis Lynnon ftuf and Dyaper belongynge his
Lordfhipis

Lordſhipis Dormount Boke and Weryng Boke Which parcells of Lynnon be not daily accupyede in no Offices in his Lordſhipis Hous In full contentacion for ther hole Yere Fee for ſtandinge chargede for kepinge of the ſaim Stuf to be paid ones a Yere at Michalmas —— xiij s. iiij d.

ITEM My Lorde uſeth ande accuſtomyth to pay yerly owt of his Lordeſhipp Coffures to them who ſomever they be of my Lordes Servaunts that ſtands chargede with the Kepinge of all manor of my Lordis Lynnon Stuf perteinyng my Lordis Dormunt Book and Weringe Book Which Parcells of Linnon be not daly accupyede in no Offices in my Lordis Hous ande they to have for the Waſchynge of the ſame ſtuf for the hole Yere To be payd ones a Yere at Michalmis —— xx s.

ITEM My Lorde uſeth and accuſtomyth to pay yerly owt of his Lordſhips Coffures to the Yomen of his Wardrob for the tyme beynge for fyndynge of all maner of Threde belongynge the Sewynge of all manor of Stuf which is ſhapen and cutt in my Lordis Wardrob as well concernynge my Lorde my Lady my Lordis Childeren As thos which ar at my Lords fyndynge In full Contentacion for his Fee for an hole Yere for that caus to be paid ones a Yere at Michaelmes —— xiij s. iiij d.

ITEM My Lorde uſeth and accuſtomyth to pay yerly owt of his Lordeſhips Coffures to one of his Lordſhipis Servaunts which hath the overſeight of his Lordſhipis Armory and alſo the overſight of the Armorer Which kepith his Lordſhips Armory at his Lordſhip place wher the ſaid Armory ryſtyth In full Contentacion for his ſaid Fee an Hole Yere for that caus to be payd ones a Yere at Michalmis — xx s.

ITEM

ITEM My Lorde uſith and accuſtomyth to pay yerely out of his Lordſhips Coffures for the Weſhinge of all manor of Lynnen bilongynge his owen body Viz. Shertts Al maner of Kurcheifs ande Hed-kercheifs Breeſt-Kercheifs * Heede-Kercheifs and all maner of Lynnon pertenynge his owen boddy what-ſom-ever it be After iiij s. a Quarter in full Contentacion for the Hole Yere ——— xvj s.

ITEM My Lorde uſeth and accuſtomyth yerly to pay out of my Lordis Coffures for the Waſhynge of al manor of Lynnen belongeinge my Lady if ſhe be at my Lords fyndynge ande not at hir owen x s. Ande alſo my Lord uſed and accuſtomede to pay yerely owt of his Lordſhips Coffures for the Waſhynge of al manor of Lynnon Stuf belonginge my Lord Percy my Lords Eldeſt Sone yerly v s. and for every of my Lords other Sonnes by Yere After ij s. vj d. for aither of them — v s. In all ——— xx s.

ITEM My Lorde uſeth and accuſtomyth to pay yerly out of his Lordſhip Coffures for the Waſchynge of all the Lynnen of the iij Hanſhmen if his Lordſhip kepe anny in his Hous daily which be at my Lords fyndynge and not at ther frends after vj d. a Quarter for the Waſhinge of ther ſaid Lynnon And after ij s. a Yere for every of them ——— vj s.

ITEM My Lorde uſeth and accuſtomyth to pay yerely owt of his Lordſhipis Coffures to his Purſevaunt if he take no Houſholde Waiges nor be not promotede by Patent In full contentacion for his yerly Fee accuſtomyde for hym to have by Yere To be paide at ij tymes of the Yere Viz. at our Lady day in Lent and Michalmis after xxvj s. viij d. at aither Day ——— Liij s. iiij d.

ITEM

* Perhaps 'Hande-Kercheifs.'

ITEM My Lorde useth ande accustomyth to pay yerely owt of his Lordshipis Coffures if he make ij Kepers more uppon his Carre of Arom of his Lordshipis Tenaunts ther than is accustomede for Kepynge of my said Lords Carr of arrom for overseyinge of my Lords Fysch ande Swanes ther for ther Fee After iij *s*. iiij *d*. to aither of them to be paide ones a Yere at Michealmes ——— vj *s*. viij *d*.

ITEM My Lorde useth and accustomyth to gyf every of the iiij Parsones that his Lordschip admyted as his Players to com to his Lordship yerly at Cristynmes Ande at all other such tymes as his Lordship shall comande them for Playing of Playe and Interludes affor his Lordship in his Lordshipis Hous for every of ther Fees for an Hole Yere ———

ITEM My Lorde useth ande accustomyth to gyf as in An-nuitie by Warraunt to be paide owt of his Lordeshipis Coffures to that Parson that standith chargede with the kepinge of my Lordis ij Evidens Houses at Lekenfeld and Wresill wher all his Lordshippis Evidences and other Wry-tyngs pertenynge his Lordships Lands doith remayne Ande for standynge charged with the delyvray of my said Lordis Evidences owt and for receyvynge of them in again To be paid quarterly after xx *s*. a quarter and for the hole Yere ——— iiij *l*.

ITEM My Lorde usith and accustomyth to pay yerly owt of his Lordshipis Coffures to hym that standith chargede with the Kepynge of his Lordshipis Cariages yerly Viz. Hor-lyters ——— Chayers ——— Close - Carres ——— Charryats ——— and Carttis Ande that he shall mende yerly all such Defauts as is faltie from tyme to tymein the Tymbre Warks of the said Cariagis Which my Lorde gyfyth him yerly for his Fee for
standynge

ſtandynge charged with the kepynge and mendenge of the forſaide Cariages To be paid ones a Yere at Michalmes for the hole Yere —— xs.

ITEM My Lorde 'uſith' and accuſtomyth to pay yerly owt of his Lordſhipis Coffures to a Bower for ſeynge and Dryſ-ſynge of all my Lordis Bowes in the Yoman of the Bowes kepynge from tyme to tyme Viz. for Settynge Pullynge and Skynnynge of them yerely as oft as they nede at his owen coſt and charge And to fynde Horne Glewe and all maner of other things that they lak for mendynge of them when they be faltid Which my Lorde gyffith to hym yerly for his Fee for mendynge and ſeynge to my ſaid Lordis Bowes to be paid ones a Yere at Michalmes for the hole Yere —— xxs.

ITEM My Lord uſyith and accuſtomed to pay yerly owt of his Lordſhipis Coffuris to a Flecher for ſeynge to all my Lords Shaif Arrowes and all other Arrowes in the kepynge of the Yoman of my Lordes Bowes and for Dreſyinge of all the ſaid Arrowes when they ned And he 'to' fynde Feders Wax Glewe Silke and al maner of other things that laks for mendyinge of the ſaid Arrowes from 'tyme' to tyme Which my Lord gyffith hym yerly for his Fee for mending and ſeyng to my ſaid Lordis Arrowes To be paid to him ones a Yere at Michalmes For the hole Yere —— xxs.

ITEM My Lorde uſith and accuſtomyth to pay yerly nowe owt of his Lordſhipis Coffures to his Lordſhippis Armorer that ſtandyth charged with his Lordſhipes Armory for fyndynge of all the Emery and Oyle for the makynge clean of all ſuch Harneſe of my Lords from tyme to tyme as in his Lordſhipis ſtandynge Armory where his Lordſhip lyeth And alſo for fyndynge of Bukilis Lether and Nalles from

tyme

tyme to tyme As the faide Herneffes laks for fynyfhynge
of it Which my Lorde gyffyth hym yerly for his Fee for
that caus To be paid unto hym at ij tymes of the Yere Viz.
at our Lady Day in Lent and Michaelmas after x s. at ather
Day over and befides Liij s. iiij d. paid to him for his Houshold Waiges for ftandynge chargede with the faid Armory
——— xx s.

ITEM My Lorde ufith and accuftomyth to pay yerly owt of
his Lordfhipis Coffures to one that fwepith and kepith
clyne the Leddis of the Caftell of Wrefill Which my
Lorde gyfyth hym yerly for his Fee for that caus To be
paid to hym ones a Yere at Michealmas for the hole
Yere ——— vj s. viij d.

ITEM My Lorde ufeth and accuftomyth to pay yerly owte
of his Lordfhips Coffures to the Yoman and Grome of his
Lordfhips Pantre Which ftandith chargede with the faide
Pantre for as much Chippings of Trencher-Brede and other
Brede of ther Vaillis as doith ferve for the fedyinge of my
Lords Howndis daily thorow owt the Yere Ande fo to be paid
unto them for that caufe at ij tymes of the Yere Viz. at our
Lady Day and Michalmes After vj s. viij d. at aither Day in
full Contentacion for the hole Yere ——— xiij s. iiij d.

Z z   AL

AL MANNER OF THINGS Yerly Yeven by my
Lorde for his MAUNDY ande my Laidis and his
Lordfhippis Childeren As the Confideracion WHY
more playnly hereafter folowith.

FURST My Lorde ufeth ande accuftomyth yerely uppon
Maundy Thurfday when his Lordfhip is at home to gyf
yerly as manny Gownnes to as manny Poor Men as my
Lorde is Yeres of Aige with Hoodes to them and one for
the Yere of my Lordes Aige to come Of Ruffet Cloth
after iij yerddes of Brode Cloth in every Gowne and Hoode
Ande after xij *d.* the brod Yerde of Clothe.

ITEM My Lorde ufeth ande accuftomyth yerly uppon Maundy Thurfday when his Lordfhip is at Home to gyf yerly
as manny Sherts of Lynnon Cloth to as manny Poure Men
as his Lordfhipe is Yers of Aige ande one for the Yere of
my Lords Aige to come After ij yerdis dim. in every Shert
ande after . . . . the yerde.

ITEM My Lorde ufeth ande accuftomyth yerly uppon the faid
Mawndy Thurfday when his Lordfhipe is at home to gyf
yerly as manny Tren Platers after ob. the pece with a Caft
of Brede and a Certen Meat in it to as manny Poure Men
as his Lordfhip is Yeres of Aige and one for the Yere of
my Lordis Aige to come.

ITEM My Lord ufed ande accuftomyth yerly upon the faid
Maundy Thurfday when his Lordfhip is at home to gyf
yerely as many Efhen Cuppis after ob. the pece with Wyne
in them to as many Poure Men as his Lordefhip is Yeres of
Aige and one for the Yere of my Lordis Aige to come.

ITEM

ITEM My Lorde ufeth and accuftomyth yerly uppon the faid Mawndy Thurfday when his Lordfhipe is at home to gyf yerly as manny Purffes of Lether after ob. the pece with as manny Penys in every purfe to as many poore men as his Lordfhip is Yeres of Aige and one for the Yere of my Lords Aige to come.

ITEM My Lorde ufeth ande accuftomyth yerely uppon Mawndy Thurfday to caufe to be bought iij Yerdis and iij Quarters of Brode Violett Cloth for a Gowne for his Lord-fhipe to doo fervice in Or for them that fchall doo fervice in his Lordfhypes Abfence After iij s. viij d. the Yerde And to be furrede with Blake Lamb Contenynge ij Keippe and a half after xxx Skynnes in a Kepe and after vj s. iij d. the Kepe and after ij d. ob. the Skynne and after Lxxv Skynnys for Furringe of the faid Gowne Whieh Gowne my Lord werith all the tyme his Lordfhip doith fervice And after his Lordfhip hath don his fervice at his faid Maundy doith gyf to the poureft man that he fyndyth as he thynkyth emongs them all the faid Gowne.

ITEM My Lorde ufeth and accuftomyth yerly upon the faid Mawnday Thurfday to caus to be delyvered to one of my Lordis Chaplayns for my Lady If fhe be at my Lordis fyndynge and not at hur owen To comaunde hym to gyf for her as manny Groits to as manny Poure Men as hir Ladyfhipe is Yeres of Aige and one for the Yere of hir Aige to come Owte of my Lordis Coffueres if fche be not at hir owen fyndynge.

ITEM My Lorde ufeth and accuftomyth yerly uppon the faid Maundy Thurfday to caus to be delyvered to one of my Lordis Chaplayns for my Lordis Eldeft Sone the Lord
Percy

Percy For hym to comaunde to gyf for hym as manny
Pens of ij Pens to as manny Poure Men as his Lordfhipe is Yeres of Aige and one for the Yere of his Lordfhipis age to come.

ITEM My Lorde ufeth and accuftomyth yerly uppon
Mawndy Thurfday to caus to be delyvetit to one of my
Lordis Chaplayns for every of my Yonge Maifters my
Lordis Yonger Sonnes To gyf for every of them as Manny
Penns to as manny Poore Men as every of my faid
Maifters is Yeres of Aige and for the Yere to come,

XLV.

XLV.

THE ORDER OF THE NOMBRE OF THE HORSSES whiche my Lorde and his Counſell thynks covenyent to be kept yerely in WYNTER in his Lordeſhips Stable at the charge of the Houſe And to what uſe they ſhall be exerſiſed HEREAFTER FOLLOWITH And this Nombre not to be exeedet without my Lordes Knowing upon 'any' Conſideracion.

NAGGES to be kept in my Lords Stable in WYNTER And for what Cauſes.

FIRST A Nage for my Lorde to ryde on.

ITEM A Nagge to be ledde for my Lorde for chaunge

ITEM A Nagge for my Lordes Secounde Son to ryde upon

ITEM A Nagge for my Lordes Thurde Son to ryde upon.

THE NOMBRE of the NAGGES is —— iiij.

HORSSES to be kept in my Lords Stable in WYNTER Whiche muſt neds be had for the CARYADGE

CARYADGE of my Lords STUFF when my Lorde rydes.

FIRST A Horffe for my Lordes Maile for the Grome of the Roobbes to ryde affore.

ITEM A Horffe for my Lordes Cloth-Sak with his Bedde.

ITEM A Horffe for my Lordes Cloth-Sek with his Apparell of his Body.

ITEM A Horffe for the Grome of the Ewry to ryde before my Lorde 'with' Shavynge-Baffynge and Ewer.

THE NOMBRE of the HORSSES for CARYADGE of STUFF —— iiij.

HORSSES to be kept in my Lords Stable in WYN-TER for thois PARSONES that muft nedes be at my Lords HORSSYNGE.

FIRST The Horffe that the Yoman of the Hors rydes on Whiche ftonds in my Lordes Stable | His Hors.

ITEM A Horffe for one Gentillman that is at my Lords Horffynge Whiche Horffe ftondes in my Lords Stable | His Horffe.

ITEM A Hors for the Grome of the Styroypp to ryde upon That ledes my Lords Spare Nagge | His Horffe.

ITEM

ITEM A Hors for the Grome of the Stable to ryde upon
That ledes the Cloth-Sek Horſſe that caryeth my Lords
Truſſynge Bed and all thyngs belongynge yt when he rydes
| His Hors.

ITEM A Hors for the Grome of the Stable to ryde upon
That ledes the Cloth Sak Hors that caryeth my Lords
Cloth - Sek with his hoſe Appareil of his Body | His
Hors.

ITEM A Hors for one of the Groomes of the Chambre
whiche is at my Lords Horſſynge to ryde upon that ſhall
goo beffore daylye when my Lorde rydes For dreſſynge and
makynge redy of my Lords Chambre agaynſt he com |
His Hors.

ITEM A Hors for another Grome of the Chambre to ryde
upon Whiche is at my Lords Horſſynge Whiche ſhall
be allwayes aboute my Lorde at his makynge redy |
His Hors.

THE NOMBRE OF HORSSES that muſt be Keept for
theis PARSONES that muſt be at his Lordeſhip
HORSSYNGE —— vij.

THE HORSSES that my Lorde allowith the LORDE
PERCY his Son and Heire to have ſtondynge in his
Lordſhipes STABLE When he is at Yeres to ryde
and is at my Lords Fyndynge.

FIRST A Gret Doble Trottynge Horſſe for my Lorde Percy
to travell uppon in Wynter.

ITEM

ITEM A Great Doble Trottynge Hors called a Curtall for his Lordeſhip to ryde on owte of Townes.

ITEM An outher Trottynge Gambaldynge Hors for my ſaide Lorde Percy to ryde upon when he comes ynto Townes.

ITEM An Amblynge Hors for his Lordeſhip to Journey upon Dayly.

ITEM A proper Amblynge Litle Nagge for my Lorde Percy to ryde upon when he goith on Hawkynge or Huntynge.

ITEM A Gret Amblynge Geldynge or a Gret Trottynge Geldynge to cary my ſaide Lorde Percys Maile with his Stuffe for his Chaunge when he rydes.

THE NOMBRE of the HORSSES that my Lordes allowes my Lorde PERCY to have in his Lordſhip Stable in WYNTER ys ——— vj.

THE HOLLE NOMBRE of all the foreſaide HORSSES appointed to Stonde in my Lords Stable in WYNTER at Harde Mete at the Charge of the Houſe ys ——— xxj.

XLVI.

XLVI.

THE ORDER OF THE NOMBRE OF THE PAR-
SONES thought 'meet' by my Lorde and his Counfell
to be within at MEATE and DRYNKE Daily in my Lordis
Hous And no mo to be in nombre When he kepes his SECRET
HOUS At the tyme of the takinge of his Accompts And
the Nombre of the faide PARSONES appoynted to attende
upon his Lordefhip and my Lady And how they fhall ferve in
Ordur yn every Roome HEREAFTER FOLLOWITH
And this faide Nombre not to be exedit but allwayes
thus kept at all fuche tymes when my Lorde breks up his
HOUSE Yerely at Michaellmes for the takynge of the
ACCOMPTS of the Offices in his Houfeholde As the
Wardrob and other.

MY Lorde

MY Ladye

TO SYT AT MY LORDS REWARDE

MY Lordes Eldeft Soṅ and Heire

A a a   PARSONES

PERSONES THAT SHALL ATTENDE upon my LORDE at HIS BORDE Daily Ande have no more but his REVERCION Except BREDE and DRYNK.

MY Lordes Secounde Son to ferve as Kerver.

MY Lordes Thurde Son as Sewer

A Gentillman that fhall attende upon my Lords Eldeft Son in the rewarde and appoynted Bicaufe he fhall allwayes be with my Lords Sonnes for feynge the Ordurynge of them.

MY Lordes firft Hannefhman to ferve as Cupberer to my Lorde.

MY Lords ij^{de} Hanfhman to ferve as Cupberer to my Lady.

ITEM A Yoman Ufher o'the Chambre to attende upon the Door at Mealis.

ITEM A Yoman of the Chambre to kepe the Cupborde at the Seller.

A Yoman or a Grome to awayte upon the Cupborde as Panteler.

A Yoman or a Groome to awayte upon the Cupborde as Butler.

ITEM The Yoman or Groome of the Ewry to awayte upon the Ewrye-Boorde.

A

A Yoman or a Grome Ufher of the Hall for Orderynge and Servynge of the Hall at the Firft Dynner and to be at the Revercyon.

A Grome Offycer of the Buttre or Pantre that fhall kepe and ferve the Offices as Seller Buttre and Pantre And to Breve And to be at the Revercion.

THE Clarke of the Kechinge that fhall ferve my Lorde at the Dreffer and fo the fervice frome the Kechinge to all other And to be at the Revercyon.

THE Porter that fhall kepe the Gaits and appoynted to be at the Revercion.

THE Yoman or Groome Cooke that fhall ferve at the Dref-for Servys to the holle Houfe And to be at the Revercion.

THE Childe of the Kechinge that fhall help the faide Yoman or Groome to dreffe my Lords Metes and Servyce for the Howfeholde And to be at the Revercion.

THE NOMBRE OF THE PARSONES IS —— xvj.

PARSONES THAT SHALL SYT at the KNYGHTS BOORDE in my Lordes GREATE CHAMBRE And to dyne at the FIRST DYN-NER.

THE Firft Gentillwoman to my Lady.

THE Secounde Gentillwoman to my Lady.

THE

THE Firſt Chamberer to my Lady.

THE Sccounde Chamberer to my Lady.

THE Thirde Chamberer to my Lady.

THE Deane of my Lordes Chappell or an outher Chappelayn for Sayinge of Grace to my Lorde.

ITEM A Gentillman Usſher o'th' Chambrè to dyne at the Firſt Dynner for takynge up my Lords Borde.

ITEM Another Gentillman Usſher of the Chambre to Dyne at the Firſt Dynner and to brynge yn the Towell and to ferve my Lorde with Water when his Lordeſhip goes to Dynner and when his Lordeſhip ryſſes frome Dynner.

THE NOMBRE OF THE PARSONES YS —— viij.

PARSONES APPOYNTID TO SYT in the HALL and to dyne at the FIRST DYNNER and to awayte upon my Lorde at AFTER DYNNER.

THE Preſt that ſtonds charged with the Payments of the Booke of my Lords Foren Expences.

THE Yoman of the Chambre that ſhall attende upon my Lady at After-Dynner.

                                        THE

THE Secounde Clarke of the Kechinge the whiche ſhall breve at after Dynner.

THE Clark of my Lords Foren Expenſis.

THE Clerke that ſhall ſyt with them that ſhall take the Accompts of the Offices in my Lords Houſe.

THE Yoman of the Bedds that ſtaunds chargid with my Lords Warderob Stuff For the Delyvre of the ſaide Stuffe at the accompt.

THE Skynner that is in my Lords Warderob For the hel= pynge to receyve the ſaide Stuffe when it is charged agayne into the Office.

A Grome of the Warderob For the berynge of the Stuff to the Warderob agayne when it is charged at the Accompt to the Offyce.

ANother Grome of the Warderob For the Berynge of the ſaid Stuffe to the Warderobe agayne when it is charged at the Accompt to the Office.

THE Clerke that ſhall wryte clere up the Booke of my Lords Foren Exſpences under the Clerke of my ſaide Lords Foren Expences.

A Grome of the Chamber For the kepynge of Fyre in the Jewell-Hous and Lyberary and Houſes in the Garden and outher places where my Lorde ſhall ſyt aboute his Books.

THE NOUMBRE OF THE PARSONES YS —— xj.

ALLWAYES

ALLWAYES ORDEYNYDE by my Lorde and his Counſell that anny of the forſaide PARSONES that ſytts at the FIRST DYNNER and mete to bere Dysſhis Be taken frome the Firſt Dynner to bere Dysſhis to my Lorde as well at the FIRST COURS as SECOUNDE COURS.

THE NOMBRE OF THE PARSONES YS ——— xxxviij.

XLVII.

XLVII.

THE ORDERYNGE OF MY LORDES CHAP-
PELL in the QUEARE at MATTYNGIS MAS
and EVYNSONGE To ſtonde in Ordure as Hereafter
Followith SYDE for SIDE DAILYE.

THE DEANE SIDE	THE SECOUNDE SYDE
THE Deane	THE Lady-Maſſe Prieſt
THE Subdeane	THE Goſpeller
A Baſſe	A Baſſe
A Tenor	A Countertenor
A Countertenor	A Countertenor
A Countertenor	A Tenor
A Countertenor	A Countertenor
	A Tenor

THE

THE ORDURYNGE of my Lordes CHAPPELL
for the Keapinge of our LADYES MASSE
thorowte the WEIKE.

SONDAY

Maſter of the Childer a Countertenor

A Tenoure

A Tenoure

A Baſſe

MONDAY

Maſter of the Childer a
Countertenor

A Countertenoure

A Countertenoure

A Tenoure

TWISDAY

Maſter of the Chillder a
Countenour

A Countertenoure

A Countertenoure

A Tenoure

WEDYNSDAY

Maſter of the Chillder a
Countertenor

A Countertenoure

A Tenoure

A Baſſe

THURSDAIE

THURSDAIE	FRYDAY
Mafter of the Chillder a Countertenor	Mafter of the Chiilder a Countertenor
A Countertenoure	A Countertenoure
A Countertenoure	A Countertenoure
A Tenoure	A Baffe

SATTURDAY	FRYDAY
Mafter of the Chillder a Countertenor	And upon the faide Friday th'ool Chappell and every Day in the weike when my Lorde fhall be prefent at the faide Maffe.
A Countertenor	
A Countertenoure	
A Tenoure	

THE ORDURYNGE for keapynge Weikly of the ORGAYNS Oon after An Outher As the NAMYS of them hereafter followith WEIKELY.

The Maifter of the Chillder yf he be a Player The Fyrft Weke.

A Countertenor that is a Player the ij^{de} Weke.

A Tenor that is a Player the thirde Weike.

A Baffe that is a Player the iiijth Weike.

Ande every Man that is a Player to kepe his cours Weikely.

B b b   THE

THE ORDURYNGE for ſtonding RECTOR-CHORE at the Deſke As to ſay at Mattyngis Highe-Maſſe and Evyn-Songe Oon on aither ſyde As the NAMYS of them hereafter followith WEIKELY.

THE Firſt Weike a Tenoure on the oone Side and a Countertenor on the outher ſide.

THE Secounde Weike a Countertenor on the oon ſide and a Tenor on the outher ſide.

THE Thirde Weike a Tenor on the oon ſide and a Countertenor on the outher ſide.

THE Fourth Weike a Countertenor on the oon ſide and a Tenor on the outher ſide.

THE ORDURYNGE of the PREISTIS Weikely of my Lordes Chappell for keapynge of MAS Dayly and Weikely.

THE Fyrſt Preiſt Subdean to ſynge Highe Mas on Doble Feiſtis and to eas outher Preiſtis of Maſſe when he ſeith they ſhall nede.

THE

THE Seconde Preiſt to ſing oure Lady Mas the Firſt Weike and to be Goſpeller at the Highe Maſſe.

THE Thirde Preiſt to ſynge Highe Maſſe the ſaid Weike and when he ſyngith Lady Mas to be Goſpeller at the Highe Maſſe.

THE ORDURYNGE of my Lordes Chapell in the QUEARE at Mattynges Mas and Evyn Songe to ſtonde in Order as hereafter followith SYDE for SYDE.

THE DEANE SYDE	THE SECONDE SYDE
THE Deane	THE Lady Maſſe Preiſt
THE Subdeane	THE Morrowe Meſſe Preiſt
THE Goſpiller	A Countertenor
A Countertenor	A Baſſe
A Baſſe	A Tenor
A Countertenor	A Countertenor
A Tenor	A Baſſe
A Baſſe	A Countertenor
A Countertenor	A Tenor

THE

THE ORDURYNGE of my Lordes Chappell
for the keapinge of oure LADY MASSE thorowe
oute the WEIKE.

SONDAY

THE Maifter of the Chill-
dren a Count-Tenor

A Countertenor

A Tenor

A Countertenor

A Baffe

MONDAY

THE Mafter o'th Chilldren
a Counter-tenor

A Countertenor

A Tenor

A Tenor

A Baiffe

TEWYSDAY

THE Mafter o'th Chilldren
a Countertenor

A Countertenor

A Tenor

A Countertenor

A Baiffe.

WEDDEYNSDAY

THE Mafter o'th Chilldren
a Countertenor

A Countertennor

A Countertennor

A Tennor

A Baffe

THURSDAY

THURSDAY

THE Mafter o'th Chilldren a Countertenor

A Tennor

A Countertenor

A Countertenor

A Baiffe

FRIDAY

THE Mafter o'th Chilldren a Countertenor

A Countertenor

A Tennor

A Countertenor

A Baiffe.

SATTURDAY

THE Mafter o'th Chilldren a Countertenor

A Countertenor

A Tennor

A Countertennor

A Baiffe

FRYDAY

UPPON Fryday the Hoolle Chappell and every day in the Weike when my Lorde fhall be prefent at the fayde Lady-Maffe.

THE ORDURYNGE of the BASSES in my Lordes Chappell for the fettynge of the QUEARE dayly at Mattynges Maffe and Even-Songe thorowe owte the Weike As the NAYMES of them With the DAYES and TYMES that they fhall kepe Here-after Followyth.

THE BASSES.

THE Fyrft Bais to fet the Queyre all Sonday and at Mat-tyngs on Friday.

THE

THE ij^d Bais to fet the Queare all Monday and at Mas on Fryday.

THE iij^d Bais to fet the Queare all Tewifday and at Evyn-Song on Friday.

THE iiijth Baffe to fet the Queare all Weddynfday and at Mattyngs on Satturday.

THE vth Bais to fet the Queare all Thurfday and at Maffe on Satturday.

THE ORDURYNGE for the keapynge Weykely of the ORGAYNES oone after an outher as the NAMES of them hereafter followith.

THE ORGAYNE PLAYERS.

THE Mafter o'th Chilldern if he be a Player the fyrft Weike.

A Countertennor that is a Player the Secounde Weike.

A Tennor that is a Player the Thyrde Weyke.

A Baiffe that ys a Player the Fourthe Weike.

And every Man that ys a Player to kepe his Cours Weykely.

THE ORDURYNGE for ftondynge RECTOR-CHORE at the Defke Viz. at Mattyngs Highe Mas

Mas and Evyn-Songe one after an other SYDE
for SYDE as the NAMYS of them hereafter
followith.

MONDAY.

Fyrſt a Bayſe on the oon Syde

And a Baiſe on the outher Side.

TEWISDAY.

A Bais on the oon Syde

And a Baiſe on the outher Syde

WEDDYNSDAY.

A Countertenor on the oon Syde

And a Countertenor on the outher Syde

THURSDAY.

A Countertenor on the one Syde

And a Tenor on the outher Syde

FHYDAY.

A Tennor on the oone Syde and

A Countertenor on the outher Syde

SATTURDAY.

A Countertenor on the oon Syde

And a Tenor on the outher Syde.

THE

THE ORDURYNGE of the PREISTIS Weikely of my Lordes Chappell for keapinge of MASSE Dayly and Weikely.

THE PREISTIS FOR KEAPINGE OF MAS DAILY.

THE Firſt Preiſt the Subdean to ſynge Highe Maſſe on Double Feiſts and to eaſe outher Preiſtis of Maſſe when he ſeith they ſhall nede.

ITEM The Seconde Preiſt to ſinge oure Lady Maſſe the Fyrſt Weike and to be Goſpeller at the Highe Maſſe.

THE Thirde Preiſt to ſynge Highe Maſſe the ſaide Weike and when he ſynges our Lady Maſſe to be Goſpeller at Highe Maſſe.

THE Fourth Preiſt to ſynge oure Lady Maſſe the Seconde Weike and to be Goſpeller at the Highe Maſſe the ſaide Weike.

XLVIII.

THYS YS THE BILL OF THE NAMYS of the HOUSES at my Lordes Mannour of LEKINGFELDE at his Lordfhipes NEW LOGE in his PARKE ther And what CHAMBRES they be which fhall have FIERS kept in theym yerly And how myche FEWILL fhal be allowid to every Hous by the Daye Weke and Monneth As well Billett Wodde as Fagot And what Dais in the Weke they fhall have Fiers made in them at all fuch tymes in Winter that my Lorde lies not ther Yerly from All-Hallowtide to Shraftide As the Namys of the faid Houfes And what Houfes they bee And what every of them fhal be allowide by the Day Weke and Monthe And what Dais they fhall have Fiers kept in theym HEREAFTER FOLLOWITH in this Bill Signed with my Lordes Hande.

THE NAMYS OF THEES CHAMBRES ande HOUSES within my Lordes Mannour of LEKING-FELDE Which fhall have FIERS kept in theym in WINTER when my Lord lieth not there From ALHALLOWTID to SHRAFTIDE.

FURST My Lords Jewelhous within the Mannour of Lek-ingfelde to have Monday Wedinfday and Fryday thorout the Weke ij Shids and a Fagott Contenyng in the Weke vj Shids and iij Fagotts And in the Monneth in Shides xxiiij

and

and in Fagotts xij And in the iij Monnethes Lxxij Shides
and xxxvj Fagotts Which amontithe in every Monthe in
Money after v Shids j*d.* — v*d.* And in Fagotts after v j*d.*
— ij*d.* ob. Sum of all the faide Fewell for the faid Hous
in the Weke is j*d.* ob. quad. In the Monneth vij*d.* ob.
And for the iij Monthes bitwix Alhalowtid and Shraftide
— xxij*d.* ob.

ITEM My Lords Lybrary within the Mahnor of Lekingfelde to have on Monday Wedinfday and Fryday thorowt
the Weke ij Shides and a Fagott Contenyng in the Weke
vj Shids and iij Fagotts And in the Month in Shids xxiiij
and in Fagotts xij And in the iij Monnythes lxxij Shids
and xxxvj Fagotts Which amontith in every Monneth in
Money after v Shids j*d.* — v*d.* And in Fagotts v j*d.* — ij*d.*
ob. Sum of all the faid Fewell for the faid Hous in the
Weke is j*d.* ob. q*d.* In the Monneth vij*d.* ob. And for
the iij Monneths bitwix Alhallowtide and Shraftide ——
xxij*d.* ob.

ITEM My Ladies Lybrary within the Mannour of Leking-
felde on Monday Wedinfday and Fryday thorowt the
Weke ij Shids and a Fagott Contenyng in the Weke vj
Shids and iij Fagotts And in the Monneth in Shids xxiiij in
Fagotts xij And in the iij Monthes in Shids lxxij and xxxvj
Fagotts Which amontith in every Monthe in Money after v
Shids j*d.* — v*d.* And in Fagotts after v j*d.* — ij*d.* ob. Sum
of all the Fewell for the faide Hous in the Weke is j*d.* ob.
q*d.* In the Monneth vij*d.* ob. And for the iij Monnethes
bitwix Alhallowtid and Shraftide —— xxij*d.* ob.

ITEM My Lords Lybrary over the Chapell Dour within the
Mannour of Lekingfelde to have on Monday Wedinfday
and Fryday thorout the Weke ij Shids and a Fagott Contenyng in the Wek vj Shids and iij Fagotts In the Monthe
in

in Shids xxiiij and in Fagotts xij And in iij Monthes
Shids lxxij and xxxvj Fagotts Which amontith to in every
Monneth in Money after v Shids j*d.* —— v*d.* And in Fagots after v j*d.* — ij*d.* ob. Sum of all the Fewell for the
faid Hous in the Wek is j*d.* ob. q*d.* In the Monnyth
vij*d.* ob. And in the iij Monnethes bitwix Alhallowtide
and Shraftide —— xxij*d.* ob.

ITEM The Evidens Hous over the Chapell Stair within the
Mannour of Lekenfelde to have on Monday Wedinfday
and Fryday thorowt the Weke ij Shids and a Fagott
Contenyng in the Weke vj Shids and iij Fagotts In the
Monneth in Shids xxiiij in Fagotts xij And in the iij
Monthes lxxij Shids and xxxvj Fagotts Which amontith
in every Month in Money after v Shids j*d.* — v*d.* And in
Fagotts after v j*d.* — ij*d.* ob. Sum of all the Fewell for
the faid Hous in the Wek is j*d.* ob. q*d.* In the Monthe is
vij*d.* ob. And for the iij Monnethes bitwix Alhollowtide
and Shraftide —— xxij*d.* ob.

ITEM Th'Uper Hous of the Tour in the Gardyn within
the Mannour of Lekingfield to have on Monday Wedinfday
and Fryday thorout the Weke ij Shids and a Fagott Contenyng in the Weke vi Shids and iij Fagotts In the Monneth
in Shids xxiiij And in Fagots xij And in the iij Mannethes
In Shids lxxij and xxxvj Fagotts Which amontith in every
Monthe in Money after v Shids j*d.* — v*d.* And in Fagots
after v j*d.* — ij*d.* ob. Sum of all the Fewell for the faid Hous
in the Wek is j*d.* ob. q*d.* An the Monthe vij*d.* ob. And in the
iij Monnethis bitwix All - hallowtide and Shraftide ——
xxij*d.* ob.

ITEM The Nether Hous of the Tour in the Gardyn within
the Manor of Lekingfield to have on Monday Wedinfday
and Fryday thorout the Weke ij Shids and a Fagott
Contennyng

Contennyng in the Wek vj Shids and iij Fagotts In the
Monneth in Shids xxiiij in Fagots xij And in the iij
Months in Shides lxxij and xxxvj Fagotts Which amontith
in every Month in Money after v Shids j d. — v d. In
Fagots after v j d. — ij d. ob. Sum of all the Fewell for the
said Hous in the Wek is j d. ob. q⁴. In the Monnyth is vij d.
ob. And in the iij Monnethes bitwix Alhallowtide and
Shraftide — xxij d. ob.

ITEM Th'Ynner Chambre of th'Uper Hous in the Gardyn
within the Mannor of Lekingfield to have on Monday
Wedinsday and Fryday thorowt the Weke ij Shids and a
Fagott Contenyng in the Wek vj Shids and iij Fagottes
In the Monneth in Shids xxiiij And in Fagotts xij And
in the iij Monneths lxxij Shids and xxxvj Fagotts Which
amontith in every Moneth in Money after v Shids j d. — v d.
And in Fagotts after v j d. — ij d. ob. Sum of all the Money
and Fewell for the said Hous in the Weke j d. ob. q⁴. And
in the Monyth vij d. ob. And in the iij Monthes bitwix
Alhalowtid and Shraftide — xxij d. ob.

ITEM The Wardrobe within the Mannor of Lekinfield to
have on Monday Wedinsday and Fryday thorout the Weke
ij Shids and a Fagot Contenyng vj Shids and iij Fagots In
the Month in Shids xxiiij and in Fagots xij And in the iij
Monthes in Shids lxxij and xxxvj Fagotts Which amontith in
every Month in Money after v Shids j d. — v d. In Fagots
after v. j d. — ij d. ob. Sum of all the Fewell for the said Hous
in the Wek is j d. ob. q⁴. In the Month vij d. ob. And in the
iij Monnethes bitwix Alhallowtid and Shaftid — xxij d. ob.

ITEM Th'Armory within the Mannor of Lekingfield to have
on Monday Wedinsday and Fryday thorowt the Weke ij
Shids and a Fagotte Contenyng in the Wek vj Shides and
iij Fagotts And in the Month in Shids xxiiij and in Fagots
xij

xij And in the iij Monthes in Shids lxxij and in Fagotts
xxxvj Which amontih in every Month in Money after v
Shids jd. — vd. And in Fagotts after v jd. ij d. ob. Sum
of all the Fewell for the said Hous in the Wek is jd. ob.
qᵈ. In the Moneth is vijd. ob. And in the iij Monthes
bitwix Alhallowtid and Shraftide — xxijd. ob.

ITEM The Vestry within the Mannor of Lekingfield to
have on Monday Wedinsday and Fryday thorout the Wek
ij Shids and a Fagott Contenyng in the Wek vj Shids and
iij Fagotts In the Month in Shids xxiiij and in Fagots xij
And in thre Monnethes in Shids lxxij and xxxvj Fagotts
Which amontith in all every Monthe in Money after v
Shids jd — vd. And in Fagotts after v jd. — ij d. ob. Sum
of all the Fewell for the saide Hous in the Wek jd. ob. qᵈ.
In the Monthe vijd. ob. And in the iij Monnythes bitwix
Alhallowtide and Shraftid —— xxijd ob.

THE NAMYS OF THES CHAMBRES and
HOUSES within my Lordes NEW LOGE in
his Lordshipes PARK of Lekingfelde Which
shall have FYERS kept in theym in WINTER
from Alhalowtide to Shraftide as Hereafter Followithe.

FURST The Garret within the New Loge to have on
Monday Wedinsday and Frayday thorout the Weke ij
Shids and a Fagot Contenyng in the Wek vj Shids and
iij Fagotts And in the Moneth in Shids xxiij and in Fa-
gotts xij And in the iij Monethes lxxij Shids and xxxvj
Fagotts Which amontith in every Monthe in Money after v
                                                    Shids

Shids j*d*. — v *d*. And in Fagots after v j *d*. — vij *d*. ob. Sum of all the faid Fewell for the faid Hous in the Wek is j *d*. ob. q*d*. In the Monneth vij *d*. ob. And in the iij Monthes from Albalowtid to Shraftide ——— xxij *d*. ob.

ITEM The Chambre next the Chapell within the New Loge to have on Monday Wedinſday and Fryday thorout the Weke ij Shids and a Fagot Contenyng in the Weke vj Shids and iij Fagots In the Moneth in Shids xxiiij and in Fagotts xij And in the iij Monthes in Shids lxxij and xxxvj Fagotts Which amontith in every Month in Money after v Shids j *d*. — v *d*. And in Fagotts after v j *d* — ij *d*. ob. Sum of all the Fewell for the faid Hous in the Wek is j *d* ob q*d*. In the Moneth vij ob. And in the thre Monnethes bitwix Alhallowtid and Shraftide ——— xxij *d*. ob.

ITEM The Gret Chambre within the New Loge to have on Monday Wedinſday and Fryday thorout the Weke ij Shids and a Fagott Contenyng in the Weke vj Shids and iij Fagotts And in the Month in Shids xxiiij in Fagotts xij And in the iij Monethes in Shids lxxij and xxxvj Fagotts Which amontith in every Morneth in Money after v Shids j *d*. — v *d*. And in Fagotts after v j *d*. — ij *d*. ob. Sum of all the faid Fewell for the faid Hous in the Wek is j *d*. ob. q*d*. In the Monthe vij *d*. ob. In the iij Monethes bitwix Alhalowtid and Shraftid ——— xxij *d*. ob.

ITEM The Chambre in th'end of the Gret Chambre within the Newe Loge to have on Monday Wedinſday and Fryday thorowt the Weke ij Shids and a Fagott Contenyng in the Weke vj Shids and iij Fagotts In the Monneth in Shids xxiiij and Fagotts xij And in the iij Monnethes in Shids lxxij and xxxvj Fagotts Which amontith to in every Month in Money after v Shids j *d*. — v *d*. And in Fagots after v j *d*. — ij *d*. ob. Sum of all the Fewell for the faid
Hous

Hous in the Weke is jd. ob. q^d. In the Month vij$d$. ob. And in the iij Monthes bitwix Alhalowtid and Shraftid. —— xxij$d$. ob.

ITEM The Chambre over the Hall within the said New Loge to have on Monday Wedinsday and Fryday thorout the Weke j Fagott and ij Shids Contenyng in the Weke vj Shids and iij Fagotts In the Month in Shids xxiiij in Fagotts xij And in the iij Monethis in Shids lxxij And in Fagotts xxxvj Which amontith in every Month in Money after v Shids jd. — vd. And in Fagots after v jd. — ij$d$. ob Sum of all the Fewell for the said Hous in the Wek is jd. ob. q^d. In the Moneth vij$d$. ob. And for the iij Monthes bitwix Alhallowtid and Shraftid —— xxij$d$. ob.

ITEM The Chambre over the Keching within the said New Loge to have on Monday Wedinsday and Fryday thorout the Weke ij Shids and a Fagott Contenyng vj Shids and iij Fagotts in the Weke In the Month xxiiij Shids and xij Fagotts And in the iij Monethes in Shids lxxij and xxxvj Fagotts Which amontith in every Monyth in Money after v Shids jd. — vd. And in Fagotts after v jd. — ij$d$. ob. Sum of all the Fewell for the said Hous in the Weke is jd. ob. q^d. In the Month vij$d$. ob. And in the iij Monthes bitwix Alhalowtide and Shraftide —— xxij$d$. ob.

ITEM The Hall within the New Loge to have on Monday Wedinsday ande Fryday thorout the Weke ij Shids and a Fagott Contenyng in the Wek vj Shids and iij Fagotts In the Monthe in Shids xxiiij and in Fagots xij And in the iij Monthes in Shids lxxij and in Fagotts xxxvj Which amontith in every Moneth in Money after v Shids jd. — vd. In Fagotts after v jd. — ij$d$. ob Sum of all the Fewell for the said Hous in the Weke is jd. ob. q^d In the Month vij$d$.

vij *d.* ob. And for the iij Monnethes bitwix Alhallowtid and Shraftid —— xxij *d.* ob.

THE HOLL NOMBRE of } { SHIDS Miiij^{xx} xvj. *
FEWELL apointed for the } In { FAGOTTS v^c xLviij.
foresaid HOUSES is }

Wherof

IN SHIDES for the Houses at the MANNOURE vj^c Lxxij.

IN SHYDS for the Houses at the NEWE LOGE cccc xxiiij.

IN FAGOTTS for the Houses at the MANNOUR ccc xxxvj.

IN FAGOTTS for the Houses at the NEW LOGE cc xij.

THE HOLL SOM of the MONEY }
for all the foresaid FEWELL. }
After ij *s.* iiij *d.* the c HARDWOD. } is —— xxxvj *s.*
After ij *s.* the c FAGOTT }

ITEM It is ordynede to provide yerly for xxx Saks of Charcoill for Stilling of Bottells of Waters for my Lord As the Namys of the said Waters that his Lordeshipe is accustomyd to caus to be stillide yerly Herafter Followith Viz. Water of Roses — Water for the Stone — Water of Buradge — Water of Feminytory — Water of Braks — Water of Columbyns — Water of Okynleeffe — Water of Harts Tonge — Water of Draggons — Water of Parcelly — Water of Balme — Water of Walnot Leeffs — Water of Longdobeeff — Water of Prymeroses — Water of Saidge — Water

* All these Reckonings are at the Rate of Six Score to the Hundred.

— Water of Sorrell — Water of Red Mynt — Water of Betany — Water of Cowflops — Water of Tandelyon — Water of Fennell — Water of Scabias — Water of Elder-Flours — Water of Marygolds — Water of Wilde Tanfey — Water of Wormwodde — Water of Wodbind — Water of Endyff — and Water of Hawffe And to be allowed for filling of every Bottell of Water of a Pottell a pece on with another j Bufhell of Chercoill After iiij Bufhell in the Sek And after ij Suaks to a Quarter And after j Quarter for ftilling of every viij Bottells with Water.

XLIX.

THE BOOKE OF THE ORDRE FOR THE HOUSHOLDE for the Hede Officers ande thois that ftandeth Chargide with my Lordes ande the Clarkes of the Kechynge How they fhall apoynt the Marfhalls ande Ufhers of the Hall to order allow and apoynte the CARIAGES at every REMEVALL of my Lord When my Lord fhall brek upe his Houfe from place to place For the faid Marfhalls and Ufhers of his Hall to affigne the faide Cariages How they fhal be occopyede And how the faid Carriages fhall be apoyntide And what they be that fhal be apointed to every Cariage And what Cariages fhal be apoyntide for every Caus HERAFTER FOLLOWITH in this Booke in order one after another.

FURST Yt is Ordygnede that the Wardrobe Stuff fhall have at every Remevall iij Cariages allowed befides my Lordes Chariot And that they fhall have remanynge no moir Stuff (concernyng the Wardrobe in the place wher my Lord fhall remove fro) left to cary at the day of my Lordes Departour but onely the Stuf that doith hange and Beddes As to fay the Stuf in the Chambre wheir my Lord and my Laidy Lyeth The Stuf in the Chambre wheir my Lord Dyneth The Stuf in the Greate Chambre And the Stuf in the Chambre wher my Lorde makes him redy And the Beddes with the Stuf belonging them in the Chambres wher my Lordes Children lieth | iij Cartes Viz. One Cart for the Stuf of the Dynyng Chambre and Gret Chambre Ande the outher Carte for the Stuf in my Ladies Chambre and in

the

the Chambre wher my Lord makes him redy With the Gentilwomen Stuf and the Stuf that remanes in my Lordes Chambre confernyng my Lordes felf Ande the iij^de Cart for fuch Stuf remanynge in the Wardrobe which might not be remevide nor fent before unto my Lordes departour.

ITEM Yt is Ordynede that the Veftry Stuf fhall have at every Remevall One Carte As to fay for the Caryinge the iiij Antyfoners The iiij Grailles The Hanginges of the iij Alters in the Chapell The Surplaffes The Alter Clothis in my Lords Clofet and my Ladies And the Soit of Veftments and fingle Veftments and Coopes accopied daley And all outher my Lordes Chapell Stuff to be fent afore by my Lords Chariot before his Lordfhipe remeve.

ITEM Yt is Ordynyd that ther fhall be a Caryage apontide at every Remevall for the Cariage of my Lordes Childre Stuff which be at aidge For ther Apparell and the Stuf of him apontid to have the overfight of them With the Stuff of ther Servaunts that attendes upon 'them' When they have non allowance for Cariage of ther Beddes bicaufe they have ther Beddes allowid out of the Wardrobe.

ITEM It is Ordyned that the Stuff of the Offices followynge fhal be jonyd at every Remevall to one Cariage bicaus the Sellar hath but Cupbord-Clothes and Barrell-Feries The Pauntrey Towelles Purpaynes Coverpayns Chipping-knyffs The Buttry Cannes Cupes and Crufes And th'Ewry Chaffers Bafings and Ewers Table-clothis Ewry-clothis Napkins Carver and Sewer Towells Viz. the Sellar the Pantry the Butrey and Ewry and all the Parfons Stuff with ther Bedding which be Officers belonging the faide Offices Viz. Sellar Pantre and Ewry And one for the Butry to be caryed in the faid Cariage And to have non outher Cariage allowid them.

ITEM

ITEM It ys Ordynede at every Remevall that the Stuf of the Kechinge Squillery Lardre and Paftrey fhall be apontide ij Cariages Viz. One Cariage for the Keching ftuff as Spittes Pottes Pannes Traffetts Raks And Paftry-ftuf as Pryntes and outher Stuf And th'outher Carriage for the Squyllery-ftuf as Veffell and Dreffer-Clothes with the ij Beddes for the iiij Cookes to ly in And all the Parfans ther apparrell and other Stuff to be caried in the faid Cariages And to have non other Cariage allowid theime.

ITEM It is Ordyned at every Remevall that the Stuff be-longinge the Bakhous With the Bedde for the Bakers The Bedde for the Brewers The Bedde for the Grom-Ufhers o'th Hall And for ther apparrell and outher Stuff fhal be apontid to have On Cariage for the cariage of it And to have non outher Cariage allowed them but onely the faide Cariage.

ITEM It is Ordyned at every Remevall that my Lordes Attourney if he be in Hous daly with my Lorde My Lordes Auditurs in Houfhold daley The Gentilmen of Houfholde as Carvers Sewars and Cupberers and Gentilmen-Waters fhall have apontid theime One Cariage for carying of v Beddes Viz. a Bedde for the Attourney a Bedde for the ij Auditurs a Bed for the ij Carvers a Bedde for the ij Sewers and a Bed for the ij Gentilmen Waters And all ther Apparrell And other Stuf to be caried in the faid Cariage and to have no more Cariage allowid theym but one Cariage.

ITEM It is Ordyned at every Remevall that the Gentilmen Ufhers of my Lordes Chambre Yomen Ufhers of the Chambre Marfhalls and Yomen Ufhers o'th Hall fhall have apontid for them One Cariage for the cariage of v Beddes Viz. the Gentilmen Ufhers ij Beddes The Marfhalls a Bed

Bed The Yomen-Ushers o'th Chambre a Bedde And the
Yoman Ushers o'th Hall apontid And all the Aparrell
and outher Stuf to be caryed in the said Cariage And to
have no more Cariage allowid theme but the said On
Carlage.

ITEM Yt is Ordynyd at every Remevall that the Deyn Sub-
dean Prestes Gentilmen and Children of my Lordes Chapell with the Yoman and Grome of the Vestrey shall have
apontid theime ij Cariadges at every Remevall Viz. One
for ther Beddes Viz. For vj Prests iij Beddes after ij to a
Bedde For x Gentillmen of the Chapell v Beddes after ij
to a Bedde And for vj Children ij Beddes after iij to
a Bedde And a Bedde for the Yoman and Grom o'th
Vestry In all xj Beddes for the furst Cariage. | And the ij^de
Cariage for ther Aparells and all outher ther Stuff And to
have no mo Cariage allowed them but onely the said ij
Cariages allowid theime.

ITEM It is Ordyned at every Remevall a Cariage to be
asyned for the Clark of my Lordes Foren Expenses The
Clerk o'th Warks And the Clerk that haith the oversight
ande payment of the Book of my Lordes Expenses and
Reparacions And the Clerk that writes under my said
Lordes Clerks Viz, For ij Beds for the said iiij Parsons after
ij to a Bedde And for a Gret Standert Chist for carying
of ther Bookes with them And also for Cariage of ther
Aparell and outher ther Stuff And to have no mo Cariages
alowid them but onely the said one Cariage.

ITEM It is Ordyned at every Remevall a Cariage to be
affined for the Hede Clark of the Keching The ij^de Clark
o'th Keching The Clerk o'th Brevements And the Clerke
Avener Viz. ij Beddes for the said iiij Clerks after ij to a
Bedde And a Gret Standart Chist for carying of ther Books
with

with them And alſo for the Cariage of ther Aparell and all outher ther Stuff And to have no mor cariage allowed them but onely the ſaid One Cariage.

ITEM It is Ordynyd at every Remevall that the ij Chapleyns The Officers of Armys The iiij Yomen o'th Chambre The iiij Yomen Waters And the Porters to have On Cariage apontid theime Viz. for the cariage of vij Beddes Viz. On Bedde for the ij Chapleyns One Bedde for th'Officers of Armell | ij Beds for the iiij Yomen o'th Chambre after ij to Bedde. | ij Beddes for the iiij Yomen Waters after ij to a Bedde A Bedde for the ij Porters | And alſo ther Aparell and all other ſtuff to be caried in the ſaid Cariage And to have no moir Cariages allowid them onely the ſaid On Cariage apontid theime.

ITEM It is Ordyned at every Remevall that my Lordes Warkmen in Houſholde as his Joner his Smyth and his Paynter With the ij Mynſtralles and the ij Hunts ſhall have apontid theime at every Remevall one Cariage Viz. For the Cariage of the Smythes Toilles The Joners Toilles And the Paynters And alſo for the Cariage of v Beddes Viz. a Bed for the Smyth a Bed for the Joner a Bedde for the Paynter a Bedde for the ij Mynſtralles and a Bed for the ij Hunts And all ther Aparell and all other Stuf to be caried in the ſaid Cariage And to have no more Cariages allowid theime but onely the ſaid On Cariage apontid theime.

ITEM It is Ordyned and apontid by my Lord and his Counfail that thois Parſons that ſtands chargid with my Lords Hous as his Hede Officers or other the Clerk of the Keching with the Gentilmen and Yomen Uſhers o'the Chambre and Marſhalls and Yeomen and Grom Uſhers o'th Hall Which be Herbigers Shall allwais Yerly befoir the
Remevall

Remevall of my Lord at Mychelmas fe all my Lords Veftry-Stuf and Wardrobe-Stuf caried by my Lords own Chariot unto the place wher my Lord fhall remove to Except the Stuf of the faid Offices apontid to be occupied daly to ferve my Lord unto his Lordfhipe remeve Bicaus my Lord fhall be put to no further charge of Cariages than nedeth Seing the Cariage with my Lords own Chariot may fave the fame Charges And that the Stuf be gone at the leift a Fortnet afoir my Lords Remevall.

THE NUMBER OF CARRAGES AT EVERY RE-'MEVALL BESIDE THE CHARIOT —— xvij.'

L.

L.

THIS IS THE ORDOUR of all my Lordes CLERKIS in his Houfe How they fhal be chargid Yeirly at Mychaelmis And what Chargis every of them fhall taike for the Yeire And what BOOKIS of REKENYGES they fhal be chargid with | As well the Books of the HOUSHOULD as the Bookes off my Lordes FOREN EXPENSES and REPARACIONS AS well thoes that fhall Yeirly MAIKE the Bookis As thoes that fhall CORRECKE the Bookes Yeirly under my Lorde As thoies that fhall INGROICE Yeirly the faid CORRECKING BOOKS.

FURSTE That the Perfonne or Perfonnes Whatfomever he be That fhal be apointid at Mychaelmas in the Chequirroill for the Yeire to ftand chargid for the Houfhold and the Receite of th'Affignement for the fame for Keaping of the faid houfe Shal have for his Fee for the fame by Yeire, —— xx l.

ITEM That he that fhal be apointed at Mychaelmes in the Chequirroill for the Yeir as Clerke Comptroller Shall Yeirly keape a dailly Correcking Jornall Book And to fe the Parcells dailly entrid in the Clerre Jornall Booke truely And to correcke the Caitour Parcells dailly if ned be And to fee th'Entrie of the Necantoures Brafiauntours and Fur-
neountours

neoustours dailly And to fee the Service at the Dreffour fervid And the Stuf ftrekynne owte in the mornyng to ferve for that 'day' And alfo to fe all maner of Breid weid at the Bakhoufe at every Baiking AND he to have for his Waigis for thies caufes —— liij s. iiij d.

ITEM That he that fhal be apointid at Mychaelmes in the Chequirroill for the Yeir as Second Clerke o'the Kechynne Shall Yeirely blok * up the Chequiroill and Billis of every Quarter for my Lord to correcke And alfoo keape dailly a Correcking Booke of Raiting of Meallis And he to have for his Houfhold Waigis Lxvj s. viij d. AND the faid Secound Clerke o'th Kechin fhall ftand chargid Yeirly at Mychael-mes with the Booke of my Lord Reparacions at Wrefill And he to have for his Waigis for that xx s. AND fo the faid Secound Clerke o'th Keachynne haith now for his Waigis by Yeire —— iiij l. vj s. viij d.

ITEM That he that fhal be apointid at Mychaelmes in the Chequirroil for the Yeire as Clerke o'th Spicery for the Houfhould Shall Yeirly ingroice the Jornall Booke of the Hous Dailly as the Parcells comes in And to keape the Brevying Booke of the Houfe of Meate and Drinke Dailly And to ingroice up the Chequirroill and the Billes maide of every Quarter after they be Correckid by my Lorde And he too have for the fame for his Houlfhoulde Waigis xxxiij s. iiij d. AND alfo the faid Clerke o'the Spicery fchall ftand chargid Yeirely at Mychaelmes with the ingroffing of my Lordes Booke off Reperacions at Wrefill And he to have for it vj s. viij d. AND foo the faid Clerke o'th Spicery haith now for his Waigis —— xL s.

ITEM That he that fhall be apointid at Mychaelmes in the Chequirroill for the Yeir as Clerke o'the Brevements Shall Yeirly helpe the Clerke Comptroiller to fe the Service

E e e Servid

* Sic MS.

Servid at Dreſſour And to helpe to write in the Countinghous
dailly for th'Entrie of Parcells and Fynnyſhing up of the
Books And he to have for his Houlſhould Waigis xxxiij s.
iiij d. AND alſo the ſaid Clerke o'th Brevements ſhall
Yeirly at Mychaelmes ſtand chargid as Clerke o'th Werkis
at Lekynfeld And to ingroice Yeirly the Clerre Booke of my
Lordis Foren Expenſes And the ſaid Clerke o'thé Brevements
to have for that by Yeire xx s. And alſo to ingroice up Clerre
into my Lordis Regeſtre al maner of Grauntis that paſſith
from my Lord in the Yeire AND ſo the ſaid Clerke o'th
Brevements haith by Yere ——— Liij s. iiij d.

ITEM That he that ſhal be apointid at Mychaelmes in the
Chequirroil for the Yeir as Clerke o'th Countinghous
Shall Yeirly ingroice dailly the Booke off Raiting of Mealls
for the Expenſes of the Houlſhould And to taike for his
Houlſhould Waigis xx s. AND alſo the ſaid Clerke of the
Countinghous ſhall Yeirely at Mychaelmes ſtand chargid as
Clerke o'th Werkis at Topclif And to ingroice Yeirly my
Lordes Booke off Reparacions at Lekynfeld And the ſaid
Clerke o'th Countinghouſe to have for his Waigis for that
cauſe xiij s. iiij d. AND ſo the ſaid Clerke o'th Counting-
houſe haith for his Waigis by Yere ——— xxxiij s. iiij d.

ITEM That he that ſhal be apointid at Mychaelmes in the
Chequirroill for the Yeire as Clerke Avener Shall keape
dailly the Brevyng Booke of Leveries of Horſe Meate and
Fewell And too be dailly in the Garners And to ſe the delivery of Horſmeate And alſo to be dailly at the Houſe
apointid to ſe the Feuwell dailly delivert And to taike away
with him the Key after the ſaid Leveries be ſervid AND the
ſaid Clerke Avener to have for his Waigis ——— xx s.

ITEM That he that ſhal be apointid at Mychaelmes in the
Chequirroill for the Yeire as Coufferer To ſtand chargid
with

with all my Lordes Receites for the Yeire And as Gentillman Huysſher And to ſtand chargid with my Lordis Plaite and Jewell With oithur aſignid and joined unto him AND he to have for his Houlſhould Waigis for that cauſe —— Lxvjſ. viij *d*.

ITEM That he that ſhall 'be' apointed at Mychaelmes in the Chequirroil for the Yere as Clarke of my Lords Forin Expenſes Schall ſtand chargid with the maiking of the Booke of my Lordes Forin Expenſes And to correcke the ſame with my Lorde Ande he to have for his Houlſhould Waigis Lxvjſ. viij *d*. AND to correcke under my Lorde the Booke of my Lordes Reperacions of Lekynfeld And he to have for that by Yeir xxſ. Alſo to correcke under my Lorde the Booke of my Lordes Reperacions at Wreſill And he to have for that by Yeir xxſ. And to correcke under my Lorde the Booke of my Lordes Reperacions at Topclif And he to have for that by the Yeire xiijſ. iiij *d*. And this iiij Marks to be paied owt of my Lorde Couffers ALSO the ſaid Clarke o'th Forin Expences ſhall taike the payne with him or theim that ſtandes chargid with my Lordes. . . . . To Sett ᵇ at Brevementes and to ſe th'Officers examoned at the Brevementis as well for Meate Drinke Fewell as Horſe Meate And the ſaid Clerke o'th Forin Expenſſis to have for ſeing of this dailly hourely ſurly truely keape ᶜ and done And th'Officers ſurely examonid at the Brevementis To haive owt of the xx *l*. that they have that ſtandes chargid with the Affignement for doing of it —— Lxvjſ viij *d*. ——

THIS

ᵇ i. e. 'ſit.' ᶜ i. e. 'kept.'

THIS IS THE BOOKE OF ARTICLES off th'Ordour of the TYME and HOURES of all my Lordes CLERKIS in Houlhould for an houl Yeir HOW they have their TYMES expreffid Dailly Hourely Wekely Monithly and Quarterly for th'Ordour of theire TYMES in the houl Yeire As well his Lordfhip COUFFERERRE as his Lordfhip CLERKES of his Forin Expenffis and Reparacions at Wrefill Lekynfeld and Toppclif as CLERKES belonging the Coun- tinghoufe for th'Ordour of the Houfe AND how they be ordonid and apointid by my Lorde and his Counfeill to keippe the faid Houres ande Tyme apointid to theim AND what thing they fhal be accupied with and to doo in the faid Houres at tymes Houryly Dailly Wekely Mointhly Quarterly and Yeirly HEREAFTUR FOLLOWITH in order How my Lorde haith hordeinid the faid Clerks to be ordorid and occupied for their Tymes concernyng their Bookes which they be chargid with Heraftur Followith in this Booke in Articles to be keapt Yeirly by my Lordis CLERKS IN HOUSE.

TH'ORDOUR for HYM which fhal be apointid yeirly to be my Lordes COUFFERER.

FURSTE The faid Couffurer fhal have Leafure every Sounday throwowt the Yeir to maike up his owne Rekenyngis and to rekene with the Clerke o'th Forin Ex- penfs and oithur And to difcharge with theim all fuch Somes of Money as they rekenid receyvid of him in the Weke befoir As well for my Lordes Forin Expenffis Reperacions Houfhold or any oither ufe.

ITEM

ITEM The said Coufferer wheir any perticuler Receyvour comes in with any money Or any oither manour of Perfonne to deliver Money to his handes for my Lordes Ufe The said Coufferer fhal have Leaffour at all fuch tymes to receyve the faid Money And to maike up his Acquitaunce And to entier the Receiptie into his Booke And to bring it to my Lorde to figne or [a] he deliver his Acquitaunce to him or theim that bringis the faid Money.

ITEM That the Coufferer fhall every Satterday caft up his owne Booke of Receptie of Money from Michaelmes to that Day and his Delivery togeither And to bring my Lorde in a Bill what Money remaynes in handes.

ITEM That the faid Coufferer fhall at all tymes wheir any Recepties comes in come to my Lord to know his Lord-fhipis pleafure whoe fhal be prevey with 'him' for the Receptie of the faid Money becaufe his Booke fhall be chargid with noo les thanne to 'him' comes.

ITEM The faid Couffurer fhall in like caife every Satter-day bring my Lord a Bill what his Deliveries haith benne in the Weke And what the Expenfes drawes too in the Weke That he may fhue my Lorde what fhall remaynne in handes or ells what he laikes for the full Paymente of the faid Weike.

ITEM That the faid Coufferer at all fuch tymes as he fhall bring his Booke to my Lorde to figne the Parcell of his Receptes 'Shall' know my Lordes pleafure befoir he bring his Booke Who his Lordfhip wol haive to be by him whenne he figne his faid Couffers Receptis.

THE'ORDOUR

[a] i. e. 'before.'

TH'ORDOUR for hym which fhall be apointid Yeirly to be CLERKE of my Lordes FORIN EXPENCIS.

FURST The Clerke o'th Forin Expenffis fhall every Sonday maike up his Rekenyngis with the Coufferer And to difcharg with him all fuch Money as he haith receyvid in the Weke befoir of the faid Coufferer.

ITEM The faid Clerke o'th Forin Expences after that he haith chargid himfelve with 'fuch' Moiny as 'he' haith receyved of the Coufferer The faid Clarke o'th Forin Expences thanne fhall charge in his owne Booke the Titles what Money he haith receyvid the faid tyme And for what caufe it was receyvid.

ITEM The faid Clerke o'th Forin Expenffis fhall every Monday caill 'the Clerk' of the Brevementes to ingroice up into the Clere Booke the Weke o'th Forin Expenffis correckid by my Lord the 'Satterday' befoir in the Correking Booke.

ITEM The faid Clerke o'th Forin Expenffis fhall every Tuefday at vj o'th Clocke at morow haive an houre Laifour to examoine the Weke Correckid o'th Forin Expenffis by my Lord o'th Satterday befoir To fe that it be truely ingroicid into the Clere Booke as it is Correckid by my Lorde.

ITEM

ITEM The Clerke o'th Forin Expenſſis ſhall wekely every Turiſday and Friday have laiſour all the ſaid ij daies oonely to entier his Parcells laide owt by him in that Weke And to rekene with all mainer off Menne what is owing unto theim which aughte to be paied in the ſaide Weike.

ITEM The ſaid Clerke o'th Forin Expencis ſhall every Satterday wekely throw-owte the Yeire bring unto my Lorde every Satterday in the mornyng afoir vij o'th Cloke his Correcking Booke of his Lorſhip Forin Expenſſis which maike mencion of the Parecells laid owt to be paied the forſaid Weke For my ſaid Lord to correcke the Parcells of the ſaid Booke laide owt for the ſaid Weke.

ITEM The Clerke of the Forin Expenſſis ſhell ſett uppon the heade of every Parcell which my Lord correctis which ſhal be paied the ſaid Weike to write upponne the heade of the Parcell paied.

ITEM That the ſaid Clerke o'th Forin Expenſſis ſhall every Satterday wekely red unto my Lord when my Lord haith correcte the Parcells of the Weike in the ſaid Booke furſt the Title if prieſt * of every Man ſent owt That my Lord may ſtrike owt thoies which be rekynid with and entered in the Weke.

ITEM The Clerke o'th Forin Expenſſis ſhall every Satterday wekely in like caiſe read unto my Lord whenne my 'Lord' haith correckid the Parcells of the ſaid Weike the title of prieſt-money That my Lord my ſee wheither all ſuch preiſt-money delivert to any Perſonne in that Weike be truely enterid in the ſaid title to woſomer it was delivert and for that cauſe And to ſtrike owt ſuch preiſt as be rekenid with.

ITEM

* Prieſt here and below is the ſame as 'Impreſt.'

ITEM The said Clerke o'th Forin Expenſſis ſhall every Saterday after my Lord haith correckid wekely the Parcells of the Weike red unto my Lord the Title of all manner of Money lent by his Lordſhip to anny manner of Perſonne in that Weike That my Lord may ſe wheither it be truely enterid in the ſaid title or not and for what cauſe And to enter When it was lent.

ITEM That the ſaid Clerke of the Forin Expenſſis ſhall every Satterday Wekely title the Some at th'ende of the Weke what th'ole Some of the ſaid Weke comes too And to devide what is Clere paied of it in the Weik and what is reſpectid of it.

ITEM That the Clerke of my Lordes Forin Expencis ſhall every Satterday Weikely after my Lord hath correcke his woke Know my Lordes pleaſure who his Lordſhip woll apointie to be by at the payment of the money of the ſaid Weke to ſe that the Perſons ſhall be truely paied.

ITEM The ſaid Clerke of my Lord Forin Expenſſis ſhall every Satterday 'afoir' he bringis my Lord his Booke of his Forin Expenſ to correcke Know whoe his Lordſhip wol have to fett with him when his ſaid Lordſhip cauſes his ſaid Clarke of his Forin Expencis to correcke his ſaid Booke.

TH'ORDOUR

TH'ORDOUR for him that fhall be apointid
Yeirely to be CLERKE of my Lordes WERKES
at WRESILL.

FURSTE The Clerke of my Lorde Werkes at Wrefill fhal
have laifour every Friday to rekenne with the Werkemenne
and to entier in his Correcking Booke all the Werke
donne at Wrefill in the faid Weke.

ITEM The faid Clerke of my Lordes Werkes at Wrefill
fhall every Satterday at afternoon from On o'th Clocke
to ij o'th Clocke bring my Lord his Correcking Booke
of the Reparacions at Wrefill which maikes mencion of
the Parcells of all Werks fynifhid in the faid Wekes to be
paied For my Lord too correcke the faid Parcells that the
Werkemen may be paied.

ITEM The faid Clerke of my Lord Werkes at Wrefill fhall
every Sonday ingroice up clere the Booke of my Lord
Werkes at Topclif for all manier of Werkes donne their
the Weike befoire After it be correckid the Satterday
befoir by my Lorde.

ITEM The faid Clerke o'th Werkes at Wrefill fhall every
Monday afoir-non caill of the Clerke o'th Spicery for
th'ingroicing up cleere all the Werkes donne at Wrefill
the Weke befoir and correckid by my Lord And whenne it
is ingroicid examoine it by the Correcking Booke to fe that
it be truely ingroicid as it is correckid.

ITEM

ITEM The said Clerke of my Lordes Werkes at Wresill afoir he bring his Booke to my Lord to correcke 'Shall' know his Lordship pleasure 'who' his Lordship woll have to sett by him at the correcking of his said Reparacions.

ITEM The said Clerke of my Lordes Werks at Wresill shall every Satterday wekelie after my Lord haith correckid his Weke of his Booke of his Lordship Werkes at Wresill Knowe my Lord pleasur who his Lordship woll apointie to be by at the payment of the Money of the Werkes of the said Weke To se that the Poure Foulkes whome shal be paied Be truely paied.

ITEM The said Clerke o'th Werkes at Wresill shall every Satterday wekely totall the Some at th'ende of the Weke What th'ole Some of the said Wek comes to And to devide what is paied of it and what is respected.

ITEM The said Clerke o'th Werkes at Wresill shall every Satterday wekely after he haith correckid his weke with my Lorde red unto my Lord the Parcells of the Remaynith remainyng As well of Stuf boughte as of Stuf savid of old Werkes which my Lord alters or amendes That my Lord may se that it be truly enterid wekely that which remaynes.

TH'ORDOUR for him that shal be apointid Yeirely to be CLERKE of my Lordes WERKES at LEKYNFELD.

FURSTE The Clerke of my Lordes Werkes at Lekynfeld shall have Laisour every Friday to reckynne with Werke-
men

men and to entier in his Correcking Booke all the Werkes
donne at Lekynfeld in the faid Weke.

ITEM The faid Clerke of my Lordes Werkes at Lekinfeld
fhall every Satturday at After Noon from ij o'th cloike to iij
o'th cloike bring my Lorde his Correcking Booke of the
Reparacions at Lekynfeld Which maike mencion of the
Parcells of Werkes fynifhid in the faid Weke to be paied
For my Lord to correcke the faid Parcells that the Werke-
men may be paied.

ITEM The Clerk of my Lordes Werkes at Lekinfeld fhall
every Sonday and Monday if ned be ingroice up the Clere
Booke of my Lord Forin Expenfis for the Weke by paft
And to fe it examonid with the Clerke o'th Forin Expenfis
that it be truely ingroicid.

ITEM The Clerke of my Lordes Werkes at Lekynfeld fhall
every Sonday caill of the Clerkes of my Lorde Werkes at
Topclif for th'ingrocing up clere of the Weke of my Lordes
Reperacions at Lekynfeld endit the Satterday befoir And
when it is donne to examoune it truely to fe that it agre
with the Correcking Book.

ITEM The Clerke of my Lordes Werkes at Lekynfeld afoire
he bring his Booke to my Lorde to correck To know his
Lordfhip pleafure Whoe his Lordfhip wol have to fett by
him at the Correcking of his faid Reperacions.

ITEM The faid Clerke of my Lordes Werkes at Lekinfeld
fhall every Satterday wekely after my Lord haith correcked
his Booke of his Lordfhip Werkes at Lekinfield Knowe
my Lordes pleafur Whoe his Lordfhip woll apointe to be
by at the Payment of the Money of the Werkes of the
faid

Weke To fe that the Perfons which fhal be paied be truely paied.

ITEM The faid Clerke o'th Werkes at Lekenfeld fhall every Satterday wekely totall the Some at th'ende of the Weke what th'ole Some of the faid Weke comes to And to devide what is paied of it and what is refpectid.

ITEM The faid Clerke o'th Werkes at Lekynfeld fhall every Satterday wekely after he haith correcked his Weke with my Lorde rede unto my Lord the Parcells of the Re- manith remanyng As well of Stuf bought as Stuff favid of old Werkes which my Lorde alters or mendes That my Lord may fe that it be truely enterid wekely that which remanes.

TH'ORDOUR for him that fhall be apointid Yeirly to be CLERKE of my Lord WERKES at TOPCLIF.

FURSTE The Clerke of my Lordes Werkes at Topclif fhal have Laifour every Friday to rekene with the Werke- men and to enter in his Correcking Booke all the Werkes donne at Topclif in the faid Weike.

ITEM The faid Clerke of my Lordes Werkes at Topclif fhall every Satterday at After Noon from iij o'th cloike to iiij o'th cloike bring my Lorde his Correcking Booke of Repa- racions at Topclif which maikes mencion of the Parcells of all the Werkes fynifhinde in the faid Weke to be paied
For

For my Lord to correcke the faid Parcells that the Werke-men may be paied.

ITEM The Clerke of my Lordes Werkes at Topclif fhall every Sonday ingroice up clere the Booke of the Workes at Lekynfeld donne the Weke befoir after it be correkid by my Lorde.

ITEM The Clerke of my Lordes Werkes at Topclif fhall every Monday afoir noon caill of the Clerke of my Lordes Reparations of Wrefill to ingroice up clerre the Booke of my Lordes Werkes at Topclif donne in the Weike befoire.

ITEM The faid Clerke of my Lordes Werkes at Topclif afoir he bring his Booke to my Lorde to correcke ' Shall ' know his Lordfhip pleafur who his Lordfhip wol have to fitt by him at the correking of his faid Reperacions.

ITEM That the faid Clerke o'th' Werkes at Topclif fhall every Satterday wekely after my Lord haith correcte his Weike of his Booke of his Lordfhip Werkes at Topclif Know my Lord pleafur whoe his Lordfhip woll apointe to be by at the Payment of the Money of the Werks of the faid Weike To fe that the Perfons which fhal be paied be truely paied.

ITEM That the Clerke o'the Werkes at Topclif fhall every Satterday wekely totall the Some at th'ende of the Weike What the houl Some of the faide Weke comes to And to divide what is paied of it and what is refpectid.

ITEM The faid Clerke of the Werkes at Topclif fhall every Satterday wekely after he haith correctie his Weike with my Lord rede unto my Lorde the Parcells of the Remanyth remanyng as well of Stuf boughte as of Stuf
favid

favid of old Werkes which my Lord alteris or mendes
That my Lord may fe that it be truely enterid wekely
that which remaynes.

TH'ORDOUR of the HEADE OFFICERS or any oithur which ftandes chargid alon or with any oithur jointely With the CHERGE of the HOULSHOULD YEIRLY.

FURST He that ftandes chargid with the Houfe 'to' have
Leafour dailly from v o'th cloike at morow to vij o'th cloike
As well for feing the Larder ordert for ftriking owt of the
Service for the houlle day As for the fetting o'th Clerkes
o'th Countinhoufe in ordour what they fhall be occupied
with for the houlle day followinge.

ITEM That he that ftandes chargid with the houfe be dailly
at the Dreffour or ells the Clerke Comptrollour for to fe
the Service at the Dreffour fervid that their be no Bribing
at the faid Dreffour of the Service.

ITEM He that ftands chargid with my Lordes Houfe to be
dailly at the Countinghoufe at the houris following Furft
every Mornyng at vj o'th clocke to fett the Clerks at Werke
And alfo at every aftir-noon and at On o'th' Clocke to fe the
Brekefaftis and Dynner breivd Ande every Night inmediate
at After Souper to keape the Countinghoufe for Breving of
Drinkingis Souper-Leverres Fewell and Hoifemeate To keape
the faid Countinghoufe for thies caufes unto the houre at viij^th
o'th Cloike o'th night that Leveres be fervid And that the
Booke be caft up the faid night or the Clerkes goo to bed of
the Raite of th'Expenffis for that day.

ITEM

ITEM He that ſtandes chargid with my Lordes Houſe to have Leaſour every Satterday all the day wekely through owt the Yeir to keape the Countinghouſe for peruſing over the Necantours Braſiauntoures and Furniountoures of the Weke bipaſt And to peruſe over the Caitoures Parcells to ſe if they be enterd and keapte And wheither the Prices be reaſonable or not That they may correcke the Caitour Parcells if ned be And alſo to ſe what Proviſion ſhall ned to be maide in the Weke following.

ITEM He that ſtandes Chargid with my Lordes Houſe to have On Day clere owt at th'ende of every Monith throughe owt the Yeire to caiſte up the Houll Monith bipaſt cailled the Pie of th'Ependuntur of the Monith To ſe how it ſtandes And to ſett owt the Parcells with the Prices of the Difficens of every Office ſingulerly by it ſelve in a Booke that my Lord may ſe it What Difficiens every Office rynnes in every Monith And wherin And in what Parcells.

ITEM He that ſtandes chargid with my Lordes houſe for the houll Yeir if he may poſſible Shall be at all Faires wheir the Groice Empcions ſhal be boughte for the houſe for the houlle Yeire As Wyne Wax Beiffes Multons Wheite and Maltie And if he may not Thanne to apointe the Clerke Comptroillor with ſuch oithur Perſons as he thinkis good To go to the ſaid Faires for bying of the forſaid Groice Empcions.

TH'ARTICLES

TH'ARTICLES for the CLERKE COMP-TROILLER.

FURSTE The Clerke Comptroillour fhall every day caille upponne the Clerkes o'th Countinghoufe after iiij be ftrei-kynne o'th cloike And to fett the faid Clerkes in hand with their Bookes As to fey the Secound Clerke o'th Kechynne for maiking up the Booke of Raiting of Mealis dailly The Clerke o'th Spicery to goo in hande with th'Empcion Booke dailly The Clerke o'th Brevementes to goo in hande with the Ingroffing the Booke of the Raiting of Mealis dailly And the Clerke Avener to breive the Leveries of Horfmeate and Fewell.

ITEM The faid Clerks Comptroiller fhall every Mornyng caill up the Cooks after iiij o'th cloike 'be' ftreikenne.

ITEM The faid Clerke Comptroillour fhall every mornyng at v o'th cloike taike the Key of the Lardour owt of the Countinghoufe with him And to go into the Lardour And to caill the Cookes to him And to ftrike owt the Meaffes which fhal be apointid to be fpende for that day.

ITEM The Clerke Comptroillour fhall fe noo Keys of noo Offices which is broughte upp into the Countinghoufe over the night delivert on the morow to viij o'th cloike dailly that the houre is apointid to ferve Brekefaftes.

ITEM The faid Clerke Comptroillour fhall every day fe the Caitour Parcells enterid bitwixt the houres of vij and viij^th o'th cloike And that he fuffer not the Caitour to enter noo
Parcells

Parcells but that he knowes furely he dede bring in And to fe the faid Parcells him felve examonid or he fuffer theim to be enterid into the Jornall Booke And alfo that he fuffer not th'Officers to have noo Keyes delivert theim to they ferve the Brekefaftis.

ITEM The faid Clerke Comptroillour fhall dailly caille for the Keyes of th'Officers into the Countinghoufe at thies Houres following Viz. ixth 'oth' cloke After Brekefaft be donne Inmediate after the Latter Dynner be donne At iij o'th cloike at After-Drinkingis be donne And alfo every ninght inmedeately at After-Souper Alfo every night after Liveres be fervid.

ITEM The faid Clerke Coumptroillour to be dailly at the Dreffour to fe the Service fervid from the Dreffour Bicaufe of Bribing of fervice at the Dreaffour. Viz. Bitwixt viijth and ixth o'th cloike in the mornyng to fe the Brekefaftis fervid Bitwixt x and xjth o'th cloike on th'Etting Daies And bitwixt xjth and xijth of the Fafting Daies to fe the Dynner fervid And bitwixt iiij and v o'th cloike at after Dynner to fe the Souper fervid.

ITEM The faid Clerke Coumptroller every 'day' in the mornynge afoire Brekefaft and an oithir houre To ftudy And every after noon afoir Drinkingis perufe over in the Booke of Ordoures of the Houfe As well th'Articles of the Houres Dais Weikes Monithes and Quarters by | he fhall fe theim obfervid according to th'Ordours in the faid Booke.

ITEM The faid Clerke Coumptrollour fhall at every Baiking be in the Bachoufe And to fe the Breid weaid that it keape the weight according to the faid ftinte in the faid Booke 'of' Ordours.

G g g   ITEM

ITEM That the faid Clerke Coumptroillour fhall fe dailly the Necantoures Braffiauntoures and Furneuntours truely enterd in the Jornall Booke befoir him felve by the Clerke o'th Brevements And to fe the Tail writynne upponne.

ITEM That the Clerke Comptroillour fhall dailly have an Ey to the Slaighter Hous at all tymes whenne any Viaundes fhall be flaine their | And their to fe the Suette clynne taikynne owt withoute any Bribe And their weaid and brought into the Storhoufe belonging the Countinghoufe and from thens by the Clerks delivert to the Chaundler be weighte from tyme to tyme at he fhall occupie it And alfo that he fe the Slaighter Manne maike the Vaillis noo larger thanne he oughte to doo.

THE END.

N O T E S

O N
THE PRECEDING
H O U S H O L D   B O O K.

N O T E S.

Page 2.

" **REMANETH.**"] This is a Corruption of the Lat. Word *Remanet*, being the account of all such Stuff as remains unspent, (See p. 15.) Such an account is still intitled the *Remanet*, in our College Books in the Universities. See also p. 65.

Ibid.

" Stots and Whies."] A STOT is the name still used in Yorkshire for a young Ox or Bullock : A WHIE that of a young Heifer that has never had a Calf, called in Scotland a Quhey.

Ibid.

" Seftrons," are Cisterns.

Page 3.

" Wax wrought in Quarions."] A Quarion was a square lump of Wax with a wick in the center: Round Lumps of the same are still used in the Royal Nursery under the name of Mortises.

Page 6.

" Gafcoin Wine, viz. Red Wine—White Wine—Claret Wine."] " The CLARET Wine was what the Gafcoigns call at present *Vin Clairet*, being a pale red Wine, as distinguished from the deeper Reds ; and was the produce of a district near Bourdeaux called *Graves :* whence the English in ancient times fetched the Wine they called CLARET, and concerning which many very particular regulations may be found in the old *Chronique de Bordeaux.*

The

The RED Wine mentioned above was the coarfe red Wine, the growth of what they call the *Palus* or deep low clayey Countries; of which there is a great diſtrict near Bourdeaux, that ſtill produces this fort of Wine.

The WHITE Wine was probably what we now call *Vin de Graves* and *Priniac*, both of them the produce of that Country, which was generally called Gaſcony by the Engliſh; who antiently applied this name to all that part of Fance, which ſtretches away from the Loire to the Pyrennean Mountains."

This account is communicated by a gentleman of diſtinction, who long reſided at Bourdeaux, and had particularly ſtudied this ſubject.

Page 11.

" Hops for Brewing."] This ſeems to contradict the old received account, that HOPS and HERESY came into England both in the ſame reign: See Baker's Chronicle, among the Caſualties of Henry the VIIIth's Reign, viz.

" About the 15th of Henry VIII. it happened that diverſe
" things were newly brought into England, whereupon this
" Rhime was made,

" Turkies, Carps, Hoppes, Piccarell and Beere,
" Came into England all in one year."

This perhaps may relate only to the Cultivation of HOPS, when they were firſt planted in England, tho' the produce might be imported before from Flanders.

The " BREWING OF BEER" however is the ſubject of an intire Section in this book, vid. Sect. XXII. p. 137.—but it is obſervable that TURKIES are not once mentioned among the Fowls to be provided for the Table. See Sect. XIX, &c.

Page 19.

" Granes" are probably what are now called " Granes of
" Paradiſe."

"Paradife," fmall pungent feeds brought from the Eaft Indies, much refembling Cardamum feeds in appearance, but in properties approaching nearer to Pepper. See Lewis's Materia Medica, p. 298.

"Saunders." This fragrant wood, brought from the Eaft Indies, was principally ufed for colouring the confections red: as "Saffron" was for tinging them yellow. See Lewis, p. 517.

"Gallinga," Lat. *Galanga*, is the root of a graffy-leaved plant brought from the Eaft Indies,. of an aromatic fmell, and hot biting bitterifh Tafte, anciently ufed among other Spices, but now almoft laid afide. See Lewis, p. 286.

Page 41.

"Yoman Cook for the Mouth."—"Grome 'Cook' for "the mouth."] Thefe two attended hourly in the Kitchen at the "*Haiftry*," i. e. the Fire Place (ftill called the "*Haifter*" in Shropfhire,) to fee to the roafting of the Meat ufed at Breakfaft and other Meals, (fee page 325, 326.) Thefe and moft of the other Titles of Office which occur in this book, ftill are, or were very lately, kept up in the Royal Houfhold.

Page 42.

"A Taberett—a Luyte—and a Rebece."] The TABRET, or Tabour, and the LUTE need no explanation. The REBECK was a kind of Fiddle confifting of three Strings.

Page 60.

"Liveries," are things 'livered, i. e. delivered out.

Ibid.

"Taillis of the Furniunturs" (fo it fhould have been printed.] The Taill and Swatch are I fuppofe the Tally and its Counterpart.—"Furniuntur," corrupt for *Furniantur*, is

the

the account of things Baked, from the barbarous Latin Word *Furniare*, to Bake.

" Brasianturs" is the account of the Liquors Brewed from the Barb. Lat. *Brasiare*, to Brew.

" Necanturs" is the account of the Slaughter-house, from Lat. *Necare*.

Anciently all Houshold Accounts were kept in Latin, as they still are in our Colleges in the Universities, and the above Latin Words became a sort of Technical Terms for the heads of the several Accounts.

Page 65.

" Expenduntur" is the Account of the Things expended.

" The Pye of the Expenduntur" was the Sum Total of the Expences, as they still say in some of the Colleges, *In Pede Computi*. We have the Word, PYE, tho' used in a somewhat different sense, yet manifestly proceeding from the same Derivation, in the Title of the " Court of Pye-powders."

Page 68.

" St. Elyn Day," was I suppose what is called in the Roman Kalender *Dies Helenæ reginæ*, which is the 21st of May.

Page 80.

" Scamlynge Days in Lent."] These are elsewhere (p. 85.) called " Scamblynge Days," and (p. 57.) " Scam-" lyngs." Our present Word ' Scrambling' was anciently written SCAMBLING : so that Scambling Days in Lent, were Days when no regular Meals were provided, but every one scrambled and shifted for himself as he could.

So Shakespear in his Play of Henry Vth. Act. I. Sc. I. in the old original Editions, speaks of

" the scambling and unquiet time."

which

which modern Editors have altered to ' Scrambling.' See Johnson's Dictionary, and, the Glossary to the Oxford Edition of Shakespeare (2d Impression, 1771.)

Ibid.

" Reversion," is what is left at Table, (see page 362.) The " Pantler" was the Officer who presided over the Pantry: as the " Butler" over the Buttery: and the " Haistiller" over the Haistery, see above, p. 415.

Page 81.

" My Lady's Chamberer."] The CHAMBERER was a Female Attendant, being included under the Title above of " My Lady's Gentlewomen ;" besides the Officer, who attended my Lord in his Bedchamber, is called his CHAMBERLAIN, see page 85. It is a corruption of the French *Chambriere*, a Chambermaid. See Cotgrave's Diction.

Page 85.

" The Ewery" was the Office where the Ewers were kept. Our Ancestors always washed before and after dinner, as they used no Forks. This custom of Washing in form out of a Silver Ewer, is still kept up on solemn days in some of the Colleges in our Universities.

The use of FORKS at Table, did not prevail in England till the reign of James Ist. as we learn from a remarkable Passage in Coryat: the insertion of which may be pardoned, among the petty Collections here raked together. The Reader will laugh at the solemn Manner in which this important discovery or innovation, is related.

" Here I will mention a thing that might have been spoken
" of before in discourse of the first Italian towne. I ob-
" serve'd a custom in all those Italian Cities and Townes
" through the which I passed, that is not used in any other

" country

" country that I faw in my travels, neither do I thinke that
" any other nation of Chriftendome doth ufe it, but only
" Italy. The Italian and alfo moft Strangers that are com-
" morant in Italy, doe always at their meals ufe a LITTLE
" FORKE when they cut their meat. For while with their
" Knife, which they hold in one hand, they cut the meate out
" of the difh, they faften the Fork which they hold in their
" other hand upon the fame difh, fo that whatfoever he be
" that fitting in the company of any others at meale, fhould
" unadvifedly touch the difh of meat with his fingers from
" which all at the table doe cut, he will give occafion of
" offence unto the company as having tranfgreffed the lawes
" of good manners, in fo much that for his error he fhall
" be at the leaft brow-beaten, if not reprehended in wordes.
" This form of feeding I underftand is generally ufed in all
" places of Italy, their Forks being for the moft part made of
" yronn, fteele, and fome of filver, but thofe are ufed only
" by Gentlemen. The reafon of this their curiofity is, be-
" caufe the Italian cannot by any means indure to have his
" difh touched with fingers, feeing all mens fingers are not
" alike cleane. Hereupon I myfelf thought good to imitate
" the Italian fafhion by this forked cutting of meate, not
" only while I was in Italy, but alfo in Germany, and of-
" tentimes in England fince I came home : being once quip-
" ped for that frequent ufing of my Forke, by a certain
" learned Gentleman, a familiar friend of mine, Mr. Law-
" rence Whitaker; who in his merry humour doubted not
" to call me at table *Furcifer*, only for ufing a Forke at feed-
" ing, but for no other caufe."

Coryat's Crudities, p. 90, 91. 4to, London 1611.
Even when Heylin publifhed his Cofmography, (1652)
Forks were ftill a Novelty, fee his 3d book, where having
fpoke of the Ivory Sticks ufed by the Chinefe, he adds, " The
" ufe of Silver FORKS with us, by fome of our fpruce Gal-
" lants

" lants taken up OF LATE, came from hence into Italy, and
" from thence into England."

Page 100.

" Reveſtry" from the French *Reveſtir*, contractedly writ
VESTRY, as in page 389.

Page 103.

" My Lord's Boord-end."] In the Houſes of our ancient
Nobility they dined at long Tables. The Lord and his principal Gueſts ſate at the upper end of the firſt Table, in the
Great Chamber, which was therefore called the Lord's BOARD-
END. The Officers of his houſhold, and inferior Gueſts, at
long Tables below in the Hall. In the middle of each Table
ſtood a great Salt Seller, and as particular care was taken to
place the Gueſts according to their rank, it became a mark
of diſtinction whether a perſon ſate above or below the Salt.

This and the following Section, which relate to the Order
of ſerving up the Victuals, will be much illuſtrated by the
following ſhort Memoirs communicated to the Editor.

I.

" An Account how the EARL of WORCESTER lived at Rag-
" land Caſtle, before the Civil Wars [begun in 1641."]

" AT eleven o'clock the Caſtle Gates were ſhut, and the
" Tables laid; Two in the Dining-Room; Three in the Hall;
" One in Mrs. Watſon's Appartment, where the Chaplains
" eat, (Sir Toby Matthews * being the firſt;) Two in the
" Houſe-keeper's Room, for the ladies Women.

H h h 2 " The

---

* This was probably the noted Sir Toby Matthews, enumerated
among Mr. Walpole's Painters, who wrote the famous Character of
Lucy Percy, Counteſs of Carliſle, printed by Fenton in his Notes on
Waller's Poems. He was Son of an Archbiſhop of York, but turn-
ing Papiſt had probably accepted the Place of Chaplain in this great
Earl's Family, who was a Roman Catholick.

" The Earl came into the Dining-Room, attended by his
" Gentlemen. As foon as he was feated, Sir Ralph Black-
" ftone Steward of the Houfe retired. The Comptroller Mr.
" Holland attended with his Staff: As did the Sewer Mr.
" Blackburn; the Daily Waiters, Mr. Clough, Mr. Selby
" and Mr. Scudamore; with many Gentlemen's Sons, from
" two to feven hundred Pound a Year bred up in the Caftle;
" my Lady's Gentleman–Ufher Mr. Harcourt; my Lord's
" Gentlemen of the Chamber, Mr. Morgan, and Mr. Fox.

" At the FIRST TABLE fate the noble Family, and fuch
" of the Nobility as came there.

" At the SECOND TABLE in the Dining-Room, fate
" Knights and honourable Gentlemen, attended by Footmen.

" In the HALL, at the FIRST TABLE fate,
" Sir Ralph Blackftone, Steward.—The Comptroller, Mr.
" Holland.—The Secretary.—The Mafter of the Horfe, Mr.
" Delawar.—The Mafter of the Fifh-ponds, Mr. Andrews.
" —My Lord Herbert's Preceptor, Mr. Adams.—With fuch
" Gentlemen as came there under the degree of a Knight;
" attended by Footmen, and plentifully ferved with Wine.

" At the SECOND TABLE in the HALL (ferved from My
" Lord's Table, and with other hot meat) fate
" The Sewer, with the Gentlemen Waiters, and Pages,
" to the Number of twenty-four.

" At the THIRD TABLE in the HALL, fate
" The Clerk of the Kitchen, with the Yeomen Officers of
" the Houfe, * two Grooms of the Chambers, &c.

[Other OFFICERS of the HOUSHOLD †, were]
" Chief Auditor, Mr. Smith.—Clerk of the Accounts,
George

---

* I know not whether this Article fhould come in above or below the enfuing Title. † fc. which, tho' included in the above
Account, are not there particularly enumerated.

" George Wharton.—Purveyor of the Caftle, Mr. Salifbury.
" —Uſhers of the Hall, Mr. Moyle and Mr. Cooke.—Clofett-
" keeper.—Gentleman of the Chapel, Mr. Davies.—Keeper
" of the Records.—Maſter of the Wardrobe.—Maſter of the
" Armoury.—Maſter Groom of the Stable, for the War-
" horſes 12.—Maſter of the Hounds.—Maſter Falconer.—
" Porter and his Man.

" Two Butchers.—Two Keepers of the Home Park.—
" Two Keepers of the Red-deer Park.

" Footmen, Grooms, and other menial Servants to the
" Number of 150. Some of the Footmen were Brewers and
" Bakers.

" OUT-OFFICES.

" Steward of Ragland, William Jones, Efq.—The Go-
" vernor of Chepſtow-Caftle, Sir Nicholas Kemeys, Bart.—
" Houſe-keeper of Worceſter Houſe in London, James Red-
" man, Efq.

" Bailiffs, thirteen.

" Two Councel for the Bailiffs to have recourfe to.

" Sollicitor, Mr. John Smith."

What follows may be confidered, as a fomewhat later
eftabliſhment, being the Orders of that Lord Fairfax, who
had been General of the Parliament Forces.

II.

LORD FAIRFAX's ORDERS for the Servants of his Houſhold
[after the Civil Wars.]

" ORDER for the Houſe Remembrance for SERVANTS.

" That all the Servants be ready upon the Terras at ſuch
" tymes as the Strangers do come, to attend their alight-
" inge.

" PRAYERS.

" That one of the Chapel Bells be rung before the Prayers
" one

" one quarter of an hour; at which Summons the Butler
" muſt prepare for Coveringe, but not Cover.

" PORTER.

" When Prayers ſhall beginne (or a very little before) the
" Gates on all ſides muſt be ſhutt and locked, and the Porter
" muſt come into Prayers with all the Keyes; and after Service
" is done, the Gate muſt be opened until the Uſher warne to
" the Dreſſer.

" BUTLER.

" The Buttler with the Yeoman of the Chamber, or ſome
" other Yeoman muſt go to Cover. The Prayers done,
" Formes and Cuſſins, where the Ladyes and the reſt did ſit,
" muſt be removed.

" SERVANTS after SUPPER.

" After Supper (I mean of the Servants) they muſt pre-
" ſently repaire into the Dyning Chamber, and there remove
" Stooles, ſee what other things be neceſſary, and attende fur-
" ther directions until Liveryes be ſerved, which they muſt be
" ready for upon the Warninge; and in the meane tyme let the
" Buttler (with one to helpe him) make them ready, And let
" not theſe Servants depart until the beſt ſort of Strangers
" have taken their Lodgings; And the Porter muſt locke the
" Doores and keep the Keys.

" MORNING.

" Let the Servants attend by ſeaven of the Clock in the
" morning in the Hall.

" BREAKFASTS.

" The Clerk of the Kitchen muſt appoynt the Cooks, what
" muſt be for Breakfaſts for the Ladyes in their Chambers, and
" likewiſe for the Gentlemen in the Hall or Parlour, which
" muſt

" muft be ferved by eight of the Clock in the Morninge and
" not after.

" Dinner muft be ready by Eleven of the Clock, Prayers
" after Tenne, and the Orders obferved as is before faid.

" The HALL.

" The Great Chamber being ferved, the Steward and
" Chaplaine muft fit down in the Hall, and call unto them
" the Gentlemen if there be any unplaced above, and then the
" Servants of the Strangers as their Mafters be in Degree.

" The USHER's words of DIRECTIONS.

" Firft when they go to Cover, Hee muft go before them
" through the Hall, crying " By your leaves Gentlemen,
" ftand by."

" The Coveringe done He muft fay " Gentlemen and Yeo-
" men for Plate."

" Then he muft warn to the Dreffer, " Gentlemen and
" Yeomen to Dreffer."

" And he muft attend the Meat going through the Hall,
" crying " By your leaves, my Mafters." Likewife he muft
" warn for the Second Courfe, and attend it as aforefaid.

" If Bread or Beere be wanting on the Hall Table, he muft
" call aloud at the Barre " Bread or Beere for the Hall."

" If any unworthy Fellow do unmannerly fett himfelf down
" before his Betters, he muft take him up and place him lower.

" For the CHAMBER.

" Let the beft fafhioned, and apparelled Servants attend
" above the Salte, the Reft belowe.

" If one Servant have occafion to fpeake to another about
" Service att the Table, let him whifper, for noyfe is uncivil.

" If any Servant have occafion to go forth of the Chamber
" for any thing, let him make hafte and fee that no more
" than

" than twoe be abfent.   And for prevention of Errands, let all
" Sauces be ready at the Door ; for even one meffe of Muftard
" will take a Man's attendance from the Table : but leaft
" any thing happen unexpected, let the Boy ftand within
" the Chamber Door for Errants.   And fee that your Water
" and Voyder be ready foe foon as Meate is ferved and fett
" on the Table without.   Have a good eye to the Board for
" empty Difhes and placing of others, And let not the Board
" be unfurnifhed.

" The Cup Board.

" Let no man fill Beere or Wine but the Cup-board Keeper,
" who muft make choice of his Glaffes or Cups for the
" Company, and not ferve them hand over heade.   He muft
" alfo know which be for Beere and which for Wine ; for
" it were a foul thing to mix them together.
" Once againe let me admonifh Silence, for it is the greateft
" part of Civility.
" Let him which doth order the Table be the laft Man
" in it [fc. the Room,] to fee that nothing be left behind that
" fhould be taken away.
" Many things I cannot remember which I refer to your
" good care, otherwife I fhould feeme to write a Booke
" hereof."

Page 104, 105, &c.

In looking over the Lift of Birds and Fowls which are
enumerated in this XIXth Section, it may not be improper to
obferve, that

Cranes, are now judged to have forfaken this Ifland.   (See
Mr. Penant's Britifh Zoology) but they were then almoft as
common as the Heron or Heron-few.

Wypes, are what are now more generally called Lapwings.
Wipa is ftill the Swedifh Name.   Ibid.

Stints,

Stints, are Birds, that frequent the banks of rivers, and sea-shores in Winter. They are described under the name of Purre in the British Zoology, Vol. II. p. 374.

The Redshanks, the Bytters or Bitterns, the Reys (or Ruffs and Reeves) the Sholards or Shovelers, Knots, &c. are all well known, or may be found described in the above Book.

The Tern, is the Sea-swallow, Ibid. By Great Birds was probably meant, Fieldfare, Thrush, &c. by Small Birds Sparrows, Larks, &c.

In the List of Birds here served up to Table, are many Fowls, which are now discarded as little better than rank Carrion.

Page 109.

" Carre of Arom."] A CARR is a Word still used in the North, for swampy ground full of tufts of Rushes, &c. and intermixed with small pools of Water.

Page 110.

" As ye woll exchewe that at my ensewe," &c.] i. e. As ye will avoid that which may befall you: Escape the Consequences, &c. The Royal Stile here is remarkable.

Page 114.

By way of supplement to the Warrants for Deer, given in this and the preceeding pages, may not improperly be subjoined from an ancient Inquisition,

" An ACCOUNT of all the DEER in the Parks and Forests
" in the North belonging to the EARL of NORTHUMBER-
" LAND, taken in the 4th Year of Henry VIII. Anno 1512.

" In NORTHUMBERLAND.

" Huln Park	—	Fallow-Deer	879
" Cawledge Park	—	Ditto	586
" Warkworth Park	—	Ditto	150

I i i   " Acklington

" Acklington Park	—	Ditto	144
" Rothbury Foreft	—	Red-Deer	153

" In YORKSHIRE.

" Topcliff Great Park	—	Fallow-Deer	558
" Topcliff Little Park	—	Ditto	291
" Syofforth Park	—	Ditto	180
" Spofforth Wood	—	Ditto	43
" Wreffel Park	—	{ Red Deer 42 } { Fallow 92 }	135
" Wreffel Litle Park	—	Fallow	37
" Newfham Park	—	Ditto	324
" Leckinfield Park	—	Ditto	249
" Catton Park	—	Ditto	79

" In CUMBERLAND.

" Langftrothdale Park	—	Red and Fallow	456
" Adylthorp Park	—	Ditto	307
" Ditto Old Park	—	Ditto	205
" Helaugh Park	—	Ditto	319
" Wafdale	—	Red Deer	230
" Ditto	—	Fallow	21
" Weft-Ward	—	Fallow-Deer	225

Total of Deer   5571

exclufive of thofe in SUSSEX and other Counties in the South.

Page 116.

" The ftriking out of Meffes."] This is a cuftom ftill kept up in fome of our Colleges, where the Cook cuts out a piece of meat for four Perfons, to divide as they pleafe among themfelves, who are faid to MESS together.

Page 119.

" Hors greffing."] i. e. Grazing, or turning out to Grafs. Not Greafing in the modern fenfe.

Page

Page 128.

Th' officers necks of houfhold,"] So it is in the MS. but evidently a miſtake of the Tranſcriber for " Weeks of " Houfhold," ſee below, p. 167, 168.

Page 136.

" Habberdyn-Fiſh,"] (See alſo p. 179.) This is the Northern Term for Barrelled Cod, (vid. Willoughby, 166,) ſo called from Aberdeen, anciently famous for curing this kind of Fiſh.

Page 145.

" Waigeth," is here uſed for Wages (v. p. 149. 189.) So before in Page 118. " Cauſeth" for Cauſes.

Page 162.

" OR it be entered :" i. e. BEFORE it be entered. OR in old Engliſh ſignified BEFORE, as it does ſtill in Shropſhire, where it is pronounced ORE. So in Shakefpeare's Kg. John, Act 4. ſc. 5.

" Twill be,
" Two long days journey, Lords, OR E'ER we meet."
that is, ' before ever we meet.'

So again in the old Tragedy of " M. Arden of Feverſham, " 1529." 4to. the Wife ſays,

" He ſhall be murdered OR [i. e. before] the Gueſts " come in." Sign. H. 3.

The Phraſe OR E'ER is not rightly underſtood by ſuch as imagine E'ER here ſignifies " before," or is the ſame as ERE : E'ER is merely the contraction of EVER, and is barely augmentative; it is the Word OR or ORE which ſignifies " before," and is ſynonymous to ERE. *Veteres Angli* ER *et* OR *fine Diſcrimine ſcribebant*; ſays Lye in Junii Etymol. ad verb. ERE.

Page 188.

" Bere muſt be made Bigger in Somer thann in Winter for

Iii 2 " Turn-

"Turninge," (fo it is here in MS. as in page 134, not "Tunninge" which is an Erratum.) i. e. the Beer fhould be made ftronger in fummer than Winter to prevent its turning four. BIG is alfo the name of a fpecies of Barley, of which the Malt might poffibly be made; and then BIGGER may mean more impregnated with BIG.

Page 207.

"Warrants to be fervide out."] SERVIDE is an Erratum; the MS. has SEWIDE. To SEW or SUE out a Warrant was the ancient proper Phrafe : from the Fr. *fuivir*.

Page 220.

"WILLIAM WORME, my Cofferer and General Receyvour, &c."] This WILLIAM WORM, who is here invefted with fuch great Trufts, and whofe name occurs before fo familiarly, as to be ufed inftead of his Office, (vid. p. 56.) continued to be employed under the fixth Earl of Northumberland, when he had the ftill more important Poft of that Earl's Treafurer; at length he fell under a fufpicion of treachery, and of betraying his Mafter to Cardinal Wolfey, who appears to have treated that young Lord in a very arbitrary and imperious manner. I have now before me a Series of Letters writ by this fixth Earl of Northumberland (Son of the Author of our Houfhold Book); in one of which he mentions a very particular inftance of the Cardinal's tyranny, in feizing upon the furniture of his Father's Chapel, particularly the fine Service Books, and applying them to his own ufe. As this Letter gives us a curious Picture of the Manners, as well as Literature of our firft Nobility at that time, I fhall here infert a great part of it; and that the rather, as it is a full vindication of this Earl of Northumberland from the Charge of Ingratitude, in being the perfon employed to arreft the Cardinal at his Caftle of Cawood. He had been placed under

the

the Cardinal's Roof by his Father, among other young Noblemen, who accepted of menial Offices under that proud Prelate; but it plainly appears from these Letters, that he had been treated with so much harshness and contempt, as to be under no great obligation to him on that account. In a former Letter he tells his friend, that the Cardinal had wrote to forbid him attending the Funeral of his own Father to Beverly, and had treated him with many other Indignities.

These Letters are written soon after that Earl's Death in 1527, and are directed " To his beloved Cousyn Thomas Arundel, " one of the Gentlemen of my Lord Legates Prevey Cham- " bre," whom he addresses with the familiar Appellation of " Bedfellow" as a term of Endearment: Which however strange it may appear now, was consistent with the stile of manners in the middle ages: Holingshed in his Chronicle, tells us of that Lord Scrope, who was one of the Conspirators against K. Henry V. " The said Lord Scroope was in such " favour with the King, that he admitted him sometime to " be his BEDFELLOW; in whose fidelity the King reposed " [much] Trust," &c. Vid. Vol. 3. sub. Ann. 1415.

✝

" Bedfellow, After my most harté recomendacion: Thys " Monday the iiid off August I resevyd by my Servaunt, Letters " from yow beryng datt the xxth day off July, deliveryd unto " hym the sayme day at the Kyngs town of Newcastell; wher " in I do perseayff my Lord Cardenalls pleasour ys to have " such Boks as was in the Chapell of my lat lord and ffayther " (wos soll Jhu pardon) To the accomplyshement of which at " your desyer I am confformable, notwithstanding I trust to be " able ons to set up a Chapel off myne owne. But I pray " God he may look better upon me than he doth. But me " thynk I have lost very moch, ponderyng yt ys no better " regardyd; the occasion wher off he shall persayff.

" Fyrst,

" Fyrſt, the long lyeng off my Treſſorer * ; with Hys very
" haſty and unkynd words unto hym, not on my parte deſ-
" ſerved.

" Alſo the news off Mr. Manyng, the which ys blon obroud
" over all Yorkſher ; that neyther by the Kyng †, nor by my
" Lord Cardenall I am regardyd : And that he wyll tell me at
" my metyng with hym, when I come unto Yorkſher ;
" which ſhall be within thys month, God wyllyng : but I ffer
" [fear] my words to Mr. Manyng ſhall deſpleas my Lord ;
" ffor I will be no Ward.

" Alſo, Bedfellow, the payns I tayk and have taykyn ſens
" my comyng hether, are not better regardyd ; but by a
" ffateryng Byſhope off Carell [Carliſle] and that fals
" WORM ‡ ſhall be broth [brought] to the meſſery and
" carffulneſs that I am in ; and in ſuch ſlanders, that now and
" my lord Cardenall wold, he can not bryng me howth [out]
" theroff.

* * * *

" I ſhall with all ſped ſend up your Lettrs. with the Books
" unto my Lords Grace, as to ſay iiij Anteſſonars §, ſuch as
" I thynk wher nat ſeen a gret wyll ; v Gralls ; an Ordeorly ;
" a . Manuall ; viij^th Proſſeſſioners. And ffor all the reſſidew,
" they not worth the ſending, nor ever was occupyed in my
" Lords Chapel. And alſo I ſhall wryt at this tyme, as ye
" have wyllyd me.

" Yff my Lords Grace wyll be ſo good Lord unto me as to
" gyff me Lychens [Lycence] to put Wyll^m WORME with-
" in a Caſtell of myn off Anwyk in aſſurty, unto the tyme
" he have accomptyd ffor more money rec^d than ever I rec^d,
" I ſhall gyff hys Grace ij C.^li and a . Benyſſis off a C. worth
unto

* That is, his long continuance with the Cardinal. † He had
probably diſobliged the King, by his attachment to Anne BULLEN.
‡ Willm. WORME, whom he mentions in a former Letter, as the
Perſon who betrayed him. § See below, Note to p. 387.

" unto his Colleyg *, with such other thyngs refferved as his
" [Grace] shall defyre ; but unto such tyme as myne Awdytore
" hayth takyn accompt off him : Wher in good Bedfel-
" low do your beft, ffor els he shall put us to fend myfelff, as
" at owr metying I shall show yow.

" And alfo gyff fecuer credens unto this Berer, whom I
" affur yow I have ffonddon a marvellous honeft man, as ever
" I ffownd in my lyff. In haft at my Moneftary off Hul-
" Park the iij^d day of Auguft. In the owne hand off

" Yours ever affured

" H. Northumberland."

" To my bedfellow
" Arundell."

I know not whether the above offer was accepted, or the
faid William WORME committed to durance in Alnwick
Caftle : but there is a tradition in the place, that an Auditor
was formerly confined in the Dungeon under one of the
Towers, till he could make up his Accounts to his Lord's
Satisfaction.

Page 330.

It is perhaps needlefs to obferve that " Yeven," or Yoven,"
was anciently ufed for " Given :" fo " Yef," in p. 291.
for " Give," and " Yates" for Gates," &c. " Leck" in
this page is evidently a contraction for Leckinfield.

Page 243.

The ALB was an ancient linen Garment worn at the ad-
miniftration of the Communion, but differed from the Surplice, in being made to fit the body clofe like a Caffock, with
clofe fleeves, and tyed round the middle with a girdle or fafh.
It was fometimes embroidered with various colours and adorned with Fringes. See Wheatly on the Com. Prayer. pag.
107.

It

* fc. the College, which Wolfey had then newly founded at Oxford, originally " Cardinal College," now " Chrift Church."

It seems also to be used here for the fine Linen Cloth, employed the Altar.

Page 254.

"Haunsmen," or "Hanshmen," (more frequently written "Henchmen" or "Henxmen") was the old English Name for the Pages, so called from their standing at their Lords HAUNCH or side. The Earl of Northumberland had three young Gentlemen who attended him in this capacity, (p. 344.) and are classed along with his Wards, &c. (p. 355.) and next to his own Sons (vid. p. 361.)

Ibid.

"Aumer," i. e. Almoner (vid. p. 44.) This sort of contraction is familiar in our Language; so the Ambry in Westminster is corrupted from Almonary, Eleemosunary.—It is not easy to account why the name of "Under-Almoner" should be given to the Servant, who supplied the Grooms of the Chamber with wood (vid. p. 45. 255.)

Ibid.

The PISTOLER was the Clark, who read the Epistle: The GOSPELLER or Priest who read the Gospel, is mentioned above, see also page 44.

Page 292.

The "Dormount Book," and "Wering-Book," were Books wherein the Accounts of the Linnen (vid. p. 349) and perhaps all other sorts of Cloth, Stuffs, &c. (see p. 346.) and Wardrobe Accounts were entered. The WERING BOOK probably contained Entries of all such parcels of Linen, &c. as were in actual Wear: The DORMOUNT BOOK, of such as were laid up and not in present Use.

The Year, as to Houshold Affairs, ended at Michaelmas: Of this Mode of computation, a relique is still preserved in the Custom of Hiring Servants at Michaelmas in the Midland Counties.

Page

Page 302.

" The Clark Avenar," was the Clark who kept account of the Oats and Corn ufed in the Stables, &c. Lat. *Avena*, (fee p. 307.) One of the Towers in the outward Court at Alnwick Caftle is ftill called the AVENAR's TOWER.

Ibid.

BROACHES are Spits ; " a child for the Broches," was a boy to turn the Spits. To BROCHE is to fpit, or run through ; hence the fame verb is applied to a hogfhead or veffel of wine, &c. fee page 58. where it is ordered that Vinegar be made of broken Wines ; and that when they are paft drawing and can be fet no more " of broche," [i. e. a-broach] that then the "Laggs" or Lees be put by in a Veffel to make Vinegar. In a fecondary fenfe a BROCHE came to fignify a Lady's Bodkin, and fo occurs in Shakefpeare and other old Englifh Writers.

Page 310.

" To Ten of the Clock * that my Lord goes to dinner."] TEN o'clock continued to be the Dining Hour in the Univerfity of Cambridge, in the Reign of Edward VI. as appears from a very remarkable paffage in a Sermon of Thomas Lever, (who was afterwards appointed firft Mafter of Emanuel College) preached at Paul's Crofs, the xiiij Dec. 1550. (fmall 8vo. B. L. fign. E. 2.)

Speaking of the Univerfity of Cambridge, he fays, " There " be dyuers ther which ryfe dayly betwixte foure and fyue " of the clocke in the mornynge, and from fyve untyll fyxe " of the clocke, ufe common prayer wyth an exhortacion of " Gods worde in a common chappell, and from fixe unto " ten of the clocke ufe ever eyther pryuate ftudy or com- " mune lectures. At Ten of the Clocke they go to Dynner,

K k k   " whereas

* The frequency of this phrafe in the Houfhold Book fhews that CLOCKS were then common.

" whereas they be content wyth a penye pyece of byefe
" amongeft iiii. havyng a few potage made of the brothe
" of the fame byefe, with falte and otemell and nothynge
" els.

" After thys flender dinner they be either teachynge or
" learnynge until v. of the clocke in the evenyng, when as
" they have a Supper not much better then theyr dyner.
" Immedyatelye after the whyche, they go eyther to reafon-
" yng in problemes or unto fome other ftudye, untyll it be
" nyne or tenne of the clocke, and there beyng wythout fyre
" are fayne to walk or runne up and downe halfe an houre,
" to gette a heate on their feete when they go to bedde."

About the middle of Queen Elizabeth's Reign the Dining
Hour was fomewhat later; tho' even then it was ftill kept
up to TEN o'CLOCK in the Univerfities, where the eftablifhed
Syftem is not fo eafily altered as in private families.
" With us (fays the Author of the Defcription of England
" prefixed to Holingfhed's Chronicle) the Nobilitie, Gentrie,
" and Students do ordinarilie go to dinner at ELEVEN before
" noone, and to fupper at five, or betweene FIVE and SIX
" at afternoone. The Merchants dine and fup feldome be-
" fore TWELVE at noone, and at fix at night efpeciallie in
" London. The Hufbandmen dine alfo at high noone as
" they call it, and fup at feven or eight: but OUT OF
" THE TEARME in our Univerfities the Scholars DINE AT
" TEN."

We have feen above (in Note to p. 103.) that ELEVEN continued to be the Dining-hour among our Nobility, down to the
middle of the laft Century. And yet one would imagine that
fo early an hour as either TEN or ELEVEN muft have very
ill-fuited the Nobility and Gentry at a time when they were
fo generally addicted to all kinds of rural fports, and made
them fo much the great bufinefs of their lives.

Page

Page 324.

" Evenſong and Complyng."] The COMPLINE was the laſt act of Worſhip at Night, by which the Service of the Day was compleated. Fr. *Compline*. Low Lat. *Completinum.*——Johnſon's Dict.

Pag 328.

" Clypping of Knottis."] The late ſtile of Dutch Gardening was only an embelliſhment of the more ancient mode; the Gardens of our old Nobility conſiſted of Beds of Flowers laid out in whimſical forms with low clipped Borders, which they called KNOTS. The Old Hiſtorian Stow, deſcribing Fair Roſamond's Bower, calls it " A houſe of " wonderful working ─' that' after ſome was called Laby-" rinthus or Dedalus Work; which was wrought like unto " a KNOT in a Garden, called a Maze." See Reliques of Anc. Eng. Poetry, Vol. II. p. 441, 2d Ed.

Page 333.

" The five Joys of our Lady."] Theſe, I ſuppoſe, are what are now called in the little Eng. Manuals of the Roſary, " The five Joyful Myſteries:" which are, 1. The Annunciation of the Bleſſed Lady. 2. The Viſitation of St. Elizabeth. 3. The Nativity of our Lord. 4. The Preſentation of him in the Temple. 5. The finding the Child Jeſus in the Temple. They are oppoſed to the Five DoLOURS of our Lord, &c. 1. Our Lord's bloody Sweat in the Garden. 2. His ſcourging at the Pillar. 3. His being crowned with Thorns. 4. His carrying the Croſs. 5. His Crucifixion.

Ibid.

" Saint Blayes Day."] The Anniverſary of St. Blaſius is the 3d of February: when it is ſtill the cuſtom in many parts of England to light up Fires on the hills on St. Blayſe Night; a cuſtom anciently taken up, perhaps for no better reaſon,

than the jingling refemblance of his Name to the word
BLAZE.

Page 334.

" When his Lordſhip crepith the Croſs."] This old Po-
piſh Ceremony is particularly defcribed in an ancient Book of
the Ceremonial of the Kings of England, bought by the
prefent Dutchefs of Northumberland, at the Sale of Manu-
fcripts of the late Mr. Anftis, Garter king at Arms. I ſhall
give the whole paſſage at length, only premifing that in 1536,
when the Convocation under Hen. VIII. aboliſhed fome of
the old fuperftitious practices, this of Creeping to the Crofs
on Good-Friday, &c. was ordered to be retained as a lau-
dable and edifying cuftom. See Herb. Life. of Henry VIII.

" The ORDER of the KINGE, on Good Friday, touch-
" inge the cominge to Service, Hallowinge of the CRAMPE
" RINGS, and Offeringe and CREEPINGE TO THE CROSSE.

" Firſte, the Kinge to come to the Chappell or Cloſſet,
" withe the Lords, and Noblemen, waytinge upon him, with-
" out any Sword borne before hime as that day: And ther
" to tarrie in his Travers until the Byſhope and the Deane
" have brought in the Crucifixe out of the Veſtrie, and layd
" it upon the Cuſhion before the highe Alter. And then
" the Uſher to lay a Carpett for the Kinge to CREEPE TO
" THE CROSSE upon. And that done ther ſhal be a Forme
" fett upon the Carpett before the Crucifix, and a Cuſhion
" laid upon it for the Kinge to kneale upon. And the Maſter
" of the Jewell Howfe ther to be ready wth the Crampe
" Rings in a Bafon of Silver, and the Kinge to kneele upon
" the Cuſhion before the Forme, And then the Clerke of
" the Cloſett be redie with the Booke concerninge the Hal-
" lowinge of the Crampe Rings, and the Amner [i. e. Al-
" moner] mofte kneele on the right hand of the Kinge holdinge
the

" the layd booke. When that is done, the King fhall rife
" and goe to the Alter, wheare a Gent. Ufher fhall be redie
" with a Cufhion for the Kinge to kneele upon : And then
" the greateft Lords that fhall be ther to take the Bafon with
" the Rings, and beare them after the Kinge to offer. And
" thus done the Queene fhall come downe out of her Clofſet
" or Traverſe, into the Chappell with La. and Gentlewomen
" waytinge upon her, and CREEPE TO THE CROSSE : And
" then goe agayne to her Clofett or Traverſe. And then the
" La. to CREEPE TO THE CROSSE likewife ; And the Lords
" and Noblemen likewife."

On the fubjeċt of thefe CRAMP-RINGS, I cannot help
obferving, that our ancient Kings, even in thofe dark times
of fuperftition, do not feem to have affeċted to cure the King's
Evil ; at leaſt in the MS. above quoted there is no mention
or hint of any power of that fort. This miraculous gift was
left to be claimed by the STUARTS : our ancient PLANTA-
GENETS were humbly content to cure the CRAMP.

Page 336.

" A Mes [Mafs] of Requiem upon the Morowe [of] my
" Lord's Father's xij Month Mynde."] A TWELVE
MONTHS Mind was an anniverſary in times of Popery, an
annual folemnity for commemorating the deceafed. There was
alfo a " Week's Mind," and a " Month's Mind ;" from
which laſt came the common phrafe of having a Month's
Mind to any thing. Among the Interrogatories and Obſer-
vations concerning the Clergy, in 1552, it was ordered that
particular inquiry be made, (Inter. VII.) " Whether there
" are any Months Minds and Anniverſaries :" i. e. xij
Months Minds. See Strype's Memorials of the Reformation,
Vol. II. page 354. Vol. III. page 305. See Ray's Proverbs, and a Note from Gray in Johnfon's Shakefpear in
Appendix to Vol. I. page 190.

Page

Page 337.

" The Holy Blode of Haillis."] This was a pretended Relique of the Blood of our Saviour, which was brought from the Holy Land and depofited in the Monaftery of Hales in Gloucefterfhire by Edmund Earl of Cornwall, (fon of Richard King of the Romans, brother of King Henry III.) It has been commonly faid to have been the blood of a Duck changed every week, of which a very diverting account is given by Collier in his Ecclef. Hift. Vol. I. page 14.

But Hearne has printed the Report of the Commiffioners, who were fent purpofely to examine it, at the Diffolution of the Monafteries; and it plainly appears to have been neither more nor lefs than CLARIFIED HONEY, " which being in a " glaffe, appeared to be of a glifterynge Redd refemblynge " partly the color of Blod."—See Petri Benedicti Vita et Geft. Hen. 2. &c. Vol. 2d. page 752.

Ibid.

" Our Lady of Walfingham."] The famous Image of the Virgin Mary, preferved in the Priory of Black Canons at Walfingham in Norfolk, was celebrated all over Europe for the great Refort of Pilgrims and the rich offerings made to it. We have a very curious and entertaining account of it given us by Erafmus, under the Name of *Virgo Parathalaffa*, in his famous Colloquy, intitled *Perigrinatio Religionis Ergo*. See alfo the Reliques of Anc. Eng. Poetry, Vol. II. B. 1. S. 13.

Page 339.

" The King's Jugler:"] Lat. *Joculator Regis*. Concerning the ancient Import of this Word, its Origin and Application, fee the preliminary Differtation to the Reliques of Ancient Eng. Poetry, Vol. I. 2d Edition, page 26, 63, &c.

Page 340.

" The Abbot of Mefx," &c.] This I find to be the real name

name of an Abbey in the Eaſt-riding of Yorkſhire. A few miles diſtance North of Leckingfield lies Watton; to the South lies Beverley (a frequent burying Place of the Percies:) and to the South Eaſt is the Abbey of *Meaux*, called in Latin *Melſa*, and pronounced by the Common People *Meuſs*: of which ſome remains are ſtill viſible.

Ibid.

" The Barne Biſhop of Beverly — Barne Biſhop of York."]
It was an ancient Cuſtom in ſuch Churches as had Cathedral Service for the little Choriſters on St. Nicholas's Day, (Dec. 6.) to elect one of their Number to the *Epiſcopus Puerorum*, the BEARN (i. e. Infant) BISHOP, or Choriſter Biſhop; who continued to preſide over the reſt, with an Imitation of all the Epiſcopal Functions, till Innocents Day, (Dec. 28.) and then after ſolemn proceſſions, and great pageantry, he laid down his Office. He was choſen on St. Nicholas's Day becauſe St. Nicholas was the Patron Saint of Children, He having when an Infant ſhewn ſuch ſingular piety (as the Legend ſays) that when he was at his Mother's breaſt, he would not ſuck on Wedneſdays and Fridays, that he might obſerve the Faſts of the Church. In the Poſthumous Tracts of John Gregory, 4to. 1650. is a full account of the Office, &c. of the *Epiſcopus Puerorum*, to which I refer the Reader; only adding here from an ancient MS. an Inventory of the ſplendid Robes and Ornaments belonging to one of theſe Bearn-Biſhops, which was communicated by Thomas Aſtle, Eſq.

CONTENTA DE ORNAMENTIS EPI. PUER.
(E Rotulo in pergamen).

Imprimis. i Myter well garniſhed with Perle and Precious Stones, with Nowches of Silver and Gilt before and behind.

Item.

Item.   iiij Rynges of Silver and Gilt, with four ridde Precious Stones in them.

Item.   i Pontifical with Silver and Gilt, with a blue Stone in hytt.

It.   i Owche broken Silver and Gilt, with iiij precious Stones and a Perle in the mydds.

It.   A Croofe, with a Staff of Coper and Gilt, with the Ymage of St. Nicolas in the mydds.

It.   j Veftment redde with Lyons, with Silver, with Brydds of Gold in the Orferes of the fame.

Item.   i Albe to the fame with Starres in the paro.

It.   i White Cope, ftayned with Triftells and Orferes redde Sylke with Does of Gold and whytt Napkins about the Necks.

It.   iiij Copes blew Sylk with red Orferes trayled with whitt Braunchis and Flowres.

It.   i Steyned Cloth of the Ymage of St. Nicholas.

It.   i Tabard of Skarlet and a Hodde thereto, lyned with whitt Sylk.

It.   A Hode of Skarlett lyned with blue Sylk.

Page 341.

" The King's Shames."] The Shalm, or Shawm was a wind Inftrument like a Pipe, with a fwelling Protuberance in the Middle. In Commenius's Vifible World, tranflated by Hoole, 1659, the Latin Word *Gingras* is tranflated by SHAWM, and the form of the Inftrument is reprefented as in the annexed Figure, viz.

Page 343.

" Pfalls" is undoubtedly Souls.—St. Nicholas was the re-
puted Patron of Children, for a reafon affigned in p. 441. See
alfo Knight's Life of Dean Collet.

Page 344.

" An Abbot of Mifrule at Chriftmas."] This, probably,
was the fame refpectable perfonage, that was known after the
Reformation (when the word ABBOT had acquired an ill
found) by the title of LORD OF MISRULE; who in the
Houfes of our Nobility prefided over the Chriftmas Gambols,
and promoted mirth and jolity at that feftive feafon. In
Scotland, where the Reformation took a more fevere and
gloomy turn, this and fome other fportive characters were
thought worthy of an Act of Parliament to fupprefs them :
for, I take for granted the Scottifh ABBOT of UN-REASON,
was no other than our Englifh ABBOT of MISRULE.

See the 6th Parl. of Qu. Marie of Scotland, 1555.—"ITEM,
" It is ftatute and ordained, that in all times cumming, na
" maner of perfon be chofen " Robert Hude," nor " Lit-
" tle John," " ABBOT OF UN-REASON," " Queenis of
" May," nor utherwife, nouther in Burgh nor to Landwart
" [i. e. in the country] in onie time to cum." And this
under very high Penalty, viz. in Burghs, to the chufers of
fuch characters, lofs of Freedom and other punifhment " at
" the Queenis Grace' Will :" and Banifhment from the
realme to the " acceptor of fik-like office." And in the
Country to the chufers a forfeiture of 10 l. and imprifonment
" during the Queenis Grace Pleafure." " And gif onie Wo-
" men or uthers about fummer, hees [hies,] fingand [i. e.
" finging] . . . throw Burrowes and uthers Landward Tounes,
" the Women . . . . fall be taken, handled, and put upon the
" Cuck-ftules of everie Burgh or Towne."

L l l   Ibid.

Ibid.

The Ceremony of crying LARGESS by the Heralds is still kept up at the Ceation of Knights of the Garter, and of the Bath, &c.

Page 347.

" Saint Christopher-gild of York."] Concerning the Gilds and Confraternities in the Dark Ages, the Original, and Design of these Establishments, see the Notes to the Eng. Version of Mallet's Description of the ancient Danes, &c. 1770. 8vo. Vol. I. Page 311, 313.—See also Baker's Preface to the Old Sermon of Bp. Fisher.

Page 354.

" Tren Platters" are " Treen," i. e, Wooden Platters or Trenchers. " Eshen Cups" are Ashen Cups.

It has been observed in the Preface, that " Pewter Plates" were too costly to be used common. In Rymer's Fædera, is a Licence granted in 1430, for a Ship to carry certain commodities for the express use of the King of Scotland, among which are particularly mentioned a supply of Pewter Dishes and wooden Trenchers, " *Octo duodenis vasarum de* " *Peuter, mille et ducentis Ciphis ligneis.*" Tom. 10. p. 470. See a Specimen of Notes on the Statute Law of Scotland, [by Sir David Dalrymple, Bart.] 8vo.

In the same cargo, was also a Cloth-sack, (so often mentioned in this Book) *Uno Cloth-sack.* Ibid.

Page 359.

" My Lord's Trussing Bed" was probably what might be trussed into a Portmanteau, or Cloth-sack, &c.

Page 361.

" When my Lord keeps his secret House."] At certain times of the year the Nobility retired from their principal Mansion to some little adjoining Lodge; where they lived private,

private, no longer kept open houſe, but put their Servants to Board Wages, diſmiſſed part of them to go to their Friends, and only retained a few of the moſt neceſſary about their per-ſon. It is remarkable that even during this privacy the Earl of Northumberland was not to be without his proper Officers of State, and therefore his younger Sons, and the young Gentlemen who were conſtantly reſident with him, were at thoſe times to ſupply Offices of Carver, Sewer, &c.

The SEWAR was the Officer who placed the Diſhes on the Table. (See Johnſon's Dict.) He and the CARVER had precedence over the other Houſhold Attendants, as being neareſt the Lord's Perſon at Table, ſtanding probably on each ſide of him.

Page 367.

It appears from this, and other Inſtances, that the Nobility about this time had great regard to the Splendour of their Choral Service; for which reaſon a ſhort account of its Origin, may not be improperly ſubjoined here.

" CHORAL or ANTIPHONAL Singing was introduced into
" the Service of the Church about the middle of the fourth
" Century, under the patronage of St. Chryſoſtome and St.
" Baſil in the Eaſt, and of St. Ambroſe in the Weſt. It was
" afterwards much improved by Gregory the Great, and
" became univerſal throughout the Chriſtian Church. It was
" looked upon to be ſo neceſſary in the celebration of Divine
" Service, that it was a conſiderable part of the duty of the
" Monks, not only to ſtudy it themſelves, but to deſſeminate
" the knowledge of it among the Laity; for this purpoſe
" Children were maintained in Convents, and taught the
" Rudiments of Song. GUIDO ARETINUS, the inventor of
" the preſent Syſtem of Muſic, in his *Micrologus* ſays, that
" by the invention of the Syllables UT, RE, MI, FA, SOL,
" LA, he was enabled to improve the Children of his Con-

L l l 2   " vent

" vent more in one Month, than others could in Twelve.
" PUTTA, an ancient Bishop of Rochester, being deprived
" of his See, travelled about the County of Kent, teaching
" the Children of the Poor to sing.   BEDE in his Ecclesiastical
" History tells us, that the Inhabitants of Britain were taught
" singing by John the Arch-Chanter of the Church of St.
" Peter at Rome ; and that he was sent hither for that pur-
" pose by Pope AGATHO.   Many years after the establish-
" ment of the Choral Service most of the Cathedrals in this
" Kingdom had a peculiar Formulary ; of these the most
" famous was that in *Usum Sarum* ; whence the Proverb *Se-*
" *cundum Usum Sarum*.   Sir Thomas MORE used to join
" with the Choir habited in a Surplice.   King HENRY the
" VIIIth. composed an Anthem in five Parts, " O Lord, the
" maker of all things," which is frequently sung in Cathe-
" drals.   Somewhat before this time Choral Service was per-
" formed in the Chapels of the greater Nobility, who ap-
" pear to have paid particular attention to this subject, and
" vied with each other in the Splendour and Ornaments of
" their Choirs. *

    " But about the time of the Reformation such abuses had
" crept into the Choral Service, which had departed from
" its primitive simplicity and dignity, that not only the
" Councel of Trent passed a Decree against " curious and
" artificial singing," but the thirty two Commissioners in the
" *Reformatio Legum Ecclesiasticarum* expressed their disappro-
" bation of it in very strong terms.   Queen MARY, who
" loved Music, and played on several Instruments, laboured
" to support it, and in her reign the formulary *In Usum Sarum*
" was republished. At the Accession of her Sister ELIZABETH
                                                          " to

    * See above, Page 429. where the 6th Earl of Northumberland,
says, " He trusts to be able some time to set up a Chapel of his
" own."

" to the crown, the Clergy were divided in their opini-
" ons about the use of Church Music ; the first Sta-
" tutes of Uniformity seemed to consider it as a thing indif-
" ferent, but the Queen by her Injunctions made it a part
" of Cathedral Worship. In this she is supposed to have had
" the concurrence of PARKER Arch-Bishop of Canterbury,
" who had been taught to sing in his youth, and was a great
" lover of Music, as was also the Queen. The Protestant
" Cathedral Service was chiefly composed by JOHN MAR-
" BUCK, of whom the Reader may see an Account in Fox's
" Martyrology."

This curious and learned memoir was communicated by
JOHN HAWKINS, Esq; of Twickenham, to whom the
World will soon be indebted for " A GENERAL HISTORY
" of the Science and Practice of MUSIC ; with MEMOIRS
" of the most eminent MUSICIANS, and Remarks on their
" Works."

There is a passage in an old Play, intitled " 𝕿𝖍𝖊 𝕴𝖓𝖙𝖊𝖗-
𝖑𝖚𝖉𝖊 𝖔𝖋 𝖙𝖍𝖊 𝖋𝖔𝖚𝖗 𝕰𝖑𝖊𝖒𝖊𝖓𝖙𝖘 :" (written about the beginning
of Henry the VIIIth's reign) which shews what high regard
was anciently paid to Church Music.

HUMANITY says,

" 𝕻𝖗𝖞𝖐-𝖘𝖔𝖓𝖌 𝖒𝖆𝖞 𝖓𝖔𝖙 𝖇𝖊 𝖉𝖎𝖘𝖕𝖞𝖘𝖊𝖉,
" 𝕱𝖔𝖗 𝖙𝖍𝖊𝖗𝖊𝖜𝖎𝖙𝖍 𝕲𝖔𝖉 𝖎𝖘 𝖜𝖊𝖑𝖑 𝖕𝖑𝖊𝖘𝖞𝖉,
" 𝕳𝖔𝖓𝖔𝖜𝖗𝖊𝖉, 𝖕𝖗𝖆𝖞𝖘𝖞𝖉, 𝖆𝖓𝖉 𝖘𝖊𝖗𝖛𝖞𝖉
" 𝕴𝖓 𝖙𝖍𝖊 𝕮𝖍𝖚𝖗𝖈𝖍 𝖔𝖋𝖙 𝖙𝖞𝖒𝖊𝖘 𝖆𝖒𝖔𝖓𝖌.

YGNORAUNCE answers,

" 𝕴𝖘 𝕲𝖔𝖉 𝖜𝖊𝖑𝖑 𝖕𝖑𝖊𝖆𝖘𝖞𝖉, 𝖙𝖗𝖔𝖜𝖘𝖙 𝖙𝖍𝖔𝖚, 𝖙𝖍𝖊𝖗𝖇𝖞 ?
" 𝕹𝖆𝖞, 𝖓𝖆𝖞, 𝖋𝖔𝖗 𝖙𝖍𝖊𝖗𝖊 𝖎𝖘 𝖓𝖔 𝖗𝖊𝖆𝖘𝖔𝖓 𝖜𝖍𝖞 :
" 𝕱𝖔𝖗 𝖎𝖘 𝖎𝖙 𝖓𝖔𝖙 𝖆𝖘 𝖌𝖔𝖔𝖉 𝖙𝖔 𝖘𝖆𝖞 𝖕𝖑𝖆𝖞𝖓𝖑𝖞

" G 𝖞

" *Gyf me a Spade ?*
" *As Gyve me a fpa, ve, va, ve, va, vade ?*
" 𝕭ut yf thou wylt have a fong that is gone
" 𝕴 have one of 𝕽obin 𝕳ode
" 𝕿he beſt that ever was made."

Sign. E. viij. jx, &c.

Page 377.

" Chambers and Houſes."] In the Caſtles of our ancient Nobility, the Apartments were of two kinds, viz. either CHAMBERS, which were principally within the Caſtle-Keep or *Dungeon*, Fr. or elſe little detached HOUSES built in the Lower Court under the ſhelter of the Walls. Theſe from the unſkilful Architecture of thoſe ſimple Times, were cluſtered together without any ſymetry or regard to external beauty. ;

Page 384.

Among the ſeveral Herbs here diſtilled, ſome few are diſguiſed by the obſolete Spelling, &c. e. g. Fumitory.—Brakes or Ferne.—Oaken-leaf.—Parſley.—Walnut Leaves.—Lang du bœuf.—Sage.—Dandelyon.—Water of Hauſe, i. e. Haws, or Hawthorn-berries.

Page 387.

The ANTIPHONAR, Lat. *Antiphonarium* (Gr. Αντι *contra* & Φωνη *ſonus)* is the name of a Book in the Latin Service, which contained the Reſponſories, Verſes, Collects, and whatever is ſung or ſaid in the Choir, called the Seven Hours, or Breviary.

GRAIL, Lat. *Gradale*, is the name of the Book, which contained all that was ſung by the Choir at High-Maſs ; the Tracts, Sequences, Halelujahs ; the Creeds, Offertory, &c. as alſo the Office for ſprinkling the Holy-Water.—See Burn's Eccleſ. Law.

As

As to the " VESTMENTS and COPES :" The COPES were a fort of Robes (often richly embroidered) worn by the Priefts over the Albs, &c. when they confecrated the Elements. At which times the Priefts and Deacons who affifted, only wore TUNICLES, viz. Silk Sky-coloured Robes, probably here called " Single Veftments."—See Wheatly on the Common Prayer.

Ibid.

The " Purpaines or Portpaines" (fee page 16.) and " Coverpaines" ufed in the Pantry, feem to have been a kind of Napkins and Table Cloths. They probably had their Name from the Latin *Pannus*. We have ftill the Word " Counterpaine" from the fame original.

Ibid.

" All other my Lordes Chapell Stuff to be fent afore by my " Lords Chariot before his Lordfhip remeve."] From this application of the CHARIOT for the conveyance of the more heavy part of the Chapel Furniture, and from the mention in the preceding page, that part of the Wardrobe Stuff was to be carried in the fame vehicle, it appears pretty evidently that my Lord's Chariot bore no refemblance to the modern carriage of that name, nor was intended for the fame ufe; but was fimply a large Waggon drawn by fix or feven of the ftronger kind of Horfes, called on that account " Large trotting Horfes," (page 127.) The CHARIOTMEN or Waggoners, who accompanied it, having a Nag or fmaller Horfe allowed them to ride by its fide. (page 128.)

It is remarkable that in all thofe paffages of Scripture where in the prefent Tranflation mention is made of WAGGONS, in the more early Verfions have the Word CHARIOT, or GHARETT uniformly in its ftead. Thus in Numbers vii. 3. " And they " brought unto the Lord fix covered Waggons;" is in the old

old Verfion by T. Matthew, Ed. 1537, rendered " **fit co=** " **vereo Charettes.**" It is the fame in Tyndal's Ed. 1551. in Miles Coverdale's Ed. 1550. in that of Hen. VIIIth. &c. — See alfo Ezek. xxiii. 24, &c. &c.

Our Word CHARIOT comes from the French Word *Chariot,* a Waggon. — See Cotgrave's Dictionary, 1632. Where we are alfo told, that the French name of *Chariot,* which primarily fignifies a Waggon, was alfo given to " a " kind of Litter borne up by an axeltree and two wheels ; " ufed heretofore by Citizen's Wives, who were not able, or " not allowed to keep ordinary Litters." Hence by degrees it became applied to the vehicles to which it is now peculiarly appropriated.

The Ufe of COACHES is faid to have been firft introduced into England by Fitz-Allan, Earl of Arundel, A. D. 1580. —(See Anderfon's Origin of Commerce, Vol. I. page 421.) At firft they were only drawn with Two Horfes. It was the favorite BUCKINGHAM *, who, about 1619, began to draw with Six Horfes, which (Wilfon tells us) " was won- " dered at then as a novelty, and imputed to him as a mafter- " ing pride." See his Life of K. James, 1653. Fol. page 130.

Before that time Ladies chiefly rode on horfe-back, either fingle on their Palfreys, or double behind fome perfon on a Pillion. Not but in cafe of ficknefs, or bad weather, they had HORSE-LITTERS, and even vehicles called CHAIRS, and CARRS or CHARRES. This appears not only from page 351 of this Houfhold Book ; but more particularly from a very curious Account of the Manner of receiving the Princefs Catharine of Spain, when fhe came over to marry Prince Arthur, A. D. 1501. The Original MS. is preferved in the

---

* About the fame time he introduced Sedan-Chairs. See Wilfon, ibid.

the British Museum, [Harl. MSS. 69. (25).] whence I
shall extract the following passages.

"	THE said Princess shall be met about Blackwall, with
"	the States [i. e. Great Personages] following: That is
"	to say, the Duke of Bucks in one Barge: The Bishop of
"	Bath in another: The Bishop of Exeter in another: The
"	Earl of NORTHUMBERLAND [the Author of this Houshold
"	Book] in another: The Earl of Kent in another, &c."—
"	[These are to conduct her to the Tower.]

* * * *

"	WHEN the Princess shall dislodge out of the Tower, It
"	is appointed that then my Lord of York [Hen. viij.] and
"	all the other Lords and Nobles, be ready at the said Tower
"	on horse-back, to convey her to the West-Door of the
"	Church of St Paul's, &c.

"	Item, That a rich Litter be ready to receive and con-
"	vey the said Princess to the West Door of the Church of
"	St. Paul's.

"	Item, That three Horsemen in Side Saddle and Harness
"	all of one Suit, be arrayed by the Master of the Queen's
"	Horse, to follow next to the said Princess's Litter.

"	Item, That a fair Palfrey with a Pillion richly arrayed
"	and led in hand for the said Princess, do follow next unto
"	the said Horsemen.

"	Item, That eleven Palfreys in one Suit be ordained for
"	such Ladies attending upon the said Princess, as shall fol-
"	low next unto the said Pillion.

"	Item, That five Charres diversely apparelled for the
"	Ladies and Gentlemen, be ready the same Time at the said
"	Tower, whereof one of the Chief must be richly apparelled
"	and garnished for the said Princess, and the other four to
"	serve such Ladies as be appointed by the Queen's Chamber-
"	lain, and that the same follow in such Order as the said
"	Chamberlain shall appoint.

M m m
"	Item,

" Item, That betwixt every of the said Charres, there be
" five or six Palfreys of such Ladies as shall come to the Feast
" for the attendance given upon the Queen's Grace."

* * * *

" THE third Day after the Day of Marriage the said
" Prince and Princess to depart from the said Palace [sc. the
" Bishop of London's adjoining to St. Paul's] towards
" Baynard's Castle, to go to Westminster with the King's
" Grace, and that the said Princess so departing shall ride
" in her LITTER or on her spare Horse, with the PILLION
" behind a Lord to be named by the King, and eleven Ladies
" on Palfreys after her, &c.

THE END OF THE NOTES.

-An

An ACCOUNT of

WRESSIL CASTLE

AND

LECKENFIELD MANOUR,

in YORKSHIRE.

TO render this Work compleat, it may not be improper to give a fhort account of the two great Manfions at WRESSIL and LECKENFIELD, which were the fcenes of the Hofpitality defcribed in the foregoing Part of this Book.

With regard to WRESSIL CASTLE, we have a very particular Defcription of it by Leland, a few Years after the Date of the foregoing Book. See his Itinerary, begun 1538, Vol. I. fol. 59.

WRESSIL CASTLE.

" From Houeden to Wrefehill, [are] 3 Miles; al by low
" Medow and Pafture Ground, wherof part is enclofid with
" Hegges.
" Yet is the Ground, that the Caftelle of Wrefehil ftandith
" on, fumwhat high yn the refpect of the very lough Ground
" therabout.
" Moft Part of the Baffe Courte of the Caftelle of Wrefe-
" hil, is all of Tymbre *.
" The Caftelle it felf is moted aboute on 3 Partes. The
" 4 Parte is dry where the entre is ynto the Caftelle.

M m m 2   " The

* i. e. The Buildings in the Bafe-Court are of Timber.

" The Caftelle is al of very fair and greate fquarid Stone,
" both withyn and withowte : wherof (as fum hold opinion)
" much was brought owt of France.

" In the Caftelle be only 5 Towers, One at eaoh corner
" almoft of like biggenes.   The Gate Houfe is the 5, having
" fyve Lougginges yn high. 3 of the other Towers have 4
" Hi∴hes in Lougginges : The 4 conteinith the Botery, Pan-
" tery, Paftery, Lardery and Keehyn.

" The Haule * and the Great Chaumbers be fair : and fo
" is the Chapelle, and the Clofettes.

" To conclude, the Houfe is one of the moft propre
" beyound Trente, and femith as newly made : yet was it
" made by a youngger Brother of the Percys, Erle of Wic-
" cefter, that was yn high favor with Richard the Secunde,
" ande bought the Maner of Wrefehil, mountting at that
" tyme litle above 30 li. by the yere : and for lak of Heires
" of hym, and by favor of the King, † it cam to the Erles
" of Northumbreland.

" The Baffe Courte is of a newer Building.

" And the laft Erle of Northumberland faving one ‡, made
" the Brew-Houfe of the Stone without the Caftelle Waulle,
" but hard joyning to the Kechyn of it.

" One thing I likid excedingly yn one of the Towers,
" that was a Study, caullid Paradife § ; wher was a Clofet in
" the midle of 8 Squares latifid aboute, and at the Toppe
" of every Square was a Defk ledgid to fet Bookes ' on
" Bookes ' || on Cofers withyn them, and thefe femid as
                                    " yoinid

* This Hall contained 8 ftanding Tables, and 8 Fermes, as
appears from an Inventory taken in 1574.   † Probably Hen. 5.
‡ This was writ after the Death of Henry Percy, the 6th Earl,
fon of the Author of this Book.   § This is called in the Inventory 1574, " Paradice, a new Studie coloured green and white."
|| Thefe two words are thought to be redundant.

" yoinid hard to the Toppe of the Clofet: and yet by
" pulling, one or al wold cum downe brifte higthe in rabet-
" tes, and ferve for Defkes to lay Bokes on.

" The Garde-Robe yn the Caftelle was excedingly fair.
" And fo wer the Gardeins withyn the mote, and the Or-
" chardes without. And yn the Orchardes were Mountes
" Opere topiario, writhen about with Degrees like Turninges
" of Cockelfhilles, to cum to the Top without payn.

" The ryver of Darwent rennith almoft hard by the
" Caftelle; and aboute a mile lower goith ynto Owfe. This
" Ryver at greate Raynes ragith and overflowith much of the
" Ground there aboute, beyng low Medowes.

" There is a Parke hard by the Caftelle."

THREE of the Apartments in Wreffill Caftle, were adorned
with POETICAL INSCRIPTIONS, as mentioned in the Preface
(p. xxii.) Thefe are called in the MS.

" PROVERBES in the LODGINGS in WRESSILL."

1. " The Proverbes in the Sydis of the Innere Chamber
" at Wreffill." This is a Poem of 24 Stanzas, each containing 7 Lines: beginning thus,

" When it is tyme of cofte and greate expens,
" Beware of Wafte and fpende by meafure:
" Who that outrageoufly makithe his difpens,
" Caufythe his goodes not long to endure, &c.

2. " The Counfell of Ariftotill, whiche he gayfe to Alexan-
" der, kynge of Maffydony; Whiche ar wrytyn in the Syde
" of the Utter Chamber above the Houfe in the Gardynge at
" Wrefyll." — This is in Diftichs of 38 lines; beginning
" thus,

" Punyfhe moderatly and difcretly correcte,
" As well to mercy, as to juftice havynge a refpecte, &c.

3. " The

3. " The Proverbis in the fyde of th' Utter Chamber above
" of the Hous in the Gardying at Wrefyll." A Poem of 30
ftanzas, chiefly of 4 lines, &c.

" Remorde thyne ey inwardly,
" Fyx not thy mynde on Fortune, that delythe dyverfly, &c.

WRESSIL CASTLE continued in all its Splendor, till the
fatal Civil Wars broke out in 1641 : It was then garrifoned
with Soldiers for the Parliament ; and notwithstanding the
Earl of Northumberland had efpoufed their Caufe, the Damage
he fuftained there by his own Party before Michaelmas 1646,
was judged to amount to a thoufand Pounds, * in the Deftruc-
tion of his Buildings, Leads, Outhoufes, &c. by the Garrifon :
their havock of his Woods, Inclofures, &c. without including
the Loffes he had fuftained in the Non-payments of his Rents,
in confequence of the Contributions levied on his Tenants.

On the decline of the King's Party, it fhould feem, that
the Northern Counties enjoyed fome refpite : but in 1648,
fome Attempts being made or expected from the Royaliffs,
frefh Troops were fent into the north ; and in May that
Year, Major-General Lambert, ordered a fmall Detachment
of 60 Men to garrifon Wreffel Caftle, of which Major Charles
Fenwick had all along continued Governor for the Parliament, with the intire approbation of the Earl of Northumberland.

About the Beginning of June 1648, Pomfret Caftle was
feized for the King, and underwent a Siege of ten months :
to prevent any more Surprizes of this kind, a refolution was
taken for demolifhing all the Caftles in that Part of England :
And

* Extracted from a " Brief View of the Arrearages, and Loffes
" fuftained by his Lp. occafioned by the late unhappy Warres,"
MS. dated Michas. 1646. The Sum total of his Loffes even then
amounted to 42,554 l.

And while the Earl of Northumberland was exerting all his influence above, to save this noble Seat of his Anceſtors, a Committee at York ſent a ſudden and unexpected Order to diſmantle it: which was executed with ſuch precipitation and fury, that before the Earl could receive notice of the deſign, the miſchief was done.

The following Letters, ſelected from a Series on this ſubject, will ſhew the Spirit of the Times, and how little reſpect was ſhown to this great Nobleman, by the low People, who had wreſted the power into their hands.

I. A Letter to Mr. Prickett at York.

" Sir,

" I am very ſorrye to ſee the ſpoyle that is alreadye made
" of his Lordſhips Caſtle with this forenoones worke: there
" is 15 men throwing downe the Out-Battlemt; I thinke by
" to morrow noone they will have gone rownd about the
" Caſtle. The Stones are for the moſt parte all maſhed to
" pieces, and if their be not ſome ſpeedy courſe taken for to
" preſerve the Timber, Lead, Glaſſe, and Wainſcott, by
" taking them downe att his Lordſhips coſt, they will be all
" ſpoyled and broaken to peeces. I pray ſee if you can get
" an Order from the Committee to ſtay the proceedings till
" we can take courſe to preſerve thoſe things for his Lord-
" ſhips uſe: the workemen doe not looke to ſave any of the
" materiels but take the readyeſt courſe to throw downe the
" wall; which they will doe inward upon the ſloores and ſea-
" ling, as well as outward upon the ground. I dare ſay his
" Lordſhip had better have given 150 li. then theſe 15 men
" ſhould have done this dayes worke. Good Sir, let me in-
" treat your paines to come over as ſhortly as poſſiblye you

" can,

" can. In the mean time my beſt care ſhall not be awanting:
" I have ſent you a Copy of the workemans warrant. *
" This in great haſt from

" Decemb. 28th.　　　　" Your aſſured true friend
　　1648.　　　　　　　　" To ſerve yow,
　　　　　　　　　　　　　　Wm. Plaxton.

" His Lordſhip had better take downe the Caſtle att his
" owne charge, then ſuffer the ſpoyle that will be done by
" the Countryemen,

　　　　　　DIRECTION.

" For his very friend Mr. Marmaduke
" Prickett, theſe with ſpeede."
" Leave this Letter at Mr. James Black-
" beards next the Minſter Gates;　and
" I deſire it may be delivered as ſoon as
" poſſible may be."

II. A Letter to Mr. Potter, at Northumberland Houſe.

" Sir,

" Yours I received; and ſince I writt my laſt, on the ſame
" daye, the Commiſſioners ſett on workmen to pull downe
" and deface that ſtately Structure.　They fell upon the Con-
" ſtables Tower, and hath with much violence purſued the
" work on thurſday and ffryday.　Their Agents wold ſhowe
" noe care in preſerveinge any of the materialls, but pitched
" of the Stones from the Battlements to the ground; and
" the Chymneys that ſtood upon the Lead downe to the
" Leades, which made breaches thorough the roofe where
" they fell. All the Battelements to the roofe, on the ffront
　　　　　　　　　　　　　　　　　　　　　　　" of

＊ This is not preſerved in the Family.

" of the Castle (excepting the High Tower over the Gate)
" are bett downe. What materialls could bee fav'd Mr. Plax-
" ton did fett on fome Tenants to take awaye, and laye in
" the barne. Believe it, Sir, his Lordfhip hath fuftain'd very
" deepe loffes in his houfe; I conceive 2000l. will not re-
" paire the ruynes there: But I hope their work is at an
" end; for this day the Major and Mr. Plaxton are fett for-
" ward to attend Major Generall Lambert with the Lord
" Generall's order to him: And in the meane tyme the fol-
" diers are to hold them of, from doinge further violence to
" the Caftle; which I wifh had bin done by order 2 dayes
" fooner *

" Your true ffriende and fervant,

Wr. 30. 10^{brie}

48°   " ROB. THOMSONE.

DIRECTION
" To my much honored Friende
" Hugh Potter Efquire, thefe I pray
" prefent with Care and Speede att
" Northumberland Houfe, London."

From this 30th of December, 1648, no further outrages
were committed, till the year 1650. And then, notwithftanding all the endeavours of the Earl of Northumberland
to preferve it, an Order was iffued out for the further demolifhing of Wreffil Caftle. The only indulgence he obtained
was that the execution of the Order fhould be intrufted to his
own Stewards, and that part of the principal Building fhould
be fpared, to ferve for a Manor-Houfe.

III. The ORDER for demolifhing WRESSIL CASTLE.

" In purfuance of the Orders of Councell [of] State to us
" directed, for the making Wrefle Caftle inteneable, as alfoe

N n n   " of

* The Remainder of the Letter relating to private bufinefs is here
omitted.

" of a further Order of the Committe of Militia of the County
" of Yorke to that purpoſſe ; Theſe are theerefore to require
" you to proceede in making the ſayd Caſtle inteneable with
" all ſpeede : Which we conceave will be by throwing downe
" to the ground all that ſide wheerein the Hall ſtands, to the
" Towre adjoyning, leaving only the South Side remayning ;
" wherein we require you alſoe That Windowes be broken
" forth of eight foote breadth and heighth, and eight foote
" diſtance round about all that ſide which remaynes ; And
" that it be down by the 17th of May next ; that the Coun-
" try may be ſecured from any danger that may happen
" thereby. Given under our Hands at Wreſle this 17th of
" Aprill, 1650.

" You are alſo to throwe   " PHIL. SALTMARSH,
" downe all the Battle-   " CHA. FEINWICKE.
" ments round about.   " ED. KIR - LEWE.
                          " THO. ATHROPPE.

DIRECTION.
" ffor Mr. William Plaxton or other
" the Lord Northumberland Officers
" at Wreſle."

In conſequence of this Order, three Sides of the Square,
which formerly compoſed WRESSIL CASTLE, were entirely
demoliſhed. However the whole South-Front, which was
the moſt conſiderable, and contained ſome of the principal
State-Rooms, ſtill remains, and is very magnificent. It is
flanked by two large ſquare Towers ; and theſe again are
mounted by circular Turrets of a ſmaller ſize : on the top of
one of the turrets is ſtill preſerved the Iron Pan of the Beacon,
anciently uſed to alarm the country.

The whole Building, which is of the fineſt maſonry, ſtill
contains the Great Chamber or Dining-Room, the Drawing-
Chamber, and the Chapel, beſides many of the inferior Apartments.

ments. In all these the finishing and ornaments seem to be left nearly in the same state that they were in the time of this HOUSHOLD BOOK. The Cielings still appear richly carved, and the sides of the Rooms are ornamented with a great profusion of ancient Sculpture, finely executed in wood, exhibiting the ancient Bearings, Crests, Badges and Devises of the PERCY Family, in a great variety of forms, set off with all the advantages of Painting, Gilding and Imagery. In the two principal Chambers are small beautiful Stair-Cases of very singular contrivance with octagon Screens, imbattled at the top, and covered with very bold sculpture, containing double flights of Stairs, winding round each other, after the design of Paladio.

The Chapel appears to have been fitted up in a ruder style and at a more early period than the other apartments. In this the sculptured Badges, &c. are still tolerably entire, and some of the painted glass unbroken. The Cieling is inscribed with the following Motto, *Esperance en Dieu ma Comforte*. The Chapel is now used instead of the Parish-Church, which was situate about a bow-shot from the Castle. Of this one ruined end-wall only remains, in which at present hang two Bells. The Pulpit now stands as on a pedestal, upon the great stone Altar of the Chapel, and the Communion is administered at a Table in the middle of the room.

LECKINFIELD MANOUR-HOUSE,

OR, as it is not improperly stiled in the Title-page, LECKINFIELD CASTLE, (for it was fortified by a Licence from the Crown in 2 Edw. II. *) is now so entirely destroyed that the area on which it stood (forming a parallelogram of 4 acres) now affords a rich green pasture, being still inclosed by the ancient Mote, which is wide and deep, and full of water.

N n n 2   The

* Dugd. Baron. I. 273.

The Caftle is thus defcribed by Leland, in his Itinerary, (Vol. 1. fol. 50.) as it was about the Year 1538.

" Al the way bytwixt York, and the Parke of Lekenfeld ys " meetely fruteful of corn and graffe, but it hath little wood. - - -

" Lekingfeld is a large Houfe, and ftondith withyn a great " Mote yn one very fpatious Courte. Three partes of the Houfe, " faving the Meane Gate that is made of brike, is al of tymbre. " The fourth parte is made of ftone and fum brike.

" I faw in a little ftudying Chaumber ther caullid PARA- " DICE, the Genealogie of the PERCYS.

" The Park thereby is very fair and large and meetely welle " woddid. There is a fair Tour of brike for a Lodge yn the " Park. From Lekingfeld to Beverle 2 Miles."

The following Apartments in Leckinfield had poetical In- fcriptions : as mentioned in the Preface, p. xxii.

" PROVERBS in the LODGINGS at LECKINFIELD."

1. " The Proverbis of the Garrett over the Bayne at Le- " kyngfelde." This is a Dialogue in 32 ftanzas, of 4 lines, between " The Parte Senfatyve," and " the Parte Intel- " lectyve ;" containing a poetical Comparifon between fen- fual, and intellectual Pleafures.

2. " The Proverbis in the Garet at the New Lodge in the " Parke of Lekingfelde." This is a Poem in 32 ftanzas, of 4 lines, being a Defcant on Harmony, as alfo on the manner of Singing, and playing on moft of the Inftruments then ufed: fc. The Harps, Clavicordes, Lute, Virgynall, Clarifymballis, Clarion, Shawme, Orgayne, Recorder. The following ftanza relates to the SHAWME, defcribed in p. 442, and fhows it to have been ufed for the Bafs, as the RECORDER was for the Meane or Tenor).

" A SHAWME makithe a fweete founde for he tunithe BASSE, " It mountithe not to hy, but kepithe rule and fpace. " Yet yf it be blowne with a too vehement wynde, " It makithe it to mifgoverne oute of his kynde."

3. " The

3. " The Proverbis in the Rooffe of the Hyeft Chawmbre " in the Gardinge at Lekingfelde." If we fuppofe this to be the room mentioned above, where the Genealogy was kept; the following jingling reflections on the family Motto (in 30 Diftichs) will not appear quite fo mifplaced;

" *Efperaunce en Dyeu,* *
" Trufte in hym he is moft trewe.

" *En Dieu efperaunce;*
" In hym put thine affiaunce.

" *Efperaunce* in the Worlde ? nay;
" The Worlde varieth every day.

" *Efperaunce* in Riches ? nay, not fo,
" Riches flidithe and fone will go.

" *Efperaunce* in exaltacion of Honoure ?
" Nay it widderithe . . . lyke a floure.

" *Efperaunce* in bloode and highe Lynage ?
" At mofte nede, bot efy avauntage.

The concluding Diftich is,

" *Efperaunce en Dieu,* in hym is all :
" Be thou contente and thou art above Fortune's fall."

4. " The Proverbis in the Roufe of my Lorde Percy Clofett " at Lekyngfelde." A poetical Dialogue containing inftruc- " tions for Youth, in 142 Lines.

5. " The Proverbis in the Roufe of my Lordis Library at " Lekyngefelde." 23 ftanzas of 4 Lines, whereof take the following Specimen :

" To

* The FOURTH EARL of Northumberland, father of the Author of the Houfhold-Book, gave his Motto fomewhat different, fc. *Efperance ma comforte :* And this Motto was engraven over the great Gateway at Alnwick Caftle.

> " To every tale geve thou no credens.
> " Prove the caufe, OR * thou gyve fentens.
> " Agayn the right make no dyffens
> " So haft thou a clene Confciens."

6. " The Counfell of Ariftotell, whiche he gave to Alexan-
" der kinge of Macedony ; in the fyde of the Garet of the
" gardynge in Lekynfelde." This confifts of 9 ftanzas, of
8 Lines : Take the laft ftanza but one :

> " Punyfhe moderatly, and difcretly correct,
> " As well to mercy, as to juftice havynge a refpect ;
> " So fhall ye have meryte for the punyfhment,
> " And caufe the offender to be fory and penitent.
>
> " If ye be movede with anger or haftynes,
> " Paufe in youre mynde and your yre reprefs :
> " Defer vengeance unto your anger affwagede be ;
> " So fhall ye mynyfter juftice, and do dewe equyte."

The above documents, however mean and homely the verfe,
are not unworthy the notice of any great perfonage in the
moft polifhed age or nation.

As the Reader may be curious to know how our firft Nobility were accommodated with apartments in their largeft manfions, I fhall fubjoin a Lift of all the Rooms of every kind,
that were in LECKINFIELD MANOUR HOUSE : being nearly
double the number that were in WRESSEL CASTLE, as appears
from an Inventory of them both now before me, taken in the
year 1574. The names of the apartments in both were fo
much alike, that the enumeration of one was thought fufficient.

The Furniture of the Apartments in both thefe Manfions
confifted of nothing but Long Tables, Benches, Cupboards,
and Bedfteads, and contained nothing curious ; otherwife the
Inventory fhould have been printed at large.

It

* i. e. " before." See the above Note to p. 162.

It is obfervable that in upwards of Fourfcore Apartments, there do not feem to have been more than three or four deftined for the reception of the noble Owners and their Guefts : thefe were probably, the Drawing-Chamber, the New Chamber, the Carved Chamber, and the Great Chamber or Dining-room : all the reft were meerly offices, or cabins to fleep in.

I fhall premife, that the GREAT CHAMBER contained only " a Long Table upon a Frame, a Cupboard with a dore ;" and the HALL " Six great ftanding Tables, with fixe Formes, " three Cupbourds, - - - - two Dores, nether Locks nor " Keyes."

The APARTMENTS at LECKENFIELD.

1. " The Gallery. 2. The Chapel. 3. My Lord's Chamber. 4. The Gentlewomen's Chamber. 5. The Nurfery. 6. My Lady's Clofett. 7. The Drawing Chamber. 8. The New Chamber. 9. The Great Chamber. 10. The Carved Chamber. 11. Paradice and the Lower Houfe. 12. The Hall. 13. The Pantry. 14. The Buttery. 15. The Larder. 16. The Scullery. 17. The New Larder. 18. The Kytchen. 19. The Paftry. * The Chamber over the Hall. 20. The Inner Chamber. 21. The Chamber over the Pantry. 22. The Utter Chamber. 23. The Landry. 24. The Milkhoufe. 25. John Bone's Chamber. 26. My Lady's Buttery. 27. The Green Tower. 28. The Auditor's Chamber. 29. The Upper Chamber. 30. My Lady Percy's Chamber. 31. The Muficians Chamber. 32. The Utter Chamber. 33. The Bayne. 34. The Bakehoufe. 35. The Brewhoufe. 36. The Garners. 37. The Chamber adjoining to the Milne. 38. The Groom's Chamber. 39. Tho. Bingham's Chamber. 40. The Smethie. 41. The Stable Tower. 42. The Stables. 43. The Chamber over the Gate. 44. The Utter Chamber. 45. The Porter's Lodge. 46. Alfourth Tower. 47. The Towres Chamber. 48. The Clarke's Chamber. 49. The Checker.

Checker. 50. The Spicery. 51. The Storehoufe. 52. Edw. Graie's Chamber. 53. John Coke's Chamber. 54. The Chamber under the Clarkes Chamber. 55. 56. The two next Chambers. 57. The Gardyner's Chamber. 58. The Ewery. 59. The Study at the Starehead. 60. The next Chamber called the Scole-howfe. 61. The Waredropp. [Wardrobe]. 62. The Waredropp of Beds. 63. The Store-howfe under the Waredropp. 64. Dudlayes Towre. 65. Mr. Mychell ͻ hamber. 66. The Bayleys Chamber. 67. The Carter's Chamber. 68. Jenytt Perfonnes Chamber. 69. Per-fonne Ralliff's Chamber. 70. Stokaies Chamber. 71. Peter Garnet's Chamber. 72. 73. 74. Three next Chambers. 75. Mrs. Percy's Chamber. 76. William Twathes Chamber. 77. The Corner Chamber. 78. 79. 80. Three next Chambers. 81. Charlton's Chamber. 82. The next Chamber. 83. The Hawk's Mew."

At the end of the above INVENTORY, the Surveyors report that they find the " Decayes of the Howfe at Leckinfield, " to be much greater, and of more charge, than of that at " Wreffel; and that the greateft part of the faid Howfe, as " well the Lead Cover, as Tyle, muft be taken of, and new " tymbered, &c. &c." They conclude their Report in the following words, " We cannot fpeke of the particular harmes " of the faid Howfe, the Wafte is fo univerfal."

Thence-forward, it was probably never repaired; but after fome time pulled down and demolifhed : for I have feen an account fent up to the fucceeding Earl of Northumberland in James the Firft's reign, of the Quantity of Timber, Painted Glafs, and Carved Images in the Ceilings, &c. which were removed by his order from Leckenfield to Wreffel Caftle.

EXTRACT

EXTRACT from LELAND's Itinerary,

Vol. 7: fol. 66.

' The Earl of Northumberland's ancient TITLES.'

Erle of Northumbr. Lord of the Honors of Cokermouth and Petworth. Lorde Percy, Lucy. Lorde Poyninges, Fitzpaine, Brian. Cokermouth came by [Maud, Lady] Lucy. Petworth by gift of a King [Hen. II.]

Fitz-paine and Brian's landes cam to Poyninges, and by Poyninges heire general al thre to Percy.

The Erle of Northumbr. CASTELLES and MANORS.

Cokermouth [caftel] in CUMBRELAND, a 700li. by yere.

Alnewik, Werkworth caftel, Langely and Prudehow [caftels] in NORTHUMBRELAND, Rothebyri lordefhip on Koket, a vii Miles above Anewik . . . Corbridge lordfhip, wher appere great tokens of buildinges by fquare ftones. Chatton lordfhip upon Tille, a mile from Chillingham.

In YORKSHIRE, Semar, Hundemanby near Semar. Poklington market 2 miles from Semar. Lekingfeld 2 miles from Beverlé. Wrefil Caftel 2 miles from Howeden market, where the bifhop of Durham hath a faire palace. Catton wher is a parke, as is [to] almofte [all] of the lordfhipes afore reherfid. Spofford a greate village 2 miles from Oteley upon Eyre river. Topclif on Suale a goodly maner houfe yn a parke. Tadcafter and Helé, Lyndeley by Spofford . . .

He had yn KENT a 500 mark of Poyninges landes.

In South-Sax [SUSSEX] Poyninges lordfhip, [and] Petworth.

Torre-Bryan in SOMERSETSHIRE that Mr. Kitfon boute.

The lorde-marquis of Excefter had much of his londes in DEVONSHIRE.

He had Caftelles yn WALES and was there a great Lorde Marcher. Peraventure Paine caftel by Wy, was his: for he bare the name of the lorde Fitz-paine.

He had fome lande yn Southfolke [SUFFOLK] and CAMBRIDGE-SHIRE.

He had Taulaughar a caftel about the mouth of Tevy, cumming from CAIRMERDINE.

HACTENUS.

[N. B. The foregoing Account might be much inlarged and im-proved from the ancient Rentals of the Family, but it was thought proper to keep here to LELAND's own Words.]

INDEX to the NOTES.

Necantur

I N D E X.

F I N I S.

ERRATA.

Page 58. For ‘ Counter,’ read ‘ Counterfeit Veffel.’

  — 60. (near the Bottom) read, ‘ Furniunturs.’

  — 71. Note †. The Contraction is ‘ Pcs.’

  — 72. for ‘ Yardwood,’ read ‘ Hardwood.’

  — 151. for ‘ Renewalle,’ read ‘ Remevalle.’

  — 207. for ‘ fervide,’ read ‘ fewide.’

  — 235. for ‘ Dobfon,’ read ‘ Hobfon.’

  — 352. (near the Bottom) for ‘ Nalls,’ read ‘ Nails.’

  — 406. for ‘ Hoifemeat,’ read ‘ Horfemeat.’

  — 419. for ‘ contractedly writ.’ read ‘ alfo writi.’

  — 435. read ‘ BROACHES (Fr. *Broches.*) are Spts.

  ⁎ ‘ Cator,’ or ‘ Catour,’ is almoft every where ufed for ‘ Ca terer :’ but this contraction is in the MS.

A LETTER

DESCRIBING

THE RIDE TO HULNE ABBEY

FROM ALNWICK IN

NORTHUMBERLAND.

A

LETTER TO THE REV. MR. L**.

ALNWICK, in NORTHUMBERLAND,
August 5, 1765.

Dear SIR,

AT parting you defired I would fometimes write to you, and defcribe whatever I faw moft curious in the North. In compliance with your requeft, I fhall at prefent attempt a defcription of one of the beautiful Rides we have from this Caftle; and fhall the rather felect the following, as it prefents views fo different from what we have in the South of England, and alfo as the whole extent of it lies within one of the ancient Parks belonging to this great Barony, called HULNE or HOLNE PARK.

IN a right line from the great Gate of ALNWICK-CASTLE, a wide handfome road leads to a beautiful Gothic Gateway; which reprefenting, as it were, an outwork from the Caftle, is with great propriety ornamented with Battlements and a Portcullis.

HENCE between borders of flowering fhrubs, and young plantations of beautiful foreft trees, the path winds down a fteep romantic Hill; at the bottom of which we crofs a Rivulet, and turning to the left defcend into a deep fequeftered Valley. Here we we pass under a high Cliff, with over-hanging trees, watered at the foot by a clear running Brook, which after a shower affords one or two very fine Water-Falls.

FROM this Valley we begin to ascend some wild swelling Slopes; whence the eye is thrown to the left over a rough uncultivated Scene, all broken into hill and dale. Passing on, we cross thro' two Gates and enter upon another scene of Heath Ground: a little narrow Valley full of young trees lying to the right; a small swell of planted Ground to the left.

THEN crossing over some corn-fields and upland pastures, thro' which the path very agreeably winds with a gentle ascent, we begin to gain a fine extensive prospect towards the east, terminated by the Sea. In the middle of this beautiful landscape we have a very pleasing view of ALNWICK CASTLE, standing on an Eminence, the foot of which is washed by the River ALNE. And as we continue to ascend the Hill, the swelling Towers of that noble edifice, seen at a distance, make a very striking and picturesque appearance.

PROCEEDING on, we ascend some wild Heath Grounds, and afterwards enter young plantations of Fir-trees, till by degrees the vast Swellings of CHIVIOT begin to appear towards the west, and at length emerge from behind the interposing hills, presenting an immense Group of pyramidal Mountains, the highest tops of which are, for the most part, covered with the clouds.

THESE are seen at a great distance to the left; near at hand, to the right, the eye is charmed with the

sight

fight of a fine circular Hill we are about to afcend;
clothed to its very fummit with thriving plantations
of young trees of various forts and forms. This may
be termed the Flowery Head of CARMEL; as this
Hill * may, with great propriety be called, for a reafon that will be given below.

PROCEEDING on, a path to the right leads to a rude
Cave amid the Cliffs of the Rocks, which is to be adorned with the Statue of a Hermit, not ill adapted to the
retired fituation of this fine romantic folitude.

THE former path being refumed, winds for a quarter of a mile round the Edge of a moft aftonishing
Precipice, which from a vaft height, prefents a noble,
wild profpect of wide extent, and at an amazing
depth below the Path from which it is feen. The
firft Object the eye looks down upon at the foot of
the Mountain, is the River ALNE, winding in the
moft beautiful and whimfical irregularities... This
is to be received into a large Lake on the right, which
will cover 200 acres of ground. On a little Hill
on its margin, are feen, as in a picture held far below
the eye, the fine Remains of HULNE ABBEY : more
to the left are little Swellings, the hollows of which
are fringed with a chain of fmall rough Thickets.
Beyond thefe rifes a vaft extent of wild naked Plains,
with here and there a fingle Farm or Plantation fcat-
tered like folitary iflands in a wide unbounded ocean.
Over thefe the eye gradually rifes to where the vaft
Mountains of CHIVIOT erect their huge conic heads ;
between.

* Called by the Country People BRISLEY HILL.

between the openings of which, the fight gains a glimpfe of the ftill more diftant blue Hills of TIVIOT-DALE in Scotland. The top of Chiviot is diftant more than twenty miles: the Hills in Tiviotdale near forty or fifty.

TURNING off from the Edge of this high natural Terrace, we crofs a little level Plain, and then gain the higheft point of this Britifh Carmel. Elevated as its lofty fummit is, it is all clothed with young Plantations of evergreen and foreft Trees, with fpacious Avenues left for the paffage of Wheel-Carriages, which eafily afcend to its topmoft point. Here in a little Plain, furrounded by a Circus of young Trees, is to be erected a noble Tower fifty feet high: which will command an aftonifhing extent and variety of profpect. Here we fee, as in one general map, what we have hitherto admired in detached parts.

To the Weft we have ftill a more extenfive view of that amazing wild Profpect towards Chiviot, which is but faintly defcribed above. Thofe rude Mountains now appear finely contrafted with a great Variety of Hills and Slopes to the North, which are cultivated up to their very fummits. — To the Eaft are fine green Vales, in the midft of which the Town of ALNWICK, overlooked by the Caftle, hath a moft picturefque appearance: below it, the River ALNE is feen beautifully winding towards the Sea. But above all the SEA itfelf moft nobly terminates this fine profpect to the Eaft and South, extending itfelf all along the Coaft from beyond the FARN ISLANDS to the north, almoft

down

down to TYNEMOUTH CASTLE; yet not so distant but the Shipping may be plainly seen many miles from the land. On the margin of the Sea the Ruins of DUNSTANBURGH-CASTLE, and the little Port of ALNEMOUH, are two of the most striking objects. — To the South-west a wild rude Moor, part of the ancient Forest of HAYDON, rises still higher than the Mountain on which we stand; yet clothed on one side to its very top with infant plantations which are at present struggling with the inclemencies of its situation, but promise fair to surmount them. And here and there are interspersed some of those rude Pyramids of Stone erected in ancient times for Land-marks, and called by the inhabitants CAIRNS or KERNS.

AND now the eye being fully glutted with these great and wild views of nature, we descend from this eminence in order to contemplate other Scenes more confined and more cultivated. For winding down to the bottom of the Mountain, we cross the River, and find that HULNE Abbey, which before appeared so low beneath our feet, is really situated on a Hill of no inconsiderable height, to which we again ascend from the River.

HULNE ABBEY was the first Monastery of CARMELITE Friars in these Kingdoms. The account of its Foundation is thus given by ancient Writers. Among the British Barons, who went to the Holy Wars in the reign of King Henry III. were WILLIAM DE VESCY, Lord of Alnwick, and RICHARD GRAY, two eminent Chieftains in the christian army. Led by curiosity or devotion, they went to visit the Monks of MOUNT CARMEL, and

there

there unexpectedly found a countryman of their own,
one RALPH FRESBORN, a Northumberland man, who
had distinguished himself in a former Crusade, and in
consequence of a vow had afterwards taken upon him
the monastic profession in that solitude. When Vescy and
Gray returned to England they strongly importuned the
Superior of the Carmelites to let their countryman ac-
company them home : which was at length granted,
upon condition that they would found a Monastery
for Carmelites in their own country. Soon after their
return, Fresborn, mindful of their engagement, began
to look out for a place for their Convent. After
examining all the circumjacent solitudes he at length
fixed on the present spot, induced, it is said, by the
great resemblance which the adjoining Hill bore to
Mount CARMEL : And indeed whoever looks into
" MAUNDREL's Travels," will find that the Draught
of that Mountain given in his Book bears a strong
likeness to this before us.

THE above WILLIAM DE VESCY * gave a Grant of
the Ground, consisting of II or I2 acres in his Park of
HOLNE, but FRESBORN is said to have erected the
Buildings himself. The Foundation was laid about A.D.
1240, and Fresborn gathering a proper number of Monks,
became the first Abbot of the Order, and having presided
here with great reputation of sanctity, at length died, and
was buried in this Monastery about the year 1274.

THIS

* Not his son JOHN, as it is in Leland, Bale, &c. This appears
from the Original Charters, of which I have seen Extracts in MS.
as also from Dugdale's Baronage, vol. i. p. 93. 763.

THIS Grant of William de Vefcy was afterwards con-firmed and enlarged with new privileges by his Sons John and William ; and when in the beginning of the next century their Barony came into the poffeffion of the PERCY Family, their Charters were confirmed by the fucceffive Lord PERCIES of ALNWICK, fome of whom gave additional marks of their favour to this Abbey, as appears by their Charters of 1310 and 1334.

AT length HENRY PERCY, fourth Earl of NORTHUM-BERLAND, built in it a fine Tower as a place of refuge for the Monks to retire to, in times of danger. For in the fudden irruptions of the Borderers of both nations, thefe rude men fpared no places or perfons however facred, but laid all wafte with fire and fword.

THIS Tower having been preferved more intire than any other part of the Abbey, has been lately repair-ed by the prefent noble Poffeffors, who are fitting it up in the old Gothic Style, and have fhown an admi-rable tafte both in the choice and adaptation of the ornaments. Near it, in ancient Englifh, is this curious

INSCRIPTION.

[I.] n the year of crift Jhu̅ M CCCC IIII VIII
This towe̅ was bilded by Sir henr̅ Percy
The fourth Erle of Northu̅berlad of gret hon̅ e worth
That efpoufed Mand ye good lady full of virtue and bewe̅
Daught̅ to fr willm̅ harb'rt right noble and hardy
Erle of Pembroch whos foulis god fave
And with his grace cofarve ye bilder of this tower

DESCEND-

DESCENDING from these venerable Ruins we wind
along a fine romantic Valley, with hanging Woods
to the left, and the River ALNE to the right, beyond
which rises a rough Hill covered with small Thickets.
The River here accompanies the path for near two
miles, sometimes approaching near to the Wood, at
other times receding from it; one while gliding along
in a smooth Canal of clear water, at other times foam-
ing down among Craggs and interposing Stones.

AND first we pass close under a fine impending
Wood; whence emerging we enter a green spacious
Meadow, here and there interspersed with trees. This
is agreeably contrasted with a large succeeding Shrubbery, in the midst of which rises a fine Chalybeat
Spring, that will probably be distinguished by a little
overhanging Grotto. Passing the Shrubbery, which
also affords a large nursery for future plantations, we
ford the River, and travel round another beautiful
Meadow, from the center of which the eye is carried,
to the right, over a succession of fine swelling Slopes,
till it rests on the top of CARMEL. Soon after a very
pleasing Landscape is seen to the left thro' an opening
in the Trees that hang over the River.

Now we enter some beautiful Plantations, which by a
gentle rise and fall in the ground, afford a great variety
of pleasing Scenes in beautiful succession, till at length
ALNWICK CASTLE begins to emerge from among the
trees, and presents itself to the eye more than once in
this conclusion of the Ride. Here also the Battlements of
the Tower, belonging to the once-famous PRIORY of
ALNWICK, are seen below to the left, close embowered
amid

amid the trees. As the Tower is the only ancient part now remaining of that once-extensive building, the rest being a meer modern house, it was all that was worth disclosing to the eye. Soon after we regain the Gothic Gateway by which we entered; and now having compleated a circuit of six or seven miles, we return back to Alnewick Castle, having to the left a charming view over a country most beautifully diversified.

I HAVE now brought my long narrative to a conclusion, in which be pleased to observe that some things are mentioned not as Objects of Attention, but merely as Landmarks, the better to distinguish and divide the several Parts of the Ride; yet most of the particulars above described, afford great and striking beauties.

I am, &c. &c.